PLAYS FOR YOUNG AUDIENCES

featuring The Emerald Circle
and other plays by

MAX BUSH

edited by
ROGER ELLIS

MERIWETHER PUBLISHING LTD.
Colorado Springs, Colorado

Meriwether Publishing Ltd., Publisher
P.O. Box 7710
Colorado Springs, CO 80933

Executive editor: Theodore O.. Zapel
Typesetting: Sharon E. Garlock
Cover design: Tom Myers

Library of Congress Cataloging-in-Publication Data

Ellis, Roger
Plays for young audiences by Max Bush : edited by Roger Ellis.
1st ed.
p.   c.m.
ISBN 1-56608-011-8 (paperback)
1. Children's plays, American.   2. Young adult drama, American.
{1. Plays.} I. Ellis, Roger, 1943 May 18- II. Title.
PS3552.U821P57 1995
812'.54—dc20   95-2382
                                                                  CIP
                                                                  AC

    2   3   4   5   6   7   8   9   99   98   97

For Rosemary, Alex, and Jeremy

CONTENTS

EDITOR'S PREFACE

It gives me great pleasure to present the plays of Max Bush in this collected edition of his best work. Some of the plays here have been unpublished until now, and naturally I'm proud to be able to introduce these to a wide readership. Others, of course, already enjoy the reputation of long production histories or the prestige of regional and national awards standing behind them. All the dramas, however, have been successfully produced on community, educational, and professional stages across the nation, giving tens of thousands of young spectators and their families moving experiences from their hours spent in the playhouse.

Having worked with Max on numerous occasions over the past fifteen years, I've come to regard him as one of those very special kinds of playwrights, a brilliant author who *prefers* to write for young audiences. And as a writer, Max understands these audiences very well: their impatience to be entertained, their desire to be awed, their suspicion of condescension or preaching, their delight in experiencing a good tale, and their highly vocal, highly emotional involvement in the world of the play.

Max's scripts are filled with all these elements, and more. For the adventurous imagination, he offers characters like the courageous (and swashbuckling) Queen Meaghan in *Voyage of the Dragonfly*, or the quietly-heroic wizard Robin of *The Crystal*. In *The Emerald Circle*, Max deals with the painful and often embarrassing emotions associated with friendship, dating, and competition; while *Rockway Cafe* explores the problematic fantasy life that many teens enjoy with their television heroes and heroines, as well as with their parents. Finally, Max's adaptations of classical tales drawn from the works of the Brothers Grimm or Charles Perrault offer "old Kool-aid in new bottles": stories that have captured the imaginations of millions, yet presented here afresh without old-fashioned sentimentality or condescending moralizing.

Broadly speaking, the plays in this collection can be classified under three categories: adaptations of classical tales (*Puss In Boots, Rapunzel, Hansel and Gretel*, and *The Boy Who Left Home to Find Out About the Shivers*); heroic fantasy-adventures (*Voyage of the Dragonfly, 13 Bells of Boglewood*, and *The Crystal*); and contemporary plays of social and psychological issues affecting young adults (*Rockway Cafe, The Emerald Circle*, and *Ghost of the River House*.)

While the *range* of Max Bush's plays is certainly very impressive, what is most remarkable to me is the *modern sensibility* that infuses all of them. Even with his adaptations of classical tales where he adheres closely to all the original details of his sources, treating them with great respect, he will flesh-out his characters with a modern psychological understanding that makes them accessible to contemporary spectators. And his constant use of folklore and myth in all his plays makes them enjoyable and provocative for adults as well as for younger audiences. The reader, the teacher, or the stage director will find in these scripts very little sappy, "feel good" escapism; but instead, will discover much challenge for a young theatregoer's sense of ethical behavior, personal identity, and psychological health.

It is this feature more than any other — the modernity of Max's inspiration — that first enticed me to undertake the task of assembling his plays in one volume. And having edited three previous anthologies of new American playwriting, I felt more attention needed to be drawn to the impressive outpouring of new work devoted to young audiences. This is a sector of the American theatre that has suffered great neglect for too long, despite the fact that the past two years have witnessed a surge in professional children's theatre productions across the United States that has spelled box office success for many producers.

More important, however, than this recent renaissance in playwriting for young audiences, is the fact that children's theatre in the U.S.A. — and abroad — has undergone a subtle yet readily identifiable shift in its rhetorical posture towards the spectator. No longer, that is, are producers with "sugary breakfast cereal" the only purveyors of children's theatre. Scripts that contain packaged wisdom blandly handed down from one generation to the next, plays that razzle and dazzle but which remain far removed from the problems facing modern youth, or plays that resemble the puerile "kidvid" escapist entertainment which gluts our television programming and movie theatres are gradually being pushed aside by more thoughtful, serious writing. The growing trend towards *modernity* in new writing for young audiences — modernity in themes, characters, situations, dialogue — is everywhere apparent; and Max's work ranks among the very best that American writers have been producing over the past ten years.

Finally a word must be said for what I like to call the literary quality of these plays. I have only seen six or seven of them in actual performance, the others I've read several times. But even just on the printed page, Max's scripts contain a life that is vital, vivid, and makes for compelling reading. Max is truly a "wordsmith." And this is no accident, I know from working with him as his editor: there were times when he spent weeks laboring over the choice of phrase, deliberating the appropriateness of a stage direction, or berating me for changing his punctuation, before finally giving me approval to go ahead with a script. Additionally, Max religiously attends as many

2

rehearsals and productions of his new plays as possible, regarding each script as a "work in process," before committing himself to a final version. In so many places, therefore, Max Bush's writing— both in prose and lyric poetry—is muscular, engrossing, and rich with the resonance that evokes feelings of pity, fear, awe, compassion, and delight.

Pulitzer Prize-winning author Tony Kushner has decried the state of children's theatre in the United States, calling it the reflection of "a society that seems to offer its children only a future of diminished expectations." He calls instead for a repertoire of "dangerous" plays for young audiences: plays which challenge the failing *status quo*, and which unflinchingly address those social and psychological problems that have affected young people throughout history.

I think it is within the context of this psychological, social, and spiritual no-man's-land of modern society that Max's plays are best understood and appreciated. For young spectators they are like a beacon; for the adult viewer they are engrossing and provocative intellectual adventures; for directors they are wonderful theatre; and for producers I would venture to say they can be the keys to box office success.

— R.E.

INTRODUCTION

by Scot E. Copeland
Producing Director of the Nashville Academy Theatre

The problem with writing an introduction to this beautiful, weight-heavy and expensive anthology of Max Bush's plays is that I can't really try to discuss Max's work without raising the subject of psychology. Please do not run screaming for the hills. This is not a self-help article. Though Max has risen above his background in psychology, his art is rooted there, so I can hardly avoid the subject, try though I might.

Let's start with the name "Jung." Now, don't, please, start crying. I know. Even Max begged me to "stay away from that Jungian stuff, you'll scare everyone to death." Yet I'm afraid I have to go there — but only with a layman's perception, so perhaps it will not be so terribly annoying to you. The important thing to understand is Jung's concept of the "collective unconscious."

Jung posited that the continuing evolution of the brain is aided by a multigenerational engagement with certain basic patterns of experience. As a result, certain universal archetypal images can stimulate a rapid recognition and response within the collective unconscious of the human mind. These archetypes communicate within the unconscious through symbol and metaphor, not as an image substituting for an idea, but as an expression of an intuitive perception incorporating our own experience with the genetic residue of our collective psyche. The philosopher Kant referred to this tenet of human understanding as "knowledge *a priori*": knowledge that is a given, knowledge that is present even in innocence, knowledge that awaits only synthesis with our own life experience to become understanding.

I am experiencing a flashback to my undergraduate philosophy class. "So, Mr. Copeland," asks the kindly professor, "does this desk actually exist or not?" It doesn't matter. Really. *It does not matter.* Remember this one? Ninety-nine monkeys on an isolated island are taught to ring a bell and get a banana, and the fabled "Hundredth Monkey" in a totally different place rings a bell to get a banana without having been taught. He knew because the others knew. I love that story, even though I suspect all one hundred monkeys probably came to a bad end.

We have no universal rites of passage in contemporary society, a function that earthier civilizations understand. "It has always been the prime function of myth and rite to supply the symbols that carry the human spirit forward," wrote Joseph Campbell. "In fact, it may well be that...the decline of such [myths and rites have left us] fixated to...infancy and...disinclined to the necessary passages of our adulthood." The power of archetypal images is so essential to our development that if they are not supplied by ritual and myth, they will have to be announced to us directly from our unconscious in dreams. The healthy manage to assimilate the dream archetypes and make passage — from childhood to adulthood, from innocence to enlightenment, from selfishness to self-awareness — without those rites and rituals, but some of us do not.

Some of us require the collective reinforcement that ritual exploration of the archetypes provide. Even those healthy, stalwart individuals who do not require such reinforcement will benefit from engaging the collective message in a collective setting.

It is amidst the age-old rituals of the theatre that Max Bush enacts the basic passage towards maturity. It is upon the collective unconscious that Max Bush builds the psychological matrix of his work. He structures his plays like dreams — waking dreams, *accessible* dreams. On the surface is the story of the play: valid, interesting and entertaining on its own merits. Below the surface are the archetypal images and metaphoric situations that we respond to on an intuitive, usually unarticulated level — images of growth and passage shadowed by the ever-present threat of regression.

Max's plays invariably concern themselves with a central protagonist in a universal struggle or crisis of emotional, psychological or spiritual health. The playwright presents the hero with a door, a choice, a turning point, a primal scene. The challenge to the hero is to find the guts to step through that door. It is a choice that requires tremendous courage, for on the other side of the door awaits change, growth and health — maturity with all its mysteries and uncertainties. On this side of the door lie the sweet seductions of regression, for there is no status quo. We are encouraged to take the step, by proxy, in our own identification with the hero. When we do, we experience both an aesthetic and psychological catharsis and celebrate the health of the healthy as one. Jung wrote that "the moment when the mythological situation appears [in art] is characterized by a peculiar emotional intensity...as though chords in us were touched that had never resounded before...at such moments we are no longer individuals but the [collective human] race."

Max offers the adolescent as mythic hero. True, his protagonists are not always of adolescent age. They are sometimes younger. They are sometimes older. Nonetheless, they all face internal struggles towards healthy realization of growth. We all experience such passages many times in our lives, but we all directly face primal manifestations of that heroic struggle in adolescence. In each play, the playwright strives to externalize the internal struggle of the adolescent hero, so that the remaining characters within the plays can be seen as archetypal realizations of the hero's own psyche as it fights its way towards positive development. At the same time, they can be seen as people, struggling with the cause and effect of real life and real relationships. The characters, therefore, inhabit two worlds at once: standing with one foot in the function and progress of the surface story and one foot in the archetypal functions of the underlying dream world. "A horse is a horse," wrote D.H. Lawrence, "but a horse is also a metaphor."

In Max's plays, as in real life, the archetypal world of the unconscious and the real world of the conscious exist together, each taking from and feeding on the other. That duality can make his work misunderstood by the casual reader for it doesn't easily fit in with our notions of clear divisions in theatrical style. We can readily recognize the archetypes of expressionistic artists, for the familiar guideposts are there in the distorted, Caligari-like visuals and the non-linear plot. These works, though interesting, can be emotionally unsatisfying because, like a dream relayed, they have no reference point for us. We more easily identify with realistic art because we can personally identify with the frame of reference inherent in cause and effect and slice-of-life visuals. Knowledgeable theatre practitioners perceive these two forms to be antithetical. Indeed, expressionism — with its Jungian components — was, historically, a reaction against the Freudian-inspired tenets of realism, so it is not surprising that we are slow to recognize a deliberate and successful fusion of the two.

Children more naturally respond to the dual nature of myth than their more experienced, cynical and unimaginative elders. Their perceptions have not yet been conditioned to dismiss the wisdom inherent in the metaphor, nor have they yet chained their perceptions in the dungeons of the literal. In making this case to my own company during the process of directing five of the ten plays in this anthology, I have invariably been asked, "Do you really expect the kids to get all that?" Well, yes, I do, albeit on an inexpressible level. The metaphors and archetypes of the collective unconscious communicate to us in dreams as inferences that do not require verbalization or even conscious retention in order for the message to be received and stored for later use within our individual psyche.

Likewise, the same collective allegories communicate with our unconscious through the ritual of the theatre. If asked, children will describe the surface story and its ramifications, but the deeper mytho-poetic level of the experience, unarticulated, has subtly and quietly found its mark as well.

This is the essential strength of Max's work, just as it is the essential transcendental, indefinable power of the theatrical ritual itself. I cannot prove this hypothesis. It cannot be surveyed, tabulated or documented in any way whatsoever. Yet I accept its truth in full faith, for it is knowledge *a priori*. I know it to be true because I know it to be true.

Those who produce Max's plays must trust that the unarticulated will be absorbed by the audience in the proper way; otherwise the collaborative team may attempt to present the underlying psychological matrix as the surface play. Certainly the artists involved must fully explore that matrix as subtext, but they must then tell us the surface story — and tell it well — and trust that the dream world will take care of itself. Once the effort has been successfully made, the producer will be rewarded with a theatre experience that thoroughly engages, entertains, amuses and moves its young audience in more depth than they or we need to express.

Considering the playwright's interest in our psychological journeys and his skill in utilizing the power of archetype, it is not surprising that he would be drawn to the similarly inclined lexicon of fairy tales. Some voices in the field of theatre for young audiences advocate the abandonment of the fairy tale world, but I am not one of them. Fairy tales are a valid, truthful, relevant expression of the folklore of any and all cultures, embodying the everyday common wisdom of the people. Those who perceive fairy tales as nonsensical elitist fluff — as well as those who regard the stories as dangerously sexist — have fallen victims to the truncations provided by British Victorian daddies who re-interpreted the stories to reflect their own view of the world. They made the stories "safe" for the nursery, "safe" for their children and particularly "safe" for their daughters. Considering the earthy wisdom inherent in the original tales — the undercurrents of individual empowerment and sexual development — one can understand why they made such an effort to repress it.

Only the Victorians could spin *Rapunzel* into a story about a girl locked in an ivory tower who should have known better than to fall for that Prince's smooth line of talk. The Victorian attitude destroys the psychological matrix by imposing an antithetical moral: "Poor girl, she should have stayed safe in that tower, she shouldn't have asked so many questions, she should have kept her hair to herself." From the deepest deeps of the Victorian daddy's heart comes the voice of Peter Pan, begging us not to grow up. But the older, wiser, truer voice of the fairy world urges us to the contrary. It is to that voice that Max pledges his loyalty when adapting a fairy tale to the stage.

Max's Rapunzel, on the other hand, emerges from self-centered adolescence to a mature, healthy understanding of herself and her responsibility to the world around her. She is no longer a child who clings to her mother for nurturing. She has become the nurturer. It is Rapunzel's tears of compassion for her husband that restore his eyesight. Thus brought to enlightenment, they both turn their eyes on their children and "live long and happily together." In *Puss in Boots*, the childlike Claude unleashes reason as embodied in the title character, and achieves a greatly elevated station in life as a metaphor for successful passage from ignorance to intelligence. *Hansel and Gretel* (the feminine and masculine aspects of one central child protagonist) are empowered by the White Bird to face the dangers ahead of them rather than return to the illusion of safety at home. *The Boy Who Left Home to Find Out About the Shivers*, in his search for self-realization, journeys through a fascination with the mysteries of morbidity, ultimately rejecting that preoccupation in favor of full commitment to life and joyful maturity as embodied by the symbolic dousing in the water of life.

13 Bells of Boglewood provides an enlightening bridge between Max's fairy tale adaptations and his original plays because it is a non-adaptive work that strives to apply general aspects of classic fairy tales to a contemporary sociological issue.

The examination of the playwright's use of the dream world within the fairy tale adaptations will give the reader informed access to the playwright's application of that matrix within his original work. Though these plays demonstrate a much more three-dimensional realization of character and relationships within the surface story than do the adaptations, the archetypes and metaphors to psychological rites of adolescent passage are still Max's primary interest.

The Emerald Circle presents an adolescent who is tormented by a pivotal event in his life, which the playwright raises to theatrical expression as a "primal scene." Each time he returns to the primal scene, young Dave is faced with the choice of whether to deal with the full implications of the event or not. With the support of his mother and (most importantly) his best friend, he completely engages the truth of the dream and begins his journey beyond it.

Similarly the protagonist of *Ghost of the River House* — a young girl suffering the pain of her father's subtle rejection — repeatedly confronts the ghost of a woman who has drowned herself in tragic-romantic response to the rejection of her lover. In *Voyage of the Dragonfly*, a small group of men and women band together in a mutual quest for a powerful warming Flame, but their success is complicated by the traps they lay for each other in mutual suspicion. In *Rockway Cafe* the playwright explores a contemporary reference for the interweaving of the conscious and the unconscious by utilizing the dramatic device of television to dance back and forth between dream world and real world.

The Crystal is, perhaps, the most complex example of the playwright's approach. I shall leave the reader to his or her own journey into this piece unhindered by my interloping, except to point out that in this play, the playwright has fully stepped beyond the every-day concerns of folklore and well into the spiritual dimensions of myth. It is a delightfully absorbing, thoroughly satisfying puzzle as well as a richly-engrossing play.

It is important to remember that (in spite of this essay's neces-sary focus on the psychological ramifications of Max's repertoire) these plays are well-structured, emotionally satisfying, humorous and touching works of art. We in the audience laugh when we expe-rience them. We share tension and release. We are moved. We are entertained.

Here's another thing I like about Max Bush's plays: he is unlike-ly to linger on about the ending. When the play is over, it's over — ring the bell, get the banana and let's go home.

GHOST *of the* RIVER HOUSE

by MAX BUSH

CHARACTERS

JENNY 10

LARRY . . . . 11, Jenny's brother

LAWRENCE. . . . . 33, Jenny's father

GRAMPA. . . . . 55, Jenny's grandfather

SONDRA. . . . . 19, a ghost

THOMAS . . . . 24, a memory

The roles of Lawrence and Thomas are to be played by the same actor.

TIME: Evening, in October of the present year.

PLACE: A ruined house near a river.

RUNNING TIME: Approximately fifty-five minutes.

DEDICATION: *Ghost of the River House* is dedicated to Joe Dulin and Jeannie Averill.

"I Love You Truly," from *Seven Songs* by Carrie Jacobs-Bond, MCMVI.

Ghost of the River House was commissioned by the Grand Rapids Circle Theatre, funded in part through a grant by the Michigan Council for the Arts and Cultural Affairs, and opened on June 14, 1993, with the following cast and crew:

CAST

JENNY . . . . Megan Dullaghan

LARRY . . . . Preston Koning

LAWRENCE. . . . . John S. Douglas

GRAMPA GEORGE . . . . Jack Gillisse

SONDRA. . . . . Amy Gaipa

THOMAS. . . . . John S. Douglas

PRODUCTION STAFF

Managing Director. . . . . Joe Dulin

Director . . . . Max Bush

Scenic Design . . . . Tom Lohman

Lighting Design . . . . . . Matt Taylor

Music Composer . . . . . . Linda Missad

Costume Designer . . . . . Heather Edwards

Light Board Operator. . . Andrew Fraser

Sound Board Operator. . Amy Tenbrink

Producers . . . . Carol LaMange,
Sally Schaafsma

Acknowledgements . . . . Myra Bush, Debra Olsen,
Rosanne Steffens, Joe Zainea,
Susan Hinkle, Waters Corp.

(At rise we see the foundation of a ruined house framed by large shade trees. All that's left standing is the fieldstone chimney and the low, crumbling foundations of the walls. Weeds, wild flowers and bushes grow up through the cracks in the floor. Vines hang off the trees, crawl over the foundation and on to the floor. A broken, skeletal pear tree with a twisted trunk and twisted branches stands behind the house, all that remains of the backyard orchard. Most of the usable boards and bricks have been removed. Various articles remain from the house and are scattered about: a kitchen chair, a number of badly damaged paintings, a cushion, a toy boat, a book, a rusty shovel head, a deflated ball, a disconnected well pump, a sink, a set of disconnected stair steps, etc. It's evening in autumn, the colors of the trees are rich and vibrant; colored leaves lay scattered over the entire scene.)

(LARRY, his FATHER and GRANDFATHER enter carrying fishing poles and tackle, heading past the ruined house. GRAMPA also carries a lantern.)

FATHER: Fishing in the river isn't like fishing in the lake. In the lake you go to where the fish are waiting. Here in the river, you wait for the fish to come to you.

LARRY: What bait do you think I should use, Grampa?

GRAMPA: Night crawlers.

FATHER: That's right.

LARRY: *(To FATHER)* But I want to use the new lure you gave me—it's for walleyes.

FATHER: But if you use a night crawler you'll catch more fish.

GRAMPA: Sure, Larry, on a night crawler you'll get walleye, but then again you might hook a catfish or even a smallmouth bass.

LARRY: But what I want is a walleye.

FATHER: *(Supportively)* All right, then use your new lure.

JENNY: *(Off)* Wait! Dad! Dad, wait!

FATHER: Jenny...

LARRY: I thought you said she had to stay in the house with Gramma and Mom.

FATHER: What has she got?

JENNY: *(JENNY runs on carrying a fishing pole.)* I found a pole. So I can come along.

LARRY: I don't think so.

JENNY: I found a pole in Grampa's basement, I'm coming along.

FATHER: Jenny—

JENNY: I'll put on my own night crawler.

LARRY: Well, give it up, you're not coming.

FATHER: Larry, I told you, stay out of it.

LARRY: You said just the three of us were going. You said that yesterday, remember?

FATHER: I know what I said, son. *(To JENNY)* I told you in the house. This is something I promised Larry we'd do together. Just him and me. And Grampa if he wants. Larry and I need to spend some time together alone, with a little peace and quiet, please. Why don't you play in the haunted house, here?

JENNY: We don't spend time together, alone.

FATHER: We do too.

JENNY: When?

FATHER: Jenny, relax.

LARRY: Yeah, Jennifer, relax.

JENNY: My name is Jenny, Lawrence. Why do you have Mom's camera? Does she know you took it?

LARRY: Yes. I'm going to take a picture of the ghost and send it to the "National Inquirer." Going to make a million bucks.

JENNY: Oh, righto, Lar. Dad, why can't I —

FATHER: Jenny, come on, let it go.

GRAMPA: I'll stay with you, Jenny.

FATHER: Yeah?

GRAMPA: *(Handing LARRY the lantern)* Yeah, I can fish here any time.

FATHER: Sure, stay with Grampa. Let him tell you about the haunted house, and the box of money. You know we never found that.

JENNY: Why can't I go? I'm not going to do anything wrong. Why can't I go? It's just fishing. I'll sit and I won't talk.

LARRY: Yeah, right.

JENNY: Mom says you have to talk to Larry. I won't talk. I won't listen. I'll just fish. Then when you're done, I want to talk to you, too.

FATHER: This is something for Larry and me to do. You're just going to have to understand that.

JENNY: Why do I have to understand? Why doesn't Larry have to understand?

FATHER: Jenny, calm down!

LARRY: God, Jenny, you're going to blow.

FATHER: There's no reason for you to get this emotional.

JENNY: I want to go! I just want to go! I just want to go with you! Let me go, please, Daddy!

FATHER: No! That's it, little lady! Now, no more! You stay here with Grampa or you go back to the house. *(JENNY starts to speak.)* No! I don't want to hear any more! Don't you make

16

this any worse for you. And if you say anything more, you will, I guarantee it. Larry. *(He exits. LARRY moves to JENNY, takes her pole, then goes off. JENNY watches them go, then sits.)*

JENNY: *(Softly, to herself)* **I could go. It would be all right. I could go.** *(She pulls her knees up to her chest.)* **I never went fishing in the river before.**

GRAMPA: **Do you want to go fishing with me? I know where the best runs are for walleye. You could use my fishing pole.** *(She indicates no.)* **Do you mind if I stay with you?** *(She indicates no.)*

JENNY: **We would have fun. When we went perch fishing, I caught the most, didn't I?**

GRAMPA: **You caught the most and the biggest.**

JENNY: **Why won't he let me go, Grampa?**

GRAMPA: **Well, he said he needed to spend time alone with Larry.**

JENNY: **He does. All the time. What's wrong with me? He hates me.**

GRAMPA: **There's nothing wrong with you, Jenny. I do know that. So it's got to be something else. Maybe he does have some things to talk over with Larry.**

JENNY: **I know why. Why he won't let me go.**

GRAMPA: **Why?**

JENNY: **I do. I know why.** *(GRAMPA waits for an answer.)* **It's because Larry's a boy.**

GRAMPA: **Is that what you think?**

JENNY: **I know. He loves Larry more than me. Because Larry's a boy.** *(He sits next to her, puts his hand on her.)* **I can't help it I'm a girl.**

GRAMPA: **No, of course not.**

JENNY: **It's not my fault. I don't know what to do.**

GRAMPA: **You did something. You told me about it. That's important.**

JENNY: **You think it's true?**

GRAMPA: **I don't know. Right now you think it is, though.**

JENNY: **It is. Just because he's a boy. Doesn't anybody notice? Larry's like his best friend.** *(A wind begins to blow. GRAMPA hears it, looks up. He wraps his arm tighter around JENNY.)* **I wanted a basketball for my birthday and he finally bought me one — a girl's basketball — but he doesn't play with me. He bought Larry a new glove and they play catch all the time. I can throw almost as far as Larry and I bet I could beat him in basketball but he's too chicken to play me. What can I do so Dad will be different about me?**

GRAMPA: **Have you talked to your dad about it?**

JENNY: Yeah. He just says it isn't true.

GRAMPA: Well, keep talking. I know he's got a lot on his mind, working too hard, taking care of bills, but nothing is more important than you.

JENNY: I was going to talk to him again tonight but... *(The wind blows stronger.)*

GRAMPA: Ah, that's a cold wind. *(JENNY rises, sensing something in the wind.)* I think your dad sees himself in Larry. Larry reminds him of himself when he was a boy.

JENNY: Yeah, Dad named him after himself — Lawrence.

GRAMPA: You'd look funny wearing a name like that.

JENNY: Yeah. So does Larry.

GRAMPA: I guess when I named your dad I should have named him something like Shirley; then maybe he'd of named you after himself.

JENNY: Shirley, Grampa? I'd be Shirley?

GRAMPA: Yeah!

JENNY: "Welcome to your first day of school. What's your name, little girl?" "Shirley." That is so bad.

GRAMPA: That's what I would have named my daughter, if I had one.

JENNY: She's lucky you didn't. *(A VOICE begins to emerge [miked] in the wind, a woman's whispering voice. The words are indistinct. Another VOICE — this time a man's — seems to join in the whisper. We're able to make out fragments of a conversation.)* Who is that? Do you hear that?

GRAMPA: What?

JENNY: It sounds like...like people talking...somewhere.

GRAMPA: I don't hear anything.

JENNY: Listen, Grampa, don't you hear...?

GRAMPA: A man and a woman?

JENNY: Yeah, maybe, but...

GRAMPA: They're having an argument?

JENNY: Yeah, about...a dream...money. Money. *(The MALE VOICE fades out but the FEMALE VOICE fades in clearer.)*

VOICE: Jenny...Jenny...

JENNY: Who...? Do you hear somebody calling me?

GRAMPA: Calling you? By your name?

JENNY: Yeah.

GRAMPA: Your dad you mean?

JENNY: No, like a woman.

GRAMPA: Your mom?

JENNY: No. Listen, Grampa.

VOICE: Jenny...

JENNY: There. My name.

VOICE: Jenny, stay...stay...

JENNY: What?

VOICE: Stay...

JENNY: *(The VOICE is gone, the wind is dying out.)* **Hello!...What?**
(The wind fades out. To GRAMPA) **I heard someone calling
me.**

GRAMPA: From where?

JENNY: Over...I don't know. I couldn't tell.

GRAMPA: A woman's voice?

JENNY: Yeah.

GRAMPA: Far away, but yet right next to your head?

JENNY: Yeah. Who is that?

GRAMPA: Sondra.

JENNY: The ghost?

GRAMPA: That's the way it sounds.

JENNY: Why would a ghost call me? How would Sondra know
my name?

GRAMPA: She doesn't usually call people by their name,
though. Especially somebody she doesn't know.

JENNY: Why me?

GRAMPA: I don't know. Maybe she likes you.

JENNY: Uh uh. Nope. Nope. It didn't sound like it. *(She walks
towards river.)* **If she likes me she can go scare Larry. And
make him fall into the river...How long do you think
they'll be gone?**

GRAMPA: A while.

JENNY: Can we wait here for them?

GRAMPA: You want to wait *here*?

JENNY: Maybe Dad will change his mind and then he won't
have to go so far to find me. Do you think he'll change his
mind?

GRAMPA: I don't know, but if you change your mind and want
to go fishing with me I'd love to take you. Because you're
the best fishergirl this side of the Peckawanee River.

JENNY: *(She smiles.)* **The Peckawanee River, where's that?**

GRAMPA: Somewhere between here and Utah.

JENNY: Thanks, Grampa.

GRAMPA: So you want to go?

JENNY: No. Stay. I want to stay. *(Turning to the ruins)* **Do you
believe Sondra hid all that money out here?**

GRAMPA: Yeah, I do. I talked with old Thomas once. He was
here that last day in 1920 and he swore she had a box of
money and jewels. And I think it's why she scared everybody away after she died—no one could live here. She was
protecting that money.

JENNY: If she hid it in the house it's probably gone. You know
why?

GRAMPA: Why?

JENNY: The house is gone.

GRAMPA: Over the last sixty years people tore it down board by board to find it, but they never did.

JENNY: Where are all the boards?

GRAMPA: I took some to build my barn, other people took some. They'd build huge bonfires — in the middle of the day — to keep the spooks away. Then they'd get frustrated 'cause they couldn't find any money and take anything they could use — boards, bricks, sinks, bathtubs, tables, chairs. *(He has picked up the old kitchen chair and now puts it right side up, dusts it off.)*

JENNY: Have you looked?

GRAMPA: *(He sits in the chair.)* I've been known to look a time or two, but not for long. I don't like it here. At night the mist moves up the river banks and hangs over the house; makes the air smell like a rotten cellar. The mist works into the trees and they crack; sounds like the clacking of bones. And Sondra, she won't stay down. She's a restless soul, mournful and angry. And she doesn't like the living; hates us I think, for what happened to her when she was alive. She moves through the trees like a cold wind; she clouds the light of day. She comes whispering in your ear, touching you with her cold hands and freezing your blood. And all that hurt and anger inside her goes right into you and you feel like dying.

LARRY: *(Suddenly appearing, soaked to the bone)* **Jenny!** *(Startled, JENNY turns to him.)*

JENNY: Larry! It's Larry.

LARRY: There you are.

JENNY: What happened to you?

LARRY: You know what happened to me. I fell in the river.

JENNY: You fell in the river?

LARRY: Yeah, I fell in the river.

JENNY: *(Laughing)* **You fell in the river!**

LARRY: *(Pushing her)* **Very funny, Jennifer. It ruined Mom's camera.**

JENNY: *(Pushing him back)* **Why you pushing me, stupid?**

LARRY: *(As they struggle)* **You did it!**

GRAMPA: Hey, Larry—

JENNY: *(GRAMPA tries to separate them.)* **Did what? What are you talking about? I didn't do anything!** *(GRAMPA separates them.)*

GRAMPA: Jenny!

LARRY: You were spying on us, then you snuck up and yelled at me — "Lawrence!" — and I slipped and fell in. Then you

20

ran back here.

JENNY: No, I didn't. I was here the whole time. Don't blame me because you're so stupid, Lawrence.

LARRY: It was you, I recognized your voice. I could have drowned.

JENNY: I thought you could swim.

LARRY: You see?! You did do it, Jennifer!

JENNY: I did not. I was here the whole time!

LARRY: You were not!

GRAMPA: Yeah, she was.

LARRY: She was?

GRAMPA: Yeah, right here. The whole time.

JENNY: You see?

LARRY: Then who...I heard your voice. It sounded just like you.

JENNY: Some fisherman. "I'm fishing. Nope. I fell in the river. I must be swimming. But I still have my clothes on. I must be a dork."

GRAMPA: You'd better go up to the house and dry off.

LARRY: Would you...would you walk with me, Grampa? I...

JENNY: You know the way.

LARRY: Will you walk with me? I just would like you to walk with me.

JENNY: I'd like you to stay here with me, Grampa.

GRAMPA: Jenny and I were about to look for that money, Larry.

LARRY: Why don't you come with us, Jen? It's not very far.

JENNY: Grampa, Larry is usually irritating and obnoxious and calls me Jennifer. He just called me Jen. Why do you think he did that?

LARRY: Come on, Jen...ny.

JENNY: Did Dad say I could come fishing with you now?

LARRY: We just got there. We didn't even talk about anything, yet. So Dad didn't say anything about you.

JENNY: Then I want to look for the money. You can run to the house, it's not very far. *(He hesitates, shakes. JENNY picks up a board, walks over to LARRY, fans him.)*

LARRY: Oh, nice.

JENNY: Say, Larry, would you like an ice cream cone?

LARRY: Very funny.

JENNY: *(A fake laugh)* Ha-ha-ha-ha-ha.

LARRY: Stop it. Jenny, stop it. Stop it!

JENNY: *(Sees he's genuinely cold and scared.)* Gees, he's freezing. You better go with him, Grampa.

LARRY: Yeah.

GRAMPA: That's nice of you, Jenny.

JENNY: *(Surprised at herself)* Yeah.

LARRY: **Yeah, thanks, Jenny. Oh, Jenny—** *(A wet LARRY suddenly embraces a surprised JENNY.)* **You're so good to me. I love you, sister!** *(He kisses her, rubs himself onto her. JENNY wipes the kiss off, shakes off the water LARRY rubbed onto her.)*

GRAMPA: *(Leading him away)* **But you can go on yourself, Larry. You'll be all right, just swim on over to the house and tell your grandmother what happened so she can find you some warm clothes.** *(LARRY hesitates.)* **She won't follow you all the way to my house.**

LARRY: **Who won't follow me?**

GRAMPA: **The ghost.**

LARRY: **She won't?**

GRAMPA: **No, go on.** *(He runs off. JENNY stands, still wet and in shock, holding her arms out to dry.)*

JENNY: **Grampa, do you think that Larry's, like, a normal boy?**

GRAMPA: **He's as normal as the rest of us.** *(GRAMPA laughs a goofy laugh. JENNY laughs, echoing him.)* **Yeah, he's all right. He's all right.**

JENNY: *(JENNY's focus shifts to the house.)* **I bet this is the living room.**

GRAMPA: **Living room, front door, back door over there. My father, your great-grandfather George, was born in the bedroom, here. So was Sondra. Their mother died in the same room — in the same bed — when Sondra was twelve.**

JENNY: **So Sondra was my...**

GRAMPA: **She was my aunt so she's your great-great aunt.**

JENNY: **Wow.** *(JENNY gets on her hands and knees and searches.)*

GRAMPA: **What would you do with a box of money?**

JENNY: **Spend it! I'd buy a boy's basketball.**

GRAMPA: **Made of gold? There's a lot of money out here.**

JENNY: **No, Grampa, a basketball made of gold wouldn't bounce. And I'd buy a fishing boat for my dad. He wants one but he can't afford it. Then he'd take me fishing — all the time. Wouldn't that be great?**

GRAMPA: **I guess so.**

JENNY: **Yeah! And then, if I had all that money, Larry would have to listen to me. And I'd build a double Ferris wheel in our front yard. And I'd take a trip, on a jet. I've never done that before. To Hawaii. And I'd swim in the ocean, I never did that before either. And go to that place where you can swim with dolphins. Wouldn't that be fun, Grampa, swimming with dolphins! I can talk to them.** *(She speaks dolphin to GRAMPA. GRAMPA speaks back something in dolphin. JENNY speaks dolphin back to him. He speaks back. JENNY looks at ruins.)* **Sondra is a bad housekeeper.** *(She holds up* *painting.)* **NICE PICTURE.** *(She drops it. She sees the deflated ball, picks it up, tries to bounce it, it doesn't bounce.)*

GRAMPA: Must be made of gold.

JENNY: *(JENNY picks it up and throws it at GRAMPA.)* **Think fast!** *(He catches ball and throws it right back at her.)*

GRAMPA: Think faster! *(She catches it, throws it back.)*

JENNY: Faster!

GRAMPA: *(Back again)* **Faster!**

JENNY: Faster! *(She fakes, fakes again, fakes again, he ducks, she throws ball and hits him.)* **Slam-dunked.** *(She picks up another badly damaged painting.)* **NICE PICTURE.** *(She drops it. She spies an old doll under something, picks it up. It's dirty and dusty; she shakes it out, tries to straighten it up. The doll wears a wedding dress. To doll.)* **And who are you? Oh, you are a mess. What's happened to you? Don't you have anyone to take care of you? Oh, look at your hair. Were you Sondra's doll when she was a little girl? Did she make your little shoes? And your pretty dress? Is it a wedding dress? Someone used to love you very much. They dressed you all up. And then they left you here? Oh, you poor, lost thing. Did Sondra look like you? Do you have any money on you?** *(She looks.)* **In you?** *(She shakes doll — none.)* **What happened here?** *(She turns doll to look at house.)* **Remember? The day she hid the money? Remember that day?** *(She shakes the doll's head yes.)* **You know, don't you.** *(Shakes the doll's head yes.)* **Yes, I knew you did. Where is it? Where's the money?** *(She looks doll in the face.)* **What? I can't understand you.** *(Holding doll up to her ear)* **I can't understand you. Where is that money?** *(Face to face)* **Talk to me — talk to me —** *(She hits doll's head on her forehead.)* **Talk to me — I can't hear you! Don't you want me to know?** *(The doll shakes head no.)* **You don't?** *(She smells doll, pulls a face.)* **Pah! Take a bath!** *(She throws it down. She sneezes. Silence. She sneezes again. GRAMPA laughs.)*

GRAMPA: Bless you. *(We hear a flutter. She looks up. More fluttering. He also hears it.)*

JENNY: Sondra?

GRAMPA: That's her.

JENNY: *(The flutter fades out, then fades in again, louder.)* **Sondra?** *(The noise stops.)* **Where's-that-money?**

GRAMPA: I don't think she'll tell you, Jenny. It's why she's here, right now, watching us; to protect the money.

JENNY: Sondra, I know you're here. Where is the money? *(Seemingly impossible, the toy boat begins to move. JENNY jumps back.)* **Grampa, the boat...** *(It moves up on a pile of boards, stops.)* **Do you think...** *(She moves towards the* boards.)

GRAMPA: Are you sure you want to do that?

JENNY: *(JENNY gingerly moves to boat, pushes it over with her foot. She carefully pushes boards apart with her foot, sees something. She bends over and, out of the dirt, picks up an old silver dollar.)* **Ha! A coin!**

GRAMPA: I don't believe it.

JENNY: *(She blows off the dirt, rubs it on her jeans, looks at it.)* **"One dollar. Nineteen...nineteen..." "No, eighteen. Eighteen...** *(She scratches away some dirt.)* **Eighteen ninety-seven." Eighteen ninety-seven! This must be worth a lot. There must be more.** *(She tosses aside some boards and a bucket, stops short.)* **Grampa...** *(She reaches down and pulls from the dirt a necklace with a large, jeweled pendant.)* **Look at this. Look at this, Grampa!**

GRAMPA: A necklace? *(The wind begins to blow again.)*

JENNY: It's beautiful. It shines. Can I have this? *(GRAMPA begins to answer her.)* **Thank you. Thank you very much.**

GRAMPA: You're welcome.

JENNY: It looks like jewels. Are they real? *(GRAMPA begins to answer.)* **Yes they are! Look at this. What kind of jewels are these, Grampa?** *(He begins to answer.)* **Red ones! And blue ones!**

GRAMPA: It's beautiful.

JENNY: I'll bet this was Sondra's. Is there more? *(She gets on her hands and knees and searches. GRAMPA joins her in tossing aside boards, pans, logs, etc.)* **Here, money, money. It's me, Jenny. You were calling me. Remember?**

GRAMPA: Keep looking, Jenny. You've already found more than anybody else. I looked over every inch of this ground and I didn't find any jewelry, any coins. She's talking to you.

JENNY: I'm listening. I'm listening.

GRAMPA: *(The wind blows louder. A mist begins to float in from the river. JENNY doesn't see it coming but GRAMPA does. He stops searching, rises.)* **But be careful. She might want something back. If you get too scared, just run back to my house. Sondra doesn't move far from here.**

JENNY: You know, Sondra could have just dropped one coin. Or someone could have found all of it and dropped one as they were leaving. I wish I knew what really happened. *(The light dims. Not noticing this, JENNY keeps searching. GRAMPA notices it.)* **Then I'd know where she put the box...if there was a box.** *(The light continues to fade.)*

GRAMPA: Jenny. *(She looks up and notices the light, the wind, and the fog. She stands.)*

24

JENNY: What is it? What's happening?

GRAMPA: I'm not sure. What do you think?

JENNY: I don't know.

GRAMPA: Is she talking to you?

JENNY: No.

GRAMPA: Do you hear voices?

JENNY: I don't think so. *(The light has completely altered; darkness surrounds the house which is shrouded in mist.)*

GRAMPA: Come here.

JENNY: *(SONDRA materializes out of the mist.)* **Grampa!**

GRAMPA: I see her.

JENNY: Is that...?

> *(SONDRA is tall and striking. She's dressed in a calf-length, white skirt, white stockings and white shoes; a white, lace blouse that is belted at the waist and worn outside her skirt; and a rose-red choker. Her hair is very long, full and loose. Her skin is pale. THOMAS enters through the mist, behind her. He's dressed simply in a shirt, slacks and suspenders; he has a moustache, wears his hair parted in the middle and combed tightly to his scalp. He's a hard-working, earthy man, maybe a carpenter or a mason. SONDRA and THOMAS will act as if the house is standing with everything as it was in 1920. Which is what JENNY and GRAMPA are watching through the mist, part of an event that happened long ago.)*

THOMAS: Give me the money.

SONDRA: So you see, you can leave work.

THOMAS: Sondra, give me the money and I'll give it all back to your father.

—JENNY: It's Sondra!

SONDRA: What?

THOMAS: *(Advancing on her)* **Where is it?**

—JENNY: Grampa, what are they doing?

SONDRA: What's the matter?

THOMAS: I won't steal another man's money. Where is it?

—GRAMPA: I'm not sure.

SONDRA: That money belongs to me, and you.

THOMAS: You're dreaming, Sondra. This is some dream of yours.

SONDRA: It's our dream. I thank God for you, Thomas Hanson. You've brought me back to life again. It's a miracle that you want what I want.

—JENNY: They don't even see us.

THOMAS: *(He grabs her, holds her.)* **Where is it?**

SONDRA: *(She pulls away, moves from him.)* **I hid it, where only I can find it.**

THOMAS: I'm trying to help you, Sondra.

SONDRA: Do you know what he'll do to me if he finds out I took it?

THOMAS: You should have thought of that before.

SONDRA: You may have it if we go.

THOMAS: I won't go with your father's money.

SONDRA: Then we'll take the jewels, just my mother's jewels.

THOMAS: Sondra—

SONDRA: *(Stunned, afraid)* Then without them. We'll go without them.

THOMAS: How can I go with you? My God, you're a thief.

SONDRA: A thief?

THOMAS: Stealing from your own family, what kind of woman is that?

SONDRA: You know him, you know part of that money belongs to me, you said so.

THOMAS: Yes, but this — isn't — right! *(He turns from her, begins to leave.)*

SONDRA: Thomas! *(They freeze. Pause. They begin again, exactly as before.)*

THOMAS: Give me the money.

SONDRA: So you see, you can leave work.

THOMAS: Sondra, give me the money and I'll give it all back to your father.

—JENNY: He said that before.

SONDRA: What?

THOMAS: Where is it?

SONDRA: What's the matter?

THOMAS: I won't steal another man's money. Where is it?

—JENNY: It's the same. It's all the same.

SONDRA: That money belongs to me, and you.

THOMAS: You're dreaming, Sondra, this is some dream of yours.

SONDRA: It's our dream. I thank God for you, Thomas Hanson. You've brought me back to life again. It's a miracle that you want what I want.

—JENNY: She looks just like I thought she would.

THOMAS: *(He grabs her, holds her.)* Where is it?

SONDRA: *(She pulls away from him.)* I hid it, where only I can find it.

—GRAMPA: That's *old* Thomas.

THOMAS: I'm trying to help you, Sondra.

SONDRA: Do you know what he'll do to me if he finds out I took it?

THOMAS: You should have thought of that before.

SONDRA: You may have it if we go.

THOMAS: I won't go with your father 's money.

—JENNY: This is that last day.

SONDRA: Then we'll take the jewels, just my mother's jewels.

THOMAS: Sondra...

26

—GRAMPA: How do you know?

—JENNY: I just know.

SONDRA: *(Stunned, afraid)* **Then without them. We'll go without them.**

THOMAS: **How could I go with you? My God, you're a thief.**

SONDRA: **A thief?**

THOMAS: **Stealing from your own family, what kind of woman is that?**

SONDRA: **You know him, you know part of that money belongs to me, you said so.**

THOMAS: **Yes, but this — isn't — right!** *(THOMAS turns from her, starts to leave.)*

SONDRA: **Thomas!** *(They freeze. Pause. They begin again, exactly as before.)*

THOMAS: **Give me the money.**

SONDRA: **So you see, you can leave work.**

—JENNY: **Again, it's the same.**

(Now the two conversations run simultaneously. The volume of the repeated conversation diminishes to allow focus on JENNY and GRAMPA.)

GRAMPA: **I think she wants to show you something, Jenny.**

THOMAS: **Sondra, give me the money and I'll give it all back to your father.**

JENNY: **What?**

SONDRA: **What?**

GRAMPA: **Do you know why she wants you to see this?**

THOMAS: **Where is it?**

JENNY: **Why?**

SONDRA: **What's the matter?**

GRAMPA: **I don't know, do you?**

THOMAS: **I won't steal another man's money. Where is it?**

JENNY: **I wanted to know what happened that last day.**

SONDRA: **That money belongs to me, and you.**

(Now just THOMAS and SONDRA.)

THOMAS: *(Full volume)* **You're dreaming, Sondra, this is some dream of yours.**

SONDRA: *(She turns to JENNY, speaks directly to her.)* **This is our dream.** *(THOMAS and SONDRA disappear into the fog.)*

JENNY: **She looked at me. Did she look at me? She looked at me when she said: "This is our dream." Did you see her?**

GRAMPA: **Yeah.** *(The light returns to normal, the wind dies out. They turn back to the ruins.)*

JENNY: **Did you ever see that before?**

GRAMPA: **Nope.**

JENNY: **Did you ever see anything like that before?**

GRAMPA: **Nope. Did you?**

JENNY: **Nope.**

GRAMPA: I *heard* pieces of it out here before, but I never *saw* anything like it.

JENNY: They talked about the money.

GRAMPA: There *was* money, a lot of money. I always knew there was.

JENNY: But they stopped before we saw what happened to it.

GRAMPA: Yeah. But why did she give you the necklace, why show us this? Something...she's never done anything like this before. Something is wrong.

JENNY: What?

GRAMPA: She's a ghost, she should be down. The dead should stay down. She wants something, she's always wanted something, probably something she can never have, which is why she haunts us. But you, I think you're something special to her, and I don't like that. Do you want to go back to the house? You have a real treasure already, worth a lot of money.

JENNY: I want to stay and look some more.

GRAMPA: Why don't we go back to the house and you can show everybody what you found. Then you can decide exactly what you want to do. *(There is a fluttering sound, the lights dim, GRAMPA suddenly grabs his thigh in pain.)* **Ah! Ow—**

JENNY: What? What is it?

GRAMPA: A cramp or something in my leg.

JENNY: Grampa, what are you doing?

GRAMPA: No, Jenny, I — *(He tries to straighten his leg out, to stand on it.)* **Ah! Good Lord that hurts.** *(He can't put weight on it.)* **Bring me that chair, will you?** *(She brings him the chair and he sits down.)*

JENNY: Why do you have this? Have you had it before?

GRAMPA: No. I don't know why I have it. It's just a cramp but I can't — Ow! I can't walk. What were we...? What was I just saying?

JENNY: About going back to the house?

GRAMPA: Yeah. Going back to the house. I think we should — *(A stab of pain)* Ah! What was I saying?

JENNY: You wanted me to go back to the house.

GRAMPA: Yeah. Because — *(Pain)* Ah. Because — *(Pain)* Ah! Do you remember why?

JENNY: What's the matter, Grampa?

GRAMPA: I don't know. *(He laughs.)* There's something wrong, though. Isn't there, Jenny?

JENNY: Yeah.

GRAMPA: What's wrong?

JENNY: Your leg hurts.

GRAMPA: Yeah. *(LARRY runs on.)*

28

LARRY: There you are. It took me forever to find you.

JENNY: I thought you knew the way.

LARRY: Yes, I know the way. I must have run right past you.
Do you want to come fishing with us now, Grampa?

JENNY: He can't. His leg hurts. He has to stay with me.

LARRY: Do you, Grampa? We really want you to go fishing with
us. And I don't want to get lost again.

GRAMPA: You go ahead, Larry. I'm going to stay with Jenny.
(LARRY starts off.)

VOICE: *(Distantly, faintly, seemingly coming from all around them
[miked]. They do not directly hear this.)* La la la la la la la la
la...

LARRY: *(He wanders, gets lost.)* Then, can you tell me exactly
how to get there?

GRAMPA: Yeah, it's always been straight down the path.

LARRY: There?

GRAMPA: Yeah, right where you found it the last time.

LARRY: All right. *(He runs and trips, falls.)* Ah!

JENNY: Larry?

LARRY: What was that? It felt like someone stuck out their
foot and tripped me.

VOICE: *(Whispering)* Larry...Larry...here...here I am...

LARRY: *(Suddenly, frantically)* Who's touching me? Someone's
touching me. Who's there? *(With some effort, GRAMPA moves
to him.)*

VOICE: *(LARRY begins to hear her.)* Here...here...

LARRY: *(As if someone is poking him)* Ow. Ow! Who is that?
(GRAMPA wraps his arms around LARRY.)

VOICE: Drown, into the river and down, drown.

LARRY: What?...Me?...

VOICE: The river will swallow you, swallow...

LARRY: Who said that?

GRAMPA: Said what?

VOICE: Down...drown...

LARRY: Said the river will s—, will swallow me.

GRAMPA: We have to get out of here. *(Letting go of LARRY)* Larry,
go on. And stay off the river bank.

VOICE: La la la la la la la...

GRAMPA: *(LARRY starts off the wrong way.)* Hey, Larry! Down the
path. That way.

LARRY: Oh, yeah. *(He runs off.)*

GRAMPA: Come on, Jenny. Come on, come on, come on. *(GRAM-
PA starts to walk, the pain hinders him. Determinedly, he continues; JENNY helps him. We hear a WOMAN [miked] singing "I
Love You Truly," hauntingly and slowly; they do not hear it con-
sciously. The pain fades in GRAMPA's leg, but now he is very*

sleepy. The song continues under the lines.)

VOICE:

> **I love you truly,**
> **Truly, dear.**
> **Life with its sorrow**
> **Life with its tear.**
>
> **Fades into dreams**
> **When I feel you are near.**
> **For I love you truly**
> **Truly, dear.**

GRAMPA: We need to...we need to... *(He yawns.)* **Need to...I need to sit down.** *(JENNY goes to get the chair, GRAMPA sits on ground, leans against a tree. JENNY leaves chair. He yawns again.)* **Jenny, I'm just going to lay here a while.** *(He sings a line of the song with the VOICE to JENNY.)*

GRAMPA & VOICE: When I feel you are near.

JENNY: Are you singing, Grampa?

GRAMPA & VOICE:

> **For I love you truly,**
> **Truly, dear.**

JENNY: That's nice. I love you too, Grampa.

GRAMPA: Aw, what a sweetheart.

JENNY: Sondra must be doing this to you. You've never sung to me before.

GRAMPA: I think, I think you'd better go back to the house, kid.

JENNY: I'm going to stay here with you. *(The VOICE begins again, sings the second verse under the following lines. The light begins to slowly dim.)*

VOICE:

> **Ah, love, 'tis something**
> **To feel your kind hand.**
> **Ah, yes, 'tis something**
> **By your side to stand.**
>
> **Gone is the sorrow**
> **Gone doubt and fear.**
> **For you love me truly**
> **Truly, dear.**

GRAMPA: I don't know if that's the best idea you had today.

JENNY: *(Noticing the light dimming)* **I'm staying here and keeping you awake.**

GRAMPA: I don't think you can. Jenny, remember — remember... remember what? *(He laughs at himself.)* I can't remember. Oh — *(He gets it.)* She wants something from you.

JENNY: I want something from her, too.

GRAMPA: You don't have to give her anything you don't want to. *(He sings another line of the song with the VOICE.)*

GRAMPA & VOICE:
For you love me truly,
Truly, dear.

JENNY: Grampa, what is she doing to you?

GRAMPA: I think I'm just going to sleep.

JENNY: *(Shaking him)* No.

GRAMPA: Go back to the house. She can't follow you. Don't let her...she... *(He lies back, asleep. The light has completely changed.)*

JENNY: Grampa? Grampa, wake up. George, wake up! George! *(SONDRA enters, dressed as before. However, her hair is wild, her face even paler.)* Sondra? *(JENNY runs toward river.)* Dad!

SONDRA: *(Stepping in her path.)* Jenny. *(JENNY turns and runs completely off toward GRAMPA's house. SONDRA steps toward GRAMPA. Angrily)* George.

JENNY: *(Running back on, standing between SONDRA and GRAMPA)* You leave him alone.

SONDRA: *(Advancing on him)* He told you to run away. Old fool has never understood—

JENNY: No — *(Protecting GRAMPA)*

SONDRA: — never understood enough about me to know—

JENNY: Don't hurt him.

SONDRA: — to know what the truth is. *(SONDRA stops advancing.)*

JENNY: A ghost.

SONDRA: Jenny. Stay.

JENNY: What do you want?

SONDRA: *(She laughs.)* What do I want? What do you want?

JENNY: You know what I want.

SONDRA: Haven't I given you enough? The jewels in the necklace are real, like you. They're worth a lot of money. But it looks so pretty on you. I hope you don't sell it. It was my grandmother's, your great-great-great-grandmother's. Sell the coin. That was my father's. *(SONDRA begins to advance on JENNY.)* Jenny... *(JENNY retreats up to GRAMPA, but then holds her ground, protecting him.)* Don't...I just...You're so...warm.

JENNY: What do you want?

SONDRA: Just once I want that day to be different. *(SONDRA* *turns, walks into the house.)* **My house is such a mess. I am a bad housekeeper, I've been told.** *(She reaches down and picks up painting.)* **"NICE PICTURE."**

JENNY: I thought so, too.

SONDRA: I painted these nice pictures.

JENNY: Oh, sorry.

SONDRA: *(Putting painting down)* **The pictures I could paint now.** *(She sees doll on the ground, picks it up.)* **But I can only really do what I did before.** *(She tries to straighten up the doll.)* **The same words, the same pictures, the same feelings, the same dead days over and over.** *(She gives up on the doll, drops it. Deeply tired)* **And over...**

JENNY: Then, what are you doing now?

SONDRA: Haunting you, Jenny. *(She sits where JENNY sat and repeats as JENNY.)* **"I know why. Why he won't let me go...I do...It's because Larry's a boy. He loves Larry more than me. Because Larry's a boy. I don't know what to do."**

JENNY: Why did you say that?

SONDRA: You said that.

JENNY: Because it's true.

SONDRA: Would you really buy a boat for your father if you found the money?

JENNY: We'd go fishing, then. He'd take me fishing, then.

SONDRA: It won't work. I tried, with Thomas. I offered him all that money. Didn't you see?

JENNY: Yeah.

SONDRA: Do you think your father will ever change? And what if he doesn't? What will *you* do?

JENNY: I don't know.

SONDRA: Anything you find is yours, Jenny, not his, not your family's. I want you to have it. And you spend it the way you want. On your big dreams. *(She throws some silver dollars near JENNY.)* **Jenny, you're alive!** *(JENNY sees what they are, picks them up.)* **And I'll bet you're going to be an artist of some kind. Can you sing?**

JENNY: Yeah, a little.

SONDRA: Can you draw?

JENNY: Yeah.

SONDRA: You can?

JENNY: I think so. I love to draw.

SONDRA: Of course you do. Can you dance?

JENNY: I hate dancing.

SONDRA: You're going to be a dancer! *(She laughs.)*

JENNY: I am not.

SONDRA: Because you have to dance with boys! You'd rather beat them in a foot race.

JENNY: In a basketball game.

SONDRA: You can do anything! *(She throws her a handful of silver dollars.)* You can be anything! You already are...everything. *(She squats, looks at JENNY who is on her knees and who has finished gathering coins.)* You could be me. *(JENNY looks up at her.)* You could be my child. I would have loved you dearly. *(Rises.)* Will you come here? *(JENNY starts toward her, stops.)* Have I hurt you? Haven't I given you things? Haven't I done what you asked? Showed you that last day? You wanted that awful Larry to fall in the river and he did.

JENNY: You did that?

SONDRA: Because you asked me to. And you laughed.

JENNY: Yeah.

SONDRA: Will you come here? *(She goes to SONDRA. Once near her, JENNY shivers from the cold.)* Oh, so warm.

JENNY: Cold. *(SONDRA reaches out slowly, almost touches JENNY's face. JENNY recoils in pain.)* Ah — cold.

SONDRA: So warm.

JENNY: That hurts.

SONDRA: Jenny... *(She reaches out with both hands; JENNY backs away in pain.)*

JENNY: Ah! I can't, you can't do that.

SONDRA: I'm sorry.

JENNY: You can't do that, it hurts.

SONDRA: I know, I'm sorry.

JENNY: What do you want?

SONDRA: I want to show you parts of my life that no one will ever know about if you don't see them. They'll be lost forever. Not just that last day. The day I painted that picture, the day I went to the fair and rode the Ferris wheel, my ninth birthday. I can't have the children I would have had, I can't paint the nice pictures, but I can show you and you can remember.

JENNY: Oh. That's what you want?

SONDRA: And, I want you to come back. Often. And tell me all about what's happening to you. All about everything. And when you're older, if you have children, I want you to bring them here. And show me pictures of where you live. And the pictures that you paint. A whole lifetime of pictures you paint. All right?

JENNY: Well...

SONDRA: Now, you tell me what *you* want.

JENNY: A fishing boat. To go fishing with my dad.

SONDRA: What else?

JENNY: Um, oh yeah, to go swimming with the dolphins in

Hawaii.

SONDRA: What do you want from me?

JENNY: To see the rest of what happened that day.

SONDRA: The money. Everyone wants the money, even you. *(SONDRA considers a moment, seemingly looking for — and finding — an answer in JENNY's face.)* **I would have loved you dearly.** *(Sings.)*

> **Ah, love 'tis something**
> **To feel your kind hand.**
> *(GRAMPA stretches and yawns.)*
> **Ah, yes, 'tis something**
> **By your side to stand...**

(JENNY moves to him as SONDRA exits.)

JENNY: Grampa?

GRAMPA: Jenny. Hi, kid. What are you doing... *(Noticing where he is)* **here? What happened?**

JENNY: Sondra, she's here and she— *(She looks, sees SONDRA is gone.)* **She was here. She talked to me.**

GRAMPA: Right to you? Did you see her?

JENNY: Yeah, and look, she gave me more money.

GRAMPA: More money?

JENNY: Yeah, and she told me the necklace was her grand-mother's. And she sang to me — like you did. And she tried to touch me and it hurt and she told me —

GRAMPA: *(He rises.)* **She hurt you?**

JENNY: When she touched me.

GRAMPA: Are you all right?

JENNY: Yeah, but we have to stay here because —

GRAMPA: No, no, let's go back to the house and you can tell me all about it.

JENNY: No, we have to stay.

GRAMPA: We don't know what she's doing. *(He pulls them toward house.)*

JENNY: No, Grampa, we have to stay; she's going to show us what happened. *(The light dims, both of them notice this, and turn toward the house.)* **I told her I wanted to see what happened that last day.**

GRAMPA: You can't be sure that's what she's doing. She's a ghost. She hurt you. *(Finally pulling her along)* **Come on, Jenny. We're going back to the house.** *(Seemingly from nowhere, SONDRA steps out, reaches and almost touches GRAMPA in the chest.)*

SONDRA: No! *(He recoils, gasping for breath and in pain.)*

GRAMPA: Ah —

JENNY: Grampa!

SONDRA: Stay, you old fool.

JENNY: We will.

SONDRA: Listen to her. She knows more than you. She understands more than you. It's what she wants. It's what you want. *(She touches him again, he backs away in pain, sits.)*

JENNY: Stop it.

SONDRA: It's what you all want. *(She advances quickly on him. JENNY steps between them.)*

JENNY: He'll stay. We're staying.

SONDRA: You're great fun, George, all of you: bankers, farmers, lawyers, relatives, you and your son Lawrence; building fires in the middle of the day to keep me away, screeching and stumbling out of here like you'd seen a ghost. You understand nothing about what you found, about that money, about me. *(Mist begins to roll in from the river.)* Now is the time, George. It's what you came for. Listen to her. *(She exits.)*

JENNY: Are you all right?

GRAMPA: Yeah, if I can catch my breath. Did you say she touched you?

JENNY: Yeah, not like you, she was nice to me, but it still hurt.

GRAMPA: Yeah, took the breath out of me. *(Mist continues to thicken.)* Cold... *(She takes his hand.)* You're warm. *(She rubs his hand.)* That feels good.

JENNY: *(Noticing the thickening fog)* But we have to stay. All right?

GRAMPA: Are you sure? I don't want her touching me, again, or you. Her money's not worth feeling like this.

JENNY: She's not going to hurt me. You were right. I think she likes me. And she's going to show us! There she is! She's going to show us that last day! *(SONDRA appears through the mist, followed by THOMAS.)*

GRAMPA: Are you sure you want to see it?

JENNY: What do you mean?

SONDRA: What do you mean?

THOMAS: I just said I wanted to go to the fair with you. I never said I'd run away with you.

SONDRA: That's what you want.

THOMAS: Sondra, I've only been seeing you a month.

SONDRA: I bought this dress for you, for today; it's a wedding dress.

THOMAS: What?

SONDRA: My wedding dress. Do you like it?

THOMAS: Yeah, you look beautiful.

SONDRA: I do?

THOMAS: You always do.

SONDRA: And look — *(Showing him her right hand)* **My mother's wedding ring. We'll go anywhere you want. Just get in your automobile and go.**

THOMAS: Sondra, I can't just leave, leave my work. And I don't have any money.

SONDRA: We have money. See? *(She holds out the necklace.)*

THOMAS: A necklace?

—JENNY: The necklace!

SONDRA: My mother's jewelry.

THOMAS: Where did you get it?

SONDRA: Where my father hid it — in the cellar. My mother would want me to have it, so I'm taking it with us. And — *(She holds up a silver dollar)* I found all of father's money — in the cupboard, under his bed, in his shaving kit—in his shoes, Thomas. He hides his money in his Sunday shoes. I have it all in a box.

THOMAS: All your family's money?

SONDRA: Yes, my *family's* money. He's never given us anything. When we need something he lies and says he doesn't have any money. You've seen him.

THOMAS: Yes, but—

SONDRA: He won't be angry I'm gone, he'll miss his money.

THOMAS: Yeah, that's probably true.

SONDRA: You see? You understand. You understand. *(Embracing him)* We can go. It will be all right. We can go.

THOMAS: But you don't have the right to take all your family's money.

SONDRA: What I'm taking is rightfully mine. One third of it. I'll leave the rest. My mother would want me to take it. And so would Georgie. We'll save it for our children, Thomas; we're going to have lots of children and they'll all look like you.

THOMAS: Where is the box of money? In your suitcase?

SONDRA: Thomas? *(He exits, she follows.)*

JENNY: She was only going to take part of it.

GRAMPA: Georgie. That was her brother — my father. *(SONDRA enters as before, followed by THOMAS.)*

THOMAS: Give me the money.

SONDRA: So you see, you can leave work.

THOMAS: Sondra, give me the money and I'll give it all back to your father.

SONDRA: What?

THOMAS: *(Advancing on her)* Where is it?

SONDRA: What's the matter?

THOMAS: I won't steal another man's money. Where is it?

36

SONDRA: That money belongs to me, and you.

THOMAS: You're dreaming, Sondra, this is some dream of yours.

SONDRA: It's our dream. I thank God for you, Thomas Hanson. You've brought me back to life again. It's a miracle that you want what I want. *(He grabs her, holds her.)*

THOMAS: Where is it?

SONDRA: *(She pulls away from him.)* I hid it, where only I can find it.

THOMAS: I'm trying to help you, Sondra.

SONDRA: Do you know what he'll do to me if he finds out I took it?

THOMAS: You should have thought of that before.

SONDRA: You may have it if we go.

THOMAS: I won't go with your father's money.

SONDRA: Then we'll take the jewels, just my mother's jewels.

THOMAS: Sondra...

SONDRA: *(Stunned)* Then without them. We'll go without them.

THOMAS: How can I go with you? My God, you're a thief.

SONDRA: A thief?

THOMAS: Stealing from your own family, what kind of woman is that?

SONDRA: You know him, you know part of that money belongs to me, you said so.

THOMAS: Yes, but this — isn't — right! *(He turns, begins to exit.)*

SONDRA: Thomas!

THOMAS: *(Moves to front door, turns back.)* And I could support a family—I will, when I'm ready. I won't need another man's money. *(Coming back to her)* If you don't give me the money now, I'm going to town to tell your father you took it. *(She stands resolute.)* It was you who took it, not me. *(As he exits)* I never wanted his money. *(He leaves. Stunned, she goes out the door after him.)*

SONDRA: Thomas! *(He's gone. She watches him go, opens her hand and the necklace and coin fall to the ground. She moves into the house, trying to understand what has just happened. She goes to the fireplace, loosens a corner stone and slides it over. SONDRA pulls out a large, ornate, wooden jewelry box, then slides the stone back. SONDRA picks up box, opens it, revealing money and jewelry. The jewelry box is a music box and plays an old love song.)*

JENNY: There! *(SONDRA takes the paper money in her hands, clenches it and holds it to her breast. Then she stuffs the money back in the box, shuts it, and runs out the front door toward the river.)*

GRAMPA: No.

JENNY: *(Stepping in front of SONDRA)* No! *(SONDRA, still in 1920 and not responding to JENNY, stops, turns back to house and considers.)* **Yes, put it back. Put the money back, Sondra.** *(SONDRA hesitates, takes a step back toward the house.)* **You put it back, didn't you?** *(SONDRA runs off toward river. JENNY starts after her.)*

GRAMPA: *(Holding her back)* **You know what she does in the river.**

JENNY: **Did she jump in with the box? Did she take the money with her?** *(She stops trying to pull away, is searching for SONDRA who has disappeared.)* **Where...where'd she go? Do you see her? Grampa, where'd she go?**

GRAMPA: **I don't think she wants you to see what she did.** *(The light changes to late evening.)* **All these years. All of us tearing down this house board by board, scared half out of our minds, looking for money that wasn't here. She was laughing at us old fools.**

JENNY: **Maybe she brought it back and put it behind the stone.** *(She runs to the stone and tries to loosen it.)*

GRAMPA: **No wonder she doesn't stay down. We're too damn entertaining.**

JENNY: **Grampa, help me. Help me.** *(He helps her. They loosen it, move it over.)* **It's not here. She could have put it somewhere by the river. A hole in a tree or under a rock.**

GRAMPA: **Why would she do that?**

JENNY: **Why would she take it with her into the river? That would be stupid. Come on, Grampa, let's go look. She ran this way.** *(She starts to pull him off.)*

GRAMPA: **Jenny, she was hurt and angry.**

JENNY: **Not at me.**

GRAMPA: **She didn't know you then.** *(SONDRA enters, appearing to both of them.)* **Jenny —** *(He stops them, pulls JENNY away from SONDRA.)*

JENNY: *(Getting free of GRAMPA, moving to SONDRA)* **Where is it? You put it somewhere, didn't you? That's why no one could find it.**

SONDRA: **I took it with me into the river.**

JENNY: **Why did you do that? You lost all that money. Now no one can spend it.**

SONDRA: **I know.**

JENNY: **You took that money away from everybody. You took it away from me.**

SONDRA: *(Going to JENNY)* **If I would have known —**

JENNY: **Don't touch me.**

SONDRA: *(Keeping her distance)* **Jenny, I didn't —**

JENNY: **That was stupid. That was just stupid.**

SONDRA: **You're right.**

JENNY: Drowning yourself in the river! Stupid! That was stupid!

SONDRA: Yes, it was.

JENNY: *(Turning away)* **Stupid.**

SONDRA: If I would have known that one day you would come, Jenny, I would have left it for you. I didn't know what to do. And what I did was stupid. I lost our money — but so much more: I lost the children I would have had; my painting, a lifetime of paintings, and... *(To herself; relieved, exhilarated)* Oh, I'll never be the same. To show you the rest of the day, something I did not think I could ever show anybody. *(To GRAMPA)* I even showed you. *(She sighs deeply. To JENNY)* I gave you all there was left. The coins and the necklace. You have everything. And you can keep it all, can't she, George.

GRAMPA: Oh, yes.

SONDRA: You'll keep her father from it?

GRAMPA: It's hers.

SONDRA: I believe you. *(To JENNY)* The necklace is worth a lot of money, enough to buy a boat for your father, if that's what you still want. *(To herself)* Oh, I can't remember when I've ever felt so tired. *(Back to JENNY)* I'm glad you know my secret. I'm so glad it's you I told. I know that one day you'll understand everything. Thank you, Jenny. *(She starts off, toward river.)*

JENNY: Sondra? *(SONDRA stops.)* When I come back, will I see you again?

SONDRA: I don't know. I'm very tired.

JENNY: You said you wanted to show me things, so that I could remember them.

SONDRA: I'm not sure that's what I want, anymore. I think I showed you what I wanted to show you.

JENNY: But I want to see you again.

SONDRA: Here... *(She takes off her ring.)* This was my mother's wedding ring.

JENNY: I know.

SONDRA: She wanted me to wear it on my wedding day. Hold out your hand. *(She drops ring in JENNY's hand.)* Wear this and you'll remember me. *(JENNY reaches out her hand toward SONDRA.)* Jenny, you don't have to... *(JENNY holds her hand close to SONDRA'S face. JENNY winces but keeps her hand there. SONDRA loves the warmth.)* So warm...

JENNY: Thanks. Thanks for everything. *(SONDRA walks off.)* Good-bye, Sondra. *(JENNY moves to GRAMPA, cold and in pain.)* Oh, Grampa. *(GRAMPA rubs her hand. FATHER and LARRY are heard laughing and talking Off-stage. JENNY pock-*

ets the ring and necklace. They enter.)

GRAMPA: How'd you guys do?

LARRY: Dad only caught one—a dogfish.

FATHER: Larry fell in and scared all the decent fish away.

LARRY: You guys find anything?

FATHER: Yeah, did you find that box of money?

GRAMPA: No, we didn't find that box of money.

FATHER: Well, I guess nobody caught anything much, tonight. We're going back to the house. You want to walk with us, Jen?

JENNY: I think...Grampa, will you go fishing with me for a while?

GRAMPA: Yeah?

JENNY: Yeah. I just need to talk to you. Spend some time alone with you.

GRAMPA: Sure. Sure, Jenny. Be happy to. *(GRAMPA takes tackle box and poles from LARRY.)*

LARRY: Nothing's biting but the bugs.

FATHER: See you at the house.

LARRY: Race you back, Dad. All right? Ready? Go! *(He takes a quick couple of steps, FATHER dashes, LARRY stops, calls to him.)* **You win!** *(LARRY grins, FATHER strolls back to him.)*

FATHER: You'll pay for that.

LARRY: Oh, not my allowance.

FATHER: Worse. *(He puckers, kisses the air.)*

LARRY: Oh, kissing Gramma again?

FATHER: *(He laughs an evil laugh.)* **Come on.** *(FATHER and LARRY start off.)*

JENNY: Dad? *(They stop.)*

FATHER: Yeah?

JENNY: I found this — *(She holds up the necklace.)* **And some old silver dollars.**

FATHER: A necklace? *(He takes necklace.)* It *is* a necklace. Look at this. Are these jewels real, Dad?

GRAMPA: Yeah. Belonged to Jenny's great-great-great-grandmother.

FATHER: This must be worth a fortune.

JENNY: I was going to buy a boat, a fishing boat. But now, I think I'm going to keep the necklace.

GRAMPA: Yeah.

FATHER: Where did you find this?

JENNY: Over there under some stuff.

FATHER: You found it here?

JENNY: Yeah.

FATHER: I don't believe it. You don't know how often I've looked out here. And Grampa, too. And we never found anything.

JENNY: Sondra showed me where to find it.

FATHER: Sondra? Are you all right?

JENNY: I'm fine.

FATHER: Are you sure? She can scare the devil out of you. Believe me, I know.

JENNY: I'm fine.

LARRY: Did you see her?

JENNY: Yeah, talked to her, too.

FATHER: She never let us see her. Why did she let you see her?

LARRY: Yeah, and why did she tell you where the necklace was?

JENNY: I'll meet you at the house, then I'll tell you the whole story.

FATHER: Where's the rest? Did she tell you where the money is?

JENNY: I just need to talk to Grampa awhile. Then I'll tell you what happened. I'll tell you everything, all right? *(She holds out her hand for the necklace.)*

FATHER: I should keep this for you. I don't know if you know what you found here, Jenny. This is an heirloom, a family treasure, worth a lot of money. It's not a toy.

JENNY: Dad —

FATHER: And she might want it back. You don't know what she'll do. She's angry, very angry.

JENNY: She won't take it back from me. She's not angry at me.

GRAMPA: Give her the necklace, Lawrence. I believe it's her's. *(FATHER gives her the necklace.)*

FATHER: What happened here, Dad?

GRAMPA: Jenny will tell you. *(FATHER and JENNY face each other. In the silence, the FATHER waits for something. JENNY stands her ground, gives him nothing.)*

FATHER: See you back at the house. *(FATHER and LARRY exit. GRAMPA sits.)*

JENNY: I'll bet these silver dollars are worth enough. Grampa, do you want to go to Hawaii with me?

GRAMPA: Jenny, you don't have to take me to Hawaii. You don't have to give me anything. I'll still love you.

JENNY: I know. I'm not saying I can pay for you. I just want you to go with me. Will you go with me? *(She sits on his lap.)*

GRAMPA: Sure. We'll go swimming with those dolphins.

JENNY: She gave me some nice things. *(Holds up wedding ring.)*

GRAMPA: She gave you some beautiful things.

JENNY: *(She puts wedding ring on, holds out her hand, looks at ring.)* It's a little big for me, yet. *(And, in the same manner*

as with SONDRA, she slowly reaches over and touches
GRAMPA's cheek. Then she kisses his other cheek, sighs, and
relaxes into him.)

GRAMPA: Jenny... *(Pause)*

JENNY: Come on, Grampa. *(They pick up their gear and go off
together.)*

THE END

HANSEL AND GRETEL

THE LITTLE BROTHER AND THE LITTLE SISTER

~by~
MAX BUSH

CHARACTERS

HANSEL

GRETEL

MOTHER

FATHER

WHITE BIRD

WITCH

TIME: Once upon a time.

PLACE: Near the Woodcutter's cottage on the edge of the forest, in the deep forest, outside the Witch's house.

RUNNING TIME: Approximately fifty minutes.

This play is based on the manuscript and early editions of the Brothers Grimm.

This adaptation was commissioned by the Emmy Gifford Children's Theatre of Omaha, Nebraska, and opened there on October 25, 1991, with the following cast and crew:

CAST

HANSEL	Kevin Barratt
GRETEL	Laura Mar
MOTHER	Pam Carter
FATHER	Earl Bates
WHITE BIRD	Jenny Coyan
WITCH	Amy Kunz

PRODUCTION STAFF

Director	James Larson
Assistant Director	Stephanie Anderson
Set Design	Film & Stage Services
Light Design	Film & Stage Services
Costume Design	Sherri Geerdes
Music Design	James Larson
Incidental Music	John Kunz
Properties	Tracy Thies
Make-Up	Cea Larkin

SCENE 1

(At rise we see the Woodcutter's house, the forest in the background. Trees, stumps, bushes; a patch of multi-colored stones. Near the house, a large water pitcher.)

(HANSEL runs on carrying a worn, soft, leather ball about the size of a melon, leans against a tree, blinds his eyes and counts. GRETEL runs on, checks to see if he's peeking, dashes behind a bush. She decides better of it, runs, and dives behind a tree. She jumps up in indecision, starts toward a tree, stops, hesitates, moves behind stump just as HANSEL wheels and yells.)

HANSEL: I see you! *(He doesn't. He tosses ball up and down as he scans the area and walks around the home tree. He quietly sneaks up on a deserted bush, all the while facing home. He suddenly bolts toward a stump, jumps up on it, prepares to throw the ball.)* **Caught!** *(GRETEL moves farther away from him by moving behind a tree. HANSEL turns and quickly runs to the home tree.)* **Gretel? Gretel! Where are you? We said you couldn't hide in the forest. Are you in the woods?** *(He dashes and takes a quick look behind house. GRETEL moves behind a stump and closer to the home tree. He runs back.)* **You will never get home free again.** *(He sees her foot sticking out behind the stump.)* **I'll sit and wait for you.** *(He sits but immediately begins to crawl toward GRETEL. She peers over stump, sees him, looks for her way out. She picks up a stone, tosses it behind HANSEL. HANSEL stops, looks, laughs to himself, then continues to crawl toward her. She peers over stump, sees him moving closer. She starts to crawl out, stops when she realizes he would see her. She desperately looks for an escape. There is none. HANSEL crawls up to the other side of stump, begins to slowly rise. GRETEL jumps up and screams in his face.)*

GRETEL: Hansel! *(He starts for a moment as she squeals and runs toward home. HANSEL recovers, chases her and, when he's close, throws ball and hits her. He then runs for home but she trips him.)*

HANSEL: Aaaahhh! Gretel! *(She chases down ball, picks it up, throws, hits him and runs toward home. He frantically crawls toward ball but it's too late.)*

GRETEL: *(Touching home-tree)* ***Free! Ha! Twice! Free! Free!***

HANSEL: You tripped me. That's not fair.

GRETEL: We never said we couldn't trip.

HANSEL: *(Hitting her with the ball)* **We can't trip.**

GRETEL: All right. Not anymore.

HANSEL: I would have won.

GRETEL: I won, Hansel. Twice. You have to get the water from the stream.

HANSEL: I don't know why we have to get the water. We always get the water.

GRETEL: *(Handing him the pitcher)* Go on.

HANSEL: I'm too hungry and tired to go all the way to the stream.

GRETEL: Hansel, it's for our soup.

HANSEL: It's not good soup. It's stick soup. She makes it with sticks. It tastes like water with sticks in it.

GRETEL: She won't cook us anything if we don't get the water.

HANSEL: Let's play again.

GRETEL: I'm still free. *(Running after ball)* And you still have to get the water.

HANSEL: You won't win this time. Give me the ball. *(She throws it to him.)* And no tripping.

MOTHER: *(Calling from within house)* Hansel?

HANSEL: The water — *(He runs to the pitcher, picks it up.)*

GRETEL: She's coming. *(He hands pitcher to GRETEL, runs and hides. She hurriedly sets it down, hides. MOTHER enters from the house, sees pitcher.)*

MOTHER: Ah. Good. *(She picks up pitcher.)* Empty. Gretel? *(She looks but can't see them.)* I told you I needed water from the stream for soup. Hansel? Your father will be home from the market, and he'll be thirsty and hungry. Gretel! *(HANSEL playfully pushes GRETEL out, but the MOTHER doesn't see her. GRETEL hides again.)* If you don't get the water you won't eat. *(The CHILDREN stay hidden.)* Gretel! You have to help me! You know you have to help me. Hansel! *(FATHER enters pulling a wagon with firewood stacked high on it.)*

FATHER: Finally...home... *(Setting down wood)* What a time to live. *(She embraces him warmly.)*

MOTHER: You look exhausted.

FATHER: *(Seeing pitcher)* Ah, water.

MOTHER: No, empty. I asked the children to bring some up for you.

FATHER: They didn't?

MOTHER: I heard them playing and thought they had...You couldn't trade any wood?

FATHER: There's no food.

MOTHER: None?

FATHER: The stocks are full of thieves — people like you and me — who tried to steal food, just to live. The streets are crowded with peddlers, fortunetellers, barbers, surgeons, cobblers, all starving.

MOTHER: What are people doing?

FATHER: They're dying.

MOTHER: And their children...?

FATHER: How are we to feed our poor children when we have nothing for ourselves?

MOTHER: No one is going to help us. We must do something.

FATHER: What?

MOTHER: I have thought about this — and so have you, I know. *(Soothingly)* Tomorrow morning we will take the children into the thickest part of the forest. We will light a fire, and give each of them a piece of bread; then we will go do our work and leave them.

FATHER: I could never leave my children alone in the forest.

MOTHER: Will you find us food?

FATHER: No child deserves to be left in the wood.

MOTHER: Will you find us food?

FATHER: I have until now. We've eaten until now.

MOTHER: But our food is almost gone — look in our cupboards. You and I may be able to survive until crops are replanted.

FATHER: The wild animals would tear them to pieces.

MOTHER: Then we will all die of hunger.

FATHER: They're our children.

MOTHER: I know they're our children. I can't watch them starve to death. Can you? Gretel is so pale already. And maybe, in the forest, somehow, they'll find a way to survive.

FATHER: They'll never survive alone.

MOTHER: We don't know. We won't know. I'll never know. *(She picks up pitcher, exits toward stream.)*

FATHER: Wait. Wait! *(He exits after her. HANSEL and GRETEL step out, look after their parents, stunned. GRETEL sits on the ground, cries. He drops ball, watches it roll away.)*

HANSEL: We'll have to find our way back.

GRETEL: At night?

HANSEL: I'll find our way back.

GRETEL: How, in the dark?

HANSEL: I'll...tonight, when the moon is out, I'll go out and gather the white stones that shine in the moonlight. I'll fill my pockets and when we go into the forest, I'll drop them one by one. Then we can follow them back home.

GRETEL: Hansel! *(She hugs him.)*

HANSEL: Don't worry, Gretel. Don't worry. I'll find our way back. *(Music, dim-out. End Scene 1.)*

SCENE 2

(Evening in the deep forest. Very large trees, large rocks; two stacks of wood, one prepared for a fire, the other to feed the fire. Occasional bird songs; strong silences. This is a rich, earthen place; deep color with brilliant patches of bright flowers, lichens, and light. It's teeming with old and new life and full of unchecked energy and possibility. FATHER enters, followed by MOTHER, GRETEL, and HANSEL. GRETEL runs ahead gathering wild flowers.)

FATHER: **It's just a little further.**

GRETEL: *(Picking a flower)* **Another yellow one.** *(HANSEL stops, turns back, drops a white pebble.)*

FATHER: **Here's the fire I built for you.** *(HANSEL runs to check out fire.)* **Isn't this a beautiful place?**

GRETEL: **We've never come this far before.**

FATHER: **There's a stream, see?**

MOTHER: **And bushes with berries.**

GRETEL: *(Picking a flower)* **I've never seen a flower like this.**

MOTHER: **Here, children. Some of your favorite cake for your supper. I made this for you last night.**

GRETEL: **Will you have some with us, Mother?**

MOTHER: **We...have to get wood before it gets too dark.**

GRETEL: **I'll give you part of mine.**

MOTHER: **But it's so small; and I made it for you. I want you to have your favorite cake. And here's some water.**

GRETEL: **Cake is better with milk.**

MOTHER: **I wish I had milk to give you.**

HANSEL: *(To FATHER)* **Why did we come so far in the forest?**

FATHER: **A good question, Hansel. You are a smart boy, aren't you?**

HANSEL: **There's wood near the house.**

FATHER: **Very smart.**

HANSEL: **And how are you going to bring the wood back? You didn't take your wood cart.**

MOTHER: **Father will light the fire and you eat.**

FATHER: *(As he lights the fire)* **The fire will burn slow, all night. See how I built it? And there's more wood.**

HANSEL: **But we don't need a fire all night.**

FATHER: **No...no...but you don't need to be afraid of animals with a fire like this. And it will keep you warm.**

MOTHER: **When you've eaten, lie down by the fire and rest yourselves. When we're finished, we'll come back for you.**

GRETEL: **Here.** *(She gives her MOTHER the bouquet of wild flowers.)*

MOTHER: **Gretel...**

FATHER: **Yes, you sleep while we gather wood and...we'll come back for you.** *(MOTHER starts off, FATHER hesitates.)* **You...you're**

smart, Hansel, very smart. And you're brave, aren't you, Gretel? *(He kisses her.)* **Very brave.** *(He exits, followed by MOTHER.)*

GRETEL: **I'm not brave.**

HANSEL: **I'm smart.**

GRETEL: **Will they come back?**

HANSEL: **They said they would. Father said he would.**

GRETEL: **They wouldn't leave us here. Not here.** *(Standing next to an enormous trunk)* **These trees are big...It's getting dark already.**

HANSEL: **We're safe by the fire.** *(Eating)* **Cake. See, she made us our favorite cake.**

GRETEL: **It's good. Cinnamon.**

HANSEL: **I'm so hungry I could eat a mountain of cake.**

GRETEL: **A mountain of cake.** *(A wind passes through the forest. The CHILDREN hear it, look around and up. Then they hear a sound like the distant, slow chopping of wood.)* **Listen...**

HANSEL: **That's Father, chopping wood, right over there. See? Father said he'd come back. I want milk with this cake.** *(Behind GRETEL the WHITE BIRD glides in on the wind, lands, screeches and flutters its wings. Her screech is piercing, frightening. She resembles a large bird of prey more than a duck or dove.)*

GRETEL: **Hansel!** *(HANSEL stands in horror for a moment, then picks up a stick, pulls GRETEL behind him.)*

HANSEL: **Father! Mother! Father!**

GRETEL: **Scare it away. Get it away.**

HANSEL: **What does it want?**

GRETEL: **Scare it away; kill it!**

HANSEL: **Father!**

GRETEL: **He said the fire would protect us from the animals.** *(The BIRD spreads her wings, moves toward them, cooing. GRETEL screams, HANSEL pulls her away from the BIRD.)* **Hansel!** *(The BIRD glides toward an opening in the trees. She turns, screeches, hops toward path. She turns, sees HANSEL and GRETEL aren't moving, then glides back into clearing.)*

HANSEL: **Stay behind me.** *(He starts slowly toward BIRD.)*

GRETEL: **Hansel, what will you do? It'll bite your throat. It'll claw your eyes!** *(HANSEL walks cautiously up to the BIRD, reaches out to touch her. The BIRD turns her head to be petted. HANSEL suddenly strikes BIRD with the stick, she squawks.)*

HANSEL: **Go!**

GRETEL: *(Joining him as she sees BIRD move away from HANSEL)* **Go! Go!**

HANSEL: **Hah! Hah! Hah!** *(They chase the squawking BIRD around the trees, yelling, stomping, swinging and throwing sticks. The BIRD is reluctant to go. She moves off, however. HANSEL runs*

51

back to the fire.) **Free!**

GRETEL: *(Joining him)* **Free!**

HANSEL: **That bird won't come back.**

GRETEL: **Not by us.**

HANSEL: **You see, Gretel? Don't worry.** *(They sit by fire, pick up their cake. The BIRD enters quietly, coming up unseen behind them.)* **She didn't give us very much cake.**

GRETEL: **It's not enough for a whole day.**

HANSEL: **Not for a whole day. Can you see the moon?** *(GRETEL looks, but sees BIRD, screams. BIRD screeches with her.)* **Stay by the fire.**

GRETEL: **Why did it come back?**

HANSEL: **Stay by the fire.**

GRETEL: **What does it want?** *(HANSEL charges BIRD; it flees toward GRETEL. GRETEL runs around fire, the BIRD seems to pursue her while HANSEL chases the BIRD. GRETEL runs away from the fire, the BIRD follows her, followed by HANSEL. GRETEL runs between trees, the BIRD breaks off pursuit, flies off. HANSEL throws a large stick at her. The BIRD, off, squawks loudly. HANSEL yells and runs off after her.)* **Hansel? Hansel! Don't leave the fire! Hansel, come back!** *(She is suddenly alone. She searches through the trees.)* **Hansel, come back to the fire...** *(To the forest)* **Mother...Mother...** *(Silence. HANSEL runs on.)*

HANSEL: **It flew away. I hit it with the stick. Did you see?**

GRETEL: **It squawked.**

HANSEL: **Just like you when I hit you with the ball. You squawked.**

GRETEL: *(Taking his hand, pulling him)* **Let's go to where Father is chopping wood and tell him and Mother about the bird.**

HANSEL: *(He stops them.)* **He's gone.**

GRETEL: **No, he's over there. I hear him.**

HANSEL: **He tied a stick to a dead tree; the wind's blowing it against the trunk. That's what we hear. I saw it while I was chasing the bird.**

GRETEL: **Then he left us. They left us.**

HANSEL: **It's all right, Gretel. The moon is up and look, there, on the ground...there, see? Gretel, look.**

GRETEL: **The white stones.**

HANSEL: **You can see them, now. And they will lead us right to our house.**

GRETEL: **You are smart; very smart.**

HANSEL: **Come on.** *(He takes her hand, leads her off. Music, dim-out. End Scene 2).*

SCENE 3

(Dawn at the Woodcutter's house. A despondent FATHER sits near house. HANSEL and GRETEL run on.)

GRETEL: Home!

HANSEL: We're home! I told you! We're home free!

GRETEL: Free!...Father!

HANSEL: Free, free, free, free, free!

FATHER: Gretel? But — Hansel! You've come back. *(He embraces them.)* You've come back to me. I was so worried about you. Oh, you're home. You're home!

GRETEL: We walked all night.

HANSEL: Then the moon went down and we couldn't see —

GRETEL: So we had to wait until the sun came up —

HANSEL: But then we could see the house.

GRETEL: Hansel did it!

FATHER: Hansel!

HANSEL: And we saw a White Bird.

GRETEL: Yes, a terrible White Bird came but we scared it away.

FATHER: A white bird?

HANSEL: I hit it with a stick.

FATHER: And you found your way back. My children are alive. *(He embraces HANSEL.)*

GRETEL: Father! *(She jumps on his back, he spins around, laughing.)*

HANSEL: Home! We're home! We're home free! Free!

MOTHER: *(Entering from house. FATHER stops spinning.)* Children...

FATHER: Both of them, and not even hurt.

GRETEL: Mother. *(They go to her and GRETEL embraces her.)* We thought we'd never see you again.

MOTHER: Children...

HANSEL: I knew we would.

MOTHER: Why did you sleep so long in the wood? We thought you weren't coming back any more.

HANSEL: We didn't sleep. We walked all night.

MOTHER: You got lost. You wandered off and got lost.

GRETEL: We weren't lost. Hansel knew the way home.

MOTHER: Hansel...

HANSEL: Do you have something to eat?

MOTHER: *(To FATHER)* Anything to eat.

GRETEL: Yes, we walked all night.

MOTHER: Hungry, you see?

HANSEL: More cake?

GRETEL: Yes, more cake. That was good.

MOTHER: There's our last loaf of bread in the cupboard. Go in now, cut it in half, and bring it to me.

HANSEL: Just bread?

GRETEL: **We want more cake.**

HANSEL: **We didn't eat anything all night.**

GRETEL: **And all we had yesterday was the cake.**

HANSEL: **And we want milk with the cake.**

GRETEL: **Yes, we want milk with the cake.**

MOTHER: **I don't have cake. I don't have milk. Get the bread, that's all there is!** *(They run into the house.)* **How could they find their way back!** *(FATHER starts into the house.)* **They must go, again.** *(He stops.)* **They must go, now. This time we'll take them further into the forest so they won't be able to find their way back.**

FATHER: **I couldn't sleep all night.** *(She stares him down.)* **I don't think I can do it.**

MOTHER: **If you did it once, you can do it again. Children!** *(The CHILDREN enter with bread.)* **We're going back into the forest.**

GRETEL: **We are?**

HANSEL: **Are we, Father?**

MOTHER: **Bring your bread with you, but save it for supper.**

HANSEL: **We're going to stay in the forest all day?**

MOTHER: *(To FATHER)* **Take your axe. We'll need to chop firewood.**

HANSEL: **Do we have to go now? Couldn't we wait awhile?** *(Kneels at pebbles, trying to sort out the white ones from the others.)* **We want to play.**

MOTHER: **We have to go now.**

GRETEL: *(Goes to pebbles, tries to sort out the white ones.)* **But Father, we have a new game we want to play with these white stones. But we need a lot of them.**

HANSEL: **We can't go yet. We'll go tomorrow.**

FATHER: **We could wait...**

MOTHER: **We have to go now so we can be back by night. Come along. Bring your bread, but remember, wait until supper.**

FATHER: **Come now. You can play in the forest.** *(Their FATHER's compliance stuns HANSEL and GRETEL and they stop sorting. HANSEL drops stones, having thought of his alternate plan.)*

HANSEL: **All right. Come on, Gretel.**

GRETEL: **But Hansel —**

HANSEL: **Don't worry. We won't get lost. I know what to do.**

GRETEL: *(Relieved, dropping stones)* **Oh. All right.**

MOTHER: *(To FATHER)* **Lead the way.** *(He leads them. HANSEL is last. He turns back to the house, drops bread crumbs.)*

FATHER: **Why are you standing still and looking back at the house?**

HANSEL: **Oh, I'm looking at my little white dove. It's sitting on the roof and wants to say good-bye to me.**

MOTHER: It's not your little dove, it's the morning glow shining on the chimney. Come along. *(Music, dim-out as they exit. End Scene 3.)*

SCENE 4

(The deep forest. FATHER has just finished lighting another fire. HANSEL drops his last bread crumbs. The MOTHER holds GRETEL's hand. The CHILDREN are exhausted.)

FATHER: Stay by the fire and you'll be safe and warm.

MOTHER: We're going further on to cut wood; when we've finished we'll come back for you.

FATHER: Here, Gretel. *(He takes off his coat, lays it on ground. GRETEL lies on it.)*

MOTHER: You'll sleep well, since you didn't sleep last night.

FATHER: Lie here, Hansel. *(HANSEL lies down.)*

MOTHER: Sleep a long, long time.

FATHER: Dream of food, a mountain of food, all the food you ever wanted. And then you'll play and play. *(He exits. MOTHER starts to follow, turns, looks back at them. GRETEL opens her eyes, sits up, looks at MOTHER.)*

GRETEL: *(A simple question)* Are you leaving us again, Mother? *(MOTHER starts to say something, stops, then exits. GRETEL lies down.)* Hansel, they left us again.

HANSEL: It's all right. We'll wait until the moon comes up, then we can see the bread crumbs I dropped to show us the way home. *(He tiredly points to where he dropped them.)*

GRETEL: Here, half my bread. *(He takes it.)* I'm going to sleep.

HANSEL: I'll eat it when I wake up and then we'll go home free, again. Don't worry.

GRETEL: I'm not.

HANSEL: Don't worry.

GRETEL: I'm not worried. *(They sleep. Quietly, the white BIRD glides in, lands. She moves towards the CHILDREN, inspects them. She stands near them, waits, seemingly standing guard. She fluffs her feathers, preens her wing. Her head pivots, searching the forest. Ominous music—the Witch's theme. The BIRD becomes alert. Out of the darkening forest comes the WITCH. She's old, near-sighted and walks with a cane. She's opulently dressed and wears jewels on her hands, wrists, neck, and hair. She sniffs the air, scenting the children. The BIRD watches her intently. The scent leads her to the CHILDREN.)*

WITCH: *(In a stage whisper)* **[Sniff]...[sniff]...I know well. A lost child is what I smell.** *(She moves close to them.)* **Ah, here. Two of them. Two. And no one else here but me. And you.** *(To BIRD)* **Shoo! Away with you, filthy bird. Shoo.** *(The BIRD* *moves, but not off.)* **These are mine.** *(She looks closely, sniffs.)* **A girl...and a boy...young, sweet, far from home and hungry, so hungry, we are so hungry. I will give you food, my little ones, all the food you want. Here...** *(She places a little cake by GRETEL. Sings, as she moves to HANSEL.)* **"You, you, you must be true to me."** **And here, a little cake of hope.** *(Another cake near HANSEL)* **And more, much more than you are dreaming of now. Sleep well, my darlings, while I cook for you, prepare a feast for you, a feast for all of us.** *(She starts off, stops. Ominously)* **You are with me, now. Find me, little ones. Follow your noses.** *(She swings at BIRD with her stick.)* **Fly away.** *(She goes off. The BIRD moves to path, spies a bread crumb, eats it. She moves, scratches ground, bends, pecks, eats the bread crumb. She exits, searching for bread crumbs.)*

HANSEL: *(Moaning in his sleep)* **No, no, I can't...don't—** *(Awakening in a panic)* **No! We'll never find our way!**

GRETEL: **Hansel?**

HANSEL: **We won't know what to do!**

GRETEL: **Hansel, what is it?**

HANSEL: **Oh...I was...Was I dreaming?**

GRETEL: **I was. About an old woman with a gold necklace, I think, who smelled like a swamp.**

HANSEL: **I don't know what I was dreaming. Just that we couldn't find our way home.**

GRETEL: **Hansel, look.** *(She holds up cake.)* **A little cake. Mother must have left me a cake.**

HANSEL: **Me too, I have one, too. It smells like—**

HANSEL & GRETEL: **Gingerbread!** *(They bite cake, roll on the ground in ecstasy.)*

GRETEL: **Mmmm, it is gingerbread.**

HANSEL: **With berries and nuts.**

GRETEL: **Where did she get nuts?**

HANSEL: **I could eat a mountain of gingerbread.**

GRETEL: **Gingerbread with berries and nuts. Mmmm...**

HANSEL: **There isn't very much of it.**

GRETEL: **I can't eat it slow. It's going to be gone.**

HANSEL: **Save some—**

GRETEL: **I can't.**

HANSEL: **Neither can I.** *(They finish them.)* **It's gone.**

GRETEL: **Hansel, the moon is up.**

HANSEL: **We should be able to see the crumbs I dropped. I dropped the last one here...around here...do you see it?** *(They're standing where the WHITE BIRD ate the crumbs.)*

GRETEL: **No. Are you sure it was here?**

HANSEL: **Yes, just by this tree. Don't worry, the next one is** right there—here...near here...somewhere here...

GRETEL: Hansel—

HANSEL: But I dropped it here!

GRETEL: I think I know where they—

HANSEL: I know I did. What could have happened to them?
(With a screech the WHITE BIRD glides in between HANSEL and GRETEL, forcing them apart.)

GRETEL: The birds! The birds in the forest ate them. They ate the crumbs.

HANSEL: I didn't think of the birds.

GRETEL: Now we'll never get home. There's no way home!

HANSEL: Why didn't I think of the birds?

GRETEL: We don't even know what direction it is. Do you remember?

HANSEL: This is the way.

GRETEL: No, this is the way.

HANSEL: Is it?

GRETEL: I can't remember.

HANSEL: *(Taking her hand.)* **This way.** *(He pulls her.)*

GRETEL: *(The WHITE BIRD screeches, GRETEL stops, pulls HANSEL back to the fire.)* **Not at night! We should stay by the fire!**

HANSEL: **Come on, Gretel.** *(He pulls her. The BIRD screeches, GRETEL stops them, pulls HANSEL back to the fire.)*

GRETEL: Not in the dark. The animals will —

HANSEL: They won't hurt us if we're not afraid of them. *(The BIRD moves in front of him, squawks, denying them the path.)* **Get out of our way.** *(He swings at the BIRD.)* **Away! Go away!** *(He tries to walk around BIRD.)*

GRETEL: No, Hansel, no. *(The BIRD moves in front of HANSEL. HANSEL again tries to go around BIRD.)* **Hansel, no.** *(The BIRD cuts them off.)* **You see, we shouldn't go. She doesn't want us to go.** *(The BIRD reacts to this; bows, coos.)* **She heard me. I think she understands me.** *(HANSEL pushes the BIRD aside, tries to drag GRETEL past the BIRD. The BIRD pecks his shoulder, screeches, flaps him again and again and again. HANSEL backs off, the BIRD pursues, flapping him and screeching. HANSEL covers his head, goes to his knees and the BIRD lightly sinks her talons in his thigh. HANSEL recoils, the BIRD glides away from him, GRETEL goes to him.)* **Did she hurt you?**

HANSEL: No, it just scared me. No, *(A realization)* it didn't hurt me. It didn't hurt me. *(HANSEL tries leading GRETEL slowly off in another direction. The BIRD lumbers in front of them. He slowly tries another direction, the BIRD lumbers in front of them, stopping them. Another direction. The BIRD slowly moves in front of them, stops them. HANSEL approaches where WITCH* entered and exited. The BIRD moves out of their way.)

HANSEL: It will let us go this way. (HANSEL starts down that way, sees the BIRD isn't stopping him. He pulls GRETEL to the fire.)

GRETEL: She wants us to go that way. I think she wants to help us. (The BIRD moves to WITCH's path, starts down it, turns back to the CHILDREN, flaps, coos.) **I think she wants to show us the way home.** (The BIRD moves toward them, coos, HANSEL backs off. GRETEL moves toward BIRD, tentatively reaches out to touch her.)

HANSEL: Gretel...Gretel!

GRETEL: (She carefully reaches out, touches BIRD; BIRD coos and rubs her head on GRETEL.) **She likes me. See? She likes me.** (Pets BIRD. HANSEL stays back.) **And she's such a beautiful bird; all white; a moon bird. Like the stones. She shines in the moonlight. We'll follow her like the white stones.** (The BIRD moves to path, turns, screeches.) **She wants us to go that way.**

HANSEL: (HANSEL pulls GRETEL another way. This time the BIRD doesn't move to block their way, but turns from them.) **She's letting us go, now.**

GRETEL: (To BIRD) **Will you protect us from the other animals?** (The BIRD squawks.) **Hansel, let's follow her. She'll help us.** (She takes HANSEL by the hand and they run off following the BIRD. Music, dim-out. End Scene 4.)

SCENE 5

(Outside the WITCH's gingerbread house. A long table is set out, elegantly prepared to receive guests — dishes, silver, candelabra, napkins, food. The large oven. The small stable. The forest surrounds the house. The WHITE BIRD glides on, screeches. HANSEL and GRETEL run on, stop in amazement.)

GRETEL: It's someone else's home.

HANSEL: Look at that. (The table) **A table set for a meal. A big meal.**

GRETEL: A big meal.

HANSEL: I wonder who it's for.

GRETEL: They must have a lot of food if they need this many dishes.

HANSEL: There aren't many chairs. Only two.

GRETEL: For all these dishes?

HANSEL: I smell cooking.

GRETEL: Sweet cooking.

HANSEL: Do you smell gingerbread?

GRETEL: And pancakes. (They move toward house.)

HANSEL: Gretel...the house...Am I so hungry that I think...

GRETEL: It looks like...

HANSEL: It looks like it's made of bread.

GRETEL: And covered with cake. Hansel, it's covered with cake!

HANSEL: And cookies. *(He tastes window.)* This window is made of sugar.

GRETEL: It's a house made of food! A whole house made of food!

HANSEL: Let's eat it!

GRETEL: Let's eat it all!

HANSEL: The roof — *(He breaks off a piece, bites it.)*

GRETEL: The window — *(Takes out a pane, bites it.)*

HANSEL: Mmmm; sweet —

GRETEL: Sugar. They have sugar. They have everything.

HANSEL: This is better than going home.

GRETEL: I like this house better, too.

HANSEL: We can eat this forever. *(The BIRD screeches, exits. The CHILDREN watch it go.)*

GRETEL: Good bye, White Bird. I knew she would help us.

WITCH: *(From within house)* Nibble, nibble, gnaw
Who is nibbling at my little house?
(Silence. The CHILDREN freeze.)
Nibbling, nibbling, like a mouse,
Who is nibbling at my house?

GRETEL: The wind.

HANSEL: The wind.

GRETEL: The wind that blows from the sky to below. *(They resume eating. HANSEL takes a piece of the house. GRETEL rips off a shingle.)* I think this is... *(She bites it.)* Cinnamon cake...with berries. Mmmm. Cinnamon cake. Cinnamon cake, Hansel! *(HANSEL bites it, they laugh together.)*

WITCH: *(Off)* Nibble, nibble, gnaw
Who is eating my wall?

GRETEL: The wind—

HANSEL: — the wind that blows —

GRETEL: From the sky to the earth below.

HANSEL: I'm thirsty. Do you see anything to drink?

GRETEL: There might be something on the table.

HANSEL: Milk? Is there milk?

GRETEL: There must be milk.

HANSEL: There must be milk. Milk, milk, milk, milk — *(The WITCH enters.)*

WITCH: Children. *(Startled by her appearance, they drop their food.)* Children are nibbling at my house. Dear children, how did you come here? This deep into the wood.

HANSEL: The...the White Bird showed us the way.

WITCH: Ah, did she? Is that what you think? And are you so hungry you would eat my house?

GRETEL: It's made of cinnamon cake.

WITCH: I know. I baked it in my oven.

HANSEL: The roof is made of gingerbread.

WITCH: You poor dears; you will be all right. You will not come to any harm. You're just hungry. How unfair of the world to allow two such tender children to be so hungry, for so long. I've prepared a breakfast. Would you join me? We're having milk.

HANSEL: You have milk?

WITCH: Oh, yes, all the milk you can drink.

HANSEL: I knew you would have milk.

WITCH: And pancakes with sugar, apples and nuts.

GRETEL: Apples!

HANSEL: Where could you find apples?

WITCH: Sit, I will serve you. *(They sit. She hands them each a glass.)* **Here.**

HANSEL: **Milk!** *Miiilllkkk!* *(They drink.)*

WITCH: **And —** *(She lifts top off server.)*

GRETEL: **Pancakes! With nuts!** *(The CHILDREN grab very large pancakes.)*

WITCH: **And apples!** *(She uncovers a bowl of apples, tosses them each one.)*

GRETEL: Apples and nuts — apples and nuts — apples and nuts.

WITCH: **Eat.** *(They dive in.)* **Eat all you can, my little ones.** *(They eat pancakes with their hands, laugh, bite their apples.)* **Yes, that's it. A breakfast just waiting for you. A breakfast you deserve. Your breakfast. You will never be hungry again.**

HANSEL: Pancakes! Pancakes, Gretel!

GRETEL: *(Stands.)* **I-love-pancakes!** *(In her exuberance she throws her pancake into the air, catches it, bites it.)*

WITCH: **Yes, eat; play; play; eat. Have a grand feast!**

GRETEL: Hansel — *(They throw each other their pancakes, take a bite, throw them back and bite them. Smultaneously)*

| HANSEL: **Apples!** | GRETEL: **Pancakes!** |
| HANSEL: **Pancakes!** | GRETEL: **Apples!** |

WITCH: *(Almost dancing in exuberance)* **Yes, yes, pancakes, yes, yes, yes, apples, yes.** *(HANSEL picks up entire plate of pancakes, buries his face in them, comes up with some in his mouth. He growls and snorts and shakes his head. The pancakes break into pieces. GRETEL laughs. GRETEL tears a large pancake in half, holds up the pieces to her ears, barks.)*

GRETEL: **Woof! Woof! Woof!**

HANSEL: *(HANSEL sees this, howls.)* **Aaaooo!**

WITCH: *(Sings.)*
"I join the merry dancers
As nimbly as I can.
I sing of pretty children
Eating fruit and bread.
Their faces show no cares
Their laughter fills the air
Together we will feast."

(She indicates for HANSEL to come to her. He does. She takes his hand.) **Ah, my young boy, you are a fine, sweet one, aren't you.** *(Sings slowly.)*
**"Oh, you my chosen only comfort,
Be happy, be happy."**

HANSEL: *(Entranced)* I am.
GRETEL: Happy.
WITCH: *(Feeling his arm)* But you are thin. We'll change that, won't we? Would you like dessert?
HANSEL: *Yeees!*
GRETEL: Dessert!
WITCH: The sweetest—
HANSEL: Sweetest—
WITCH: Tenderest—
HANSEL: Tenderest—
WITCH: Dessert.
HANSEL: Dessert!
WITCH: And on the day you eat it, that is a day to celebrate. That is a grand feast.
HANSEL: A grand feast.
WITCH: It's in here. In here, my boy, my boy, in here. *(The little stable)*
HANSEL: In the chicken coop?
WITCH: Go in and you'll see it.
HANSEL: But I can see in there and I don't see anything.
GRETEL: Go in, Hansel, I want to know what it is.
HANSEL: But what can it be?
GRETEL: Hansel, go in and find out.
WITCH: Yes; you may be surprised, little one. *(He crawls in. She shuts the door and locks it.)*
HANSEL: I still don't see anything. Where is it?
WITCH: There, my boy, now I have you; you won't escape me.
HANSEL: What did you say? Where is the dessert?
WITCH: It's there; it's you; a meal and a dessert. *(She sings to herself under the following.)* **"A meal and a dessert. A meal and a dessert. A meal and a dessert."**

61

HANSEL: **Me?** *(He tries to get out.)* **Let me out. Let me out! You locked it? Gretel!**

GRETEL: **Why did you lock him in?**

HANSEL: **Gretel!** *(GRETEL pulls on cage furiously.)*

GRETEL: **Let him out. Let him out!**

WITCH: *(Eating food from the table)* **You, girl, fetch water from the stream, go into the kitchen and cook good food for your brother. He needs to be fattened. When he is nice and fat, I will eat him.**

GRETEL: **What?**

HANSEL: **Gretel! Father! Help, somebody help!**

WITCH: **You see? You won't be hungry ever again. We'll cook the best food for you.**

HANSEL: **Father, help!**

GRETEL: **Father! White Bird!**

WITCH: *(Throwing her a bucket)* **Go now, girl, or you will go into the oven first.**

GRETEL: **Hansel —**

HANSEL: **Call for Father by the stream.**

GRETEL: **He'll never hear me.**

WITCH: **A grand feast, a day to celebrate.**

HANSEL: **What am I going to do?**

WITCH: **A grand feast.**

GRETEL: **It'll be all right, Hansel. I'll find a way out of this.**

HANSEL: **How?**

GRETEL: **I will. Don't worry. Don't worry.**

WITCH: **Fetch the water!** *(GRETEL goes off. The WITCH sings during the fade.)*
"Their faces show no cares,
Their laughter fills the air,
Together we will feast."
(Music, dim-out. End Scene 5.)

SCENE 6

(Three weeks later. HANSEL is asleep in the stable. The oven is glowing; smoke comes out the stack, firelight flickers from within. GRETEL enters, carrying a tray of food for HANSEL. She stops, looks at oven, then continues to HANSEL.)

GRETEL: **Hansel...Hansel, breakfast.** *(He awakens.)* **I've made you a wonderful breakfast, Hansel. Eggs with onions and pepper, corn bread and cinnamon cake. And milk. I'm becoming a good cook.**

HANSEL: **I'm not hungry.**

GRETEL: **I am. She still doesn't give me anything to eat but crab shells.**

62

HANSEL: Eat some breakfast. I'll say I ate it, again.

GRETEL: If she sees me —

HANSEL: She can't see; she never sees.

GRETEL: *(She begins to eat.)* I watched her again this morning. She has jewels, all kinds and colors of jewels. She keeps them in a box under her bed.

HANSEL: Jewels will do me no good.

GRETEL: She has to hold them like this *(Holds food next to her eye)* so she can see them. She rubs them in her hands and mumbles old songs. *(GRETEL sings like her, mocking her. HANSEL laughs.)*

"I join the merry dancers
As nimble as I can.
I sing of pretty children..."

HANSEL: *(He looks at oven.)* Gretel, is there a fire in the oven? ...Gretel...

GRETEL: Early this morning, while you were asleep, we built it.

HANSEL: A fire in the oven...

GRETEL: She's baking bread.

HANSEL: She has all the bread she needs.

GRETEL: She didn't say anything about...you. Just bread. *(The WHITE BIRD glides on, screeches.)*

HANSEL: The White Bird, again. Why do you come here? What do you want?

GRETEL: *(She runs at it.)* You horrible bird! You led us to this Witch! *(GRETEL kicks at her, chases her around the stable. HANSEL kicks at the screeching BIRD through the bars.)*

HANSEL: Get away from me!

GRETEL: You helped her! Get away! *(She gets a good kick in, BIRD flies off.)* Hansel, I think I saw a key. Maybe the key to this lock. I think I saw a key in her box of jewels.

HANSEL: Can you get it?

GRETEL: The box isn't locked and I think I know where she keeps it, but she never lets me in the house alone.

HANSEL: Try to go in when she comes out; find a reason.

GRETEL: She 'll never let me in the house alone.

HANSEL: Try to go in when she checks to see how fat I am.

GRETEL: You do something to make her forget about me. You do something — she likes you when you're funny. You play; she likes you when you play.

HANSEL: What should I play?

GRETEL: But when she wants to see how fat you are, don't let her touch you. Where's the bone?

63

HANSEL: Here.

GRETEL: Only let her feel the bone.

HANSEL: I know.

GRETEL: Hansel, today, only let her feel the bone.

WITCH: *(Off)*
"I join the merry dancers
As nimbly as I can."

HANSEL: **Give me the food.** *(GRETEL gives him the food.)*

WITCH: *(Entering)*
"I sing of pretty children
Eating fruit and bread."

Come here, girl. *(GRETEL doesn't.)* **Come here.** *(GRETEL goes to her. The WITCH sniffs her.)* **Give me your hand.** *(WITCH holds out her hand, GRETEL puts hers in the WITCH's.)* **You've been eating. His food. Yes?**

GRETEL: **Yes.**

WITCH: **Do you make the food for him and not yourself?**

GRETEL: **Yes.**

WITCH: *(Swatting GRETEL's hand once, hard)* **Then don't eat it! Or you'll go in the oven first!** *(GRETEL pulls back hand, rubs it. WITCH moves to stable.)* **Now, Hansel...** *(Singing, affectionately)* *Hansel.* **My little pig! Are you eating your breakfast? Eat slowly, chew your food, enjoy yourself.**

HANSEL: **I don't feel well.**

WITCH: **No, dear one, what's wrong?**

HANSEL: **I have a fever. I have spots all over me, red spots. I have the pox. See?**

WITCH: *(Trying to see)* **Yes, I see.**

HANSEL: **And I'm dizzy and the food doesn't taste good, and I'm pale, very pale, I know I am. See?**

WITCH: *(Trying to look, as GRETEL slowly starts toward house)* **I see.**

HANSEL: **I have the plague!** *(He chokes and wheezes, pathetically.)* **The plague.**

WITCH: **Oh, my Hansel.**

HANSEL: **And I'm hot and then cold and then hot and then I'm asleep, then I'm awake and I don't know the difference. Then sometimes I don't feel like Hansel. I don't even think I'm a boy. I think I'm a...a chicken in a coop.** *(He becomes a chicken, flaps at WITCH, startling her.)*

WITCH: **Oh!** *(She laughs at herself. GRETEL goes in house.)* **You frightened me.** *(She watches him.)* **Yes, yes, good, very good, a chicken.** *(She clucks back at him.)*

HANSEL: **And sometimes I think I'm a duck.** *(He becomes a*

64

duck.)

WITCH: A duck. You sound just like a duck. *(She also quacks. They sing a kind of song together and she dances.)*

HANSEL: Or a pig in the pen. *(He is a pig.)*

WITCH: Oh yes, oh yes, yes, a pig, a beautiful, fat pig. Oh, my dear pig, you're playing, aren't you. And well you should. Today is a day to celebrate. A day for the Grand Feast. Today I will let you out of your pen, my little pig. *(She holds a large key, hanging from her waist.)*

HANSEL: *(Reaches for the key.)* **Give me the key. I'll unlock the door.**

WITCH: When all is ready, I'll let you out. Now, put your finger out for me to feel how fat you are.

HANSEL: *(Looking for bone)* **But...but I told you...I'm thin and sick.**

WITCH: Put out your finger, my Hansel.

HANSEL: I don't want to make you angry.

WITCH: Come, my little pig, your finger. *(HANSEL holds the bone to her hand, then slowly reaches for the key. The WITCH moves, HANSEL misses key.)* **Bony and thin. How can you still be so thin?**

HANSEL: I'm sick — the spots — see?

WITCH: Oh, you know I can't see. Give me your finger again. *(He does.)* **I don't understand it. You should be fattened for me.** *(Picking up food from the tray, throwing it at him)* **Food is what you want, isn't it? All the food you could ever eat? Gretel?** *(GRETEL enters from the house, gesturing to HANSEL that she couldn't find the key. HANSEL indicates WITCH has it on her waist.)* **Gretel.**

GRETEL: Yes.

WITCH: Come here. *(GRETEL moves to her.)* **Give me your hand.** *(She holds out her hand, GRETEL puts hers in it. The WITCH kisses GRETEL's hand.)* **You see well, don't you? You see all things around you?**

GRETEL: *(Seeing key on the WITCH)* **Yes.**

WITCH: And you would tell me what you saw, if I asked?

GRETEL: I do.

WITCH: Does our Hansel have spots, red spots? Is he pale? Is he still so thin?

GRETEL: *(HANSEL groans.)* **Oh, yes. White; and red spots on his arms and face. And all bones, just bones.**

WITCH: Oh, Gretel, Gretel. What shall we do? What should we do? *(She pets GRETEL's hand, feels her arm.)* **Why, dear girl, you're as plump from eating his food as he should be.** *(She takes GRETEL's face in her hands and kisses her on the cheek. Then she tastes the kiss. It tastes good.)* **No matter.** *(Dropping*

GRETEL's hand) **Today I will eat Hansel.**

GRETEL: But he's sick. He will make you sick.

WITCH: We will cook him a longer time.

GRETEL: But he's so thin.

WITCH: Fat or thin, sick or not, I will eat him today.

GRETEL: I wish the animals in the forest had eaten us, we should at least have died together.

WITCH: You may spare your tears; they will do you no good. *(The WITCH crosses to oven.)* **Fresh bread for the grand feast.** *(She opens door, pulls out the board the bread is on. Firelight flickers brightly from within the oven, smoke drifts out the door. HANSEL slumps in his cage.)* **The bread is baked. The fire is perfect. A day to celebrate. Gretel, dear Gretel, how many loaves of bread are here?**

GRETEL: Two.

WITCH: But I put in three. One must have fallen off the board. Take these loaves off. *(Using her apron to keep from burning her fingers, GRETEL takes the two loaves off the board.)* **Now, look inside, see if you can see the other loaf. I can't see very far, as you know.**

GRETEL: I can't see the other loaf.

WITCH: You must get on the board so you can see into the oven.

GRETEL: But I can see into the oven. There isn't another loaf.

WITCH: Simple girl, get up on the board and I will push you in a short way, then you must see it.

GRETEL: I don't know how I should begin to do that. Get up on the board.

WITCH: Climb up on the board.

GRETEL: I don't know how to do that.

WITCH: You're a child, aren't you? You can climb. Just climb up here, so... *(She gets half-up.)* **And look in.** *(GRETEL pulls her all the way on to the board.)* **No. I don't want to get on the board —**

GRETEL: Show me.

WITCH: It's a simple thing to do — let me down. I want you — *(GRETEL doesn't allow her to get down.)* **No!** *(GRETEL gets up on the board and pushes her toward opening.)* **No! Gretel! You horrible child!** *(The WITCH stops herself from going in. GRETEL pushes, the WITCH holds her ground.)*

HANSEL: Push, Gretel, push! Push! *(Unable to push her in backwards, GRETEL gets WITCH turned around, then GRETEL sits on the board and pushes with her foot. The WITCH turns again, grabs GRETEL's foot, tries to pull GRETEL in. GRETEL frantically grabs hold of the edge of the board and succeeds in pulling herself free. They face off. GRETEL lunges, tries to push WITCH in. The WITCH pulls GRETEL's hair. GRETEL frees her hair,* *backs into WITCH, the WITCH wraps her arms around GRETEL. GRETEL leans with her back on WITCH, grabs for the key and rips it off the chain.)*

GRETEL: Hansel, the key! Help me! *(As she throws it, the WITCH hits her arm; the key goes wide of the cage.)* **Get the key!** *(He tries desperately to get it but it's out of his reach.)*

HANSEL: I can't reach it. I can't reach the key! You have to do it. Push! Push! *(GRETEL hits the WITCH's hands, frees herself, jumps down, gets a short running start and barrels into WITCH who continues to hold her ground. She tries again, pushes WITCH into opening of oven. Holding on to the wall of the oven, the WITCH keeps from going in. GRETEL pushes, the WITCH loses her grip and GRETEL shoves her further in. The WITCH holds on to GRETEL and screams. GRETEL struggles as the WITCH tries to pull her in. GRETEL pushes the WITCH all the way in, then with both hands she shuts the door, locks the handle. She backs away from oven, listening to the WITCH's screams dying out. A burst of smoke billows from the chimney. GRETEL runs to key, picks it up, opens door. HANSEL crawls out and hugs her.)* **Thank you, thank you, thank you; you are brave.**

GRETEL: She's gone! *(They jump in joy.)*

HANSEL: You did it. You pushed her in.

GRETEL: She was going to push me in. She was going to push me in, I knew it. She's dead.

HANSEL: She's dead.

GRETEL: She's dead. We're free!

HANSEL: Free! *(They cheer.)*

GRETEL: Let's get the jewels and take them home to Father and Mother. *(They run in the house. The WHITE BIRD glides on, moves to stable, then to oven. The CHILDREN run out of the house carrying a large, ornate box of jewelry. GRETEL has on a wide, gold, jeweled necklace and bracelets. They set box down, open it, revealing jewelry.)* **Look at all these jewels. We'll never be hungry again.** *(The BIRD screeches, bows, scrapes, flaps about.)* **The White Bird.** *(FATHER runs on.)*

FATHER: Children!

GRETEL: Father?

HANSEL: Father! *(They run together, embrace.)*

FATHER: Gretel — Hansel — both of you.

GRETEL: Father, Father.

HANSEL: How did you find us?

FATHER: I followed the White Bird.

GRETEL: She showed you the way?

HANSEL: But she led us to the Witch.

FATHER: Witch? She led me to you. I knew she would.

GRETEL: **Father, look.** *(They show him jewels.)*

HANSEL: **We're rich!**

FATHER: **We are?**

GRETEL: **Yes, see? Jewels, Father! Jewels!**

FATHER: **How are these yours? And whose home is this? A witch, you say?**

GRETEL: **Where's Mother? I have this for her.** *(The necklace)*

HANSEL: *(Looking)* **Did she come with you?**

FATHER: **No, she didn't. She...I'm sorry. Mother is dead... But my children. My children are alive! I haven't had a single happy moment since I left you in the wood. How did you live? What happened here?**

GRETEL: **We'll tell. But first we want to leave this enchanted forest.** *(The WHITE BIRD squawks, flaps, indicating the way.)* **Let's follow her.**

HANSEL: **Yes, that's the way. Come on.** *(He picks up box of jewels, hands them to GRETEL.)* **We're free.** *(Dim-out as they exit.)*

THE END

The Emerald Circle

by Max Bush

CHARACTERS

SANDY 14

DAVE 14

MAGGIE . . . . . . 35, Dave's Mother

CHIP . . . . 14, Dave's Friend

MAN 28

TIME: Late Saturday afternoon in May of the present year.

PLACE: Single set. The action flows without a break between a cemetery and the basketball court in the driveway of Dave's house.

RUNNING TIME: Approximately one hour.

DEDICATION: *The Emerald Circle* is dedicated to Scot Copeland and Harvey Jackins.

The Emerald Circle was commissioned by the Nashville Academy Theatre and opened there on February 3, 1992, with the following cast and crew:

CAST

Dave	Kemper McDowell
Sandy	Melody McNair
Maggie	Rona Carter
Chip	Sean Sweeney
Man	Raymond Speakman

PRODUCTION STAFF

Director	Scot Copeland
Technical Director/Designer	Scott Boyd
Production Manager	Daniel C. Brewer
Fight Choreographer	Raymond Speakman
Costumier	Ida Bostian
Technical Assistant	Richard Neville
Technical Assistant	Ray Ingram
Technical Assistant	Raymond Speakman
Master Electrician	Richard Neville
Music Score	Dobehi Lacaden

(The stage is divided roughly in half. Right is the basketball court in Dave's driveway with the hoop on the front of the garage. Far right is a picnic table on the lawn. Left is the graveyard. The cemetery is old, encircled with large, draping spruce trees. The grave stones range from simple and small to large, ornately carved markers. Few remain in their original position. Most lean, some are broken in half, others are chipped, discolored with age. On one grave marker are the words: "Timothy, Not Dead, He Sleepeth.")

(At rise spot is up on SANDY in graveyard, half sitting, half lying in an awkward position. Spot up on DAVE standing in driveway. This is part of a dream he's remembering.)

SANDY: Dave? Dave? Where are you? Dave?

DAVE: I'm here.

SANDY: *(She turns, sees him.)* **I've been looking all over for you. Where are you?**

DAVE: Are you alone?

SANDY: I don't know. Help me.

DAVE: I can't. I can't move.

SANDY: You may kiss me if you want.

DAVE: I want to. I can't move.

SANDY: Are you thinking about me?

DAVE: I'm always thinking about you.

SANDY: Then come here. Help me.

DAVE: I don't know where I am. I think I'm underground. I can't lift it off me.

SANDY: Come here!

DAVE: I can't move!

SANDY: Did you do this?

DAVE: What? *(As spot fades on SANDY)* **Sandy...** *(Spots fade out. Lights up on basketball court in DAVE's driveway where DAVE stands, lost in thought. MAGGIE, DAVE's mother, enters carrying a tray with pop, a sandwich, a muffin and chips on it for DAVE, juice and a sandwich for herself.)*

MAGGIE: Hey, kid.

DAVE: *(Fairly cheery, getting ball)* **Hi, Ma.**

MAGGIE: Did you win?

DAVE: Yeah, but the competition was weak.

MAGGIE: Hungry?

DAVE: Not yet. *(He spins ball on his finger.)*

MAGGIE: Well, I could starve waiting for you. *(Sits at picnic table.)* **Come on, try this tuna salad. I made it without onions.**

DAVE: I will.

MAGGIE: What a beautiful day...I asked your dad to pick up your Mr. Muscle Protein Powder on his way home from

73

> work, Mr. Muscle.

DAVE: Is he going to do it?

MAGGIE: Well, sure. *(DAVE reaches for a muffin. Slapping his hand)* Muffin after sandwich, thank you.

DAVE: I'm not that hungry.

MAGGIE: I miss the onions...How'd you sleep? *(Spot up on SANDY in the cemetery, in same position as in the opening dream sequence.)*

DAVE: *(Glancing at SANDY)* Fine.

MAGGIE: I thought I heard you in the middle of the night.

SANDY: Dave?

DAVE: Nature calls, you know.

SANDY: Where are you? Why don't you come?

MAGGIE: Any nightmares?

SANDY: Come here. Help me!

DAVE: Not that I remember. *(Slow dim-out in the cemetery. He begins to shoot around.)*

MAGGIE: What do you say, you want to go back to school on Monday?

DAVE: Monday?

MAGGIE: Do you think you're ready?

DAVE: Monday? Yeah. Sure.

MAGGIE: All right.

DAVE: Great. See? I'm back! *(Tossing MAGGIE ball)* Hey! Off the injured reserve. The franchise returns! The go-to man. And they go to him!

MAGGIE: No-look. *(She tosses a no-look pass to him, he shoots a long air-ball, missing everything. He runs down ball, occasionally shoots during the following.)* The police called me at my office yesterday. When I told them how much better you were doing they wondered if you had anything more to tell them.

DAVE: I told them everything.

MAGGIE: That's what I told them you'd say.

DAVE: I told them everything.

MAGGIE: Dave...*Dave.*

DAVE: *(He stops moving.)* What? I told you, I'm not hungry right now.

MAGGIE: I'd like you to tell me what happened.

DAVE: When?

MAGGIE: That day.

DAVE: What? Why?

MAGGIE: Dave —

DAVE: What do they want me to say?

MAGGIE: I'm not asking for the police.

DAVE: What do you want to know?

MAGGIE: I just want to hear the whole story again. Start with the note.

DAVE: The note doesn't have anything to do with anything.

MAGGIE: Start with the note, then you can skip to the night, and then I'll leave you alone. But I want to hear the whole story again.

DAVE: *(He shoots.)* I'll tell you later. I want to shoot.

MAGGIE: We're going to the Wieland's for a party and Happy Day; they're showing slides of their vacation to Cleveland.

DAVE: I don't know why you want to hear it all again. It's over. It's over.

MAGGIE: It will help me. And I think it will help you.

DAVE: *(After a moment)* Can I make a deal?

MAGGIE: What?

DAVE: Can I have some money to go to the movies tonight? Chip wants to go to the movies.

MAGGIE: I think that can be arranged. *(CHIP enters carrying notebook and book, stands near DAVE. DAVE doesn't acknowledge him.)* But you may go to the movie, anyway, if you want.

DAVE: I can go anyway?...The note...I got to first hour government class and... *(He reluctantly tosses ball to her, turns to CHIP.)* I got to first hour government class and Chip was waiting for me.

CHIP: I am Fat City on this government test. *(Opening notebook, handing it open to DAVE)* Up all night draining the books. Ask me. Ask me.

DAVE: *(Reading from notebook)* "Who answers directly to the city manager?" *(CHIP screams. DAVE panics.)* We have a test?

CHIP: You didn't know?

DAVE: I did but I didn't believe Old Underarm would really go through with it.

CHIP: Who does answer directly to the city manager?

DAVE: Your dad.

CHIP: He does?

DAVE: Isn't he the assistant city manager?

CHIP: Oh, yeah. If I can't get that question right I'll never remember who founded the city.

DAVE: Someone founded the city?

CHIP: Yeah, it was...

DAVE: It was...I know this...it was...

CHIP: Amerigo Vespucci.

DAVE: Yeah.

DAVE & CHIP: *Heeelllppp!*

DAVE: *(Suddenly calm)* Hey, I'm cool.

CHIP: *(Ditto)* I'm cool.

DAVE: You are.

CHIP: **Very cool.**

DAVE: **Give me a sign. How cool are you?** *(CHIP shows how cool he is.)* **Very cool.**

CHIP: **And you?** *(DAVE does his own Gesture of Extreme Coolness.)* **Wow. You are the Prince of Cool.**

DAVE: **Rock and roll.**

CHIP: **What have I got?**

DAVE: **What have you got?**

CHIP: **What's in my pocket?**

DAVE: **What's in your pocket?**

CHIP: *(He takes out a note on folded notebook paper. Sings.)* **"A love note."**

DAVE: *(Singing along)* **"A love note."**

CHIP: **"It's a love note."**

DAVE: **"Love note. Who's it fr-om?"**

CHIP: *(Singing)* **"To Da-ve from Sandy."** *(DAVE is suddenly grim.)* **"I read it. It made me swe-at."** *(DAVE lunges for the note, CHIP pulls it away, opens it, pretends to read.)* **"Hi, Doll. How's my sweet lips?"** *(He kisses the air loudly.)* **"Did you study for that government test?"** *No.* *(DAVE takes note, reads it.)* **"I wish you could have come over last night. Were you thinking about me? I thought about you. The time you ate half my mother's birthday cake and I lied saying it was Ralph, our dog. I thought of your seventh grade haircut that looked like someone with buck teeth chewed it off."**

DAVE: *(Putting note away)* **You're jealous.**

CHIP: **I am.**

DAVE: **You are.**

CHIP: **I am jealous.**

DAVE: **You are.**

CHIP: **I am this jealous.** *(He shows how jealous. The school bell rings.)* **Who answers directly to the city manager?**

DAVE: **Amerigo Vespucci.**

CHIP: **Right. I am Fat City on this government test.** *(As he exits, he takes out his pen, writes answer on the inside of his hand.)* **Amerigo Vespucci...**

DAVE: **The note said she wanted to meet me —**

MAGGIE: *(Taking out the folded note paper)* **Here...read it.**

DAVE: **I know what it says. I read it a thousand times. It says —**

MAGGIE: **Will you read it to me?**

DAVE: *(He opens note.)* **What part?**

MAGGIE: **All of it.**

DAVE: *(Reads.)* **"My Dear —" All of it? This first stuff isn't about anything.** *(She stares him down. He reads.)* **"My Dearest Davie, hi, Doll! How are you this wonderful day?**

Did you get your algebra notebook done? Did you study for that government test?" (*To MAGGIE*) **Yes.** (*Reading*) "I wish you could have come over last night, I sure missed you! Laurie Weingarden invited me to a party next Saturday. It's going to be a beach party — I'm not sure if boys are coming or not but if they are do you want to go with me? Cheryl's going to ask Mark.

Isn't it beautiful outside?

Have you been thinking about me? I've been thinking about you. Try to get a conference with me if you can in sixth hour.

I have a feeling this is going to be a *great day*! If what I think is going to happen will happen.

Tonight can you stay at Chip's? I'm staying over with Cheryl. I'll meet you at Timothy's house in the Emerald Circle at 11:30, if you want."

MAGGIE: And Timothy's house is...

DAVE: (*With an attempt to be patient. By rote*) The grave stone in the cemetery that says, "Timothy: Not Dead, He Sleepeth." She calls the cemetery the Emerald Circle because of the big pine trees there.

MAGGIE: Go on.

DAVE: The rest is just... (*He goes on.*) "Well, I guess I'd better go now. The bell's going to ring. Sandy. P.S. I.S.L.Y.E.I.Y.D.C.V.M."

MAGGIE: And that means?

DAVE: I told you and you wrote it down.

MAGGIE: What's it mean?

DAVE: "I still love you even if you don't care very much."

MAGGIE: Why did she think you didn't?

DAVE: How should I know?

MAGGIE: So you told her in sixth hour that you were staying with Chip and you could meet her at 11:30 in the Emerald Circle. (*Moonlight up on the cemetery*)

DAVE: Yeah. Do I have to hear about it again? Dad's given me enough torture —" 11:30! Damn it, Dave, you're better than that! You were just asking for trouble." Right, Dad, it's my fault.

MAGGIE: Why the graveyard, honey?

DAVE: (*Flatly*) It's just down the block from Chip's and Cheryl's. It's like a park. And nobody goes there...we thought.

MAGGIE: Go on.

DAVE: All of it? Or just the last part?

MAGGIE: I'd like to hear it all.

DAVE: But what happened at the beginning doesn't... (*He picks up his jam-box.*) I got there first and was waiting —

MAGGIE: Was she late or were you early?

DAVE: I was early. *(He starts toward cemetery.)*

MAGGIE: And you didn't tell anyone where you were meeting her?

DAVE: No, I didn't. Do you want me to tell you what happened or not? *(He stops.)*

MAGGIE: *(Sits on picnic table, watches from there.)* Go ahead. I won't interrupt again.

DAVE: *(He continues on, stops at the edge of the graveyard, looks at it. He enters the Emerald Circle.)* Sandy? Hello? *(He sets jam-box next to Timothy's gravestone).* Timothy, wake up. And make sure none of these guys steals this, will you? Sandy? *(He looks for SANDY. It's quiet. He spies a log, picks it up, wields it like a baseball bat, swings.)* Touch 'em all. *(He hums, then sings, strumming the log like a guitar.)*
"Hey baby won't you call my name,
This waitin's drivin' me insane."
(He hits play on his jam-box. A hard-rock intro plays. Addressing the crowd of graves, speaking into log as if it were a microphone.)
Welcome. Welcome, everyone, to the Friday Night Concert In the Park. Timothy, glad you could make it. Esther, Ellen, what a couple of babes. Smokin' threads from 1878. I am The Prince, The Prince of Cool, taking you home to the Emerald Circle. And this is not your Tuesday afternoon soft favorites. This is Friday night Party Rock and Monster Roll. Get on. Get up. Rock and roll! *(He starts rocking, not dancing, but more playfully moving to the music. He jumps up as if he were the singer, slides down, sings a phrase into log directly to Timothy. He stops, suddenly self-conscious, thinking he's seen someone.)*
Sandy...? Sandy...? Hello! Who...? *(He drops log, goes to a large monument. He picks up a stone ball that is the top part of the monument, shoots it like a heavy basketball.)* Fumble. *(He dives and grabs the stone ball.)* Recovered by Bates. It's a live ball! *(He leaps up, holding the stone ball like a football and runs, weaving in and out of the gravestones.)* Fifty. Forty. Thirty. *(He bangs into monuments, stumbles, almost falls, pauses a moment to pose as the Heisman trophy and continues on.)* Twenty-five. Twenty. Fifteen. He's to the ten. One man left to beat. Can Timothy stop him? *(He bounces off a monument, twirls, falls, holding out ball.)* Touchdown! *(He jumps up, does an end-zone dance.)* High fives. Low fives. No fives. Interviews after the game. Can't make it. Got a date with The Treasurer of the National Honor Society.

SANDY: *(Running on)* Hi, doll.

DAVE: Oh, and there she is! *(He turns off jam-box.)* Hi.

SANDY: *(Handing him a rose and a card)* **I didn't take it off Dearly Departed Eliza. I bought it for you.**

DAVE: **Thanks.**

SANDY: **Read the card.**

DAVE: **"I.L.Y."**

SANDY: **If you can't figure that out you're dumb.**

DAVE: **I brought you something.**

SANDY: **You did?**

DAVE: **Yeah.**

SANDY: **You don't very often. It must be something special.**

DAVE: **It's...** *a-picture-of-me*...**the one you wanted.**

SANDY: **Thanks. I wore the other one out.**

DAVE: **And —** *(He takes card off flower, gives it to her.)* **Read the card.**

SANDY: **"I.L.Y."**

DAVE: **If you can't figure that out, you're dumber than I am.**

SANDY: **You haven't told me that and I was kind of wondering if you did.** *(He punches her shoulder.)*

DAVE: **What did you mean in your note when you said it was going to be a great day if what you thought was going to happen would happen?**

SANDY: **I'll never tell.**

DAVE: **Did it happen yet?**

SANDY: **No.**

DAVE: **What did you want to happen?**

SANDY: **If you can't figure that out you're dumber than anybody...Isn't it a beautiful night? We were all dancing outside on Cheryl's patio. What a riot. Cheryl ripped her jeans.** *(She laughs.)* **It was really a lot of fun but it was lonely without you.** *(Awkward silence as she looks, as she often does, for something from him, something that does not come. Sees stone ball, nudges it.)* **Did you win the game?**

DAVE: **Recovered a fumble. Returned it seventy yards. Timothy was not dead but he was sleeping and couldn't catch me.**

SANDY: **Give you any kind of ball and you're happy the rest of the day, aren't you?**

DAVE: *(Picking up the ball, replacing it on monument)* **Yeah.**

SANDY: **You're going to conquer the world with a ball.**

DAVE: **Well, the sports world. No, the whole world.**

SANDY: **Probably.**

DAVE: **Probably.**

SANDY: **Oh; I felt dumb at track today. Did you see me?**

DAVE: **Yeah.**

SANDY: *(This pains her.)* **How did you like my green gym suit? I look like a limesicle. I can't help it, though. My mother bought it for me.** *(Moving to him)* **Were you thinking about**

me today?

DAVE: Oh, yeah.

SANDY: What were you thinking?

DAVE: About you.

SANDY: What about me?

DAVE: I don't know. But I did. It gets me through government class.

SANDY: Well, what, though? What kinds of things do boys think?

DAVE: *(He smiles broadly. Then:)* I don't know. I think about what you said. About the things you gave me. I put them on my desk. I look at your picture. I don't know. I think about what you wear.

SANDY: *(Charmed)* What I wear?" Really? *(Suddenly horrified)* My green gym suit? Not my green gym suit.

DAVE: No, your other clothes.

SANDY: Oh.

DAVE: You dress different than I do.

SANDY: Yes I do; and you like that?

DAVE: Well, yeah.

SANDY: That's good.

DAVE: What do you think about? What do girls think about?

SANDY: I'm not going to tell *you*.

DAVE: I told you.

SANDY: I told Cheryl.

DAVE: Tell me.

SANDY: You weren't thinking you were going to kiss me tonight?

DAVE: Wowhat?

SANDY: You...haven't kissed anyone before, have you? Not really.

DAVE: Who, me? Ah...

SANDY: That's all right. I won't tell Chip. You haven't, have you?

DAVE: *(After a moment, making a joke at his expense)* My...mom. Maybe my...*gramma*.

SANDY: You may, if you want.

DAVE: You mean, with my lips?

SANDY: You could use your elbows. Then my mother wouldn't be upset. *(He punches her shoulder.)* Well, that's not exactly what I had in mind.

DAVE: And...yes.

SANDY: What?

DAVE: Yes.

SANDY: Yes, what?

DAVE: Yes, I'll go to Laurie's beach party with you. You asked me in your note, remember?

SANDY: Oh, yes. Good. *(Coyly)* Because someone asked *me* to Laurie's beach party.

DAVE: Who?

SANDY: Some man.

DAVE: Who?

SANDY: Mark.

DAVE: *(Without anger; more from confusion and vulnerability)* **Mark asked you?** What did you say?

SANDY: Why? Are you interested in what I said?

DAVE: What did you tell him?

SANDY: Oh, you are interested.

DAVE: What's he asking you for anyway? He goes with Cheryl.

SANDY: They broke up. Didn't you know? And so, I told him I had to talk with you before I could give him an answer.

DAVE: Why? Would you go with him? Do you like him?

SANDY: I don't know. That's why I told him I had to talk to you.

DAVE: So you *do* like him?

SANDY: Not like I like you.

DAVE: What does that mean? Sandy, what does that mean?

SANDY: Not like I like you.

DAVE: *(Taking her by the shoulders, trying to understand her)* **What does that mean?** What are you saying?

SANDY: *(Seeing he's serious)* **Nothing. It doesn't mean anything.** I'm just teasing you.

DAVE: You're just teasing me?

SANDY: Yeah, I'm just teasing. I'm not serious about Mark. I don't want to go with him to Laurie's party, I want to go with you. That's why I asked you. And... *(Pleased)* you're jealous...you're really jealous. Aren't you?

DAVE: I don't know.

SANDY: You are.

DAVE: *(Thinking he's seen something in the distance)* **What...who's that?**

SANDY: What?

DAVE: Did you see?

SANDY: What?

DAVE: I thought I saw...a gravestone move.

SANDY: A ghost?

DAVE: *(Staring into the night)* **Yeah. A ghost.** Timothy, who was that? A friend of yours?

SANDY: Timothy, you tell whoever that is to go away. No one else may come here. *(To DAVE)* I love this place. It's our place, isn't it? I told Cheryl I was meeting you but I didn't tell her where. I've never told anyone; have you?

DAVE: No.

SANDY: I don't think anyone else has been here in a hundred years. These graves are that old. All the people who buried these people...are buried. So no one comes here. They're afraid. I'm not. With you. *(DAVE doesn't respond much, still confused about Mark, and concerned he may have seen someone. Looking at a gravestone.)* Some of the people they buried here didn't live very long. Esther and Eliza were only nineteen; Laura was eighteen; Timothy was only twelve...Do you think...These trees are so old. They don't grow. They don't die. They just...Do you think their roots went into the coffins?

DAVE: Yeah.

SANDY: So these trees...ate what was left of the people?

DAVE: Yeah. Sucked them up into the leaves.

SANDY: So the people are in the trees, they are the trees.

DAVE: This one is old Captain Griffen.

SANDY: That one is a woman — Hatie May. She's wearing a long green dress.

DAVE: Hatie May and Ellen and Eliza, Ester and Laura. That's a big tree with big roots.

SANDY: I think they like us here...Oh; look. *(She moves to him, puts her face close to his.)*

DAVE: What?

SANDY: Look...I have make-up on.

DAVE: Oh...yeah.

SANDY: Do you like it? *(He nods yes.)* I had a dream about you last night. We went on a camping trip. You were a pretty wicked person. *(He touches her hair and kisses her. He starts to pull away but she clearly takes hold of him , holds him to her, making the kiss longer. Afterwards she lays her head against his shoulder.)* You see? You're not so dumb. You figured out why it was a great day.

DAVE: Oh.

SANDY: I trust you. I trust you, Dave.

DAVE: Were you just teasing about Mark?

SANDY: Oh, yes. It's really nothing, doll. Nothing. *(He kisses her again.)*

DAVE: *Heeey!* *(He jumps.)* *Yeeeah!* *(He does his Gesture of Extreme Coolness.)* Cool. *(He hits play on his jam-box. A hypnotic, medium-slow rock ballad plays.)*

SANDY: Oh, I love that!

DAVE: I know.

SANDY: Where did you buy it? I couldn't find it anywhere.

DAVE: I taped it off the radio for you last night.

SANDY: Thank you. Oh, I love it. I love it! *(She starts to dance; he watches her.)* Dance with me. *(Indicating graves)* Everyone else is. *(He does, but hesitantly. She becomes more involved in the music and begins circling around him. He dances more ener-*

getically.) **Now this song will always remind me of you.**
*(They dance around monuments, on graves; they sweep
through the trees. She laughs. He becomes completely free of
being self-conscious, dances with abandon. They twirl.)* **What a
beautiful night. I feel like we're flying!** *(She stops, watches
him twirl. He jumps over a monument, laughs. She turns down
music.)* **Do you promise if I tell you something that you
won't tell anyone?**

DAVE: **Yeah.**

SANDY: **You'd better. You know how mad I get.**

DAVE: *(She turns jam-box off.)* **I promise.**

SANDY: **Well...here it goes. I don't ever want you to find out
that you can live without me — I don't think I could live
without you. I never want to. They always say that good
things must end sometime. Well — I hope our sometime
comes when we die.**

DAVE: **It will with me.** *(DAVE turns to MAGGIE, deciding whether
or not to continue. He looks away; then back at SANDY and
goes on. The MAN appears. He's fairly large, rounded, in his
late twenties. He takes SANDY by the wrist.)*

MAN: **I'm not going to hurt you.**

SANDY: **What?**

MAN: **You just come with me, now.**

SANDY: **What do you want? We weren't doing anything.**

DAVE: **What's the matter?**

MAN: **I'm not going to hurt you.**

DAVE: **Who are you?**

MAN: **I won't hurt you. I promise.**

SANDY: *(SANDY begins to pull him slowly toward DAVE. MAN goes
with her.)* **Let me go then. You're hurting me. You're hurting me, now.**

MAN: **Because you're pulling. Stop. I won't hurt you.**

DAVE: **Who are you?**

SANDY: **What do you want? Let me go.**

DAVE: **Let her go!**

MAN: **Don't come over here. No, don't come over here.** *(DAVE
tries to grab her, the MAN grabs him by his hair, slams DAVE's
face into his thigh, DAVE falls. SANDY almost struggles free but
he manages to hold on to her.)*

SANDY: **Dave?** *(To MAN)* **Why did you do that?**

MAN: **It's all right, it's all right, it's all right.** *(The MAN puts a
handkerchief over SANDY's mouth and nose. She struggles, but
begins to be affected by a drug in the cloth. She sinks to her
knees. Unseen by the MAN, DAVE rises, moves to log, picks it
up, starts to swing the log. The MAN turns, DAVE hits him in the
chest, the MAN rolls. This stuns him for a moment. DAVE swings*

again, the MAN partially blocks the blow. As the MAN faces off against DAVE, SANDY, groggy but aware, staggers off. DAVE swings, the MAN ducks, then he hits DAVE in the ribs, then in the face. DAVE falls, unconscious.) **Sandy? Sandy?** *(The MAN exits searching. Short silence. DAVE gets up. He picks up his jam-box, moves toward driveway as the cemetery fades out.)*

DAVE: That's enough.

MAGGIE: What happened next?

DAVE: Sandy made it to those people's house and they called the police. You know the rest. *(DAVE sets the jam-box down.)*

MAGGIE: How are you?

DAVE: All right.

MAGGIE: Yeah?

DAVE: It gets easier each time I tell it.

MAGGIE: Yes, I see. But you know what I think, sweetheart? I think this is hurting you more than you're showing.

DAVE: What do you mean? I'm getting better.

MAGGIE: Remember last week, after it happened? You didn't sleep, you didn't change your clothes, you stank, you were skipping school, wandering around the park like a bum.

DAVE: Yeah.

MAGGIE: Now you wash, you eat, you do your homework, you shoot baskets.

DAVE: Yeah!

MAGGIE: But you can't stop the nightmares, can you? You had another one last night, didn't you. *(He starts to protest, she stops him.)* I heard you calling her name.

DAVE: Mom, she got away, it's over.

MAGGIE: Not for her; and obviously not for you. *(Short silence)* David, you're different; you feel different. You're further away. And not just from me, from everybody. Even your dad noticed it. You've hardly called Sandy. Or Chip. Whatever it is I'll still love you. *(No response)* Look at me so I know you heard what I said. *(He looks at her.)* Whatever it is I'll still love you. *(No response)* Do you believe me? *(He does not indicate yes.)* When your father and I were separated, I realized that part of my problem was what happened to me — and that happened before I even met your father. It was keeping me from him and I didn't know it. Remember? And you asked me to forget you were a kid and to talk to you like a friend and I did that, remember?

DAVE: This isn't like what happened to you.

MAGGIE: It is the same kind of thing. We talked through everything. I needed your help before I could go back with him.

DAVE: I still don't know why you did.

MAGGIE: That's not the point.

84

DAVE: Well, I don't know why. You didn't have to. We were doing fine.

MAGGIE: Dave —

DAVE: You said you weren't going to. You even bought that house and everything.

MAGGIE: I know there's a place...inside of you...In there is every sound, every thought, every feeling from that night. If you let me in there with you, I may be able to help.

DAVE: Ma, he didn't want me, he wanted Sandy. She's the one who you should be worried about.

MAGGIE: I am worried about her.

DAVE: He tried to take her, not me. And he might try again. Go do this with her.

MAGGIE: He might come after you again. You helped her get away. He might be very angry at you. You must have thought about that.

DAVE: I told the police his description. They drew a picture that looked just like him. I told them I'd recognize him again.

MAGGIE: It's not for the police, it's for you.

DAVE: If you know so much you figure out who he is.

MAGGIE: David, don't you... *(She represses her strong response.)*

DAVE: Why would anybody do that? How come nobody knew about that guy? *(Moonlight slowly comes up in the graveyard on MAN. He stands looking off, waiting.)* How come they didn't take care of him a long time ago? He's crazy! I'm not! It's not my fault he's out there! Or that the police are too stupid to catch him. I don't know who he is!

— MAN: *(Moving as if he were holding SANDY, speaking to her as if she were there.)* I know you.

MAGGIE: There must be more. Some of it just doesn't make sense to me.

— MAN: You've been easy to know.

MAGGIE: Like it was windy that night. There were tornado warnings. You never mention the wind.

— MAN: *(Now directly to DAVE as DAVE stands in driveway)* Dave.

DAVE: *(Turning to MAN, staying in driveway)* It was windy.

MAGGIE: And when I talked to Sandy, she said she fought back more than that.

DAVE: I guess she did.

—MAN: *(Directly to DAVE)* You're kind of crazy, aren't you?

MAGGIE: And all your bruises. Your face, your ribs, your shoulders. You were hit more than two or three times.

— MAN: Come on, sonny, let's see what you got.

DAVE: I told you; he must have kicked me when I was knocked out.

85

MAGGIE: Why? Sandy was getting away. Wouldn't he go look-ing for her as soon as you were down?

—MAN: You're kind of crazy, aren't you?

DAVE: I don't know. He's crazy. I don't know! *I don't know.*

MAGGIE: *(Suddenly)* Don't let him do this to you!

DAVE: He's not doing this to me, you are!

MAGGIE: I'm trying to help you! Don't let him take a part of you away forever. You don't have to. I know. You don't have to!

DAVE: I've answered all your questions. I told them everything over and over again. I told you over and over. Leave me alone. *(He starts to exit into the house.)*

MAGGIE: Dave —

DAVE: Leave me alone!

—MAN: I'm waiting.

MAGGIE: Don't let this — I didn't mean — Dave! *(He exits into the house.)* **Damn! Come on, Dave!** *(She hits the garage, then flops on to the picnic table. She pounds on table.)* **Ah! David!** *(She stomps her feet in frustration. In another voice, to herself)* **I told you he'd run. I said: "If you push too hard, he'll run from you." And what did he do?** *(In her voice)* **Two years ago he would have told me. Two years ago he would have told me everything.** *(She sighs, stares off in the distance. SANDY enters graveyard. The MAN stands in the background, watch-ing her.)* **Timothy's house...a park—no, the Emerald Circle. You'd think they'd be afraid, a cemetery at night, but —**

SANDY: *(Moving as before, speaking as if DAVE were in the ceme-tery with her)* I love this place. It's our place, isn't it? I told Cheryl I was meeting you but I didn't tell her where. I've never told anyone; have you?

MAGGIE: Your place, but...

SANDY: Timothy, you tell whoever that is to go away. No one else may come here.

MAGGIE: *(Turning to SANDY. MAGGIE stays in driveway.)* **And you thought it was going to be a great day.**

SANDY: *(SANDY doesn't register her.)* Isn't it a beautiful night?

MAGGIE: Beautiful. Very romantic. Unforgettable.

SANDY: We were all dancing outside on Cheryl's patio. What a riot. Cheryl ripped her jeans. *(She laughs; MAGGIE smiles. MAGGIE turns to MAN who is watching SANDY.)*

MAGGIE: What did you do? *(The MAN turns his head, looks at MAGGIE. DAVE enters driveway, takes a bite out of a sand-wich. MAGGIE turns to DAVE. MAN exits graveyard. SANDY sits, waits.)* **Two years ago you would have told me; you would have told me everything, just like I told you every-thing. I miss that with you. You helped me, let me help**

you. *(Silence)* **If you can't tell me, tell your dad.**
DAVE: Tell him what? All he knows is I wasn't supposed to be in the graveyard. I was supposed to be at Chip's. I'm not telling him anything.
MAGGIE: Grampa, Chip —
DAVE: You know what everybody's saying about me? About her? About why we went to the graveyard? Everybody's got big ideas and no one knows.
MAGGIE: Have you talked to Sandy? You really haven't, have you? *(Silence)* Why not?
DAVE: Am I going back to school on Monday?
MAGGIE: Yes.
DAVE: All right. *(He tosses down rest of sandwich, turns his jambox on, turns up the volume. It plays the slower rock ballad—SANDY's song — from the cemetery. He picks up ball, shoots. MAGGIE decides to let things sit awhile.)*
MAGGIE: I'm going to make myself a cup of tea. You want some?
DAVE: No. *(He shoots.)*
MAGGIE: Don't wander off. *(MAGGIE exits. He shoots.)*
SANDY: *(Moving as before, as if DAVE were in the graveyard with her)* Oh, I love that!
DAVE: *(Focused on shooting, to himself)* "Don't wander off..."
SANDY: Where did you buy it? I couldn't find it anywhere.
DAVE: *(Shooting)* I'm not going to tell you, Ma. I'm not going to tell anybody, anything.
SANDY: Thank you. Oh, I love it. I love it!
DAVE: Not until it's over. Until it's all over. *(He drives, shoots.)*
SANDY: *(She starts to dance.)* Dance with me. *(DAVE looks at SANDY. Indicating graves)* Everyone else is. *(DAVE holds ball, focuses on SANDY.)* Now this song will always remind me of you.
DAVE: It always reminds me of you.
SANDY: What a beautiful night. I feel like we're flying! *(She laughs. DAVE watches from driveway as SANDY moves as before, as if DAVE were with her in the graveyard.)* Were you thinking about me today?
DAVE: *(Laughing)* Oh, yeah.
SANDY: What were you thinking?
DAVE: I think you know. *(He shoots a long shot, gets rebound, immediately dribbles out.)*
SANDY: What about me?...What kind of things do boys think?
DAVE: Yeah, you know, don't you! About you! *(He shoots, gets rebound.)*
SANDY: You weren't thinking you were going to kiss me, tonight?
DAVE: Yes! Yes I was. And I did. And it was...sweet.
SANDY: You see? You're not so dumb.

DAVE: **That's right.**

SANDY: **I trust you. I trust you, Dave.**

DAVE: *(This cuts through all of his attitude, stuns him.)* **What?**

SANDY: **I trust you. I trust you, Dave.**

DAVE: **Sandy...** *(The MAN enters behind SANDY, stops, stares at her. DAVE darkens. He turns back to basketball. He sets, drives in, trying out a move he's been working on. It's a driving 360-degree turn-around lay-up. He misses the basket entirely. He quickly resets, tries it again. He hits rim, but misses.)*

MAN: **Come on, sonny.** *(DAVE dribbles out, sets, drives in, jumps, misses, slams into garage. He gets ball and throws it at rim.)* **I'm waiting.** *(DAVE walks over to ball, picks it up. He starts walking to his set place, looks at MAN, stops.)* **There's nothing you can do about it.** *(He moves to his set place, concentrates on basket. He drives, leaps, turns, slams into garage, misses again. He grabs ball, clutches it to his chest, leans against the garage, begins to cry. He slides down to the pavement in tears. MAN walks up behind SANDY. MAN speaks directly to DAVE.)* **No one'll hear you. No one will come. No one knows.** *(CHIP enters driveway. DAVE sees him, hides his face.)*

CHIP: **Hit the open man!** *(DAVE tosses him the ball. Cemetery fades.)* **"They surround him! Give it up, give it up, you fool. Wait, what's this? From nowhere!" Ahhhh!** *(He tries the 360 and throws ball up through the bottom of the basket and beyond.)* **I'm as good as you.** *(DAVE wipes his face and turns off music. CHIP shoots. DAVE feeds him during the following.)* **What's shakin'?**

DAVE: **Going back to school on Monday.**

CHIP: **Oh, yeah. I'll warn the cheerleaders. Track, too?**

DAVE: **Yeah.**

CHIP: **All right. Maybe coach will give us a break. Nobody's got over fourth in the high jump since you left.**

DAVE: **How'd you guys do yesterday?**

CHIP: **They squeaked by us, they crushed us, we died like flies.**

DAVE: **Sweet. Did I miss anything at school?**

CHIP: **Nothing, except in government class Laurie Weingarden went up to ask him if she could go to the bathroom and she threw up on Underarm's desk.**

DAVE: **Skanky.**

CHIP: **Yeah. Right on our tests. He had to throw them out.**

DAVE: **Ha! I wish I'd seen that.**

CHIP: **No you don't. I saw it. No you don't...And Sandy came back, yesterday.**

DAVE: **Yeah, I know.**

CHIP: **She wears this thing on her belt, now, wherever she goes — an alarm.**

DAVE: She doesn't go in the backyard without her mother going with her. *(CHIP shoots. DAVE now shoots around with him.)*

CHIP: *Everybody's* going to be asking you *questions.* You should hear some of what they say.

DAVE: What do they say?

CHIP: Cheryl says she thinks maybe that roach was watching her house that night and he followed Sandy out to meet you. And that he might come back and say, "Helllooo Cheryl. I'm the geek that stole your friend. Want a date?" And she'd say, "Ahhh!" She can't sleep.

DAVE: What's Mark say?

CHIP: He says if he had been in the graveyard he'd a kicked your guy's ass.

DAVE: Right.

CHIP: So true. So true, Mark.

DAVE: He say anything else?

CHIP: About what?

DAVE: Anything.

CHIP: I try not to listen to Mark.

DAVE: Why, what's he say?

CHIP: *(CHIP holds ball.)* What do you mean? I mean, what do you mean?

DAVE: I mean, he's got a big mouth.

CHIP: I mean, let's put a car in it.

DAVE: I mean, an Oldsmobile, in Mark's mouth.

CHIP: Going a hundred. Miles. Per hour.

DAVE: Ready.

CHIP: Go...*spleah.* *(He shoots, then positions himself to play.)* I'm warm. And I am *ready.* First out. You're doomed, my friend. The Howitzer, the Hammer, the Artiste is ready to rock. *(They go one-on-one. They play solid, aggressive basketball; both are good. After moves, block shots, etc., they celebrate with suitable exclamations and slapping. They don't play possession; the ball changes hands after each basket. After first basket or first change of possession, they hold ball and talk.)*

DAVE: What do *you* say?

CHIP: I say, we going to the movies?

DAVE: Yeah.

CHIP: Oh, yeah, movies tonight. Did you call Sandy? *(Moonlight up on SANDY standing in the cemetery, her back to the audience, looking away from DAVE)*

DAVE: Yeah.

CHIP: Is she going?

DAVE: No. She says she's not ready, yet.

CHIP: Right. *(They play. After next change of possession)* **Who is**

89

it?

DAVE: Who?

CHIP: Going with us, to the movies?

DAVE: Who?

CHIP: Cheryl. Wants to come along. In love with me as a man. Says I'll be the father of nations.

— SANDY: *(Moving as before)* Because someone asked *me* to Laurie's beach party.

DAVE: She's not going with Mark, then?

CHIP: The King of Molds and Slimes?

— SANDY: Some man.

CHIP: Mark? Go with someone? Mark just slimes around.

—SANDY: *(Moving as before)* Because someone asked *me* to Laurie's beach party.

CHIP: Nay-nay. *(Pointing to himself)* **This prince is rescuing the maiden. She's going with me.** (*They play. The following lines are spoken as they play. SANDY now watches DAVE.)* **You remember anything else?**

DAVE: Like what?

CHIP: Like what happened.

DAVE: What happened?

CHIP: Was I there?

DAVE: I told you what happened.

CHIP: All right. I'm not your dad.

DAVE: You're my dad. *(CHIP holds ball.)*

CHIP: All right, I *am* your dad.

DAVE: *Be* my dad.

CHIP: I'm sorry I'm your dad. I just thought maybe you remembered something new.

DAVE: Shut up and play.

CHIP: Are you *my* dad?

DAVE: Shut up!

CHIP: You *are* my dad. *(MAGGIE enters carrying a tray with tea, muffins, and some paperwork. The MAN enters cemetery behind SANDY. DAVE turns to him.)*

MAGGIE: It's the Chipper.

CHIP: Hey, Mrs. Maggie.

MAGGIE: Got an extra muffin here.

CHIP: *(Crawling on picnic table to get it)* **God, I missed you.**

—MAN: Come on, Sonny.

DAVE: *(To CHIP)* **We're playing.**

CHIP: Muffins! *(He stuffs one in his mouth.)*

MAGGIE: They got chocolate chips in them, mmm. Fat City.

CHIP: Chocolate's my first name.

— MAN: You want her?

— SANDY: I trust you.

— MAN: You take her.

DAVE: Play.

CHIP: **Right now this talented young hoopster has to humble that cagey veteran.**

— MAN: **You take her.** *(MAGGIE eats muffin, watches game.)*

DAVE: *(Tossing CHIP the ball)* **Play.**

CHIP: **I'm waiting for you.**

— MAN: **Come on, sonny.** *(CHIP makes a move with the ball, goes around DAVE, makes basket. DAVE moves to top of key.)*

MAGGIE: *(Applauding)* **Hot move!**

CHIP: **He scores! Muffins! Throw muffins!** *(MAGGIE does, he drops ball, catches them, bites one.)*

DAVE: **Walk.**

CHIP: **What?**

DAVE: **You took steps.**

CHIP: **No way, doctor. I jocked you off the dribble.** *(Throws extra muffins back to MAGGIE, who catches them.)*

DAVE: **Uh, uh.**

CHIP: **Pick your jock up, it's right there, I see it from here, green and ugly.**

DAVE: **You walked.**

CHIP: *(Picking up ball)* **Then you hacked me. So I got one.**

DAVE: **You didn't get anything.**

CHIP: **Play over.**

DAVE: **It's my ball.**

CHIP: **Wait a minute.**

DAVE: **It's my ball.**

CHIP: **"It's my ball?"**

DAVE: **You heard me.**

CHIP: **"It's my ball."** *(Tossing DAVE ball)* **I didn't know I was playing with Mark.** *(DAVE throws a chest pass hard into CHIP's stomach. CHIP catches ball without being hit that hard, but feels the blow. He does the same back to DAVE.)*

— MAN: **That's it. That's right. Now you got it.**

DAVE: *(After a moment)* **Take it.** *(He bounces it back to CHIP.)*

CHIP: **Yeah, I'll take it. But I didn't walk.**

— SANDY: **Dave?**

— MAN: **Now, come on. That's it.** *(SANDY's speech, the MAN's speech and the basketball game now occur simultaneously. They play. CHIP dribbles, goes up for a shot. DAVE blocks it, gets the ball.)*

DAVE: **Stuffed!** *(DAVE now has the ball. He sets, drives, tries his 360 move.)*

SANDY: **Were you thinking about me today?... What were you thinking?...**

MAN: **Come on. If you want her, come and take her. All right, go for help. You**

Well, what, though? What kinds of things do boys think?...You weren't thinking you were going to kiss me, tonight?... You may, if you want— go for help. We won't be here. And go ahead and yell! No one'll hear you. No one'll come. Nobody knows...I'm waiting. I'm waiting—

(CHIP hammers him. SANDY and the MAN abruptly stop speaking.)

DAVE: Ah!

CHIP: Foul.

DAVE: *(Slamming the ball down)* **What the hell are you doing?**

CHIP: Wasted.

DAVE: *(He pushes CHIP.)* **What the hell was that?**

MAGGIE: Hey.

CHIP: A foul. Maybe you didn't hear me. I said foul.

DAVE: You took my head off. *(He pushes CHIP again.)*

MAGGIE: Dave!

CHIP: And that's a technical.

MAGGIE: He called a foul.

CHIP: That's a T on you, sport. *(CHIP pushes DAVE back. With a hoarse yell DAVE goes for him, grabs him, throws him.)*

MAGGIE: Dave!

DAVE: Get up! Get up! Move!

MAGGIE: That's enough!

DAVE: *(He kicks CHIP in the thigh.)* **Get up!**

MAGGIE: Dave! *(CHIP jumps up, swings at him, DAVE avoids the blow.)*

DAVE: Come on. Yeah, you got it. Come on! *(MAGGIE tries to move between them. They continue to fight through and around her.)*

CHIP: Yeah, you're ready for school. Kicking me while I'm down.

MAGGIE: Both of you stop it, now! Hey — hey! Chip! *(CHIP swings again and again, missing DAVE. DAVE pushes him away, taunts him.)*

DAVE: Come on, you slime. Come on. *(MAGGIE tries to grab and hold DAVE.)*

MAGGIE: Now stop it, Dave. It's Chip. *(DAVE pushes MAGGIE out of the way.)*

DAVE: Come on. *(DAVE pushes him again, CHIP swings, hits DAVE in the body, DAVE punches him in the stomach. CHIP out of breath, falls to the ground. Rabidly)* **Get up. Get up! Come on, get up! I didn't hit you that hard.**

MAGGIE: Dave!

DAVE: *(He goes to CHIP, tries to pull him up.)* **Move! Come on! Stand up! Stand up! You little worm.**

MAGGIE: *(Grabbing DAVE from behind)* **Stop it.**

DAVE: **Let me go.** *(He pulls her off him, then shakes her violently.)* **Let me go! What is wrong with you? What are you doing?**

MAGGIE: *(Intensely)* **Take your hands off me.**

DAVE: **You don't know what you're doing!**

MAGGIE: **You let go of me, now.**

DAVE: *(He pushes her away, turns to MAN.)* **Come on!**

MAGGIE: **David!**

— MAN: **Don't come over here.**

DAVE: *(To MAN)* **Let's get this over with! One way or the other. You come back. I'm waiting, you coward. *I'm* waiting for *you*, now! It won't be that easy again. You won't walk away this time. I'll kill you, you bastard. Come on!**

— MAN: **No, don't come over here! Don't come over here!**

MAGGIE: **You will never do that again.**

DAVE: *(To MAGGIE)* **Don't come over here!** *(Lights fade in cemetery, MAN and SANDY exit.)*

MAGGIE: *(Forcefully)* **I don't care what happened to you. You will not act like this. You will not attack me like that. Or your friends. He didn't deserve that. Neither did I. You hurt me. You hurt me. Now you stay there until you're ready to apologize to both of us.**

DAVE: **Leave me alone.**

MAGGIE: **I mean it. You stay there until you remember who you are. Chip, are you all right? Chip?**

CHIP: **Yeah. He just knocked the wind out of me.**

MAGGIE: **Are you sure?**

CHIP: **Yeah, I'm all right.**

DAVE: *(To himself)* **I don't believe this. What am I doing? I don't know what I'm doing. Chip...Chip?** *(DAVE crosses to CHIP.)*

MAGGIE: **Get away from him.**

DAVE: **Here.** *(He reaches down to help CHIP up.)*

CHIP: *(He gets up by himself.)* **Get away from me. Madman.**

MAGGIE: **Leave him alone.**

DAVE: **I'm sorry.** *(DAVE sits on driveway.)* **I'm sorry.**

CHIP: **"I'm sorry. I'm a crazy man. I'm sorry, but you fouled me. So I broke your guts."**

DAVE: *(To CHIP. MAGGIE is a short distance away but can hear everything. Rapid, pressured speech)* **I keep seeing that night over and over again. I hear him. It's like he's right here, right next to me, talking to me, talking. I can't shut him up. And I dream about her. I'm underground, hiding or dead or something, and I can't breathe. I can't push the ground off me. I can't move. I keep looking for that guy. I even think I see him sometimes and I get ready and it's not him. Everywhere I go I think he's watching me. You can't see at night. Like at the movies, tonight. He could** just come up, come out of nowhere again. So I got to stay ready, I got to be ready this time. I want a gun. I think about a gun all the time. Then I'd be ready. Then that crazy bastard wouldn't get away. But I — I can't trust myself. I'll shoot somebody else, I know I will. I hit you, didn't I? I hit you! So a knife, I'll carry a knife and — and I do, all the time. I have a knife. But they don't let you have a knife in school and I know he was there, he was watching Sandy there, at school. He was watching us all over. He called her by her name. And me. He called me by my name, too. He was watching me, too. I wish he'd come back. I even went out to the cemetery looking for him, calling for him, but he wasn't there. I'm sorry I hit you. You can hit me back; I won't do anything. I'm sorry I hit you.

CHIP: He called you by your name?

DAVE: Yeah, he knew me. I'm sorry I hit you. I started it. Go ahead, hit me back. I deserve it.

CHIP: And you went looking for him?

DAVE: Yeah. To finish it, one way or the other. So, now you know. So...now what?

CHIP: What?

DAVE: I mean, you going to hit me? It's all right.

CHIP: No.

DAVE: Then...I guess...you can go.

CHIP: Oh. Yeah. All right.

DAVE: You can go. You still want to go to the movie with me? You don't have to.

CHIP: You going to go berserk again?

DAVE: I won't, no, not...You don't have to go with me. I won't go. Maybe I won't go.

CHIP: Yeah. Yeah, I'll go.

DAVE: Yeah. All right. You want to?

CHIP: Yeah. *(CHIP hesitates, then starts off.)*

MAGGIE: What else happened, Dave? *(CHIP stops.)*

DAVE: I'll walk over about eight.

CHIP: Right. *(He starts off again.)*

MAGGIE: Dave? *(CHIP stops.)*

DAVE: Then we can walk to Cheryl's.

CHIP: I think my brother will take us. I'm in the back seat with Cheryl practicing my one-on-one.

MAGGIE: What happened?

DAVE: *(Turning to MAGGIE)* What do you think happened? You tell me, what happened?

MAGGIE: I don't know.

DAVE: No, you don't. *(He sits on the ground in helplessness.)* I promised myself I wouldn't tell anybody anything until it was over. Until it was all over. But...There's nothing I can do about it. There's nothing I can do.

MAGGIE: Dave, look at yourself. You want to talk. That's why you're like this. Isn't that true? *(Lights up on deserted cemetery.)*

DAVE: Chip... *(Picking up his jam-box, going to CHIP, pulling him toward the cemetery)* That night — I mean, most of it happened just like I said, but —

CHIP: *(Stopping them)* Maybe you should tell your mom this stuff.

DAVE: No. No, you. I want to tell you.

CHIP: What am I supposed to do?

DAVE: I want to tell you, all right?

CHIP: All right. What do you want me to do?

DAVE: *(Crossing into cemetery with CHIP)* I don't know if Cheryl's right — I mean, about the guy watching her house. He might have been following *me*. Before Sandy got there I thought I saw somebody. I thought it was Sandy.

CHIP: Yeah, I remember.

DAVE: Maybe he was following me. But he could have been watching Cheryl's house that night. And when Sandy left the house he followed her. *(SANDY runs on into graveyard.)*

SANDY: Hi, doll.

— DAVE: But he was there the whole time she was. Because I know I saw somebody just after she got there.

SANDY: What?

DAVE: *(Entering scene)* Did you see?

SANDY: What?

DAVE: I thought I saw...a gravestone move.

SANDY: A ghost?

DAVE: Yeah, a ghost. Timothy, who was that? A friend of yours?

SANDY: Timothy, you tell whoever that is to go away. No one else may come here. *(To DAVE)* I love this place. It's our place, isn't it. I told Cheryl I was meeting you but I didn't tell her where. I've never told anyone; have you?

— DAVE: *(Leaves scene, talks to CHIP.)* That was him.

— CHIP: And you and Sandy never saw him anywhere else? At school, or, like, on the street?

—DAVE: Nope. Not until that night.

SANDY: Because someone asked *me* to Laurie's beach party.

DAVE: *(Re-entering scene)* Who?

SANDY: Some man.

DAVE: Who?

SANDY: Mark.

DAVE: As in Cheryl and Mark? He asked you? What did you say?

SANDY: Why? Are you interested in what I said?

— DAVE: *(To CHIP)* I should have known, somehow. I should have felt him or something. I should have been ready.

— CHIP: How could you have known?

— DAVE: I saw him. I should have known.

SANDY: I told him I had to talk to you before I could give him an answer.

DAVE: *(Re-entering scene)* You'd go with Mark?

SANDY: Why not?

DAVE: So you *do* like him?

SANDY: Not like I like you.

DAVE: What does that mean? Sandy, what does that mean?

SANDY: Not like I like you.

DAVE: *(Taking her by the shoulders, shaking her. His response is much stronger than he showed MAGGIE.)* What does that mean? "Not like I like you." What are you doing?

SANDY: *(She grimaces; he has hurt her arm.)* Nothing. It doesn't mean anything. I'm just teasing you.

DAVE: *(Again, much stronger)* What do you mean, you're just teasing me?

SANDY: *(She pulls away from him.)* I'm not serious about Mark. I'm just teasing, God. You don't have to grab me like that.

DAVE: Then what...?

SANDY: I don't want to go with Mark to Laurie's party. I want to go with you. That's why I asked you. *(She rubs her arm where DAVE hurt her.)* And...you're jealous...you're really jealous.

— DAVE: *(To CHIP)* Yeah, I was. I really was. I hurt her arm, I think.

— CHIP: No doubt.

— DAVE: I hurt her.

SANDY: But don't do that. You can't hurt me, even if you are jealous. You can't grab me and push me around like I'm on the football team or something. All right?

DAVE: Yeah, all right.

SANDY: Then don't do it again.

DAVE: *(To SANDY)* I won't.

— DAVE: *(To CHIP)* I won't.

— CHIP: Yeah. *(After a moment)* Why didn't that guy just wait until she left to go back to Cheryl's and take her then?

— DAVE: *(Exactly what DAVE's been thinking. This is not a discovery for him.)* Yeah. Yeah, that's right.

— CHIP: Why did he let you see him?

— DAVE: Yeah! You're right, Chip.

— CHIP: He must have been watching her for weeks; he waited a long time to try and take her. Why couldn't he wait one more hour?

— DAVE: Or, if he was following her that night, why didn't he take her before she got here?

— CHIP: Yeah.

— DAVE: Because he wanted me to see him. That was part of it.

— CHIP: Why?

— DAVE: He wanted me to see him. He wanted me to know. You'll see. *(He punches the slow rock song on the jam-box.)*

SANDY: Oh, I love that!

DAVE: *(In scene)* I know.

SANDY: Where did you buy it? I couldn't find it anywhere.

— DAVE: *(To CHIP)* He was watching all of this. He was close enough to hear everything we said.

SANDY: Oh, I love it. I love it! *(She starts to dance.)* Dance with me. *(Indicating graves)* Everyone else is.

— DAVE: He watched us dancing around. I forgot about seeing somebody. I forgot about everything. Except Sandy.

SANDY: What a beautiful night. I feel like we're flying!

—DAVE: And he was right there. Right there!

SANDY: *(SANDY turns down music. DAVE re-enters scene and now runs it through to the end.)* Do you promise if I tell you something that you won't tell anyone?

DAVE: Yeah.

SANDY: You'd better. You know how mad I get.

DAVE: *(She turns the jam-box off.)* I promise.

SANDY: Well...here it goes. I don't ever want you to find out that you can live without me — I don't think I could live without you. I never want to. They always say that good things must end sometime. Well — I hope our sometime comes when we die.

DAVE: It will with me. *(The MAN appears, takes SANDY by the wrist, pulls her away from DAVE.)*

MAN: I'm not going to hurt you.

SANDY What?

MAN: You just come with me, now.

SANDY: What do you want? We weren't doing anything.

DAVE: What's the matter?

MAN: I'm not going to hurt you.

DAVE: Who are you?

MAN: I won't hurt you. I promise.

SANDY: *(SANDY begins to pull him slowly toward DAVE. MAN goes with her.)* Let me go then. You're hurting me. You're hurting me, now.

MAN: Because you're pulling. Stop. I won't hurt you.

DAVE: Who are you?

SANDY: What do you want? Let me go. *(The MAN pulls her away. She struggles, trying to take his hand off her wrist.)* No, let me

go. *(With her free hand, she punches him. He takes hold of her free hand, she kicks at him, but he holds her.)* **Let me go! Dave, help me!** *(DAVE starts toward them.)*

DAVE: **Let her go.**

MAN: **Don't come over here. No, don't come over here.** *(DAVE continues.)* **I told you not to come over here.** *(DAVE tries to grab her, the MAN grabs him by the hair, slams DAVE's face into his thigh, DAVE falls. SANDY almost struggles free but he manages to hold on to her.)*

SANDY: **Dave?** *(To MAN)* **Why did you do that! Don't you hurt him!** *(She fights furiously; she hits the MAN repeatedly. The MAN tries to handcuff her. She scratches his face. He turns her around, she elbows him in the stomach. She reaches back, pulls his hair; he peels her hand away. He succeeds in handcuffing her behind her back. She stomps his foot, kicks his leg.)*

MAN: **I'm going to put you on the ground, all right? Nice and easy. It's all right. It's all right, it's all right, Sandy.** *(He puts her carefully on the ground.)*

SANDY: **Dave! Get up!**

MAN: **He can't help you, Sandy. He's not strong enough.**

SANDY: **How do you know my name? Who are you?**

MAN: **I know you. It's been easy to know you, Sandy.** *(She squirms as he tries to grab her feet; she kicks him in the face. She manages to roll away but he catches her, holds her legs and ties them with a rope.)*

SANDY: **You don't have to do that. Don't! No! What do you want? Who are you?**

MAN: **What do I want...I just want to know you, more, Sandy. I want you to know me.** *(He takes out a gag.)*

SANDY: **No, I won't scream, I won't scream, I promise. I'll just talk to you. It's all right. I'll talk to you. No!** *(He gags her. She tries to scream. DAVE begins to move, unseen by the MAN.)*

MAN: **Don't worry. I won't hurt you. You're much too important for anybody to hurt. You are to me. And don't fight because you'll just hurt yourself. You understand? You can shake your head. You understand?** *(The MAN takes a handkerchief out of baggie and covers SANDY's nose with it. She struggles but he holds it to her; she begins to pass out. He does this while DAVE moves to log, picks it up, starts to swing the log. The MAN turns, DAVE hits him in the chest, the MAN rolls. This stuns him for a moment. DAVE swings again, the MAN partially blocks the blow. They face off. SANDY lies half-conscious.)*

DAVE: **Let her go.**

MAN: **You I don't care about. You I will hurt.** *(They fight. DAVE is quicker, but the MAN is larger, stronger. DAVE swings again and again, missing MAN. DAVE swings, the MAN catches the* *log and they struggle with it. DAVE falls back, pulls the MAN over him and the MAN rolls. DAVE goes to hit him, the MAN catches log and they struggle with it again. The MAN whips DAVE around trying to pull log out of his hands. He whips DAVE into a large gravestone. DAVE holds on but the MAN knees DAVE in the stomach, DAVE lets go of log, falls. The MAN throws log away.)* **Get up. Come on, get up. Get up! Let's see what you got.**

DAVE: *(DAVE swings getting up, hits MAN squarely in the jaw.)* **I won't let you take her.** *(They fight with fists. DAVE hits him and eludes the MAN's punch. The MAN chases him down, DAVE backs up, sometimes turning and running, but always coming right back. DAVE goes to monument, gets stone ball. He faces off with MAN, then heaves ball at him. The MAN catches ball in the chest, staggers backwards, falls. DAVE runs to SANDY, loosens rope around her legs. The MAN recovers, goes for DAVE, DAVE eludes him. The MAN guards SANDY, facing away from her and towards DAVE. DAVE stands away, recovering and considering options.)*

MAN: **Come on. Come on. If you want her, come and take her.** *(DAVE looks around cemetery.)* **All right. Go for help. You go for help. We won't be here.** *(He sings out loudly.)* **And go ahead and yell! No one'll hear you. No one'll come. Nobody knows. It's just you and me.** *(DAVE takes a step back, stares at MAN.)* **I can wait; so can she.** *(Short silence. With his back to SANDY, the MAN watches DAVE. She moves. DAVE sees this.)* **She won't like being tied up so long, though. It'll cut off circulation to her legs.** *(DAVE struggles with what to do.)* **I'm waiting.** *(SANDY moves again, becoming more alert.)* **You could just go. But if you do, she's mine. I don't think you'll do that, Dave. That's not like you. No, I guess not. That's not like you, Dave. Football hero. Basketball star. Track captain.**

DAVE: **Who are you?**

MAN: **I'm like you. I like her.** *(SANDY sits up.)*

DAVE: **Why are you doing this?**

MAN: **Because if I asked her nice, she wouldn't go. Look at me. No, I don't look like you. She wouldn't go. I need her. I just need her.**

DAVE: **You crazy bastard.**

MAN: **Come on, then. You want her. You take her. Just like me. You want her. You take her.** *(Beat)* **I'm waiting.** *(Afraid that MAN will turn around and see SANDY moving, DAVE steps toward MAN.)* **That's it. That's right. Now you got it. I'll give you the first one. Maybe the first two. I will. The first one, maybe the first two. Go ahead.** *(They face off. SANDY continues to awaken. She struggles to pull the ropes off her legs.)* **Go**

on. *(DAVE swings, hits the MAN in the jaw. The MAN takes the blow.)* **Well, you're strong. Yeah, you're mad. That hurt. Try again.** *(DAVE readies and swings hard, the MAN moves, DAVE misses. The MAN then punches DAVE in the ribs.)* **I said maybe two.** *(DAVE lunges and swings at the MAN in a frenzy. DAVE's wild blows land but not strongly. The MAN protects himself until he sees an opening and knocks DAVE down.)* **You're kind of crazy, aren't you? Get up. Come on, Sonny, get up. I didn't hit you that hard.** *(He takes DAVE by the arm, and pulls him up.)* **There. Now, come on. That's it. Yeah, you like her.** *(SANDY is succeeding at getting the rope from around her legs. DAVE tries to tackle MAN. In perfect football form he hits MAN in the waist with his shoulder and drives him up against a monument. The MAN grabs DAVE's wrists, pulls them from around his waist. MAN twists one of DAVE's arms in a half-Nelson. With his other hand he grabs DAVE by the hair. MAN pushes him to his knees and pulls DAVE's hair. DAVE's head snaps back; he's unable to move.)* **Now, I'm going to take her, Sonny, and there's nothing you can do about it.**

DAVE: **No. That can't be.**

MAN: *(Smiling)* **Why? You going to take me?**

DAVE: **It can't be.**

MAN: *(Laughs a little.)* **"It can't be." I'm going to take her; and I'm going to lay you out. And there's nothing you can do.** *(MAN pushes DAVE down, he quickly jumps up. Behind the MAN, SANDY struggles to stand. DAVE swings, the MAN blocks the blow, punches DAVE in the stomach once, then again, then hammers him on the back with both fists. DAVE falls again. SANDY moves off.)*

DAVE: **You...crazy...**

MAN: **Now you better stay down. Be smart, now, Sonny. No, you stay down, now.** *(DAVE struggles to stand. Clearly in pain and struggling to breathe, he succeeds in getting to his feet.)* **All right.** *(DAVE weakly raises his fists to fight, stumbles at the MAN. The MAN easily trips him, DAVE falls again. DAVE gets up on all fours. The MAN kicks him in the stomach.)*

DAVE: **You can't...I...** *(DAVE begins to try and get up, but he can't. he rolls on his back.)* **I can't — I can't...**

MAN: *(Seeing DAVE can't stand, he turns to where SANDY was, sees she's gone.)* **Damn! Sandy? Sandy! I'll find you.** *(He exits after her.)*

DAVE: **I can't — Sandy! I can't move! I can't breathe. Chip, I can't breathe! Chip! No-no-no-no! I can't move! I can't move! Aaaahhh!**

CHIP: **Dave?** *(DAVE rolls over, away from CHIP.)* **Dave?** *(CHIP goes to DAVE, rolls him on his back.)*

DAVE: I couldn't move. I couldn't get up to help her. *(DAVE sits up.)* I couldn't move. He won; I couldn't beat him. He was too strong. Just like he said. I couldn't stop him.

CHIP: Yeah, you couldn't stop him. *(CHIP holds out his hand, DAVE takes it, CHIP pulls him up.)*

DAVE: I couldn't hurt him.

CHIP: Yeah. *(CHIP, unsure of exactly what to do, pats DAVE on the back once.)*

DAVE: Sandy was smart not to go to Cheryl's house. That's the way he went, I bet, looking for her. But she went down the other way. *(Silence, as they stand looking at each other and away)* That's what happened. Now you know everything that happened.

CHIP: Yeah, I see what you mean. He wanted you to see him.

DAVE: Yeah. *(Stunned that he has been understood)* You see?

CHIP: Yeah, that was part of it.

DAVE: I think it was. *(CHIP moves out of cemetery. He turns to DAVE, gestures for him to follow. DAVE nods, picks up jam-box and walks up to him. Long dim-out of cemetery)* So...now what?

CHIP: What?

DAVE: You going to tell everybody?

CHIP: Are you?

DAVE: I don't know. Are you?

CHIP: No.

DAVE: Okay.

CHIP: Not if you don't want me to.

DAVE: I don't know what I'll do. What about you?

CHIP: What?

DAVE: What are you going to do?

CHIP: You mean...you mean the movie? You still want to go to the movies?

DAVE: Do you?

CHIP: Yeah.

DAVE: *(In genuine disbelief)* You do?

CHIP: Yeah.

DAVE: You do?

CHIP: Yeah.

DAVE: Yeah, I do.

CHIP: We have...a date.

DAVE: I'll walk over...at eight.

CHIP: That's...great. I'll be there. Don't be late. *(Beat)* You got up four times. *(DAVE shakes his head yes.)* You did. You got up four times.

MAGGIE: Yes. I saw what he did to you. *(MAGGIE and DAVE meet, embrace.)* I am so proud of you. And you know what? That man could have taken you or killed you. You could

have run, but you didn't. Sandy got away. And you're still here. *(She embraces him again.)*

DAVE: **Thanks.**

MAGGIE: **We'll have to talk about the knife. All right? Not now; later.**

DAVE: **Sure. We'll talk later.**

MAGGIE: **Yeah?** *(She looks into him to see what he meant. Encouraged by what she sees)* **All right.**

CHIP: *(Getting ball)* **Hey, doctor, what's the score?**

DAVE: **What?**

CHIP: **I'm up, as I recall, and in the middle of your dreams.**

DAVE: **I don't feel like playing.**

CHIP: **A forfeit? Did I hear you say forfeit?**

DAVE: **No, I just don't feel like playing.**

MAGGIE: **A forfeit, Dave?** *(Sits at table.)*

DAVE: **I didn't say forfeit.**

CHIP: **All right!**

DAVE: **Chip...**

CHIP: *(Tossing DAVE the ball)* **I believe I fouled you before that last time out.**

DAVE: *(Deciding to play)* **Yeah, I got one.**

CHIP: **Foolish foul. You'd never make that shot.**

DAVE: **Oh, yeah, oh yeah I will. Ready?** *(Looking at CHIP's belt buckle.)* **I thought you said you were ready.**

CHIP: *(Looking at his belt area)* **Why?** *(DAVE dribbles by him, lays it in.)* **Hey. Hey!**

DAVE: **Scores.**

CHIP: **All right. All right, Cheap Shot, if that's the way we're playing. I'm better at this game than you. I am cheap and I am mean.** *(DAVE hands CHIP the ball. They set. CHIP suddenly looks up.)* **Who's that?** *(DAVE doesn't bite.)* **I think your mother's calling you.**

MAGGIE: *(Calling)* **Dave.**

CHIP: *(DAVE stays focused on CHIP. CHIP tries a variety of quick moves to begin a dribble but follows none of them as he is guarded well. He stops.)* **You got me.** *(DAVE relaxes. CHIP throws ball between DAVE's legs, moves and catches it, lays it in.)* **Scores! Sweet.** *(MAGGIE laughs. He rolls ball to DAVE; struts.)* **New NBA rule. That's a four-point shot.**

DAVE: **That was mean.** *(DAVE holds out his hand.)* **Good move.** *(CHIP whoops and slaps DAVE's hand.)* **You talented young hoopster.** *(MAGGIE watches. They play as the lights fade.)*

THE END

Puss in

Boots

by
Max Bush

Victor 1987

CHARACTERS

CLAUDE . . . . A Miller's Son

JEAN . . . . Claude's Older Brother, the
Oldest Child

DANIELLE. . . . . Claude's Older Sister

FATHER . . . . Claude's Father

PUSS . . . . A Cat

PRINCESS ANNETTE . . . A Princess

KING . . . . A King

HARCOURT . . . . The King's Servant

CURTIS . . . . A Lieutenant in the King's
Guard

OGRE. . . . . An Ogre

ALPHONSE . . . . Ogre's Servant

HARVESTER. . . . . A Harvester

All roles can be played by six actors.

TIME: Late 1600s

PLACE: France

DEDICATION: *Puss in Boots* is dedicated to Jon Anderson, my teacher.

Puss in Boots was originally commissioned by the Honolulu Theatre for Youth, and opened there in January, 1987, with the following cast and crew:

CAST

JEAN/OGRE/HARCOURT	David Furumoto
FATHER/KING	Kyle Kakuno
CURTIS/ALPHONSE/HARVESTER	James Pestana
CLAUDE	Kevin Reese
PUSS	Polly Kuulei Sommerfield
DANIELLE/ANNETTE	Alison Uyeda

PRODUCTION STAFF

Director	Anne-Denise Ford
Sets	Charles Walsh
Costumes	Ann Asakura Kimura
Sound	R. Suzanne Grant
Fight Choreography	Kevin Reese
Artistic Director	John Kauffman
Managing Director	Jane Campbell

(The Miller's House. Preshow music lowers in volume, playing ominously underneath the opening dialogue. PUSS sleeps on the floor, alone on the stage. JEAN, the oldest child of the Miller, runs on, looks around, calls.)

JEAN: Claude? *(Silence)* **Claude! Father?** *(Silence)* **Danielle?**

DANIELLE: *(Running on, carrying clothes basket)* **Here, Jean.**

JEAN: Danielle.

DANIELLE: What is it?

JEAN: I was called back from the mill.

DANIELLE: And I was called from the riverside.

JEAN: Is it Father?

DANIELLE: It must be.

JEAN: Father...

DANIELLE: Where's Claude?

JEAN: I sent him on ahead. He should have been here before us.

CLAUDE: *(Running on, out of breath)* **I'm here!**

DANIELLE: Why were we called back?

CLAUDE: I don't know. I just got here.

JEAN: I told you to run immediately home.

CLAUDE: There was a carriage on the road, a royal carriage, with the Princess Annette. She waved at me!

JEAN: A miller's son?

DANIELLE: Father! *(Music out. The FATHER enters, walking carefully with a cane. He sits.)*

JEAN: What is it, Father?

DANIELLE: How are you?

FATHER: It's time.

CLAUDE: Oh, Father, you're well enough.

FATHER: The time has —

CLAUDE: I'll take you for a walk today, down near the river. The leaves are beginning to change and we —

JEAN: Let him speak.

FATHER: The time has come for me to give you all that I have in this world.

JEAN: Shall I call a lawyer?

FATHER: No. They would take too much for themselves and I have little enough to leave to you. Jean...

JEAN: *(He crosses to FATHER, kneels.)* **Yes, sir.**

FATHER: To you, my oldest son, I leave the mill. Work hard, live wisely, and you will earn an honest living.

JEAN: Thank you, Father.

FATHER: Danielle...

DANIELLE: *(Kneeling)* **Here, Father.**

FATHER: To you, my second child, much less. For your dowry, I leave you my ox. Until you marry, work with your brother

Jean and you will earn your bread. I had hoped for much
more for you.

DANIELLE: *(She kisses him.)* **Thank you, Father.** *(She rises.)* **It's
enough.**

FATHER: Claude...

CLAUDE: Father, you have nothing left for—

FATHER: Kneel.

CLAUDE: *(Kneeling)* **You have nothing else, Father, I know.**

FATHER: To you, my youngest, who will need the most help
but who may surpass the others in fortune, I leave my
most important possession. Something better than a mill,
richer than gold.

CLAUDE: What, Father? What secret have you kept from us?

FATHER: I leave you — for you alone will be able to profit by it
— I leave you...my cat.

CLAUDE: Your cat? *(PUSS stretches, yawns.)*

FATHER: My cat.

CLAUDE: That cat?

FATHER: That cat.

CLAUDE: Father...that cat?

FATHER: Our Puss.

CLAUDE: You... *(He smiles)* **are joking.**

JEAN: Thank him.

CLAUDE: Father, what is it? What is your secret gift?

FATHER: Just as I've said.

CLAUDE: Your cat! *(He laughs loudly.)*

JEAN: Thank him!

CLAUDE: *(CLAUDE stops laughing.)* **Thank you, Father, for your
cat.**

FATHER: *(Slowly rising, with DANIELLE's help)* **And now, help me
to my bed, where I will pass from this world knowing all is
well with all of you.**

CLAUDE: All is well?

DANIELLE: *(Helping FATHER out)* **Claude!**

CLAUDE: Father, wait!

JEAN: He can't help you, any more. And I can't either. There
isn't enough work for you at the mill.

CLAUDE: What?

JEAN: There isn't enough business. You must go out on your
own.

CLAUDE: Me?

JEAN: I'm sorry.

CLAUDE: But you and Danielle can make an honest living, by
putting your property together. There is nothing left for
me except to die of hunger.

JEAN: Father has faith in you. He gave you his cat. *(PUSS meows.*

CLAUDE begins to protest but doesn't know what to say so he laughs.) **Good luck, brother.** *(He exits.)*

CLAUDE: But...Jean! Father! I'll starve! Unless I skin the cat and eat it. *(He dismisses the thought with a sound of disgust.)* **Father, you've condemned me to death!** *(Turning to PUSS)* **But I won't starve today. I will eat today. Casserole of Cat.** *(He draws his dagger.)* **Here, good Puss. Loyal Puss.** *(CLAUDE meows, slowly crosses to PUSS.)* **Yes, it's your new master, good Master Claude, and since I am your master it is your duty to keep me from starving. Therefore, generous servant — Voilá!** *(He lunges at reclining PUSS. In a deft and not — too — concerned move, PUSS eludes the blow. Again CLAUDE lunges, again the same results. Again. Again. In frustration, CLAUDE raises dagger to slice PUSS.)* **Stay still.** *(He swings, PUSS escapes.)* **I said stay!** *(He swings again. PUSS moves over to chair where FATHER left a cane. He picks it up, wields it like a sword with style and grace.)* **Put that cane down.**

PUSS: If you would, sir, sheathe your weapon and apologize for your attack, I would accept such an order.

CLAUDE: I am your new master, cat, and I command you to put that down.

PUSS: I won't.

CLAUDE: You will.

PUSS: Sir, I regret that what you say is impossible and I also regret that if you do not lower your weapon now, I must say to you—en garde!

CLAUDE: En garde! To me? My own Puss?

PUSS: You leave me no choice, sir. Casserole of Cat? So I say again, if you will not sheathe your weapon and apologize, en garde!

CLAUDE: Ha! *(CLAUDE attacks, PUSS defends. They fight, PUSS with finesse, protecting himself, and CLAUDE on the attack, impetuous and outclassed. In a series of stunning moves, PUSS disarms CLAUDE, stands with his cane to CLAUDE's chest.)* **Touché.**

PUSS: Reverse your position on eating your servant, sir, or I shall, with clear conscience, run you through.

CLAUDE: With a cane? Ha! *(CLAUDE grabs the end of the cane, PUSS pulls away, the cane comes apart revealing a sword. PUSS flashes more stunning moves with sword, then puts point to CLAUDE's chest.)* **Cat, I humbly apologize.**

PUSS: The casserole, sir.

CLAUDE: And will not attempt, in any way, to eat you again, in any dish.

PUSS: *(Giving CLAUDE his weapon)* **You are made of kindness, sir.**

(PUSS sheathes his weapon. Although their relationship begins with conflict, PUSS and CLAUDE must, almost from the start, demonstrate an underlying affection for one another. Their relationship is obviously contentious, with much joking at the other's expense — this is most true of PUSS — but a fast bonding and growing friendship between them is essential.) **Master, I think you had better not kill me; I shall be much more useful to you alive.**

CLAUDE: How?

PUSS: I would teach you the art of swordplay, if nothing else. You are a boy, sir; strong, with a good mind, but not well trained.

CLAUDE: Yes.

PUSS: And you *will* starve to death.

CLAUDE: Yes!

PUSS: Unless you give me a sack and a pair of fine new boots.

CLAUDE: My new boots?

PUSS: Then you will find your poor father's gift to you richer than you imagine.

CLAUDE: How can that be? A bragging cat, with a trick cane.

PUSS: You doubt me, sir?

CLAUDE: You do fight well. And I've seen you catch mice and rats. But I will not eat rats and mice.

PUSS: I will catch a rabbit.

CLAUDE: *(Helplessly)* I love rabbit.

PUSS: I will catch one.

CLAUDE: I love rabbit!

PUSS: What was that, sir?

CLAUDE: *(Completely innocently)* I love rabbit!

PUSS: *(Warmly, petting CLAUDE)* Trust me and you will eat royally.

CLAUDE: What else can I do? I'll give you your sack and your boots. Here... *(Gives PUSS a sack.)* And here...my new boots... *(Takes off his boots or picks them up and hands them to PUSS.)* These are all I have.

PUSS: You are made of generosity, sir. *(PUSS puts boots on.)*

CLAUDE: How do they fit?

PUSS: Perfectly.

CLAUDE: Shall I follow you?

PUSS: Meet me on the roadside by the Fontaine Bridge in one hour.

CLAUDE: I will.

PUSS: And I'll present you with your supper. *(Bowing)* Sir.

CLAUDE: Puss... *(PUSS runs off)* ...in my boots...rabbit...rabbit... *(He exits. Music covers scene change.)*

110

Scene 2

(A field. PUSS enters, stalking carefully, quietly, a rabbit. He spies his quarry — we don't see it yet — moves closer, stops, then moves again. He sees a rabbit — a hand puppet — moving innocently about. It disappears. PUSS continues stalking it. He reaches out, drops some lettuce in a small pile, backs off. He rolls on his back, pretends he is dead. The rabbit appears around a rock or a hedgerow; spies lettuce, starts for it, sees PUSS, panics, runs away, hides. Pause. The rabbit peers out again, sees PUSS. Rabbit moves closer to lettuce, hides, peeks up, then moves wildly, taunting and enticing the cat. No response from PUSS. Rabbit moves toward lettuce, PUSS begins to move, stops as rabbit turns toward him. PUSS freezes and the rabbit resumes eating. PUSS pounces. He wrestles with rabbit—pulls puppet from unseen hand—rolls with it, throws it up, catches it, bats it about, catches it in his mouth, shakes it sharply, then drops it in the sack.)

PUSS: **Voilà!** *(Music, as he exits with sack over shoulder.)*

Scene 3

(The roadside near the Fontaine Bridge. CLAUDE paces.)

CLAUDE: **Rabbit...rabbit...rabbit...** *(Spying PUSS Off-stage)* **Cat!**

PUSS: *(Entering with bag)* **Your rabbit, sir.** *(Throws it to CLAUDE.)*

CLAUDE: **You caught one?** *(Opens bag, looks in.)* **A fat one! A fat rabbit! Well done, Puss! Good servant!**

PUSS: *(Sincerely)* **Anything for you, sir.**

CLAUDE: **A fire. I'll build a fire. We'll cook it right here on the roadside. I brought some salt —** *(Royal trumpets sound.)* **I know that sound.**

PUSS: **Royal trumpets. They announce the king and —**

CLAUDE: **Princess Annette!**

PUSS: **They're passing down this road.**

CLAUDE: **Stay a moment and you'll see a royal beauty.** *(Courtly music. The KING, PRINCESS ANNETTE, HARCOURT, and CURTIS pass, ignore PUSS and CLAUDE, who bow deeply. CLAUDE waves; no response. He waves vigorously, walks with them, waves. No response. Finally CURTIS turns, they face each other for a moment. Then the entourage exits.)* **Did you see her?** *(He falls to his knees, weak with love.)* **She looked at me.** *(His head falls to his chest.)*

PUSS: **If only she would turn and look at you now.**

CLAUDE: **I would give everything I own to kiss her just once.**

PUSS: **Easy to say. You own nothing.**

CLAUDE: **I own you.** *(Gets up, pets PUSS.)* **You're not worth a kiss** from a princess. I couldn't get a slap from her maid for you. Puss, Puss, Puss, why was I born a miller's son and not a baron or a marquis? Why eat if I can't have what's most important to me?

PUSS: **Exactly, sir.** *(He snatches the bag from CLAUDE.)*

CLAUDE: **But I will, all the same.** *(CLAUDE snatches it back.)*

PUSS: **No, sir, you are right.** *(PUSS snatches it back.)*

CLAUDE: **I will eat this rabbit, anyway.** *(He snatches it back.)*

PUSS: **Why? If you can't live your life as you want?**

CLAUDE: *(Gives sack to PUSS.)* **You're right.** *(Calling after retinue)* **Princess! Annette! I starve to death for you!**

PUSS: **Are you young, sir, and something close to a man?**

CLAUDE: **So?**

PUSS: **You should be brave and, since you are straight of limb and not too near ugly, pursue your fortune.**

CLAUDE: **Do you think so? Not too near ugly?**

PUSS: **You should go after —**

CLAUDE: **Am I nearer to handsome?**

PUSS: **— go after her and —**

CLAUDE: **But am I nearer to handsome, Puss?**

PUSS: **You are as near to ugly as you are to handsome.**

CLAUDE: **You mean I am so-so?**

PUSS: **I mean you are ugly as a dog to me.**

CLAUDE: **Oh.**

PUSS: **And handsome enough for her.**

CLAUDE: **I am?**

PUSS: **Yes.**

CLAUDE: **Handsome!** *(CLAUDE is encouraged.)*

PUSS: **Therefore, go after her!**

CLAUDE: *(Crestfallen again)* **She won't care for me. I'm too near poor.**

PUSS: **You can still pursue her...**

CLAUDE: **You're right. Princess Annette!** *(He dashes Off-stage after her.)*

PUSS: *With a clever plan!* *(After a moment, CLAUDE slowly enters searching his thoughts without success.)*

CLAUDE: **A clever plan...**

PUSS: **An ingenious plot to make you appear worthy of a princess.**

CLAUDE: **An ingenious plot...**

PUSS: **Sir, with all respect, hunger has made you a crackbrain.**

CLAUDE: **Crackbrain?**

PUSS: **Can you think of no plots or schemes?**

CLAUDE: **None.**

PUSS: **If I could think of none I would go hang myself.**

CLAUDE: **You're right.** *(He starts off.)*

PUSS: **You need me even more than your father believed. Stop.**

(CLAUDE stops.) **Turn.** *(He turns to PUSS.)* **Listen.** *(He listens.)* **I'll present myself to the king — are you listening?**
CLAUDE: **My brain is cracked.**
PUSS: **I will present myself to the king and offer him this rabbit as a gift from your handsome self.**
CLAUDE: **He has a kitchen full of rabbits!**
PUSS: **I will say it's from you—**
CLAUDE: **A miller's son.**
PUSS: **The marquis.**
CLAUDE: **Marquis?**
PUSS: **Of...Carabas.**
CLAUDE: **I see...the marquis of Carabas...Who is he?**
PUSS: **You, Monsieur Crackbrain, are the marquis of Carabas.**
CLAUDE: *(What a joke)* **Ha!**
PUSS: **More planning later. I'll need, besides these boots, a gentleman's hat and cape to present myself to the king.**
CLAUDE: **I don't have a gentleman's hat and cape.**
PUSS: **Your ring, sir.**
CLAUDE: **My mother gave me this ring! It was the only thing she left me.**
PUSS: **I'll sell it to buy my clothes.**
CLAUDE: **My mother's ring...What's it matter? If I can't live my life as I want...Take it. Do your best.** *(Gives PUSS the ring.)*
PUSS: *(With a bow)* **Sir.** *(He exits.)*
CLAUDE: **I will be here, starving on this very roadside, if you need me.** *(He exits. Music)*

Scene 4

(The KING's palace. Courtly music. The KING sits on the throne, signing a document. The PRINCESS stands at his side. HARCOURT, the KING's servant, stands ready, next to the KING on the other side.)
KING: **Call the next petitioner, Harcourt.**
HARCOURT: **Your Majesty, Curtis Courtney!** *(CURTIS enters, bows. He is a straightforward, honest young man. PUSS puts his head around the corner, listens.)*
CURTIS: **Your Majesty.**
KING: *(His mind still half on the document)* **What is your petition?**
CURTIS: **Just this, sire.** *(He kneels.)* **I ask for your daughter's hand in marriage.** *(This startles them awake.)*
PRINCESS: **What? Oh, who? Me? Well, yes. That's me. Me?**
CURTIS: **Yes, my lady, you.**
PRINCESS: **I am honored, sir.**
KING: *(Hands document to HARCOURT.)* **You are a...**
CURTIS: **Lieutenant, sire, in your King's Guard.**

KING: And what special wealth and position of power do you offer worthy of our Princess?

CURTIS: I love her, sire, and I feel she could, in time, grow to love me. *(PRINCESS smiles at him.)*

KING: Well... *(Holding out his hand)* Your hat, Lieutenant.

CURTIS: My...

KING: Give me your hat. *(CURTIS does.)* You silly boy! *(He strikes CURTIS with the hat.)*

PRINCESS: Father!

KING: You lack the riches and power to marry our daughter.

PRINCESS: He's a young gentleman.

KING: You are no baron or marquis.

CURTIS: My lady refuses our barons and marquis.

PRINCESS: They are all old, short and fat.

CURTIS: Set me a task. Let me prove myself.

KING: What you ask is impossible. *(KING stuffs hat on CURTIS' head.)* And if you have any thought of running away with her I will find you and, on my oath as king, I will hang you, boy. She must marry for the good of the kingdom. I will hang anyone who will marry her for any other reason.

PRINCESS: We know my father is right, sir, but a proposal from such a handsome young gentleman honors both myself and the king.

KING: *(To CURTIS)* Give me your hand.

CURTIS: My...

KING: Your hand. *(He takes it, removes a ring from his hand, places it in CURTIS' hand.)* For your faithful service. We're sorry. That is all. *(PUSS sneaks out.)* Call the next petitioner.

CURTIS: *(He bows.)* My lady. *(He exits.)*

HARCOURT: Your Majesty...a *cat*.

KING: Indeed.

HARCOURT: In boots.

PRINCESS: A puss in boots?

KING: Indeed. *(PUSS sweeps in, wearing a large hat and beautiful cape, and bows gracefully.)*

PUSS: Your Majesty.

KING: Cat.

PUSS: Princess.

PRINCESS: Puss.

PUSS: Here, sire... *(He retrieves rabbit from bag, ceremoniously hands it to the KING, who holds it by the ears)* is a magnificent rabbit, killed in a warren which belongs to my lord the marquis of Carabas and which he has instructed me to offer humbly to your Royal Highness.

KING: The marquis of —

PUSS: Carabas.

KING: And where are his lands?

PUSS: Bordering the river near the Fontaine Bridge.

PRINCESS: But we hear that land is owned by a disgusting ogre.

PUSS: My master is a young gentleman.

KING: Is he married?

PUSS: Not married, My Lord.

PRINCESS: And, I suppose, he's as ugly as a dog?

PUSS: Most say he is nearer handsome.

KING: Tell your master I am pleased to accept his present.

PUSS: He sends health to Your Majesty and happiness to the Princess Annette.

PRINCESS: Tell him I thank him for his goodwill and wish the same unto him.

PUSS: In this and in all others, before and always, I am your humble servant. Sire.

KING: Cat.

PUSS: Princess.

PRINCESS: Puss. *(He exits.)*

KING: Well, that was refreshing.

PRINCESS: Do you know this marquis, Father?

KING: No, but if he is as quick and well bred as his cat, I should like to meet him. Harcourt, call the next petitioner, then take this to the cook. *(Music)*

Scene 5

(The roadside near the Fontaine Bridge. CLAUDE sits on bridge waiting for PUSS. PUSS enters, drops bag.)

CLAUDE: Did you see the king?

PUSS: Yes.

CLAUDE: Did he accept the rabbit?

PUSS: Yes.

CLAUDE: Did you see the princess?

PUSS: Yes.

CLAUDE: *(Jubilant)* Oh, you saw her? You saw Princess Annette! You saw Princess Annette! *(He embraces PUSS, PUSS purrs. Suddenly crestfallen)* So? Now what? The king will eat, again, and I will starve. Why did we do this? None of this makes any sense!

PUSS: Sir, your hat.

CLAUDE: What? My...

PUSS: Give me your hat. *(CLAUDE does.)* You silly boy! *(He hits CLAUDE with hat.)* You dishonor me and yourself and your poor father with this helplessness! Your stomach has devoured your brains! You sniveling little piggy. *(Hits CLAUDE again.)*

115

Here — *(Slaps hat back on to his head.)*

CLAUDE: **If you do that again I will throw you in the river.**

PUSS: *(Sincerely. Kneeling)* **You are right, sir. I apologize.**

CLAUDE: *(Sincerely)* **You do?**

PUSS: **I was wrong to strike you.**

CLAUDE: **I forgive you.**

PUSS: **But, master, I ask you to trust me and yourself more.**

CLAUDE: *(Genuinely)* **I will.**

PUSS: **I'm returning now to the king and will make him a second gift.**

CLAUDE: **What gift?**

PUSS: *(Holding up the bag)* **This.**

CLAUDE: *(Very interested)* **What's in there?**

PUSS: **I caught them in the field.**

CLAUDE: **Them? There's more than one?**

PUSS: **Two.**

CLAUDE: **Rabbits?**

PUSS: **No.**

CLAUDE: **What?**

PUSS: **Partridges.**

CLAUDE: **I love partridges!**

PUSS: **I shall offer them to the king.**

CLAUDE: **I love partridges!**

PUSS: **And say they are from you, the marquis of Carabas.**

CLAUDE: **Offer him one. I'll cook the other. Please; I love partridges!**

PUSS: *(To the skies)* **You are all stomach.**

CLAUDE: *(Drawing dagger)* **I am your master and I say we eat one of those birds now!**

PUSS: **You'll meet Princess Annette.**

CLAUDE: *(This stops him.)* **The princess?**

PUSS: **I will arrange it so she will pass by and you will meet her.**

CLAUDE: **But she'll expect a marquis, not a miller's son.**

PUSS: **Trust that to me, my marquis.**

CLAUDE: **But the birds...**

PUSS: **One for His Majesty, the other for your princess.**

CLAUDE: *(After a moment)* **I'll do it.**

PUSS: **You are made of courage, sir.**

CLAUDE: **But if she refuses the bird or, let's say, she doesn't much care for partridges, you'll keep hers?**

PUSS: **I will.** *(CLAUDE runs laughing up to the bridge, sits.)* **Thank you for your trust.** *(He runs off.)*

CLAUDE: *(His laughter continues for a time.)* **Princess...Princess Annette...** *(He laughs. He hums. He stops; waits. He becomes dejected.)* **How long am I supposed to wait? And what if they do come? I'm no marquis.** *(He rises.)* **If I don't eat soon** it won't matter if they come or not. Oh... *(He holds his stomach, stumbles forward, then falls to his knees and pleads with the heavens.)* **I'm starving. I'm not a bad man! Give me something to eat!** *(An Off-stage shot. Beat. A partridge falls out of the sky, hits him in the head.)* **A partridge? A partridge!** *(Looking up)* **Thank you! Oh, thank you! Thank you! Thank you!** *(He picks bird up.)* **My pretty, plump partridge.** *(He kisses it repeatedly.)* **I love you, you luscious, lovely bird.** *(He kisses it again.)* **I'll marry you. Yes. After you're cooked...if I can wait that long. Fire...sticks...** *(ALPHONSE runs on. He is a nervous, but good-natured servant.)*

ALPHONSE: **Oh, thank you, sir.**

CLAUDE: *(Clutching bird)* **For what?**

ALPHONSE: **Our bird.** *(Holds out his hand.)*

CLAUDE: **Never. Heaven sent me this bird.**

ALPHONSE: **My lord shot it on his land.**

CLAUDE: **I love this bird. She loves me.**

ALPHONSE: **He'll take it from you, sir.**

CLAUDE: **Then I'll fight him for it.**

ALPHONSE: **Do you know my master?**

CLAUDE: **It doesn't matter who he is. I'd fight the king himself for this bird. I've been too hungry for too long.** *(Draws his dagger.)*

ALPHONSE: **Put away your dagger if you value your life!**

CLAUDE: **This bird is my life.**

ALPHONSE: **Give me the bird while you still have life!** *(We hear a loud roar and a strangled scream from Off-stage. This startles CLAUDE.)* **You are a thief and a trespasser. He has killed — and eaten — others for less.**

CLAUDE: **Eaten?**

ALPHONSE: **My lord is an Ogre.**

CLAUDE: **Ogre?**

ALPHONSE: **And a shape-shifter. He will change himself into an eagle, fly over his lands and, when he spies a trespasser such as you, fly down, change into a lion and eat you.**

CLAUDE: *(Looking up)* **That isn't fair.**

ALPHONSE: **Therefore —** *(He snatches bird away from CLAUDE and runs. CLAUDE pursues him. ALPHONSE picks up a stick, turns, points it at CLAUDE.)* **Let me pass.**

CLAUDE: *(Prepares to attack, imitating PUSS in the flamboyance of his preparations.)* **If you do not put down that stick and give me that bird I must say to you —** *(À la PUSS)* **En garde!**

ALPHONSE: **En garde?** *(ALPHONSE attacks and they fight. At one point ALPHONSE holds the bird but is disarmed. CLAUDE throws him the stick and they resume fighting. In moves very much like those PUSS used, CLAUDE defeats ALPHONSE.)* **Touché.**

CLAUDE: The bird, sir, or I shall, with clear conscience, run you through. *(ALPHONSE gives him the bird.)* **You are made of generosity.** *(Helping ALPHONSE up)* **You are young, sir, strong ...enough and with a fair mind, but not well trained.**

OGRE: *(Off-stage)* **Alphonse!**

ALPHONSE: *(To CLAUDE)* **I have to have that bird! If I don't give it to him, he will eat me!**

OGRE: *(Off-stage)* **Alphonse!**

ALPHONSE: **Here, my lord!** *(To CLAUDE)* **I beg you give it up. He knows no mercy.**

CLAUDE: **I'll fight and die or I'll fight and eat. But I won't die of hunger. Let him come. I'll fight for both of us.**

OGRE: *(Enters. He is a large, frightening creature. Yet he's dressed in the fashion of a noble. He speaks in a growl.)* **Why haven't you returned with the bird?** *(ALPHONSE bows, indicating CLAUDE. CLAUDE is stunned by the OGRE. Quietly)* **You ...sir...Who are you?**

CLAUDE: **I...I...**

OGRE: **And why do you trespass?**

CLAUDE: **I...I...**

OGRE: **And why is your dagger drawn?**

CLAUDE: **My...my...**

OGRE: *(Taking CLAUDE's dagger hand, puts dagger to CLAUDE's throat.)* **Do you challenge my servant? And me?**

CLAUDE: **Me...?**

OGRE: **Ah!** *(He squeezes CLAUDE's hand. CLAUDE drops dagger. Turning to ALPHONSE, crossing to him quickly)* **Who is he?**

ALPHONSE: **My lord, the bird fell near him —**

CLAUDE: **Yes, but —**

ALPHONSE: **He picked it up —**

CLAUDE: **But I didn't —**

ALPHONSE: **When I asked him for it, he refused to give it to me saying —**

CLAUDE: **I would only give it to you, my lord, to make your acquaintance. I am Claude, my lord, an honest traveler, at your service.** *(He bows, puts down bird.)* **I drew on your man because he insisted I give the bird to him.**

OGRE: *(Taking ALPHONSE by the hair)* **Is this the truth?**

CLAUDE: **Yes.**

OGRE: **Alphonse, is this what happened?**

ALPHONSE: *(After a moment)* **It is, my lord.**

OGRE: **That's...good; very good, Alphonse.** *(He strokes ALPHONSE.)*

CLAUDE: **Are all these lands yours, my lord?**

OGRE: **The lands are mine. The river is mine. The road is mine. The birds are mine. The people are mine.** *(He strokes ALPHONSE.)* **And what are you?**

CLAUDE: A poor miller's son, seeking service to earn meat and bread from your generous lordship.

OGRE: I've no need of a miller's son.

CLAUDE: Then I will certainly starve.

OGRE: Oh, are you hungry?

CLAUDE: Yes.

OGRE: *(Picking up partridge)* Would you like this bird?

CLAUDE: I would. *(ALPHONSE signals CLAUDE to refuse bird.)*

OGRE: Cooked slowly in a thick sauce?

CLAUDE: Oh, yes. *(ALPHONSE signals no.)*

OGRE: With bread and fruit and fine wine? *(CLAUDE is unable to speak but indicates a strong yes! OGRE holds out bird to CLAUDE. CLAUDE is unsure whether or not to take it, looks to ALPHONSE who indicates emphatically no.)*

CLAUDE: Master Ogre, I couldn't just...take your... *(The OGRE again extends his hand. Again ALPHONSE pleads no to CLAUDE. CLAUDE bucks up.)* Very well. *(He crosses to OGRE, reaches out to take bird. The OGRE drops bird. Beat. CLAUDE bends down to pick it up, the OGRE kicks it away. Beat. OGRE takes CLAUDE's arm, flips him. CLAUDE lands hard and surprised on the ground.)*

OGRE: Leave my lands, beggar! Or I will shoot you as a thief! *(The OGRE grabs CLAUDE by the throat, lifts him up.)* And if I thought you were trying to steal my bird, I would have your head, sir — cooked slowly, in a thick sauce — for my supper. And feed the rest of you to my dogs! *(Throws CLAUDE down.)* Alphonse! *(They exeunt. CLAUDE lies on the ground in hopelessness, totally defeated. PUSS runs in, looks off in the distance.)*

PUSS: They're coming. They are coming! Claude? Claude! *(CLAUDE groans.)* Here you are.

CLAUDE: What's left of me.

PUSS: If you will follow my advice we'll make this day yours.

CLAUDE: So you say.

PUSS: The king and princess will pass by here immediately and they desire to meet you!

CLAUDE: Me?

PUSS: The marquis of Carabas.

CLAUDE: I'm a miller's son!

PUSS: They're coming! Stand! *(He tries to pull CLAUDE up. CLAUDE is too weak and falls down.)* The Princess Annette, sir!

CLAUDE: Let her marry herself to the Ogre. He has wealth and power enough for her.

PUSS: *(Trying to pull CLAUDE up)* Join me in the venture and your fortune is made. Take off your clothes and drown

yourself in the river.

CLAUDE: **Oh, yes, now I understand. I will make my fortune by drowning myself in the river.**

PUSS: **You are stronger and more intelligent than this.** *(Holding out his paw)* **Give me your hand, sir.**

CLAUDE: **My...**

PUSS: **Give me your hand.** *(He does. PUSS pulls him up and begins to remove CLAUDE's clothes. CLAUDE passively allows it.)* **Listen to my instructions, jump in the river, and follow my lead.**

CLAUDE: **Why?**

PUSS: **But remember, you are no longer a miller's son but the marquis of Carabas.** *(CLAUDE laughs weakly. His clothes are off. Trumpets)* **They're here. Into the river.** *(PUSS pushes CLAUDE into the river.)*

CLAUDE: **It's cold!**

PUSS: **Splash around!**

CLAUDE: **It's cold!** *You* **drown!**

PUSS: **Splash around!**

CLAUDE: **It's too cold! I'll hang myself instead.** *(He crosses out of river. PUSS stops him by sinking his claws in CLAUDE's chest.)*

PUSS: *(In the KING's direction)* **Help! Help! My lord, the marquis, is drowning!**

CLAUDE: **What are we doing?**

PUSS: **I don't have time to explain. Play this with me.** *(Pushes CLAUDE back into the river.)* **Drown yourself!** *(Cuing him)* **Help! Help!**

CLAUDE: *(Mocking PUSS)* **Help! Help!**

PUSS: *(Waving his arms frantically)* **I'm drowning!**

CLAUDE: *(Mocking PUSS)* **I'm drowning!** *(PUSS makes a loud gurgling sound. CLAUDE mocks him again. The KING, PRINCESS and HARCOURT enter.)*

PUSS: **He's drowning!**

CLAUDE: *(He sees entourage and suddenly, frantically splashes about.)* **I'm drowning! I'm drowning! Help, I'm drowning!**

PUSS: *(With a quiet, courtly respect, as CLAUDE freezes)* **Sire.**

KING: **Cat.**

PUSS: **Princess.**

PRINCESS: **Puss.**

PUSS: **The marquis of Carabas is drowning.**

CLAUDE: *(Suddenly loud and frantic again)* **I'm drowning! Help! I can't swim! The currents —**

PUSS: **The marquis of Carabas is drowning!**

PRINCESS: **Father, the marquis!**

KING: **Harcourt?**

HARCOURT: Yes, Your Majesty.

KING: Save him.

HARCOURT: Yes, Your Majesty.

CLAUDE: *(In great panic)* **Help, help, save me, I'm drowning! Help! Help! Help!**

HARCOURT: Here I am. I'll save you.

CLAUDE: **Help! Save me! I can't swim! Help me! Help me! The currents are too strong!** *(He is pulled under bridge. HARCOURT moves after him. CLAUDE fights his way back upstream. HARCOURT follows, but CLAUDE again tumbles downstream. Finally HARCOURT thumps CLAUDE on the head with his fist; this stuns CLAUDE. He stops struggling a moment, HARCOURT takes him by the head and swims them both to safety.)*

HARCOURT: **I am, sir, I am. We're almost there...you can walk now.** *(CLAUDE ends up standing next to and facing the PRINCESS. They smile at each other. PRINCESS suddenly sees that he's in his underclothes.)*

PRINCESS: **Oh!**

CLAUDE: *(Realizes the same.)* **Oh!** *(CLAUDE dashes behind HARCOURT, so the PRINCESS can't see him. The PRINCESS crosses behind the KING.)*

KING: **Well done, Harcourt, as always.** *(HARCOURT bows, as does CLAUDE so as not to be seen.)*

HARCOURT: **My pleasure, Your Majesty.** *(The PRINCESS, who has hidden behind the KING, is trying to catch glimpses of CLAUDE, who is hidden behind HARCOURT and who is trying to catch glimpses of the PRINCESS.)*

PUSS: **You must know, sire, that some robbers learned through a spy that my master was taking a great store of jewels to offer to you.**

KING: **Jewels?**

PUSS: **They laid wait for him and robbed him of his treasure.**

CLAUDE: *(Playing along)* **Thieves!**

PUSS: **Then, wishing to murder him, they threw him into the river...after they took his fine clothes.**

CLAUDE: **Rude thieves!**

PUSS: **My poor self could not stop them, nor can I — being a cat — swim.**

KING: **I am sorry we didn't arrive sooner. I would have enjoyed routing some rude thieves...** *(Shows how he would have done it.)* **Like the old days, eh, Harcourt?**

HARCOURT: **The very old days, sire.**

PRINCESS: *(To CLAUDE)* **Are you well, sir?**

CLAUDE: **Very well.**

PRINCESS: **Perhaps chilled?**

CLAUDE: Not so much chilled as hungry, my lady.

PRINCESS: Oh.

KING: Hungry?

PUSS: *(Covering)* In the heat of preparations to meet you, we missed our meal today.

CLAUDE: You wouldn't have packed a basket of food for your travel today?

PRINCESS: No.

CLAUDE: Oh.

KING: Nor clothes, I'm afraid. Harcourt, return to the castle with all speed and bring back clothes worthy of our marquis.

HARCOURT: Yes, Your Majesty.

KING: Quickly, Harcourt. *(He runs off. CLAUDE runs behind PUSS.)* Our marquis will be properly dressed in no time.

PUSS: My lord, the marquis, sire, to preserve the honor of the princess will — *(Loudly)* **Wait at a discreet distance behind the bushes.** *(CLAUDE runs off. Music plays. They all move and freeze at the same moment. They wait. They all move together, look in the direction of the castle, freeze. More time passes. They wait. They all move together in a third position, sigh together, freeze at the same time. More time passes. Finally)*

HARCOURT: *(Entering)* **Your Majesty, the marquis of Carabas!** *(All animate, music out.)*

KING: **That took forever.** *(CLAUDE enters richly dressed, but unsure of himself.)*

PUSS: *(Fixing CLAUDE's hat. He has it on backwards.)* **There you are, marquis. You look just like your handsome self. You see? You needn't have worried.** *(Short silence. "What's the next move?")* **My master thanks you, sire, for the splendid clothes.** *(CLAUDE bows awkwardly to the PRINCESS, speaks to her.)*

CLAUDE: I thank you, sire, for these...splendid clothes.

PRINCESS: My father is pleased to return a gift to such a generous and tall marquis.

PUSS: My master wishes to express his gratitude that Your Majesty has come to view his lands.

CLAUDE: *(To PRINCESS)* I thank Your Majesty for coming to...view my lands.

PRINCESS: Our pleasure, sir.

KING: How much land do you own?

CLAUDE: Puss... *(PUSS moves to CLAUDE. Quietly to PUSS)* How much land do I own?

PUSS: *(Quietly)* Along both sides of the river...

CLAUDE: *(To others)* Along both sides of the river...

PUSS: *(Quietly)* As far as one can see in that direction.

122

CLAUDE: As far as one can see in that direction.

KING: Indeed.

PRINCESS: And where do you live?

PUSS: *(Quietly)* In your humble castle.

CLAUDE: *(To PRINCESS, confidently)* In your humble castle.

KING: What?

CLAUDE: *(Something is wrong. Is it...?)* My lady. *(Silence)* My humble castle! *(He laughs. All laugh.)*

PRINCESS: You are unusual, sir.

CLAUDE: Unusual, yes. *(Silence)* How do you mean, unusual?

PRINCESS: Strangely funny. *(They laugh a little.)*

KING: And difficult to believe.

CLAUDE: I am?

KING: We won't be played with, boy. The last man to lie to us we hung for treason.

CLAUDE: What do you question, Your Majesty?

KING: We understand a fierce Ogre owns these lands.

CLAUDE: Yes.

KING: Yes?

CLAUDE: Yes, it's... *(PUSS begins to speak, but CLAUDE continues)* an old story to frighten away unwanted visitors...which is why I sent my servant with gifts and personal invitations to yourself, sire, and the Princess Annette. So you could see that I am no Ogre. But your devoted subject.

PUSS: Well said, sir. *(All look at the KING who gives no clue as to how he's responding.)* Perhaps His Majesty would do us the honor of viewing more of my lord's abundant fields.

KING: We would.

CLAUDE: Excellent, sire.

PUSS: I will run on ahead, marquis, and prepare the way for their visit.

CLAUDE: Very well, Puss.

PUSS: This way if you will, sire. *(The KING exits with HARCOURT. PUSS runs off in another direction. CLAUDE and the PRINCESS are suddenly alone.)*

PRINCESS: Are these clothes to your taste, marquis?

CLAUDE: These clothes?...Yes, they are very much like my old clothes.

PRINCESS: Would you do us the honor of riding in our carriage?

CLAUDE: The honor will be mine, my lady. *(They exeunt. Music)*

Scene 6

(An orchard. A HARVESTER is picking apples.)

HARVESTER: Ah, that's enough. I've picked my last apple today.

I've done enough for two, that's for sure. And now — *(He lies down)* for a well-deserved rest. *(He puts his hat over his face.)* And if the master Ogre appears, *(The OGRE appears)* stalking through his lands, scaring the good people, breaking our backs with work, I'll tell him to keep his growling mouth quiet out of respect...except to compliment me on my excellent labor.

OGRE: *(Quietly)* Are you resting, Harvester?

HARVESTER: *(From under his hat)* Who is that?

OGRE: If you do not rise you will not live.

HARVESTER: *(Slowly pulling hat down, to himself)* Please, it won't be — you wouldn't, dear gods, do this to me — *(He sees OGRE.)* Ah! *(He jumps up.)* Master Ogre! Forgive me, but I've worked hard today, harvested enough for four and was only resting so I could harvest more —

OGRE: Kneel.

HARVESTER: *(Kneeling.)* I was about to begin picking again when —

OGRE: The king is traveling down this road.

HARVESTER: Yes? The king —

OGRE: If he speaks to you, you will speak to him — of my kindness and generosity.

HARVESTER: Your kindness and gen —

OGRE: You will smile at his daughter and offer her an apple from my orchard.

HARVESTER: An apple, yes.

OGRE: You will do as I tell you, always.

HARVESTER: I do. I do, master Og — *(OGRE stuffs an apple in HARVESTER's mouth.)*

OGRE: Or I will roast you like a pig on a spit. *(OGRE exits. The HARVESTER spits out apple.)*

HARVESTER: I'm saved. The king's coming saved me...kindness...smile at the princess...

PUSS: *(Running on)* The king will pass by the orchard shortly and if you do not tell him this orchard belongs to the marquis of Carabas, your master, the Ogre, will have you chopped up as small as mincemeat.

HARVESTER: I say...but...why didn't he tell me himself?

PUSS: Do you question his wisdom?

HARVESTER: No, I don't ques — Who are you?

PUSS: A messenger from master Ogre.

HARVESTER: But he just passed and told me to speak generously and — *(Trumpets)*

PUSS: Look, the king comes.

HARVESTER: Just as the master said he would, and I —

PUSS: On your life, Harvester, the marquis of Carabas! *(KING,*

PRINCESS and CLAUDE enter.)

KING: *(With authority)* **Know that we are the king and we ask you: Whose orchard is this that you harvest?**

HARVESTER: **This orchard belongs to...the marquis of Carabas.**

PRINCESS: **What a splendid crop of apples.**

CLAUDE: **It's not a bad year for the harvest...although I've seen better.** *(To HARVESTER)* **You may, for your excellent service, rest the remainder of the day. Return in two days and receive full payment. Your master says this to you.** *(HARVESTER looks doubtingly at CLAUDE, then smiles broadly, proudly. He crosses to PRINCESS, smiles, gives her an apple.)*

HARVESTER: *(Smiling)* **My master is very kind and generous.**

PRINCESS: **Like no marquis I've ever met.**

CLAUDE: **I know what you mean.**

HARVESTER: **Pleasant day.** *(He exits.)*

PRINCESS: *(Pointing off)* **Is that your castle beyond the next curve?**

KING: **The very castle we heard belongs to an ogre.**

CLAUDE: **Yes, it's mine.**

KING: **We will view it now.**

PUSS: **I will run ahead, sir, and prepare for your arrival.**

CLAUDE: **No, I will run ahead and take care of any problems I find.**

PUSS: **Your place is with the princess, sir. I will go.**

CLAUDE: **Very well.**

PUSS: **You are made of wisdom, sir.**

CLAUDE: **Puss, I take my hat off to you.** *(He does. Bows to PUSS.)* **And, if we never meet again, I'm proud to have received such a rich inheritance from my wise father.**

PUSS: **Thank you, sir.** *(Exits.)*

KING: **Good servant.**

CLAUDE: **I would be a poor man without him.** *(Music. They exeunt.)*

Scene 7

(In the castle of the OGRE. A table is set for a banquet. The OGRE enters with a large, empty goblet.)

OGRE: **Drink, Alphonse!**

ALPHONSE: *(Running on, pouring OGRE a drink)* **Master, there is a cat at your door wishing to speak with you.**

OGRE: **A cat? I love cat.**

ALPHONSE: **A well-bred, well-spoken Puss.**

OGRE: **Let it come.**

ALPHONSE: *(Calling)* **Puss!** *(PUSS enters, carrying his cane, bows. ALPHONSE exits.)*

PUSS: Ogre, I greet you.

OGRE: You are welcome, cat.

PUSS: *(He is visibly stunned by the appearance of the OGRE.)* **I'm a traveler, my lord, but I did not want to pass so near the castle of such a noble gentleman without paying respect to him.**

OGRE: Pleased to have you, friend.

PUSS: *(Seeing banquet)* **I see by your generous table you are expecting guests?**

OGRE: The king is traveling through my lands.

PUSS: Yes. *(He puts his cane down.)*

OGRE: Once he has viewed my large estates he will offer his daughter to me. This banquet will celebrate the announcement of our marriage.

PUSS: I would be honored to join in such a celebration. *(ALPHONSE enters with a glass for PUSS.)*

OGRE: Sit. Drink. Talk. *(ALPHONSE sets glass down, pours drink.)*

PUSS: Certainly, sir, but first I hope you will satisfy a traveler's curiosity. I have heard in far countries of your many remarkable qualities.

OGRE: No doubt.

PUSS: Especially how you have the power to change yourself into any sort of beast you choose. A lion, for instance.

ALPHONSE: *(Involuntarily)* No.

OGRE: A hungry lion. That is quite true.

PUSS: Oh, sir, I would enjoy seeing you change into a lion.

ALPHONSE: You don't want —

OGRE: You would be amused?

PUSS: Greatly amused.

ALPHONSE: But you don't want —

OGRE: Alphonse.

ALPHONSE: Yes, master?

OGRE: Go...and wake my dogs.

PUSS: Dogs?

ALPHONSE: *(Sadly)* Yes, master. *(He exits.)*

OGRE: Now, my tender friend...a lion did you say? *(He transforms himself into a lion, leaps and growls at PUSS who leaps away in fear. The lion stalks PUSS who runs from him. PUSS goes for his cane, the lion prevents him from getting it. He tries again, picks up the cane, then tries to keep lion at a distance with it. That obviously doesn't work. PUSS draws the sword out, the lion roars. PUSS is successful at defending himself for a time, but then the lion claws the sword from PUSS' hand. The lion chases PUSS; PUSS eludes him.)*

PUSS: I see! I see! Thank you! Thank you, sir! *(The lion still pursues PUSS. ALPHONSE enters fearfully.)*

126

ALPHONSE: Master, I have awakened your — *(The lion charges him with a growl.)* **Dogs!** *(ALPHONSE screeches and runs off. PUSS uses the opportunity to hide. The lion quits his pursuit of ALPHONSE, turns to find PUSS gone. He looks for PUSS, can't find him. The OGRE resumes his shape.)*

OGRE: Cat? *(The OGRE picks up sheath and sword.)* **Cat...** *(PUSS steps out, still quite frightened.)*

PUSS: Thank you, sir. You were magnificent.

OGRE: Then you were amused. *(He laughs.)*

PUSS: Greatly amused. And I apologize for drawing my sword. You make a fierce lion.

OGRE: *(He holds out sheath and sword to PUSS.)* **I was amused by your trick cane.** *(PUSS carefully takes sheath, then sword. He holds sword at OGRE for a moment, deliberates, then sheathes his sword and sets it down.)*

PUSS: But sir, it may be easy enough for such a tall gentleman as you to change himself into a large lion; I do not suppose you could become a smaller animal — a wolf, for instance?

OGRE: A wolf? *(He begins to transform, PUSS interrupts him.)*

PUSS: Or a fox?

OGRE: Fox? *(Again he begins to transform, PUSS stops him.)*

PUSS: Or a rabbit?

OGRE: Yes, a rabbit.

PUSS: Or a rat. No, certainly not a rat.

OGRE: I can.

PUSS: So I have heard. Still, for my part, I consider that impossible.

OGRE: Impossible?

PUSS: For you.

OGRE: You doubt me?

PUSS: I do.

OGRE: *(Beat. Roaring)* Do you say I am a liar?

PUSS: I say it can't be done.

OGRE: Ah, my large, tender cat, you shall see. Then you will join our celebration...as a roast.

PUSS: A roast?

OGRE: I *love* cat. Alphonse!

ALPHONSE: *(Entering gingerly)* Yes, master.

OGRE: Lock the doors. Open them only to the king.

ALPHONSE: Yes, master.

OGRE: And build a fire under the large roasting pot.

ALPHONSE: *(Sadly)* **Puss.** *(ALPHONSE exits.)*

OGRE: A rat did you say? *(In his large cloak, he melts to the floor. A rat emerges from under his costume. Quickly PUSS runs over, snatches it up, bats it about.)*

PUSS: Voilá, master Ogre! *(He bites head off rat.)* **Delicious!** *(He* *sits in OGRE's throne and enjoys his meal. ALPHONSE enters.)*

ALPHONSE: **Master, the king and princess are** — *(Sees PUSS, is delightfully surprised.)* **Puss! But where is...** *(PUSS takes another bite.)* **Master?**

PUSS: *(Regally)* **Alphonse?**

ALPHONSE: **Yes...?**

PUSS: **Show the king in.**

ALPHONSE: **Yes...sir.** *(He goes to doorway, announces.)* **His Highness and the Princess.** *(KING, PRINCESS, and CLAUDE enter.)*

PUSS: **Sire.**

KING: **Cat.**

PUSS: **Princess.**

PRINCESS: **Puss.**

PUSS: *(Exploding)* **Claude!**

CLAUDE: **Puss!**

PUSS: **Claude!**

CLAUDE: **Puss!** *(They embrace in jubilation.)*

PRINCESS: **They are happy to see one another.**

CLAUDE: **Is he...?**

PUSS: **Gone, sir.**

CLAUDE: **This is a victory!**

PUSS: **A complete victory!** *(They both cheer.)*

KING: **What is?**

PUSS: **Ah...**

CLAUDE: **A victory that...**

PUSS: **You have come to visit—**

CLAUDE: *(CLAUDE makes, finally, a genuine, graceful bow.)* **The marquis of Carabas!**

ALPHONSE: *(Recognizing him)* **Partridge!**

CLAUDE: **Yes, Alphonse, my good servant, we'll have partridge for supper.**

ALPHONSE: **Your good** —

CLAUDE: **But now, Alphonse, bring drinks for everyone.** *(ALPHONSE wanders off.)* **Welcome, sire, to my humble castle.**

KING: **Humble! Never have I seen a finer courtyard; and these battlements! I have nothing like them in the whole of my kingdom.**

PUSS: **And in your honor, sire** — *(He indicates table of food.)*

CLAUDE: **Food...food...look at all this food!**

PRINCESS: **He is...happy to see his food.**

PUSS: **Sit! Dine! Celebrate!**

CLAUDE: **Eat! Eat!**

PRINCESS: **We will be happy to eat.** *(ALPHONSE enters, passes out drinks.)*

CLAUDE: **I toast you with this apple.** *(He takes a large bite, hands apple to PRINCESS, who attempts to understand this* *strange custom of Carabas.)* **With this croissant.** *(He bites it, hands croissant to PRINCESS, who takes a large bite out of it with like fervor.)* **With this** *(He picks up a bird leg)* **lovely, plump, partridge!** *(He bites it.)* **Mmmm! I love partridge!**

PRINCESS: **I am happy such simple things please you so much, marquis.** *(He offers partridge leg to PRINCESS. She takes a large bite out of it, enjoying the strangeness of the custom.)*

KING: *(Raising a glass)* **Your excellent qualities have won our admiration. It rests with you...sir...whether or not you will marry my daughter.**

CLAUDE: **My lady?**

PRINCESS: **I would be honored.** *(He kisses her.)*

PUSS: **Congratulations to you all.**

CLAUDE: **And you, my Puss in Boots, we all thank you.** *(Music. All cheer, drink, toast, eat, and celebrate.)*

THE END

13 Bells of Boglewood
by Max Bush

CHARACTERS

BRIAN . . . . A Young Man of 17

CASEY SMITH . . . . A Land Owner, 40

THISTLE. . . . . A Faery

LARA . . . . Queen of the Hollow Hill

THE BOGLE . . . . A Bogle

HORT. . . . . A Male Hideous Spriggan

TAUGER. . . . . A Female Hideous Spriggan

TIME: A spring morning in the present year.

PLACE: The forest.

RUNNING TIME: Approximately sixty-five minutes.

NOTES: The setting will be most effective if suggestive of the "real" forest rather than a "magical" forest or a "magical part" of the "real" forest. The magic will then be based on and grow from a tangible and familiar reality.

The sounds can be made from a large bell, small bell chimes, a bass drum, a ratchet for the pinch sound and recorded music for the food and dancing.

The tune to the Spriggans' song should be energetic and unfamiliar.

To tour, all that is needed is a stump, the log, two rocks, the three small trees and some backing flats suggestive of the forest. Daylight is the only light needed.

DEDICATION: *13 Bells of Boglewood* is dedicated to Dan, Matt, and Penelope.

The premiere production of *13 Bells of Boglewood* was presented on February 3, 1984, at Michigan State University with the following cast and crew:

CAST

BRIAN	David Andrews
CASEY SMITH.	David Magee
THISTLE.	Martie Sanders
LARA	Linda Dunlop
BOGLE.	Jordan Cohen
HORT.	Diane Crea
TAUGER.	Laura Stec

PRODUCTION STAFF

Director	Max Bush
Assistant Director.	Roger Sovis
Set Design	Noreen Walworth
Costume Design	Penelope Victor
Lighting Design	James E. Peters
Sound Design.	Steve Bridgeland
Stage Manager	Brian Stonestreet
Make-Up Design.	Kat Bolak
Technical Director	Noreen Walworth

(At rise we see a deep, climax forest in the upper Midwest: huge beech, maples, oaks and pines. There's a stump Down Right, a large rock Center Right, bushes Up Right. Left we see a large fallen, rotting tree trunk, more bushes, perhaps another stump. Up Center are three hawthorn trees surrounding a small mound. Another large boulder sits on the mound, in the center of the three hawthorn trees. It is spring and the colors are fresh and alive. The atmosphere reflects the new wildflowers, the deepening colors of the leaves and the celebration that is growing up through the forest floor. Birds are singing.)

(BRIAN runs on. He's a fairly tall, slender, animated young man who comes from a working-class home. CASEY SMITH calls from Off-stage.)

SMITH: *(Off)* **Brian? Brian, where are you?** *(BRIAN has stopped running and stands looking intently at the scenery. It's as if the forest has taken him by surprise.)* **Where'd you go? I told you to wait for me!** *(BRIAN bends over, smells a wildflower, moves to a tree, sits, leaning against it, looking up at the treetops.)* **Brian?** *(SMITH enters. The tree BRIAN is leaning against is between him and SMITH, so SMITH doesn't see him.)* **Brian? Oh...** *(He spots a wildflower.)* **Another wildflower.** *(He picks it, places it with the others he's picked. He looks up, spies the rock.)* **Ah. Here's the rock with the bell carved in it. This is the place.** *(He glances around fearfully.)* **Look at it. No wonder they say goblins and bogles live out here. Where is that boy, anyway? Brian!**

BRIAN: **Yes?**

SMITH: *(Startled)* **Ah!** *(He turns to see it's only BRIAN.)* **Oh...it's you. Don't do that out here. You'd never believe what I thought you were.**

BRIAN: **What do you have there, Mr. Smith?** *(i.e. the bouquet that SMITH carries)*

SMITH: **We might need these later.**

BRIAN: **Poison ivy!**

SMITH: **Ah!** *(SMITH drops them like they were on fire.)* **Are they?**

BRIAN: **Oh, no. Those are mostly woodlilies. I meant those are poison ivy.** *(Pointing behind SMITH)*

SMITH: **Oh, but...you were joking with me, weren't you?** *(He chuckles. BRIAN laughs. SMITH suddenly stops.)* **But it wasn't funny. Well, this is the place I wanted to show you.**

BRIAN: **You said you might be able to make me rich, Mr. Smith?**

SMITH: **I asked you here because you're the only kid in our neighborhood I can trust.**

BRIAN: About what?

SMITH: Well, boy —

BRIAN: Call me Brian.

SMITH: Well, boy —

BRIAN: My name is Brian.

SMITH: Well, boy, I bought these woods, the whole thing, and —

BRIAN: I thought old Mabel Putnam owned it.

SMITH: Well, I bought it from her. But —

BRIAN: Congratulations, Mr. Smith. It's a beautiful forest. *(Looking about)* It has some of the oldest trees in the state in it.

SMITH: I know, but that's not —

BRIAN: But how is this going to make me rich?

SMITH: *(After a moment, in a whisper)* **Gold.**

BRIAN: *(After a moment, equally as quiet and mysterious)* **In the woods?**

SMITH: *(Still quiet)* **It says so in this old book Mabel Putnam sold to me.** *(He takes out book and continues in the mysterious tone.)* **It belonged to her husband, John Putnam. He went looking for that gold in these woods forty years ago, but he never came out again.**

BRIAN: What happened to him?

SMITH: Nobody knows.

BRIAN: *(Quietly)* **Maybe he turned into Tarzan the Ape-man.** *(He jumps on the stump, bursts into a Tarzan call and beats his chest.)*

SMITH: I doubt it.

BRIAN: Who would bury gold out here?

SMITH: The book says — now don't start going crazy on me — the book says... *(Quickly)* **the gold is buried in a hollow hill and belongs to faeries and it's guarded by a faery queen and some ugly little goblins.** *(Silence. BRIAN breaks into "going crazy.")* **What's wrong with you?**

BRIAN: I'm going crazy on you! Gold, faeries, goblins!

SMITH: You laugh, but this book can make us both rich.

BRIAN: Wait a minute. I've heard that before — about strange creatures in this woods.

SMITH: So have I.

BRIAN: My grandmother used to tell me great stories about this place.

SMITH: You see?

BRIAN: *(Suddenly quite interested)* **What exactly does that old book of John Putnam's say?**

SMITH: It says invisible creatures live out here.

BRIAN: *(Truly considering the possibility)* **Invisible...**

SMITH: Yes. *(LARA and THISTLE dash on, two invisible creatures of the forest.)* **We can't hear or see them.**

THISTLE: I told you, Lara. Two thieves. *(LARA, queen of the Hollow Hill, is tall and deer-like. She's protective of the creatures around her and of the well-being of the entire forest. There is also an element of darkness in her which shows through in her more fearful moments. THISTLE, however, is smaller, more angular in appearance and character. She's dressed in purple and green and has two horns protruding from her hair. She's mischievous, whimsical, and exhibits a naiveté that leaves her vulnerable to the world. They both, as we shall see, love to play and dance.)*

SMITH: And it says they have gold out here, hidden in a hollow hill.

BRIAN: *(Looking around)* **That's what the old stories were about... gold...strange creatures...enchanted places...**

LARA: Smell him, Thistle. *(LARA and THISTLE dart up to BRIAN, smell him.)*

BRIAN: These woods are so old and magical. It looks like anything could happen here.

THISTLE: *(They like the smell of BRIAN.)* **Now him.** *(They will smell SMITH who apparently smells quite malodorous.)*

SMITH: I know what you mean. This place gives me the creeps. *(The FAERIES back away from SMITH.)* **But don't let the stories about invisible creatures scare you. The way I see it, anything you can't see can't hurt you.**

THISTLE: No? *(THISTLE makes a pinching gesture toward SMITH from about eight feet away, there is a magical sound and SMITH feels the pinch of a faery in his side.)*

SMITH: Ow!

BRIAN: What's the matter?

SMITH: *(Confused, looking around)* **Just a pinch in my side.** *(LARA laughs.)* **Now, the book says these creatures are dirty...** *(The FAERIES look at themselves and each other in confusion)* **vicious...** *(LARA and THISTLE become vicious)* **crooked...** *(The FAERIES are a little puzzled, but try to be crooked)* **ugly...** *(This they will not be)* **little devils.**

THISTLE: Devils! *(She pinches him as before, in the other side.)*

SMITH: Ow? Who pinched me? *(He wheels around to try to see who pinched him.)*

BRIAN: Maybe a vicious little faery.

SMITH: *(Smiles.)* **You're joking with me...** *(They laugh, as do the FAERIES. SMITH stops.)* **But it isn't funny. That hurt.** *(BRIAN stops laughing.)* **Now, what do you say? Would you like to help me?**

THISTLE: He wouldn't steal our gold, Lara.

LARA: He would, Thistle.

THISTLE: Not that one. He smells good.

BRIAN How do we split it up?

SMITH: You get a haa — thirr — no, one-fourth of all we find.

THISTLE: Say no.

SMITH: *(BRIAN moves away. SMITH pursues him.)* **New bikes, clothes; you can take trips—**

THISTLE: Say no.

SMITH: What do you say?

THISTLE: No!

BRIAN: Yes! I'll do it!

SMITH: Good!

BRIAN I want to be rich!

LARA: You see?

THISTLE: You hobgoblin! *(She pinches his side.)*

BRIAN: Ow!

THISTLE: Why do you smell good?

BRIAN: What was that?

SMITH: A vicious little faery. Now *that's* funny! Ha? Ha!

THISTLE: It's your fault. *(She pinches SMITH.)*

SMITH: Ow!

BRIAN: *(Looking around)* **You know, that book might be right about faeries. I have a feeling...I can't believe this. I feel something...or someone here.**

LARA: *(Impressed)* **He feels us here.**

THISTLE: You see, Lara?

SMITH: And you told me I was crazy?

BRIAN: I can't believe it either. It's like I can feel someone. Like I could see them if I would just...know how. Is there any way we can see them?

SMITH: I'll look in the book.

THISTLE: I want him to see me.

LARA: No, Thistle.

THISTLE: He thinks I'm ugly and crooked and I'm pretty and crooked...and vicious. *(She snarls in BRIAN's ear.)*

LARA: Thistle, move away!

THISTLE: *(Moving away)* **Yes...**

LARA: Go, now, and warn the Guardians of the Hill Treasure thieves are near. *(To BRIAN and SMITH)* **And for you, I shall prepare a magical feast.**

BRIAN: What's it say?

SMITH: *(Reading)* **"To see the forest creatures, eat a golden woodlily."**

THISTLE: *(Stunned)* **What?** *(BRIAN checks flowers around log to see if there are any woodlilies.)*

LARA: *(Worried now)* **They know. Warn the guardians these thieves are dangerous. I'll prepare the magical food. Go.** *(She begins to dash off. THISTLE hesitates.)*

BRIAN: These flowers you picked...some of these are **woodlilies.** *(BRIAN moves to pick up flowers.)*

LARA: *(She returns.)* **Come, Thistle, he'll see us.**

THISTLE: *(Back to playfulness)* **I want him to see me.**

LARA: **I said I forbid it. If they can see you they'll try to catch you.**

THISTLE: **He won't try to catch me.** *(With a laugh, moving near BRIAN)* **He'll fall in love with me, I know! He'll say:** *(LARA is impatient, but also amused. THISTLE as BRIAN)* **"Oh, Thistle, you are beautiful! I've fallen in love with you! And I'll say: "Then give me presents. I want ribbons! Give me ribbons!"**

BRIAN: *(Picking one out)* **This is a woodlily.**

SMITH: *(More interested than he tries to show)* **Well, eat it.**

BRIAN: **Which part am I supposed to eat?**

SMITH: **The petals.**

LARA: **Thistle, come!**

THISTLE: **But I want my ribbons!**

LARA: **Thistle, you little goblin; now!**

THISTLE: *(As she's running off)* **I'm coming. I'll be back, thief.** *(As she passes LARA)* **Run, Lara, he'll see you!** *(THISTLE laughs, they both run off. BRIAN, who has eaten the flower, wheels around to where THISTLE and LARA have just exited.)*

SMITH: **Well, what is it?**

BRIAN: **I thought I heard...no, I don't see anything.**

SMITH: *(Relieved)* **What'd you expect? Boogie men?**

BRIAN: **But I felt sure they were here.**

SMITH: **You're soft in the head, kid. Your brains are mudpies.**

BRIAN: **I guess you're right.**

SMITH: **You'll find I'm always right. Now, to find the gold —**

BRIAN: **Wait...what's that?**

SMITH: *(Startled)* **What?**

BRIAN: *(Runs to bush, reaches in, pulls something out.)* **This.**

SMITH: **That's not a faery.**

BRIAN: **It's an old sign.**

SMITH: **What's it say?**

BRIAN: *(Brushing away dirt)* **"Beware of the greedy...** *(He pronounces the "o" like the "oo" in "food")* **Boogle."**

SMITH: *(Correcting BRIAN's pronunciation. The "o" is long, as in "ogre.")* **Bogle.**

BRIAN: **What does that mean?**

SMITH: **Nothing.**

BRIAN: **It must mean something.**

SMITH: **It doesn't mean anything.**

BRIAN: *(Reading sign as if it rhymes with "toggle.")* **What's a "greedy Boggle?"**

SMITH: *(Correcting him)* **Bogle!**

BRIAN: What is it?

SMITH: Somebody put that there to scare you, that's all. Are you scared?

BRIAN: Not yet.

SMITH: Neither am I.

BRIAN: What's a greedy Bogle?

SMITH: *(With a sudden charge of excitement)* **A booglie creature that lives out here!**

BRIAN: What?

SMITH: If we give him a piece of gold he has to tell us where the treasure is hidden! I told you I'd make you rich! The book says he's tied to a tree somewhere near this rock with the bell carved in it.

BRIAN: You're serious.

SMITH: The first thing we have to do is find him. Here. A gold coin. *(SMITH takes two gold coins out of his pocket and gives one to BRIAN.)*

BRIAN: What do I do with this?

SMITH: Hold it out and call him, then he'll appear. But don't let him touch you. Where he touches you, you'll itch worse than poison ivy.

BRIAN: Great; I'd rather ask a pretty faery where the gold is. *(Tentatively, BRIAN and SMITH hold out their gold coins and call for the BOGLE. At first both take this game seriously, calling: "Here, Bogle...here, greedy Bogle..." in a variety of different voices. BRIAN becomes amused at the strangeness of their activity. He sings, accompanying himself on an imaginary guitar.)* **"Here, greedy Bogle, won't you take my gold? We're searching this place for your ugly face."** *(BRIAN breaks into a guitar solo with his imaginary guitar. He concludes, looks up at SMITH who is unimpressed. They resume calling for the BOGLE. There is an Off-stage low growl. SMITH freezes.)*

SMITH: Stop.

BRIAN: *(Freezes.)* **What?**

SMITH: A noise.

BRIAN: Where?

SMITH: There. *(He points.)*

BRIAN: Like what?

SMITH: A growl.

BRIAN: Would a Boggle growl?

SMITH: A... *(Correcting BRIAN)* **Bogle might.**

BRIAN: What did it sound like? *(SMITH growls. BRIAN is unsettled by the thought of a BOGLE that growls.)*

SMITH: Go that way.

BRIAN: Why me?

SMITH: **Earn what I'm paying you.**
BRIAN: **You're not paying me anything.**
SMITH: **I'll go next time.**
BRIAN: **There won't be a next time.**
SMITH: **Go on, boy!**
BRIAN: **My name is Brian.**
SMITH: **I don't care if it's Baby Cakes! Get over there!**
BRIAN: **All right. But I don't like this.** *(BRIAN is crossing toward BOGLE's area with SMITH right behind him.)* **Here, Boogle, Boogle, Boogle.**
SMITH: *(Correcting him)* **Bogle, Bogle, Bogle! And don't let him touch you.**
BRIAN: **Bogle, Bogle, Bogle...Sounds like a sick turkey. Bogle, Bogle, Bogle...** *(The greedy BOGLE suddenly jumps out with a long screech and chases BRIAN who screams and runs. The BOGLE grabs and fully embraces the slower SMITH, who has just turned into a solid pillar of fear.)* **Look out!**
BOGLE: **Gold!**
SMITH: **Help!**
BOGLE: **Gold-gold-gold-gold-gold!**
BRIAN: **You found him, Mr. Smith!**
SMITH: **I know I found him!**
BOGLE: **Gimme-gimme-gimme-gimme!**
BRIAN: **Look at him!**
SMITH: **Let me go!**
BRIAN: **I don't believe it.**
BOGLE: **I want it-I want it-I want it-I want it!**
SMITH: **Help me!**
BRIAN: **He won't get away from you.**
SMITH: **I want to get away from him.**
BOGLE: **Gimme-gimme-gimme-gimme-gimme!**
BRIAN: **Don't let him touch you. You'll itch something terrible.**
SMITH: **I am! Help me!**
BRIAN: **Give him the gold coin.**
BOGLE: **Yes! Yes!**
SMITH: **There, get it.** *(He tosses it up. The BOGLE lets him go, dives on the gold. SMITH runs away.)*
BOGLE: **Gold-gold-gold-gold! Ah, ah, mmm.** *(SMITH is in the agony of total body itch. He scratches, experiences relief, but immediately feels another biting itch.)*
SMITH: **Help me!** *(BRIAN scratches him furiously. Suddenly all itching subsides. SMITH breathes deeply, lies flat on his back looking up.)* **The itching is gone. I'm all right now.**
BOGLE: **Thank you, human man.** *(The greedy BOGLE, when he isn't hysterical, is working very hard at controlling his hysteria. Speaking civilly is an effort. His yellow bulging eyes are*

*hypervigilant, darting about his environment searching for any-
thing resembling the possibility of gathering more wealth. He is,
however, an intensely self-preoccupied creature. He is of medi-
um height or less, has a tail or doesn't, has deeply furrowed
eyebrows always knitted in suspicion, and large pointed ears.
His hands are focal. When he appears not to be moving, his
fists are clenched to control his hands; when excited, they open
and close rapidly as if he were grabbing things out of the air. He
is presently under control as much as is possible for him.)*

BRIAN: I don't believe it. A greedy Boggle.

BOGLE: *(Correcting him)* **Bogle!**

BRIAN: Look at him. Gives me the creeps.

BOGLE: More gold! Do you have more? You *do*. I *know* you do.
I can smell it!

BRIAN: If he is here... *(To BOGLE.)* What were those creatures I
felt before?

BOGLE: *(Whose hysteria begins to break through)* I will answer
three questions for a piece of gold.

SMITH: *(Finally sitting up, diving back in. He is matter-of-fact with
BOGLE, demonstrating no surprise as to the BOGLE's existence.)* I gave you one.

BOGLE: To let you go.

SMITH: For three answers.

BOGLE: We made no deal. The gold... *(He is escalating)* is mine?
Gimme gimme another, gimme another, gold, more gold.

SMITH: I don't have any more.

BOGLE: Liar! I can smell it. Give me.

SMITH: No!

BRIAN: Then I'll give you mine.

BOGLE: Yes, yours, for three answers.

SMITH: *(Runs to BRIAN, grabs the coin from him.)* No! That's mine.
Give it to me.

BOGLE: *(Heartbroken)* No? No?

SMITH: I have a smaller gold piece for him.

BOGLE: *(Almost breaking into bits)* Yes, another, another. Give,
give. *(SMITH takes out gold coin, pocketing the one from
BRIAN.)*

SMITH: If I give you this, you have to answer three questions.

BOGLE: Agreed. Agreed. A...greed.

SMITH: Answer the first one before I give it to you.

BOGLE: No!

SMITH: Then I won't give it to you.

BOGLE: *(Near panic)* What question?

SMITH: Where is the Treasure of the Hollow Hill?

BOGLE: *(He explodes in hysteria, then grits his teeth and hands
and goes on.)* Gold, my first, in my gold first hand...gimme

142

first, gold —

SMITH: *(He holds out the gold piece just outside the BOGLE's reach. This causes great anxiety in the BOGLE. He goes through paroxysms of indecision, pacing, grabbing. The next two speeches overlap.)* **No. Tell me where it is. Here, just one question... answer first, then the gold is yours...here it is...I'll give it to you...just one answer...**

BOGLE: **I...I can't...Yes I can! I can! No, don't, I won't — I'll tell you! — Just gimme, please — *please!*—I'll tell you! No! I can't do it, I can't do it. Help me, somebody help me, please — I want it! I want it! I want it!** *(He screams hysterically, then laughs, then cries, then faints dead away from too much inner conflict. SMITH and BRIAN approach him.)*

BRIAN: **This guy is *nuts*.**

SMITH: *(Touching BOGLE with his foot)* **Bogle? Greedy Bogle?** *(His foot then itches; he scrapes the toe on the ground.)*

BRIAN: **He's fainted.**

SMITH: **Now what?**

BRIAN: **Just give him the gold—**

SMITH: **All right.**

BRIAN: **— when he wakes up —**

BOGLE: *(Jumping up; SMITH and BRIAN jump away in fear.)* **Gold first, then three questions!**

SMITH: **Here.** *(He tosses gold at him. BOGLE doesn't catch it.)*

BOGLE: **Eek!** *(The BOGLE dives on it.)* **Mine!** *(He picks it up.)* **Mmm. I am happy now. I am happy, now.**

SMITH: **Where is the Treasure of the Hollow Hill?** *(He takes out book, prepares to write down answer.)*

BOGLE: **Yes, but they'll stop you. They'll stop you, too, my friend. The Faery Queen, and the others.**

BRIAN: **Faery Queen...**

SMITH: **Where is the gold?**

BOGLE: **Hidden in the center of three hawthorn trees. And that's one question answered.** *(SMITH writes this down.)*

SMITH: **...in the center of three hawthorn trees...**

BRIAN: **What creatures guard the hill?**

BOGLE: *(The SPRIGGANS apparently strike terror in the heart of the BOGLE.)* **The Spriggans! The Hideous Spriggans are the Guardians of the Hill Treasure...and that's two questions answered.**

SMITH: **...Hideous Spriggans guard the treasure...**

BRIAN: **Spriggans?**

SMITH: **How do we open the Hollow Hill?**

BOGLE: **You must touch it three times with a bouquet of golden cowslip wildflowers.**

SMITH: **...bouquet of cowslip wildflowers...**

143

BOGLE: *(A deliberate ploy)* **But beware of the thirteen bells. And that's three questions answered.**

SMITH: **Thirteen bells? What do you mean, "Beware of the thirteen bells"? The book doesn't say anything about thirteen bells.**

BOGLE: **I've answered your questions. Give me more gold.**

BRIAN: **What other creatures live here?**

BOGLE: **Our bargain is complete. Give more gold.**

BRIAN: **Why do faeries have gold? What do they do with it?**

SMITH: **How do we find the three hawthorn trees?**

BOGLE: **No more answers! More gold, more answers! Or set me free.** *(His old hysteria is returning.)* **I know how to help you.**

BRIAN: **Let's give him another gold piece.**

BOGLE; *(Pulls on rope.)* **Yes! Or set me free. I'll tell you about the thirteen bells. I'll tell you everything.**

BRIAN: **Why don't you just untie yourself?**

BOGLE: **You have to do it. I'll show you how.**

SMITH: **Maybe he's right. We might need his help.**

BOGLE: **Yes!**

BRIAN: **No. We can't trust him.**

BOGLE: **No.**

SMITH: **Maybe you're right.**

BOGLE: **No!**

SMITH: **Let's talk it over.** *(He motions BRIAN away from BOGLE and they confer quietly. LARA and THISTLE run on.)*

LARA: **Bogle!**

BOGLE: *(He backs up against a tree in fear.)* **Queen...**

LARA: **You have answered their questions.**

BOGLE: **They gave me gold so I gave them answers.**

LARA: **You told them of the thirteen bells without their asking.**

BOGLE: *(To BRIAN and SMITH)* **Humans! Help! Help me! Set me free!**

THISTLE: **Bogle!**

BOGLE: **I know these creatures. Stop her! Stop her!**

THISTLE: **I'll pinch you black and blue!** *(She does. He screams.)*

LARA: **Return to your bed, Bogle.**

BRIAN: *(The next two lines are delivered simultaneously.)* **Her? Who? Stop who?**

BOGLE: **She'll stop you — magic! They know magic! You need me, you need my help! Go away! Come back for me! Come back for me!**

LARA: *(LARA raises her hand, and as she closes her fist, the BOGLE's mouth closes.)* **Enough...quiet.**

BRIAN: *(Next six speeches overlap.)* **Who? Who do you mean? Who are you talking to?** *(The BOGLE tries to speak but can't open his mouth.)*

LARA: **Sleep, sleep, sad Bogle, rest your mind; curl up with your gold and sleep.** *(Instantly the BOGLE is sleepy.)* **Thistle, lead him away.** *(THISTLE picks up rope, begins to lead BOGLE off.)*

THISTLE: **Come, Bogle.**

BRIAN: **No, don't go. Who are you talking about?**

LARA: **Rest.**

BRIAN: **Bogle. *Bogle!*** *(BOGLE and THISTLE exit.)* **Wait a minute. I have that feeling again...like there's someone else here. He mentioned someone...I wonder if it's her I feel.** *(LARA carefully reaches out to touch BRIAN.)*

SMITH: **Ignore it and it will go away.**

BRIAN: **She feels...** *(She touches him lightly.)* **wonderful!**

LARA: **Wonderful...**

SMITH: **Wonderful? No. If you could feel them they'd feel evil, like the Bogle.**

BRIAN: *(LARA circles around BRIAN slowly, evaluating him.)* **Maybe you're right.**

SMITH: **I told you: I'm always right.**

BRIAN: **But I feel...** *(He tries to shake it off.)*

SMITH: **Now, what kind of trees did he say?**

BRIAN: **Hawthorn.** *(LARA backs away from BRIAN.)*

LARA: **No.**

SMITH: **Three of them...**

BRIAN: **Hawthorns...** *(BRIAN is following LARA's path as she backs away.)*

SMITH: **They must be around here somewhere.**

BRIAN: *(He walks toward LARA. She moves away, he continues on past her.)* **I'll look this way.** *(They look. BRIAN still isn't satisfied that what he feels is only in his imagination. He is trying to feel out where LARA is.)*

LARA: **I've seen enough.** *(She gestures. We hear music, a seductive, light melody that comes from everywhere. SMITH and BRIAN do not hear it.)* **They are hungry for gold. Let them be starving for food.** *(She gestures toward their stomachs. They suddenly grab their abdomens as their hunger hits them.)*

SMITH: *(A complete transformation; with great intensity)* **I'm hungry!**

BRIAN: **Me too! Just now!**

SMITH: **I'm famished!**

BRIAN: **I think I'm going to faint I'm so hungry.**

SMITH: **It just hit me.**

BRIAN: **Me too.**

LARA: **Our thieves are hungry. Bring out the food I have prepared.** *(THISTLE brings the food.)* **Put it there.** *(She places it on an oak stump. It is strangely colored and shaped fruit and herbs.)*

BRIAN: *(Each line brings them closer to each other.)* **I could eat a tree stump.**

SMITH: Maybe we should go buy a hamburger...or five or six of them.

BRIAN: Or ten pounds of baked potatoes.

SMITH: With thirty or forty steaks.

BRIAN: And fifty pizzas.

BRIAN & SMITH: Sixty pieces of pumpkin pie!

SMITH: I could eat my truck. Come on. *(BRIAN and SMITH start off. LARA moves in front of BRIAN, holds up her hand when BRIAN nears her.)*

LARA: Stop. *(BRIAN stops. SMITH continues.)* **What do you see?** *(She points to food. BRIAN turns his head, sees food.)*

BRIAN: Food! Look at this. Was this here before? *(THISTLE kneels at stump. LARA follows BRIAN over, as does SMITH.)*

SMITH, THISTLE & LARA: No!

BRIAN: It looks delicious.

SMITH, THISTLE & LARA: Yes!

BRIAN: I want it! *(The next two lines are delivered simultaneously.)*

THISTLE & LARA: Yes!

SMITH: No!

BRIAN: Why not?

SMITH: Who put it there?

BRIAN: I don't know.

SMITH: Well, I can guess.

BRIAN: Well, I don't care. It's food! *(He picks some up. Music continues.)* **I'll eat this first.**

SMITH: Stop!

BRIAN: No, this.

SMITH: Listen to me!

BRIAN: Both at the same time! *(He prepares to stuff food into his mouth.)*

SMITH: *(Pulling BRIAN's arms away from his mouth)* **Don't eat it! Don't eat any of it!**

BRIAN: But I'm starved.

SMITH: It has magic in it.

BRIAN: That sounds delicious.

SMITH: You eat this and you'll never wake up.

BRIAN: It's a bedtime snack!

SMITH: *(Earnestly)* **How do you think that food got there? The hideous Spriggans or something just as ugly put that there.**

THISTLE: I'm not ugly! *(She pinches SMITH in the shoulder.)*

SMITH: Ah! You see? *(Still more in earnest than in anger)* **Two things you never do: You don't eat their food and you don't dance with them. Remember John Putnam never left**

the woods! Maybe that's how they got him! Food, or he danced with them. *(He snatches the food from BRIAN.)* **Give me that.** *(He throws the food on the ground, stomps on it. The music stops.)* **There.**

BRIAN: *(BRIAN crumbles to his knees. In a small pathetic voice)* **Oh, I think I'm going to faint. Poor food.** *(He flops on the ground. SMITH picks up food, puts it back on tray.)*

SMITH: **Stand up.**

BRIAN: **I can't.** *(SMITH pulls him up.)*

SMITH: **We have to find the trees no matter how hungry we are.**

BRIAN: *I want pizzas.*

SMITH: **Come on.**

BRIAN: *I want pumpkin pie.*

SMITH: **Do you hear me?**

BRIAN: **I think so.**

SMITH: **Look-for-the-hawthorns.**

BRIAN: **Look for...**

SMITH: **We have to be close or they wouldn't have tried this.**

BRIAN: **The hawthorns...**

SMITH: **That's it, Brian. You're strong. You're smart. You're doing what I say.**

LARA: **Thistle, lead Brian in circles while I lead Smith away. Don't let him near the hawthorns.** *(She dashes in front of SMITH, beckons him. THISTLE does same with BRIAN. LARA sprinkles dust, THISTLE plays her pipe.)*

BRIAN: *(Following THISTLE)* **Hawthorns...this way...**

SMITH: *(Following LARA)* **This way...yes...this way...gold...I can almost see it...this way...I'm on my way...this is it.** *(SMITH and LARA exit.)*

BRIAN: *(Following THISTLE)* **They've got to be here...I feel it...I'm closer...I know it...** *(Moving away from THISTLE)* **Yes...yes...no.** *(He turns back to THISTLE.)* **This way...Yes...this way...they —** *(He stops, bumping into stump with food on it.)* **Food!** *(He dives in as music resumes. THISTLE dances, lights darken.)* **Music...I hear it now. What magical food is this?** *(He eats more. THISTLE comes into focus.)* **There...look...I *see* you. This is wonderful, look at you. I knew I felt someone here. I felt you, didn't I.**

THISTLE: **Yes.**

BRIAN: **You can't be a hideous Spriggan; you're pretty.**

THISTLE: **I know.**

BRIAN: **Who are you?** *(She moves away from him.)* **Don't run away. I like you much more than the Bogle.** *(THISTLE dances back to him, holds out her hands.)* **Stay, please, I won't try to catch you.**

THISTLE: **Come with me.**

BRIAN: *(Taking her hand)* **I can feel you! You're real!**
THISTLE: **Dance with us.**
BRIAN: *(Jumping in)* **Anything you say.**
THISTLE: **Dance.**
BRIAN: *(Suddenly stopping)* **Wait. Smith said something about dancing.**
THISTLE: **Dance, now, with us.**
BRIAN: **"Never dance with them," he said. Too dangerous.**
THISTLE: **Dance, with *me*?**
BRIAN: **No.** *(Music stops.)* **I want to. But I don't dare. I'll watch.** *(LARA runs on behind BRIAN.)* **I'll stay here forever.**
LARA: **Brian, you may stay with us...forever.**
BRIAN: *(Who is really stunned by her)* **Oh, I'm in trouble now. She's beautiful. Who are you?**
LARA: **Lara.**
THISTLE: **The queen.**
BRIAN: **The queen...**
LARA: **But we don't want you to watch us. We want you to join us.**
BRIAN: **Oh, I need help. Smith!**
LARA: **He can't hear you. You have eaten our fruit and you are with us, now, in our world.**
BRIAN: **I like it so far.**
LARA: **We are celebrating your coming, Brian. The music is for you, the food; enjoy yourself. Dance. I want you to dance with us.**
BRIAN: **Oh, no. No. No.** *(He backs up.)*
LARA: **Dance as never before. Dance wildly, magically!**
BRIAN: **I can't. Smith said no — John Putnam —**
LARA: *(Throwing dust on him)* **Dance with us!**
BRIAN: *(After a moment, completely released from fear, now enthusiastic)* **Yes. I will. Dance.** *(LARA gestures, music begins.)* **Music. Music!** *(They dance. The music is loud and fast. They come together, dance in a circle, spinning, careening wildly about, laughing.)*
THISTLE: **Faster! Faster! Faster!** *(They split apart. LARA and THISTLE dance away, then stop dancing, turning to BRIAN. BRIAN continues to dance wildly. Abruptly the music stops. Movement stops. The creatures remain still. BRIAN stands stunned, at center. He wavers, becomes dizzy and then falls flat on his face.)*
LARA: *(Sprinkling BRIAN with dust)* **You must be awakened magically, by this nightfall. If not awakened by then, you will sleep forever; a deep, dark sleep never to awaken again.**
SMITH: *(Off)* **Brian! Did you find the hawthorns?**
LARA: *(To THISTLE)* **Come. Let's warn the Spriggans of Smith.**

(They exit, THISTLE with food. Lights return to normal.)

SMITH: *(Entering)* **I couldn't see** — *(He sees BRIAN.)* **Brian!** *(He yells in BRIAN's face.)* **Hey, boy! Wake up!** *(No response)* **You wouldn't listen to me. You ate some of that food and you danced, didn't you? I ought to leave you here so you'd sleep forever. But I need your help.** *(He takes out book, reads.)* **"To break the spell of enchanted food and dancing, leave *three gold pieces on the oak stump where the food appeared!*" You're not worth three pieces, boy!** *(He counts out two pieces of gold, slaps them on stump.)* **One. Two. That's all you're worth.** *(THISTLE dashes on, pinches him.)* **Ow! All right, three.** *(He puts down another gold piece.)*

THISTLE: *(She plays her pipe over BRIAN.)* **Awaken.**

SMITH: **Come on, kid; shake a stick. I didn't wake you up just to be nice to you.**

BRIAN: **Oh...**

SMITH: *(Right in BRIAN's face)* **Hey, Brian!**

BRIAN: **Smith?**

THISTLE: **Lara! He is awake!** *(She darts off.)*

SMITH: *(SMITH feigns kindliness.)* **Brian?**

BRIAN: **Yes?**

SMITH: **I'm so happy you're all right.**

BRIAN: **Casey?**

SMITH: **Yes, son? Let me help you up.**

BRIAN: *(As SMITH helps him up)* **I kind of like these creatures, don't you?**

SMITH: *(The old SMITH returns. He drops BRIAN.)* **Think, boy. What did they do to you?**

BRIAN: *(Still charmed)* **We danced.**

SMITH: **And what were you doing just now?**

BRIAN: **Sleeping.**

SMITH: **Why?**

BRIAN: **I don't know.**

SMITH: **They cast a spell on you to sleep forever, that's why — just like they did to John Putnam.**

BRIAN: **Forever?**

SMITH: **Yes. I had to pay them three — six, no ten gold pieces so you'd wake up.**

BRIAN: **Really?**

SMITH: **Yes! What do you think this is?** *(The dust on BRIAN)*

BRIAN: **She threw it on me.**

SMITH: **Why?**

BRIAN: **They cast a spell on me. I can't believe it.**

SMITH: **You see?**

BRIAN: **Those crooked little devils! I thought they liked me.**

SMITH: **John Putnam probably felt the same way, and I'll bet**

he's still asleep somewhere around here, lying up against a tree covered with *hawthorns. Hawthorns!* *(He has spied the three hawthorns. He runs over to them.)* **One — two — three! Three hawthorns! This is it! This is it!** *(Suddenly turning to BRIAN, painfully needing reassurance)* **What is this?**

BRIAN: **Three hawthorns!**

SMITH: **Yes? Three hawthorns! I found them!**

BRIAN: **You found the hollow hill!**

SMITH: **We're going to be rich!**

BRIAN: **Yes! Rich!**

BRIAN & SMITH: **This *is* it! This is it!**

SMITH: **What is this?** *(Points to the rock in the center of the hawthorns.)*

BRIAN: *(Confused)* **A rock.**

SMITH: *(Demolished)* **Why?**

BRIAN: **A rock?**

SMITH: *(A quiet, small cry to heaven)* **No.**

BRIAN: **It would take twenty people to move.**

SMITH: *(Suddenly back in control)* **Or magic...right. What's next? What did the Bogle say?**

BRIAN: **"Touch the hill with a bouquet —"**

SMITH: **"Of golden cowslip wildflowers." Where do they grow?**

BRIAN: **In the swamp.**

SMITH: **Go get us a bunch.**

BRIAN: *(As he runs off)* **Right. Look out for the Guardians — the Spriggans.**

SMITH: *(Calling after him)* **I'll whistle so you can find me. You're going to be rich, kid! Keep telling yourself that! You're going to be rich! You're going to be rich!** *(To himself)* **Not if I can help it!**

(SMITH begins to whistle. We see someone or something moving up. We see another one. They appear and disappear behind trees. They are the two hideous SPRIGGANS, Guardians of the Hill Treasure. They are odd-looking creatures, part faery, part animal, but endearing in appearance as well as in character. They're dressed basically as a type of forest faery creature, but they also wear odd pieces of clothing they have either found in the woods or stolen from thieves. They wear wide belts that hold ropes. The SPRIGGANS are not dumb or goofy. They're serious creatures with a sense of humor. They aren't clumsy but lithe, athletic and alert in an animalistic manner. They jump here, there, hiding, popping out. SMITH wheels around, doesn't see them.)

Nothing. It's probably just a mountain lion. Keep whistling, Smith. *(He whistles for a short time, stops. He has heard a*

SPRIGGAN move.) **Who's there? Brian? Ah, he can't be that quick.** *(HORT growls.)* **I** *hate* **just standing here.** *(The SPRIG-GANS make sounds throughout their sneaking, sounds of various kinds of wildlife found in the forest.)* **Whistle.** *(SMITH tries to whistle, can't.)* **I can't whistle!** *(A SPRIGGAN does, like a bird.)* **Stay away from me, you little devils! The book. I'll read the book. Spriggans...hideous Spriggans...** *(While SMITH reads, HORT, a SPRIGGAN crawls out behind SMITH, carrying a rope.)* **Here. "Spriggans: Guardians of the Hill Treasure... Unlike most of the faery creatures, the Spriggans are not invisible to humans and can be seen." We can see them. I wonder why? "The reason we can see them is their strange appearance scares away thieves." Ha! Not me. I'm not afraid of them. What else...** *(HORT has a lasso and wants to put it around SMITH's legs. He can't if Smith just stands there, so he tickles SMITH's legs, one at a time. HORT then slips the rope under SMITH's foot when SMITH lifts it. HORT then puts rope over SMITH's toes.)* **"Each Spriggan carries a gold rope to tie up thieves. Beware, you who would steal their gold, the Spriggans are crafty, mean and strike without warning. Beware..." Ha!** *(HORT has, by now, crawled off.)* **Where are they, then? Here, Spriggan, Spriggan, Spriggan. No little devil is going to catch me off guard.** *(Suddenly the other SPRIGGAN, TAUGER jumps out down left.)*

TAUGER: Ha!

SMITH: Eeeeeyoooww? What's that?

TAUGER: Don't move, thief!

SMITH: It talks.

TAUGER: Tauger is my name and if you move a tick, I'll make you my prisoner.

SMITH: Don't threaten me, you little devil.

TAUGER: Pull it, Hort!

HORT: *(HORT pulls rope. SMITH can't escape.)* Got him!

SMITH: What? Let me go! Brian! Help!

TAUGER: Get him! *(The SPRIGGANS run up and jump on SMITH.)*

SMITH: Get off me, you little devil!

TAUGER: My name is Tauger!

SMITH: What are you doing? Stop it! Let me go! Brian! Brian, help me! Brian! *(HORT and TAUGER tie him up and gag him, saying such things as ""Thief! Thief! Hold him! Hold him! Tighter! Tighter!" They put him on the ground.)*

HORT: Got him.

TAUGER: Got you. I'm Tauger!

HORT: I'm Hort!

HORT & TAUGER: *(They sing to SMITH and dance.)*

    Guard the treasure's what we do

We're hideous Spriggans
We'll stomp on you.

When we catch a thief
We just don't care
We kick him *(They do.)*
We pinch him *(They do.)*
And pull his hair *(They do.)*
Tra la la la la
(They do a dance singing "Tra-la-la." THISTLE enters, dances with them, until they begin singing words again. Then she watches.)
When we catch a thief
We do what we choose
We kick him *(They do.)*
We pinch him *(They do.)*
And pull off his shoes!
(They do. With a quick step or two, their song ends and they bow to each other. LARA runs on. HORT and TAUGER point at SMITH.)

THISTLE: Look.
LARA: *(Delighted)* **It's Smith.**
HORT: *(To SMITH)* **Leave this woods and never return.**
TAUGER: Or worse will happen, you will learn.
HORT: You are warned, man.
TAUGER: Go!
HORT: When you can! *(They laugh.)*
LARA: Good Spriggans.
HORT: Yes.
THISTLE: Where's the other one?
TAUGER: Gone to the swamp.
THISTLE: Not for cowslips.
HORT: Yes, to open the hill.
THISTLE: No.
TAUGER: They found the hawthorns.
LARA: We'll see if he has cowslips when he returns.
HORT: Then we'll stomp his bones.
TAUGER: Hort... *(HORT takes SMITH's hat, wears it. TAUGER takes SMITH's tie.)*
HORT: *(To TAUGER)* **Hat.**
LARA: *(To THISTLE)* **Handsome.**
TAUGER: *(To HORT).* **Tie.**
THISTLE: (*To LARA)* **Ugly.**
TAUGER: Shoes! *(The SPRIGGANS each put on one shoe. They both walk on and over SMITH.)*
HORT & TAUGER: *Spriggans! (They bolt off.)*
LARA: The other one is returning. Come, let's join the Spriggans.

THISTLE: I want to watch the thieves.

LARA: You may. But don't let them see you or they'll try to catch you.

THISTLE: I won't. *(LARA exits. THISTLE perches on the log.)*

BRIAN: *(Off)* Mr Smith? Mr. Smith, can you hear me? *(SMITH tries to respond. BRIAN enters with cowslips, out of breath.)*

THISTLE: Cowslips! Thief! *(She pinches him.)*

BRIAN: Ow! What...? Who is doing that? *(He looks around.)* Smith, whistle if you hear me. *(SMITH tries to whistle.)* This is the place. There are the three hawthorns. But where is Smith...the old skunk. *(SMITH hears this and again tries to respond. "What'd you call me?" He makes a noise and BRIAN hears him.)* Eeee. Is that you, Mr. Smith? *(SMITH curses BRIAN, although no one can understand him.)* What happened? *(He runs over and unties the gag in SMITH's mouth.)*

SMITH: Spriggans, two — four — no, eight of the little devils.

BRIAN: *(He continues to untie SMITH during the following.)* Spriggans.

SMITH: Snuck up on me.

BRIAN: Are you all right?

SMITH: Of course.

BRIAN: Where are they?

SMITH: I scared them off. *(THISTLE pounds his foot.)* Ow. *(He moves away.)* I scared them off! *(She pinches his other foot.)* Ah. Wait here. And don't let those hawthorns out of your sight.

BRIAN: Where are you going?

SMITH: To get boots out of my truck. They stole my shoes!

BRIAN: But the Spriggans.

SMITH: If they come back, *(Gives BRIAN the rope)* tie them up with this rope.

BRIAN: All eight of them?

SMITH: Maybe you'll get lucky and only two will come after you. Don't move from that rock. Ow! Prickers! *(He pulls one out of his foot.)* They stole my shoes! *(He exits with cowslips. BRIAN wheels around.)*

BRIAN: Who's here? I know I feel someone here. The woodlilies... *(He runs to the woodlilies.)*

THISTLE: He'll see me. *(She begins to dash off.)*

BRIAN: I'm at least going to see what you look like, hideous Spriggans. *(THISTLE stops.)*

THISTLE: I'm not a hideous Spriggan. *(She looks around, then moves closer to BRIAN, preens a bit and prepares to be seen.)*

BRIAN: *(He's ready with rope.)* All right! Where are you?! *(THISTLE steps out. Pleasantly surprised)* It's you.

THISTLE: I know.

BRIAN: Don't you cast another spell on me.

THISTLE: Don't you try to catch me.

BRIAN: *(Throwing rope away)* **I won't try to catch you if you won't try to cast another spell on me. All right?**

THISTLE: No.

BRIAN: *(Starting for rope)* **Then I might try to catch you.**

THISTLE: No! *(She pinches him three times.)*

BRIAN: **Ow! Stop! All right! I won't catch you! I won't!** *(She stops pinching.)* **So you're the little dev — you're the one who's been doing that.**

THISTLE: *(Pointing to herself, proudly)* **Thistle, thief.**

BRIAN: **My name is Brian.**

THISTLE: **Thistle, thief Brian.**

BRIAN: **I'm not a thief—**

THISTLE: **Liar!** *(She pinches him in the nose.)*

BRIAN: **Ow!...I'm not a thief — yet.** *(THISTLE approaches him carefully, checking to see if LARA is coming.)* **What do you want?**

THISTLE: **Don't try to catch me or I'll call the Spriggans.**

BRIAN: **I won't try to catch you if you won't pinch me anymore. All right?**

THISTLE: **No.** *(She explores him, looking into his eyes, carefully reaching out and touching his face. He sniffs her. This worries her.)*

BRIAN: **You smell like a wildflower.** *(He breathes in deeply, smiles, as does she. He tries to touch one of her horns.)*

THISTLE: **No.** *(He stops. She touches his hair, then hers, then his.)* **Same.** *(She tentatively takes his hand.)* **Hand.** *(She looks up at him.)* **How old are you?**

BRIAN: **Seventeen years old.**

THISTLE: **And you're this tall?**

BRIAN: **How old are you?**

THISTLE: **Two hundred and six years.**

BRIAN: **Two hundred and six...you can't be.**

THISTLE: **Why?** *(BRIAN isn't able to think of an answer. THISTLE moves completely around BRIAN as if looking for something.)* **I want my present.**

BRIAN: **Present?**

THISTLE: **My ribbons.**

BRIAN: **You want me to give you ribbons?**

THISTLE: **You promised you'd give me ribbons.**

BRIAN: **I don't have any ribbons.**

THISTLE: **Then I want that, your bracelet.**

BRIAN: **My watch?**

THISTLE: **Yes, your bracelet.**

BRIAN: **Not my watch.** *(She raises her hand as if to pinch him.)* **OK, I'll give you my bracelet...for some of your gold.**

THISTLE: No!

BRIAN: It's a very pretty bracelet, see? It has a light on it. *(She looks at it.)* **For some gold?**

THISTLE: *(Backs up sharply)* **No!**

BRIAN: *(Advancing slightly on her)* **Why? You don't need gold, not like I do.**

THISTLE: Not the same.

BRIAN: You see? I'll trade you my *(He is now backing her up)* bracelet for just this much gold, Thistle. *(He indicates how much.)*

THISTLE: I can't. You don't know.

BRIAN: *(Stopping)* Don't know what?

THISTLE: Our gold...I...don't ask me...

BRIAN: Why? *(She suddenly wheels, listens alertly.)* What? What is it?

THISTLE: *(Turning on him)* It's your fault!

BRIAN: What is? What's wrong?

THISTLE: Thief! *(She dashes off.)*

BRIAN: Thistle? Thistle! What is it? Come back! *(To himself, as he takes his coat off and throws it on a stump.)* Boy, I blew that. *(The SPRIGGANS enter.)* What was that? Smith? Smith? No...Spriggans! *(He picks up rope.)* They wouldn't hurt me. *(He throws away rope. We hear a low, SPRIGGAN laugh.)* Yes, they would. *(The SPRIGGANS make a sound confirming this. BRIAN bolts toward where SMITH would be returning.)* Smith! Smith, come back! Casey, you old skunk! Leaving me here alone! *(TAUGER appears, disappears.)* But I'm not alone. *(He dashes behind a bush himself, hides, looks out, sees TAUGER dive behind a fallen log.)* Wait a minute. Talk to me.

(BRIAN crawls quickly from bush to rock. He then crawls slowly out. HORT crawls out opposite him. BRIAN doesn't see him because he's looking for TAUGER. Suddenly BRIAN looks forward and sees HORT. They both stop moving, face each other and remain motionless. Pause. BRIAN lets out an involuntary fearful little groan deep in his throat without moving. He then moves backward; HORT mirrors him by moving backward. BRIAN stops, HORT stops. BRIAN backs up very fast, HORT starts to, jumps up.)

HORT: Stop!

BRIAN: Eeeeyooooww! *(BRIAN backs up faster.)*

HORT: Tauger! *(TAUGER leaps out and jumps on BRIAN.)*

TAUGER: Got you, thief!

BRIAN: Help!

HORT: Hold him!

TAUGER: The rope! The rope!

BRIAN: Help! Help! Get off! Listen to me! *(HORT runs over with*

a rope, begins to wrap it around BRIAN.)
TAUGER: We're Spriggans!
HORT: We don't listen!
BRIAN Don't! Don't tie me up!
HORT: Caught!
TAUGER: Treasure stealer!
BRIAN: I haven't! I haven't stolen anything!
TAUGER: We'll stop you!
BRIAN: But I haven't done anything!
HORT: Tauger, let him go. *(TAUGER jumps off.)*
BRIAN: *(Moving away)* Thank you. I haven't taken any of your gold and —
TAUGER: Get him! *(HORT wraps rope around BRIAN's legs, TAUGER jumps back on him. They lay him on the ground.)*
HORT & TAUGER: Thief! Thief! Thief!
BRIAN: Let me go! Help! Smith! Smith, help me! Help me! Somebody help — *(They gag him.)*
HORT: We're Spriggans!
TAUGER: He can't help you!
HORT: Nobody can!
TAUGER: Caught.
HORT: Thief.
HORT & TAUGER: *(They sing and dance.)*

Guard the treasure's what we do,
We're hideous Spriggans
We'll stomp on you.
When we catch a thief
We just don't care
We shake him... *(They do.)*
Ignore him... (They do.)
And give him a scare *(They do.)*
Tra la la...*(Etc. They sing and dance to "Tra la la.")*

TAUGER: He's Hort.
HORT: She's Tauger.
TAUGER: We're Spriggans!
HORT: We're mean!
HORT & TAUGER: *(They sing and dance.)*

We just don't care if you're
Red, blue or green.
We'll give you a poke
'Cause we're jolly folk.
We'll steal from you —
A thief — as a joke. Ha! Ha!

156

(HORT steals BRIAN's belt, puts it around his neck. TAUGER takes BRIAN's coat off stump, puts it on. THISTLE runs on, hides.)

To the Hill. Haaayeeeaahh! *(They run off in opposite directions. THISTLE begins to step out but hides again as SPRIGGANS run on again.)* **Spriggans!** *(They run off together. THISTLE turns her attention to the prisoner. She glances around, then, seeing it's safe, removes gag from BRIAN, puts another woodlily in his mouth.)*

BRIAN: Thank you for coming back, Thistle.

THISTLE: Thank you for being tied up, Brian.

BRIAN: It's nothing. The Spriggans helped me do it.

THISTLE: Good Spriggans.

BRIAN: Yes. *(He tries to move.)* **Will you untie me?**

THISTLE: Will you give me your bracelet?

BRIAN: Yes, I'll give you my bracelet.

THISTLE: Will you give it to me now?

BRIAN: *(Holding out his tied hands)* **Here, take it.** *(THISTLE moves to him, he grabs her hand.)*

THISTLE: Don't! Let me go! You said you wouldn't catch me!

BRIAN: Will you tell me why you keep the gold?

THISTLE: I can't!

BRIAN: Why is it so important to you?

THISTLE: I'll pinch you!

BRIAN: Wait a minute. Here. *(He lets her go.)* **At least untie me. I'm not going to hurt you.**

THISTLE: May I have your bracelet?

BRIAN: Yes.

THISTLE: Will you give me ribbons?

BRIAN: Yes, I'll give you ribbons.

THISTLE: *(After a moment)* **I trust you.** *(Beginning to untie his legs)* **But don't tell the other ones. The queen doesn't trust you. You brought Smith cowslips from the swamp.** *(LARA enters.)*

LARA: Thistle!

THISTLE: *(She jumps back from BRIAN.)* **Lara! I —**

LARA: What have I told you?

THISTLE: To not help him.

LARA: What are you doing?

THISTLE: Helping him.

LARA: Go to my thicket.

THISTLE: But Lara, he let me go. And he said he would give —

LARA: Go to my thicket and wait for me there!

THISTLE: Yes, Lara. *(She runs off.)*

BRIAN: She trusts me.

LARA: *(Retying what THISTLE loosened)* **As I did, but you brought Smith cowslips from the swamp.**

157

BRIAN: And you cast a spell on me so I'd sleep forever.

LARA: You're trying to steal our gold.

BRIAN: Maybe if I knew why it's so important to you I wouldn't. Thistle wouldn't tell me.

LARA: She's afraid to tell you our secrets. We are all afraid of you. *(Beginning to dart off, she stops, hearing BRIAN.)*

BRIAN: But if I knew why —

LARA: I want to trust you, Brian. I want you to join us here whenever you like. *(She starts off again. Again she stops, turns back to him.)* I want to show you the wonder and magic of this forest. *(She exits.)*

BRIAN: *(Enthralled)* Oh... "The wonder and magic of this forest." I think I'm in love. *(He falls over.)*

SMITH: *(Off)* Brian!

BRIAN: *(Suddenly waking up, sitting up)* Smith.

SMITH: *(Off)* Where are you?

BRIAN: *(Looking off in LARA's direction)* Lara!

SMITH: *(Off)* Brian!

BRIAN: What am I supposed to do now?

SMITH: *(Off)* Say something! *(Silence. Off)* Can you hear me?

BRIAN: Over here!

SMITH: *(Entering, wearing boots and carrying cowslips)* Boy! What'd they do to you?

BRIAN: The Spriggans —

SMITH: Little devils. *(He unties BRIAN.)*

BRIAN: I saw them, Casey. I talked to them.

SMITH: Good boy. What did you find out?

BRIAN: They need their gold for some reason.

SMITH: So do I.

BRIAN: Does Putnam's book say why they need it?

SMITH: They need it because...they're greedy, that's all. Now, come on. The cowslips. This is it! *(Moving toward hawthorns)*

BRIAN: Smith, wait.

SMITH: Why?

BRIAN: If they need their gold —

SMITH: They don't.

BRIAN: But if...if you touch that rock they'll turn you into a swamp rat.

SMITH: What?

BRIAN: That's what they told me — a swamp rat. Maybe that's what they did to John Putnam.

SMITH: I'm not afraid of them. *(He starts to touch hill. BRIAN stops him.)*

BRIAN: But a swamp rat. You're starting to look like one already.

SMITH: *(Breaking free)* Let me go! *(He moves to hill, touches it with bouquet of flowers.)* One, two —

BRIAN: Smith —

SMITH: **Three!** *(The lights alter; a distant, low rumble is heard. Silence. Lights return to normal. Nothing more occurs.)* **Well?** *(Silence)* **I did it. Why doesn't it open?** *(Silence. He tries again.)* **One, two, three!** *(Again, lights alter; low rumble is heard. Silence. Lights return to normal.)*

BRIAN: **It's not working.**

SMITH: **There must be something else we have to do. The Bogle didn't tell us everything.**

BRIAN: **I told you we couldn't trust him.**

SMITH: **Let's wake him up.**

BRIAN: **But what if he won't tell you?**

SMITH: **He has to.**

BRIAN: *(Getting his own idea)* **Wait a minute. The Bogle has to answer the question. Any question.**

SMITH: **That's right.**

BRIAN: **Give me a gold piece.**

SMITH: *(Giving him a gold piece)* **I'll need that back. And I ask the questions.**

BRIAN: **Bogle...**

SMITH: **Greedy Bogle...**

BRIAN: **Here's gold for you.**

SMITH: **You can have it but** *don't touch me!* *(The BOGLE rushes in.)*

BOGLE: **Aaaahhh! Gooollldddd!**

BRIAN: **Look out!**

SMITH: **Don't touch me!** *(SMITH throws gold up, BOGLE catches it.)*

BOGLE: **Mine!**

SMITH: *(With arm extended, his finger pointing to the BOGLE)* **Stay there!**

BOGLE: **More!** *(The BOGLE runs up, grabs SMITH's hand.)*

SMITH: **No, don't, I told** — *(SMITH retracts his hand, backs off from the BOGLE.)* **I told you not to touch me!** *(He scratches his hand furiously.)*

BOGLE: **More gold; I'll answer more questions. Ask me questions. More gold first. Then questions. Ask about thirteen bells.**

SMITH: **Don't touch me any more, you giant mosquito!**

BOGLE: **Gold first.**

SMITH: **I'm not going to give you any more gold.** *(This cripples the BOGLE's exuberant spirit. He crumbles, from inside-out.)*

BOGLE: **No? No?**

SMITH: **No. And I want to know what else I have to do to open the hill.**

BOGLE: **No gold?**

SMITH: No! What else —

BOGLE: *(He is frantic with grief and panic.)* **No gold — No gold — No gold — No gold?!** *(He holds his head as if he were holding it together to keep it from exploding. He screams. He runs up against a tree, then covers his face, stands on his tiptoes and shakes. Then he goes limp and slides down to his knees, looking up at SMITH. In a small voice)* **You make me sad, dirty skunk.**

BRIAN: But I'll give you a piece of gold.

BOGLE: You will?

SMITH: That's mine.

BRIAN: Here — for three answers.

SMITH: No —

BOGLE: Yes! Gold! Give!

SMITH: Give me that! *(BRIAN throws it to the BOGLE.)*

BOGLE: Eeeekk!

SMITH: Boy!

BOGLE: *(With gold)* Gold, mine, gold, now, is mine, now...

SMITH: Since it's my gold I'm going to ask all the questions.

BRIAN: Bogle, why do the faeries need their gold?

SMITH: Did I just say something? I know I did. What was it?

BRIAN: *(To BOGLE)* Why is it so important to them?

BOGLE: They can't live without gold. It gives them life and magic. Without gold, queen and Thistle — all of them — would grow old and die in just one day.

BRIAN: So that's it.

BOGLE: And that's one question answered.

SMITH: And I'll ask the rest.

BRIAN: We can't steal their gold, Casey.

SMITH: Sure we can.

BRIAN: They'll die if we do.

SMITH: We'll be rich.

BRIAN: I'm not going to help you.

SMITH: I'll do it myself.

BRIAN: You don't know how to stop them.

SMITH: I'm going to find out. I have two questions left. Bogle —

BRIAN: *(Quickly, before SMITH)* Bogle, what's one and one?

BOGLE: Two! And that's two questions.

SMITH: What are you doing?

BRIAN: *(To BOGLE)* What's two and two?

SMITH: No —

BOGLE: Four! And that's three questions answered. More gold.

SMITH: But — wait a minute!

BRIAN: And that's what I'll do, Smith, every time you give him a gold piece.

BOGLE: Try again.

SMITH: **I'm not going to give him any more gold!**
BRIAN: **No?**
BOGLE: **No?**
SMITH: **No! I'm going to set him free!** *(Silence. Everyone, including SMITH, is surprised.)*
BOGLE: *(Quietly)* **Free?**
BRIAN: **No...**
SMITH: *(After a moment's reflection)* **Yes, that's what I'm going to do. I'll set him free.** *(The BOGLE explodes.)*
BOGLE: **Free! Yes, set me free!**
SMITH: **Yes.**
BOGLE: **I'll be free! I'll be happy! I'll be wonderful!** *(He jumps up and down, his arms flail about. They seem not to know how to handle this concept; they just fly around.)* **Free! Now!** *(He abruptly stops moving, arms stiffly at his side. He remains utterly stiff and unmoving throughout the following, poised and ready.)*
BRIAN: **Smith, you can't trust him. He's too crazy. Look at him.**
BOGLE: **Ready!**
SMITH: **I know what I'm doing.**
BRIAN: **I don't think so. And I'm going to stay right next to this rock.** *(He moves there, after picking up the SPRIGGAN rope and gag.)* **If you try to steal their gold, you won't get past me...either of you.** *(He puts rope on his belt during the following.)*
SMITH: *(The BOGLE growls at BRIAN.)* **We'll see about that...boy.** *(To BOGLE)* **I'll set you free if you help me steal the Treasure of the Hollow Hill.**
BOGLE: **Yes.**
SMITH: **I take all the gold and you are free.**
BOGLE: **Yes.**
SMITH: **You'll tell me everything I need to do to open this hill?**
BOGLE: **Yes.**
SMITH: **You'll help me stop the Spriggans?**
BOGLE: **Yes.**
SMITH: **And the queen?**
BOGLE: **Yes.**
SMITH: **You won't —**
BOGLE: **No.**
SMITH: **You don't —**
BOGLE: **No.**
SMITH: **You will —**
BOGLE: **Yes.**
SMITH: **You're not —**
BOGLE: **No.**

SMITH: Then we'll —
BOGLE: Yes.
SMITH: You don't —
BOGLE: No. *(Silence)*
SMITH: You can't —
BOGLE: No. *(Silence)*
SMITH: *(Very quickly)* **I'm not going to give you any of the gold.**
    (A moment, then the BOGLE lets out a stifled, inner scream.)
BOGLE: Right.
SMITH: Good. Then it's a deal.
BRIAN: Don't try it, Smith. I won't let you.
SMITH: How do I set you free?
BOGLE: To free a Bogle
    At your command,
    To do it is simple.
    Kiss his right hand!
    (He now moves, but only to hold his hand out. Silence)
SMITH: No.
BOGLE: Yes. *(Silence)*
SMITH: Oh no.
BOGLE: Oh yes. *(Silence. The BOGLE's hand now grabs at the air.)*
SMITH: No, please, no.
BOGLE: Yes, please, yes.
SMITH: My lips will itch!
BRIAN: Go on, Smith. I have to see this.
SMITH: The things I have to do. *(He tentatively approaches and carefully kisses BOGLE's hand. SMITH rubs his lips; the rope falls from the BOGLE. The BOGLE spreads his arms and runs away from rope. He does an ecstatic dance.)*
BOGLE: *Free! I'm free!*
BRIAN: Stay away! *(The BOGLE veers from BRIAN toward SMITH.)*
BOGLE: You set me free! You are my friend!
SMITH: What are you going to do?
BOGLE: I like you!
SMITH: *(Running away)* **Don't come near me!**
BOGLE: *(Embracing himself)* **I'm free...I'm wonderful...mmm...**
SMITH: What do I do to open the hill?
BOGLE: Come with me. *(The BOGLE leads SMITH away from rock and BRIAN. They talk quietly, in stage whispers. BRIAN tries to hear but can't.)* **You must first circle hill seven times round and round and then touch hill three times.**
SMITH: Right.
BOGLE: Wait!
SMITH: What?
BOGLE: Spriggans. They won't let you.
SMITH: I'm not afraid of them.

BOGLE: Don't be ridiculous. You run around hill once, they'll stomp on you.

SMITH: Then what do we do?

BOGLE: Follow my plan.

SMITH: What plan?

BOGLE: My plan.

SMITH: What *is* your plan?

BOGLE: First we stop Spriggans.

SMITH: How?

BOGLE: There is only one way to stop a Spriggan. But will you do it?

SMITH: Of course. What is it?

BOGLE: *(Very chummy)* Yes! Yes! You are my friend. You like me. I like you. We like each other, you and I.

SMITH: *(In like fashion, with a smile)* I don't like you. You give me the creeps. *(Beat)* What do I do?

BOGLE: To stop a Spriggan
    If one is about
    To do it is simple, *(Eyes bulging, mouth puckered, fists tight)*
    Turn your clothes inside-out.
    (Silence, as the BOGLE stares at SMITH who stands in disbelief.)

SMITH: What?

BOGLE: Turn your clothes inside-out.

SMITH: That's ridiculous.

BOGLE: So are they. *(That's funny to him. His laughter switches instantly to panic.)* Hurry, they'll be back.

SMITH: I don't believe this.

BOGLE: Change behind the bushes. *(SMITH begins to cross behind bushes.)*

BRIAN: Where are you going, Smith?

SMITH: *(Aloud)* Crazy! *(SMITH moves behind the bush.)*

BOGLE: What next after Spriggans? The queen? She'll use magic! They'll pinch me!

SMITH: *(Off)* What'll we do?

BOGLE: My plan. We must follow my plan. Listen to me. Ropes. Spriggan ropes. When the Spriggans come, steal their ropes.

SMITH: *(Off)* Why?

BOGLE: So we can use them.

SMITH: *(Off)* For what?

BOGLE: For my plan.

SMITH: *(Off)* What *is* your plan?

BOGLE: *(He stops, listens.)* Spriggans!

SMITH: *(Off)* Where?

BOGLE: Coming here.

SMITH: *(Off)* What do I do?

BOGLE: Come when I call. Steal ropes. *(In a whisper)* Smith.

SMITH: *(Whispers, off)* **What?**
BOGLE: *(Loud whisper)* **Smith?!**
SMITH: *(Loud whisper, off)* **What?**
BOGLE: **Quiet! Spriggans!** *(The SPRIGGANS burst on stage.)*
HORT: *(Very happy)* **Bogle?**
TAUGER: **Bogle!**
HORT: **It's the Bogle!**
TAUGER: *(This is great news.)* **Someone set him free!**
HORT: **What a wonderful day!**
BOGLE: **"What a wonderful day." Pleagh!** *(BOGLE gives them a gesture of contempt.)*
HORT: **We are happy to see you.**
TAUGER: **We are happy to tie you up again.**
BOGLE: **Go jump in the swamp.**
HORT: **We are happy to destroy you.**
TAUGER: **Destroy the Bogle!**
HORT: **Destroy the Bogle!** *(They dash at the BOGLE. He runs.)*
BOGLE: **Smith!**
SMITH: *(Dashing out)* **Spriggans!** *(SPRIGGANS stop, stare, crumble at SMITH, whose clothes are inside-out.)*
TAUGER: **No!**
HORT: **Look!**
TAUGER: **Clothes!**
HORT: **Inside-out!**
TAUGER: **Help!** *(HORT screams. The SPRIGGANS run in panic.)*
BRIAN: **What?**
SMITH: **I don't believe it.**
BOGLE: **The ropes!**
BRIAN: **Spriggans! Bogle! Smith! Stop it! Spriggans!** *(BRIAN simply adds to the chaos of the moment.)*
HORT & TAUGER: **Help! Help! Clothes inside-out! Clothes inside-out!** *(The BOGLE and SMITH chase the SPRIGGANS around bushes, over rocks and logs, around trees, etc. During the chase, SMITH picks up a stick, waits, and as HORT runs by, hits him hard in the head.)*
HORT: **Ah!** *(He falls. SMITH hits him again in the head.)*
TAUGER: **Hort!** *(SMITH raises stick to hit HORT again. BRIAN takes stick from him.)*
BRIAN: **Smith!**
BOGLE: **Get the rope! Take the rope!**
BRIAN: **Get away from him!**
TAUGER: **Hort! Wake up!** *(TAUGER is frantic, but must keep her distance from SMITH. SMITH gets the rope.)*
SMITH: **I have it.** *(SMITH takes his hat back, puts it on.)*
BOGLE: **One rope is enough.**
TAUGER: **Hort, get away!**

164

BOGLE: Give it to me. *(SMITH moves to BOGLE, TAUGER joins BRIAN with HORT.)*
TAUGER: You hurt?
SMITH: *(Gives BOGLE the rope.)* **Here.**
TAUGER: Are you hurt? *(TAUGER runs off.)*
BOGLE: My plan worked!
TAUGER: *(Off)* **Lara!**
SMITH: I still don't believe it.
BRIAN: Spriggan.
TAUGER: *(Off)* **Lara!**
BOGLE: Run!
SMITH: What?
BOGLE: The queen comes. She's not afraid of clothes inside-out. Follow me! *(BOGLE and SMITH run off. BRIAN starts after them.)*
BRIAN: Smith? Smith? *(LARA and TAUGER enter quickly.)* **Lara.** *(BRIAN moves back to HORT.)*
LARA: What is it?
TAUGER: Hort. His head is broken.
LARA: *(Bending over him)* **Hort? Poor Hort. Who did this?**
BRIAN: Smith.
TAUGER: Made us crazy with clothes inside-out.
BRIAN: Then hit this Spriggan on the head.
LARA: Why?
TAUGER: I don't know.
BRIAN: I didn't know what they were doing. I should have been more careful.
LARA: Help carry Hort to my thicket.
BRIAN: Will your gold be safe?
LARA: The Bogle knows what I'll do to him if he tries to steal it. It'll be safe until we return. *(They pick up HORT, begin to take him off.)*
TAUGER: How is Hort?
LARA: He's hurt.
TAUGER: Hort!
LARA: Hold his head up.
TAUGER: Guard the hill. Stomp on Smith. *(They take him off. SMITH and BOGLE run back on.)*
SMITH: Now, what's your plan?
BOGLE: Before they come back we must capture a faery creature, a small one, with a Spriggan rope.
SMITH: Why?
BOGLE: Once a faery is caught, she must do as you say, until she dies. They die very quickly when captured.
SMITH: So?
BOGLE: We will hide small one and tell the queen we'll let faery

die if she tries to stop us.

SMITH: **Good plan.**

BOGLE: **I am good. I am smart. You are smart, too. You do what I say.**

SMITH: **How do we catch one?**

BOGLE: **With these...** *(He holds out his hand; it is full of ribbons.)*

SMITH: **Ribbons?**

BOGLE: **I traded...** *(Painfully)* **gold for them. Hang them on bushes.**

SMITH: *(They do so quickly.)* **Just ribbons?**

BOGLE: **They like ribbons; love ribbons, greedy for ribbons; silly...they are so silly. There...over there.**

SMITH: **I'm grateful for your help, Bogle. I may even give you a couple of gold pieces when I get that treasure.**

BOGLE: **Hide, now.**

SMITH: *(Grabbing woodlilies; stuffs them into his mouth.)* **I want to see them.**

BOGLE: **Hide. Now.** *(SMITH hides, changes his clothes back right side out. BOGLE places a small pile of ribbons on the ground near the fallen log. To himself)* **I do not do this for you, Smith. I do it for me... as you will see.** *(Off, we hear THISTLE playing her pipe. He stops and listens.)* **One is coming.** *(To SMITH. He whispers.)* **Smith?**

SMITH: *(Whispers, off)* **Yes?**

BOGLE: *(Loud whisper)* **Smith!**

SMITH: *(Loud whisper, off)* **What?**

BOGLE: **Quiet! One is coming.** *(He jumps behind fallen log, hides. THISTLE enters, playing her pipe.)*

THISTLE: **Ribbons! I knew it. But who put them here?... Whose are they?...Brian put them here....For me! Ribbons!** *(She begins picking them up.)* **A blue one...gold...and here — red and green. Look at them. Lara! Spriggans! See my ribbons!** *(She spies a group, kneels by them.)* **Look. I'll give this one to Lara...no, this one. Both! This one's for Tauger. I'll give this to Hort for his new Smith hat — and this one and this one and this one. This one is for Lara's hair.** *(She holds one up.)* **Oooo. Like the sunset.** *(The BOGLE steps out and puts rope around her.)*

BOGLE: **Caught!**

THISTLE: **Let me go!**

BOGLE: **My prisoner!**

THISTLE: **Let me go or I'll pinch you, Bogle!** *(She does.)*

BOGLE: **Ow! Ow! Don't pinch me!**

THISTLE: **Spriggans! Spriggans, help me! Bogle is free! Sprig —**

BOGLE: **Quiet! You will not speak!** *(THISTLE runs frantically.)* **You are my prisoner. You must do as I say. Stop moving!** *(THISTLE instantly stops struggling.)* **You must do as I tell you.**

(Calling) **Smith! Smith! She pinched me.**

SMITH: *(Running on)* **So that's what they look like.**

BOGLE: The others will come soon. Hide her in the tree trunk.
(To THISTLE, who is already looking sad and wilted) **Come
with me. Come-come-come-come.** *(He pulls her to hollow
log.)* **Go in. Go in. Stay here and make no sound; prisoner.**
*(THISTLE crawls into log. SMITH stuffs rope in log. From Off-
stage we hear calls of "Smith! Bogle!")* **The others are coming.
Move away!** *(They move from log. Suddenly from different
directions TAUGER, LARA and BRIAN run on, all at the same
moment, shouting.)*

LARA: *(Over everyone)* **Bogle!** *(Everyone turns to LARA. To BOGLE)*
What are you doing?

BOGLE: Stay away, or the little one will die.

LARA: What little one?

BOGLE: Thistle. She is our prisoner.

LARA: No...

BOGLE: Hidden.

LARA: You know what will happen to her.

BOGLE: I'll set her free —

SMITH: — after I have the gold.

BRIAN: Smith, I told you —

LARA: Wait. *(She stops him.)*

BRIAN: You're as crazy as he is, Smith.

LARA: *(To BOGLE)* **I see your plan.** *(To SMITH)* **Beware of this
Bogle, thief. He is dangerous.**

BOGLE: Don't listen, Smith. They must go now. Tell them!

LARA: Beware of the thirteen bells.

BRIAN: Don't tell him.

SMITH: What *is* that; thirteen bells? *(TAUGER laughs.)*

BOGLE: I'll tell you! I'll tell you about bells! Tell them to go!

**LARA: Once you open the treasure, if you are not out of the for-
est by the thirteenth ring, *you* will turn into a Bogle.**

SMITH: *(Stepping away from BOGLE)* **You mean like him?**

**BRIAN: Just like him, Smith. He didn't get out of the woods by
the thirteenth ring.**

LARA: The Bogle was once human like you.

SMITH: I don't believe it.

**BRIAN: He's John Putnam, old Mable Putnam's husband. He
disappeared in this woods forty years ago.**

LARA: And he's been our Bogle ever since.

BRIAN: Ask him.

SMITH: Is that true?

BOGLE: Yes. I was John Putnam.

**LARA: You see? Tell me where Thistle is and I'll let you pass
safely out of the forest.**

BOGLE: No. They are trying to scare you away, Smith. Thirteen bells is a long time, time enough to take gold out of the woods.

SMITH: *(To LARA)* **Is that true?**

LARA: *(Enigmatically)* **Yes.**

BOGLE: You see? I know. I'll help you. Tell them to go.

SMITH: All right. I'm smarter than you. Get away from here, all of you!

LARA: Tauger, search the ferns for Thistle. I'll search the oak trees with Brian. Go! *(They exit, variously.)*

BOGLE: It worked! It worked! My plan worked!

SMITH: This is it! What do we have to do?

BOGLE: Circle the hill seven times round and round and then touch rock with bouquet.

SMITH: I'll do it.

BOGLE: *(Takes flowers from SMITH.)* **No, me!**

SMITH: We made a deal. It's my land. It's my gold.

BOGLE: *(Falling to his knees)* **But Smith. I will die!**

SMITH: *(Snatching the flowers)* **Give me those flowers.**

BOGLE: Stingy creep.

SMITH: Now, around the hill seven times. *(He begins to run around hill. As he does so he chants "Gold" over and over again. It becomes a song. The BOGLE joins in. SMITH counts out revolutions.)* **One!...gold, gold, gold...**

SMITH & BOGLE: Two!...gold, gold, gold, gold....Three!...gold, gold, gold...Four!... *(BOGLE joins SMITH running around hill.)* gold, gold, gold, gold...Five!...gold, gold, gold... Six!...gold, gold, gold, gold...Seven! *(On the seventh time around, the song and dance end with a grand finish. The rock of the Hollow Hill begins to glow and sparkle.)*

SMITH: Look at that! *(They are both on the verge of hysteria now.)*

BOGLE: I remember...touch rock three times with bouquet.

SMITH: One-two-three! *(A deep hollow drum sounds, followed by airy tinkling of chimes. The rock splits open amid a flood of light revealing a wealth of gold. The next lines are simultaneously delivered. The BOGLE pauses to allow SMITH focus on his "Laundromat" revelation, then resumes or repeats his lines.)*

BOGLE: There it is! Gold! Gold! Look at it all! Gold! I did it!

SMITH: I'm rich! I'm rich! I'm rich! I'll build — I can build anything I want! I'll build — a *laundromat!* Rich-rich-oh rich! Ha *ha! (BOGLE and SMITH run at each other, open arms; SMITH pulls up short.)* **Don't touch me!**

BOGLE: Help take it out. *(They pick it up, carry it a short distance.)*

SMITH: Oh...I'm glad you're helping me. There's so much gold I could never lift this myself. *(The first of the thirteen deep, rich, tolls of the bell echoes through the forest. They stop to lis-*

ten.)

BOGLE: Listen.

SMITH: The first of the thirteen bells. Hurry. Let's get this out of the forest. *(BOGLE puts chest down which forces SMITH to do so as well.)* **What are you doing?**

BOGLE: This. *(BOGLE shuts the rock.)*

SMITH: Why?

BOGLE: For me.

SMITH: What's going on? Help me get it out of the forest.

BOGLE: No.

SMITH: I'll never do it myself.

BOGLE: *(Circling SMITH)* **Right. You'll never do it.** *(The bell tolls.)*

SMITH: What's the matter with you?

BOGLE: You'll never get gold out of the forest.

SMITH: So *you* can take it. Is that it?

BOGLE: No.

SMITH: Then what?

BOGLE: If you don't get the gold out by the thirteenth ring... *(He is ready to burst)* **you'll be the new greedy Bogle and I'll be free to leave the forest. I'll be free and human again!**

SMITH: You tricked me.

BOGLE: Yes.

SMITH: So I'd take your place.

BOGLE: Yes! *(He jumps at SMITH and touches him all over.)* **Bogle! Bogle! Greedy Bogle!**

SMITH: *(Scratching)* **Don't touch me!**

BOGLE: You'll never get it out of the forest alone! Greedy Bogle! *(SMITH runs to chest, tries to pick it up, can't. The bell tolls.)*

SMITH: What am I going to do?

BRIAN: *(Runs on.)* **Smith, we can't find Thistle.**

SMITH: Brian! Brian, look. The gold. We're rich. Help me get it out of the forest.

BRIAN: All right.

BOGLE: No!

BRIAN: First tell me where Thistle is.

SMITH: All right, all right. She's...No. After the gold is out of the forest.

BRIAN: It'll be too late. Tell me where she is first.

SMITH: No.

BRIAN: The woods are so large we'll never find her.

SMITH: Right.

BRIAN: Then tell me.

SMITH: No.

BOGLE: I'll tell you where Thistle is.

BRIAN: Where?

SMITH: **No.** *(Bell tolls.)*

BOGLE: **She's —** *(The SPRIGGANS run on, stop between BOGLE and log. HORT wears a bandage on his head. The BOGLE backs up in fear.)*

HORT: **Bogle!**

BOGLE: **Spriggans!**

TAUGER: *(Seeing gold)* **Our gold.**

BRIAN: **Where is she, Bogle?**

HORT: **Our gold! Thieves!** *(The SPRIGGANS spring to attack.)*

BRIAN & BOGLE: **No!**

BOGLE: **No. The thirteen bells. You'll break the spell.** *(They stop.)* **I'll show you where Thistle is.**

BRIAN & SPRIGGANS: **Where?**

SMITH: *(SMITH goes for BOGLE who moves away.)* **Bogle!**

BOGLE: **I'll show you.**

SMITH: **No-no-no-no-no-no.**

BOGLE: **Here.**

SMITH: *(As he sees it's inevitable anyway)* **All right, go ahead, go ahead, go ahead.**

BOGLE: **In here. See? Hurry. In here. Here.**

BRIAN: **There she is! Help me.** *(They pull her out, put her on stump, crouch around her, holding her up. THISTLE is completely wilted and pale. SMITH begins inching chest out of forest. Bell tolls.)*

BOGLE: *(Standing apart from group)* **Wake up. You are a prisoner no more. You're free. I say so.**

HORT: **Take off the rope.**

BRIAN: **Thistle? It's Brian. Can you hear me? Why doesn't she say anything?** *(BRIAN takes off rope.)* **There, she's free.**

SMITH: **Brian, she's free. Come on.**

HORT: **Thistle!** *(Silence)* **She doesn't move.**

TAUGER: **Gone.** *(The bell tolls.)*

BRIAN: **What? No.**

BOGLE: *(Quietly)* **No...you're free.**

SMITH: **Come on, Brian. It's too late anyway.**

BRIAN: *(Shaking her)* **Thistle, wake up! You're free!** *(To others)* **There must be something we can do.** *(LARA enters.)*

TAUGER: **Lara! We found her!**

LARA: **Thistle.**

BRIAN: **She was here all the time.**

LARA: *(Quickly checks THISTLE.)* **Put her by our gold.** *(The SPRIGGANS carry her over. SMITH guards the gold, stopping LARA. BRIAN moves to SMITH, challenges him. Bell tolls.)*

BRIAN: **Back away, Smith.** *(He does.)*

SMITH: **Hurry up!** *(The SPRIGGANS set her next to gold. LARA removes gold dust from chest and sprinkles it on THISTLE.)*

LARA: Thistle, breathe, breathe. You are free again. Awaken, wildflower, awaken.

BRIAN: Thistle? *(No response. LARA takes more gold from the chest, sprinkles it on her.)*

LARA: Breathe in our gold. Breathe in its light, and energy. You are free. Awaken. *(No response. Then slowly, she moves.)*

BRIAN: She's moving! *(Bell tolls.)*

TAUGER: Thistle!

THISTLE: Lara? *(All cheer except SMITH.)* Brian. *(She slowly rises.)* You gave me ribbons.

BRIAN: What?

BOGLE: I did.

LARA: *(Just now seeing him)* Bogle!

BRIAN: He told us where to find Thistle.

BOGLE: *(To THISTLE)* You may keep the ribbons. *(Bell tolls.)*

SMITH: *(Returning to gold)* Come on now. She's all right. The gold — let's get it out of the forest.

THISTLE: Our gold.

BRIAN: Stop him.

TAUGER: We can't.

SMITH: I know.

THISTLE: The treasure is his.

LARA: He opened the Hollow Hill.

BRIAN: Then *I'll* stop him.

SMITH: What?

BOGLE: Keep him here until the thirteenth ring.

BRIAN: *(Gets opposite side of chest, holds it back. Bell tolls.)* You're not going any further.

SMITH: But it's mine! I stole it!

BRIAN: Stop!

SMITH: I'll give you a third.

BRIAN: No.

SMITH: Half.

BRIAN: No.

SMITH: I'll do anything!

BRIAN: No.

SMITH: Help me! *Please!*

BRIAN: Let go! *(He pulls it from SMITH. BRIAN takes two handfuls of gold and holds them out to SMITH.)* Look, Smith. Here, gold. Come and get it. Come on, come on.

SMITH: Mine! Mine! *(SMITH goes after it. BRIAN puts it behind his back, backs away.)* Give it to me! *(He goes for it. BRIAN runs around, avoids his hands.)* Mine! Mine! Mine! *(BRIAN drops gold.)*

BRIAN: There it is! *(SMITH goes for it, gathers it up. BRIAN returns to chest, guards it.)*

HORT: Brian is a good Spriggan. *(Bell tolls.)*

SMITH: Ten. It's the tenth ring.

BOGLE: No.

LARA: It's the eleventh ring.

THISTLE: Two more.

SMITH: Two more!

BOGLE: Two more!

SMITH: Just two more rings!

BRIAN: You can still make it, Smith. Run. Save yourself.

SMITH: Not without more gold. *(SMITH picks up a stick.)*

THISTLE: Brian! *(SMITH swings, BRIAN ducks, SMITH swings again, then again. BRIAN jumps away, SMITH drops stick, dives into treasure, grabbing gold.)*

SMITH: It's all mine! Gold! Gold! Gold! *(BRIAN comes up behind SMITH, grabs him. SMITH elbows BRIAN in the stomach, pushes him away. BRIAN rolls.)*

THISTLE, LARA & SPRIGGANS: Brian! *(LARA, THISTLE, BOGLE and the SPRIGGANS all take an immediate step toward BRIAN.)*

SMITH: *(The next two speeches are chanted simultaneously underneath the dialog that follows. SMITH begins to stuff his pockets and shirt with as much gold as he can.)* **Gimme-gimme-gimme-gimme-gimme-gimme-gimme...**

BOGLE: *(Crosses to SMITH.)* **Yes, yes, yes, yes, yes, yes, yes...** *(Bell tolls.)*

THISTLE: Brian —

LARA: Thistle!

THISTLE: Brian, get up!

LARA: Thistle, no more. *(BRIAN rises.)*
(The next six speeches overlap.)

SMITH: **Mine-mine-mine-mine-mine-** *(Etc.)*

BOGLE: Yes, that's it! That's it! More! More! *(Etc.)*

BRIAN: Smith, stop.

SMITH: **More-more-more-more! More gold! More gold!** *(Etc.)*

BRIAN: Smith — *(BRIAN takes rope from his belt, moves to SMITH and drops lasso around him.)*

SMITH: I'm rich! *(He starts to run off with an armful of gold, BRIAN tries to hold him back, but SMITH is pulling him. The BOGLE moves next to SMITH.)*

BRIAN: Stop!

SMITH: I'm rich! *(BRIAN now holds firm.)*

BOGLE: I'm free!

SMITH: I'm rich!

BOGLE: I'm free!

SMITH: I'm rich!

BOGLE: I'm free!

SMITH: I'm — *(The bell tolls the thirteenth ring.)*

BOGLE: Free! I'm *freeee!* *(The BOGLE stands tall, almost completely human. He runs off. SMITH crouches, reels BOGLE-like.)*
SMITH: *(Chanting rapidly)* **Gold-gold-gold-mine-mine-mine-yes-yes-yes.** *(He stops, frightened.)* **Noooo...not me, not me. Eek!** *(He covers his ears with his hands. His hands push upwards as if large ears were suddenly growing under them. He screams a BOGLE scream, turns, runs off.)*
BRIAN: Smith...
THISTLE: Brian!
HORT: Our gold!
LARA: We keep our gold! *(They all cheer. HORT takes SMITH's hat back, puts it on. The SPRIGGANS run up to BRIAN, give him a strange hat.)*
TAUGER: You are a good Spriggan.
HORT: Mean.
LARA: Spriggans, return the gold to the Hollow Hill. *(They pick up the chest, return it to the rock during the following.)*
BRIAN: But Smith. He'll get away. He took some of your gold.
LARA: He's our Bogle.
THISTLE: He can't leave the forest.
BRIAN: Then you're safe.
LARA: Brian. *(She embraces him.)* **Now I'll show you the wonder and magic of this forest.**
BRIAN: Oh...yes.
LARA: Spriggans, find our new Bogle and tie him to his tree.
HORT: Destroy the Bogle!
SPRIGGANS: Spriggans! *(They dash off.)*
THISTLE: I want my present now.
BRIAN: Oh, yes, my watch...bracelet. I'd like you to have this. *(He gives her watch.)*
THISTLE: *(THISTLE, after a moment's consideration, puts watch on her ankle.)* **For dancing.** *(She dances a little, holding up her foot. LARA gestures, music is heard.)* **Dance!**
BRIAN: Yes. Dance.
LARA: Dance with us.
BRIAN: I won't fall asleep?
LARA: No. You'll just dance and dance.
BRIAN: And I'll be able to leave the forest?
LARA: You may come and go as you wish. Come...dance... *(They dance wildly. As lights dim we see the new BOGLE, ears large and pointed. He is tied to the tree, mumbling, moving in the shadows, searching for a gold piece he thinks he dropped.)*
THE END

173

THE CRYSTAL

by MAX BUSH

CHARACTERS

ROBIN . . . . Seventeen-Year-Old Boy
CULLEN . . . . Twin to Robin
DOREEN. . . . . Robin and Cullen's Mother
ROSS . . . . Robin and Cullen's Father
AUDREY. . . . . Seventeen Years Old
KATE . . . . Seventeen Years Old
SLOAN . . . . Late Twenties, An Emissary
of Errigal
MORA. . . . . A Sorceress

All roles can be played by three females, four males.

TIME: Anytime.

PLACE: Merinnis, a forested island. Various locations in Errigal. The settings need not be elaborate and can be suggested by simple set pieces (except the crystal itself), sound, and lighting.

DEDICATION: To Jeff Gruszewski

The Crystal opened on November 16, 1990, at Gull Lake High School, with the following cast and crew:

CAST

Robin.	Lukas Ross
Cullen	David Long
Ross	Jeff Weyhmiller
Audrey.	Chelsea Blowers
Mora	Adrienne West
Doreen.	Cheryl Bauman
Sloan.	Brett Johnson
Darren.	Barry Weyhmiller

PRODUCTION STAFF

Producer	Robin Nott
Director.	Max Bush
Designer/Technical Director	Kevin Abbot
Costumer	Martha Bay
Stage Manager.	Amanda Cope
Weapons Master	Jenni Donnelly
Properties	Laurel Crim
Stage Crew	Angie Ludlow, Jared Boyd, Mareille Balke
Sound Tech.	Shannon Schippers, Joe Jones
Lighting Tech	Shelly Ray, Nathan Stone, Jamie Banas
Make-up	Shelly Cross
Box Office	Joanne Marcinkowski

The Crystal was subsequently produced professionally by Karamu House in Cleveland, Ohio, and opened there on April 5, 1991, with the following cast and crew:

CAST

Robin . . . . Eric Schmiedl

Audrey . . . . Kristin Kundert

Ross . . . . William Beck

Cullen . . . . Victor Dickerson

Doreen . . . . Deanna Woods

Sloan . . . . Mark Bodell

Colleen . . . . Shruti Amin

PRODUCTION STAFF

Director . . . . Jeff Gruszewski

Set Design . . . . David Dusheck

Lighting Design . . . . Marcus Dana

Costume Design . . . . Adaora Karola Nzelibe

Scenic Artist . . . . Meredith Morgan

Sound Effects . . . . Casey Jones

Stage Manager . . . . Milicent Wright

Light Operator . . . . Justin Dennis

Sound Operator . . . . Trudy Dos Reis

Sound Engineer . . . . John Rodriguez

ACT I
Scene 1

(On the island of Merinnis, in a forest clearing, ROBIN lies against a stump, dreaming. We see his dream. Music plays quietly under dream. Across the stage, a single spot comes up on AUDREY, facing Upstage. She's dressed simply, warmly, in earth tones and has long hair. She turns her head, appears to look at ROBIN.)

AUDREY: Robin...I'm here...All is well. *(Near AUDREY another spot comes up on ROSS. He's about forty, but an old forty, spiritually and physically weakened by years of intense struggle. He's blind, in a disheveled robe, lying in a heap, surrounded by darkness. ROSS awakens. Clumsily, he rises. ROBIN groans, stirs. AUDREY turns to ROSS.)* **I see.**

ROSS: *(In a harsh voice)* **Robin...** *(He feels around himself, unable to find his way. ROBIN groans again. As if he has heard this, ROSS turns to ROBIN. We see ROSS' eyes are hollow.)*

AUDREY: Rotting old bones. He wants your hands; your eyes.

ROSS: *(ROSS opens his robe; underneath is a brilliant, clean, gold robe. Painted on it is a sun in the shape of an eye. He turns toward ROBIN.)* **There.**

AUDREY: He sees you. *(ROBIN stirs.)*

ROSS: Open your eyes. *(ROBIN groans.)*

AUDREY: But I'm here. All is well.

ROSS: There is a ship.

AUDREY: Yes.

ROSS: It's your hope.

AUDREY: It's your hope. Your way is open.

ROSS: Your way is open. Come, now.

AUDREY: I'm here.

ROSS: Come, now.

AUDREY: I'll bring everything to you.

ROSS: I can't wait much longer.

AUDREY: Come into the night.

DOREEN: *(Off, not in dream, calling)* **Robin!**

ROSS: *(Turns, as if he heard her, then back to ROBIN.)* **You can't hide forever. Give us your eyes.**

AUDREY: Your wait is over. Come into the dark. I'm here.

DOREEN: *(Off)* **Robin!**

ROSS & AUDREY: It's time. *(A flash of brilliant light with the sound of a sudden rush of wind. ROSS and AUDREY disappear, music ends abruptly. ROBIN sits up, eyes open, terrified.)*

ROBIN: *Nooo!* *(DOREEN enters, carrying a basket, moves quickly to him. DOREEN's present existence is a contrast to her courtly rear-*

ing. She is a worn thirty-six.)

DOREEN: *(Bending to him)* **What is it?**

ROBIN: No-no —

DOREEN: What, Robin? *(He takes her by the throat, throws her on her back, draws back to hit her with the other hand.)*

ROBIN: I won't go! I won't!

DOREEN: Robin! Let me go.

ROBIN: I...

DOREEN: You're hurting me. *(He stares at DOREEN.)* **Were you dreaming?**

ROBIN: Mother... *(He gradually relaxes his grip and fist.)*

DOREEN: You don't have to go.

ROBIN: Mother. *(He turns away from her, confused. He turns back to her, eyes her with suspicion.)*

DOREEN: What was it?

ROBIN: That same man, calling me, over and over, calling me.

DOREEN: What does he want?

ROBIN: I don't know.

DOREEN: Who is he?

ROBIN: I don't know. He's hurt — blind I think. He's looking for me, always looking for me, stalking me like I'm an animal; and he always finds me —

DOREEN: Looking for you, finds you, though he's blind?

ROBIN: He has an eye — on his robe; an eye on his robe; he sees me. Then he calls me to...to what? I always wake up before I find out.

DOREEN: And you don't know who he is?

ROBIN: Ross?

DOREEN: Your father? No wonder you're terrified. *(Touching his face)* **Poor boy. You're still sweating.** *(She takes out a handkerchief, daubs his forehead.)*

ROBIN: Father...how could I remember him?

DOREEN: It's all right. It's just a dream. A dream can't hurt you. And I'm here. I'm here.

ROBIN: What does it mean that he's blind?

DOREEN: You're so warm. *(She opens his shirt.)* **You're covered in sweat.** *(She wipes off his neck.)*

ROBIN: Why would he want me to go to him?

DOREEN: Robin, it's a beautiful day. See? I don't want to ruin it talking about your father. Why don't you gather that firewood? *(Sees that ROBIN is deep in thought.)* **I can only tell you what I know. I don't understand your dreams.**

ROBIN: Why did he give her the crystal?

DOREEN: I told you; he was completely taken with her.

ROBIN: There must be more —

DOREEN: They walked the streets together, sailed together, he

took her to the Council's Court; he humiliated me and embarrassed everyone.

ROBIN: Did he know what he was doing?

DOREEN: The Wizard? When he disappeared with her into the forest — I knew, everyone knew — he had broken the old laws; he showed her the mysteries of the crystal, taught her its language —

ROBIN: She must have taken it.

DOREEN: He gave it to her. But even that wasn't enough. She wanted you and Cullen. But when Ross came for you, we had already sailed.

ROBIN: Would he want to kill me?

DOREEN: Mora wants to kill you. To keep you from the crystal.

ROBIN: Then what does he want?

DOREEN: It's a dream. A dream can't hurt you. Not on Merinnis. There are no blind old men, here. *(She pulls his head onto her lap.)* **They're far away...far away...I'm here...all is well...** *(He yawns, fairly falls asleep again. Sings.)*

He is strong,
An oak in the wood.
And he is young,
A mother's son.
He is a heart,
A kiss for him. *(She kisses his head.)*
A kiss for him.
What would we do without our Robin?...Isn't it a beautiful day?...All is well...I'm going to the cliff to get berries. I'd like you to fill the first row of firewood — or two — by the time I get back. Robin?

ROBIN: Yes?

DOREEN: I told Cullen to come and help you. Will you finish the first row by breakfast?

ROBIN: Yes.

DOREEN: *(She kisses him.)* **You have everything you need here.** *(She swats him.)* **Firewood!** *(She exits.)*

ROBIN: **Father...** *(He picks up a stick, then another. Then he stops, considers. His spirit fades.)* **Father...** *(He drops the sticks. A light music comes in. ROBIN looks up but it's more an inward glance at something vague.)* **Father, you...** *(AUDREY appears to us but not directly to him. At times he seems to sense her, even look directly at her, but mostly he speaks to the forest landscape.)*

AUDREY: Robin...

ROBIN: Father, what do you want? What's wrong?

AUDREY: All is well.

ROBIN: I feel like you're telling me to do something, but what?

And what I think you're telling me doesn't make any sense. First it's: "Go; sail away, now. Come to me." Then: "Wait. Stay. Everything is all right."

AUDREY: *(She laughs.)* **Poor Robin.**

ROBIN: **What do you want? What am I supposed to do? Are you my father?**

AUDREY: **I don't think so.**

ROBIN: **Are you alive? Are you voices from the crystal? Why aren't you here to answer these questions?**

AUDREY: **I am here. You know I'm here.**

ROBIN: **What are you saying?**

AUDREY: **Yes, say yes, just say yes and everything will be all right.**

ROBIN: *(Giving up)* **I know. I don't know.**

AUDREY: **Sit here with me.** *(ROBIN sits next to her. She rests her hand on him. Again, he is not directly conscious of her. He lets go of his inner debate, relaxes, gazes at the landscape.)* **There...come closer. Close your eyes.** *(He does, leans back against rock.)* **Find me. Robin...I know what you want. All will be well. The ship is here. I'm here. I'm here.** *(ROBIN hears something off, opens his eyes.)*

ROBIN: **Cullen.** *(Music out. ROBIN hides, AUDREY watches. CULLEN enters, walking quickly, looking for ROBIN. He walks past ROBIN who steps out behind him and attacks CULLEN, trying to throw him. CULLEN responds quickly, however, and throws ROBIN. He lands hard but jumps up and they face off.)*

CULLEN: **Hello, snowflake. How are you this morning? Frustrated? Or just happy to see me?** *(ROBIN dazzles CULLEN with elaborate preparations to throw him. CULLEN throws him again and he lands hard. This time ROBIN doesn't get up.)* **Good strategy, brother. Well executed.**

ROBIN: **I almost had you.**

CULLEN: *(Helping him up)* **I almost called Mother to save me from you, demon.**

ROBIN: **I knew it. You just got lucky...again.**

CULLEN: *(Slugs ROBIN.)* **Where've you been?**

ROBIN: **Out walking.**

CULLEN: **We're to gather firewood; the work you didn't do yesterday.**

ROBIN: **I couldn't work yesterday.**

CULLEN: **You will today.**

ROBIN: **I don't feel like doing anything, today.** *(He leans against the rock AUDREY sits on.)* **And, it doesn't matter. I don't have to do anything.**

CULLEN: **You don't want breakfast?**

ROBIN: **I'll eat or I won't.**

CULLEN: You know what Mother will do.
ROBIN: She'll get angry or she won't. It doesn't matter.
AUDREY: All is well. *(She puts her hand on him.)*
ROBIN: All is well.
AUDREY: Close your eyes. Come here, with me.
ROBIN: And I'm tired, I want to sleep.
AUDREY: Here, in the dark.
ROBIN: I just want to sleep. *(He closes his eyes, lowers his head.)*
AUDREY: Here I am.
ROBIN: There. *(He sighs and relaxes.)*
AUDREY: Stay with me. Sleep.
AUDREY & ROBIN: All is well. *(Silence)*
CULLEN: Robin, what is the matter with you?
ROBIN: I'm dead.
CULLEN: What?
ROBIN: I'm dead.
CULLEN: You mean, you're dead?
ROBIN: Yes.
CULLEN: How did you die?
ROBIN: I waited and waited and waited...and died.
CULLEN: And what were you waiting for?
ROBIN: I don't know.
CULLEN: *(After a moment)* Do dead people feel pain?
ROBIN: No. *(CULLEN kicks him. That wakes him up.)* Ow!
CULLEN: Well, what a wonderful surprise, you're still alive. I'm
     so happy for you. *(CULLEN grabs ROBIN by his shirt, pulls
     him up, holds ROBIN's face close to his own.)* Firewood, Robin.
     Because if you think I'll beat you or I won't, I will. Into lit-
     tle pieces of snowflake.
ROBIN: I dreamt about him again, the blind old man with eyes
     on his robe.
CULLEN: *(Tossing him)* There's some over there.
ROBIN: I feel like it's —
CULLEN: Firewood!
ROBIN: Father. *(Short pause. AUDREY rises, moves between them,
     smiling at ROBIN.)*
AUDREY: Soon. *(She exits.)*
ROBIN: He calls me. In the dream I don't want to go — no, I do
     want to go, but —
CULLEN: Why would you want to go to that jackal?
ROBIN: I don't. But...do you have any strange dreams? *(No
     answer)* You do, don't you?
CULLEN: I forget them.
ROBIN: Do you wake up at night sweating, excited; wanting
     to...to run...to go?
CULLEN: Yes, but not because of my worthless father. Maybe

184

about Kelly the wheelwright's daughter — when she's a few years older. And... *(He dismisses it.)*

ROBIN: What?

CULLEN: It's nothing that anyone could understand.

ROBIN: I might. What is it? A dark pit? A blinding light?

CULLEN: A girl.

ROBIN: A girl...a girl...What does she look like? What is she doing?

CULLEN: She...I don't know! She...sings. She just stands in the surf looking seaward and sings. She...ah, ha-ha! *(He shivers, grins.)* She looks at me then *I* want to die. She's tall.

ROBIN: What song is she singing?

CULLEN: I don't understand the words. You see? It doesn't mean anything. *(He starts picking up wood.)* What do you want? To go back to Errigal?

ROBIN: No.

CULLEN: Mora will cut off your head, stick it on a stake and burn the rest of you in the marketplace.

ROBIN: We're wizards. It's our crystal.

CULLEN: Yes it is.

ROBIN: Don't you feel —

CULLEN: I want it as much as you do — more. But I'm not crazy. She'll kill us.

ROBIN: You're a good swordsman.

CULLEN: A sword is useless against the crystal. And there'll be no one to teach us how to use it even if we did find it.

ROBIN: I feel like this island's going to open up and swallow me. There must be somewhere we can go.

CULLEN: Where?

ROBIN: I don't know. Other places —

CULLEN: And do what?

ROBIN: Go away! Find young women —

CULLEN: Oh.

ROBIN: Yes!

CULLEN: Other young...

ROBIN: You like that idea.

CULLEN: I understand that one.

ROBIN: There are no girls on Merinnis who are the age for us.

CULLEN: Grow, Kelly, grow!

ROBIN: A ship hasn't landed in six months.

CULLEN: Seven.

ROBIN: Cullen...?

CULLEN: No.

ROBIN: Cullen —

CULLEN: A ship will come. New people will arrive. As long as we stay here we're safe.

ROBIN: I can't go and I can't stay. But either way, no matter what I do, I'm going to die.

CULLEN: This again.

ROBIN: All the time, I think about it, I know it's coming and there's nothing I can do about it.

CULLEN: And if you don't get firewood it's going to be today. Mother will kill us.

ROBIN: I'm sure that's what the dreams mean. That's why I wake up screaming. I'm dying. Somehow, in those dreams, I'm dying.

CULLEN: Then you can stop worrying if it *will* happen.

ROBIN: Is that what you do? *(Silence)* Before you got here I thought I could hear that old man — with my eyes open, dreaming with my eyes open — I could hear him talking to me.

CULLEN: And what was he saying?

ROBIN: I don't know. I even asked him questions, but I couldn't understand the answers.

CULLEN: That's the difference between you and me, Robin. You're crazy and I'm not.

ROBIN: You can't understand the words she's singing to you, either...but I don't want to die without a fight. Give me **another lesson.** *(Going to get them from where he hid them earlier)* I brought the swords.

CULLEN: You'd do better to stay with your herbs and medicines and leave the swordplay to me.

ROBIN: Just a couple of passes, then we'll get the firewood. *(He holds out sword to CULLEN.)*

CULLEN: Mother will beat us with a stick if we don't have the firewood by the time she gets back.

ROBIN: She's on the cliff. *(ROBIN boots CULLEN.)*

CULLEN: Well, I could stand with a little entertainment this morning. *(CULLEN takes sword.)* This won't take long.

ROBIN: How's this stance?

CULLEN: *(Imitating ROBIN)* Charming...feet wider apart...better. *(CULLEN readies himself.)* Well?

ROBIN: Yes?

CULLEN: Come on, then. To my leg. *(ROBIN swings, CULLEN blocks.)* Again, stronger. *(ROBIN swings again, then again immediately at CULLEN's shoulder. CULLEN blocks and parries the blows.)* Stronger... *(As they fight)* ...feet apart, always. Feet first, sword second...it's like a dance...dance, Robin... better...better — *(ROBIN exaggerates his dancing, begins to sing.)*

ROBIN: La da da da da.

CULLEN: What are you doing?

ROBIN: **Dancing.**

CULLEN: **Not with me you're not.** *(CULLEN attacks, befuddles ROBIN. He advances, ROBIN retreats; again and again CULLEN swings, ROBIN blocks.)* **Don't panic! When you panic you confuse your feet.** *(CULLEN increases the strength and speed of his attack.)*

ROBIN: *(Retreating awkwardly)* **Cullen...do I...? How...?** *(ROBIN hits a rhythm, counterattacks.)* **There, you snake! Ha!...Ha-ha!...No...no! Ah!** *(CULLEN disarms ROBIN, trips him, holds sword to ROBIN's throat.)*

CULLEN: **Snake?**

ROBIN: **I was better.**

CULLEN: **Yes, better, but dead. Hah!...Snowflake.** *(His blow strikes next to ROBIN's head.)* **And when you're in the fight to your inevitable death, don't tell your opponent I taught you how to fight. Obviously I never taught you anything.** *(ROBIN sits up quickly.)*

ROBIN: **Mother!**

CULLEN: **No firewood!** *(They run, looking for a place to hide. They both settle on the same place and try frantically to hide behind the same tree. They push each other away.)* **I'm here!**

ROBIN: *I'm* **here.**

CULLEN: **I was here first!**

ROBIN: **I thought of it first!**

CULLEN: **She'll see us!** *(They both run away from tree, see the other is running from tree, turn and run back, both reaching the tree at the same time.)*

ROBIN: **I'm here!**

CULLEN: *I'm* **here!**

ROBIN: **I was first!**

CULLEN: **You ran away!**

ROBIN: **So did you!**

CULLEN: **She'll see us!** *(They both take two steps away, then immediately turn back to the tree and meet again.)* **Mine!**

ROBIN: **No!** *(They embrace each other, squeeze behind the tree. MOTHER runs on.)*

DOREEN: *(She obviously sees them. Out of breath)* **Boys!** *(They disentangle, step out.)*

ROBIN: **Mother.**

CULLEN: **We're —** *(To ROBIN)* **What are we doing?**

ROBIN: **Getting firewood.**

CULLEN: **Oh, yes, just look at all we have.**

ROBIN: **What's for breakfast?**

DOREEN: *(Trying to catch her breath)* **Listen. There's —**

ROBIN: **I asked him for a lesson, Mother. It's my fault. I'll —**

DOREEN: **There's a ship.**

187

ROBIN: A ship...

DOREEN: Off the cliff. Anchored in the cove.

CULLEN: What colors?

DOREEN: The sun in the shape of an eye.

CULLEN: *(The TWINS look at each other.)* Errigal.

ROBIN: *(Enthused)* They've come for us!

DOREEN: It can only be Mora. No one else could have found us.

ROBIN: *(Fallen)* Mora? How could she find us?

CULLEN: Did you see anyone?

DOREEN: No.

ROBIN: No boat's coming ashore?

DOREEN: No, but I don't know how long the ship's been anchored. They could have come ashore last night, this morning. Now.

CULLEN: I hope it's her.

ROBIN: What?

CULLEN: Let her come. One way or the other. *(He gets his sword, tosses ROBIN his sword.)*

DOREEN: *(Seeing something in the distance)* No...

ROBIN: What? *(Following her gaze)* I hear voices. Two people on the path.

CULLEN: Just two...What do we do? *(DOREEN is frantically trying to decide.)* Why weren't we prepared for this, Mother? What do we do? *(Still no answer from DOREEN)* Damn!

DOREEN: Don't trust her. Don't believe her. She'll lie to you, she'll know you and use your fears to take what she wants.

CULLEN: And what do we do?

DOREEN: What I tell you. Trust that I know this monster. She won't be what you expect. You listen to me.

ROBIN: We will.

DOREEN: Both of you.

CULLEN: I will!

ROBIN: I knew my dream would come true.

CULLEN: There's no blind old man, no flashing lights. *(To ROBIN)* Feet first, like dancing, remember? And don't panic, you'll confuse your feet.

ROBIN: *(Looking at his feet)* It's too late.

DOREEN: Protect him, Cullen.

CULLEN: You were always better than I let you know.

ROBIN: I was?

CULLEN: I hope so.

ROBIN: I wasn't a snowflake?

CULLEN: Just don't panic. *(They laugh. SLOAN enters carrying a shield with the Errigal emblem, a sun in the shape of an eye. His sword is sheathed. AUDREY follows him.)*

DOREEN: Cullen... *(CULLEN steps in front of ROBIN, sword ready.)*

188

SLOAN: Doreen? Doreen, yes. Yes!

AUDREY: Is it?

SLOAN: It is! They're here! Doreen! You remember me? Sloan! Sheila's son. And this is little Audrey, believe it or not! We found you!

AUDREY: Then this is Robin and Cullen. But which...

DOREEN: That's her.

ROBIN: But she's so young.

DOREEN: I told you she wouldn't be what you expected.

AUDREY: *(With a smile)* **What were you expecting?** *(She steps forward, CULLEN braces, AUDREY recoils.)*

SLOAN: There's no need for your sword. Surely you can see that. Doreen, relax your boy, here, he may be a bit confused.

AUDREY: *(To ROBIN)* **You...you're Robin.** *(Assuming she'll get a response.)* **I'm Audrey.** *(ROBIN instead turns questioningly to DOREEN.)* **Audrey.**

DOREEN: Kill her.

AUDREY: What?

ROBIN: Are you sure?

DOREEN: Kill her.

SLOAN: Doreen, you know me. You know her. You know why we're here.

DOREEN: Cullen! *(CULLEN goes for AUDREY, she runs back, SLOAN draws.)*

SLOAN: *(To AUDREY as he gives her his shield.)* **Maybe this is what Mora had planned. To kill you away from court. She could lie and no one would know the truth.**

AUDREY: Cullen, listen to me.

DOREEN: Cullen!

CULLEN: *(To ROBIN)* **Stay with Mother.** *(He engages SLOAN; then they push away.)*

SLOAN: He may not be the best mind I've met today, but he can fight.

ROBIN: If that's her why doesn't she do something to stop him?

DOREEN: *(To AUDREY)* **Did you bring the crystal? You didn't, did you? Robin and Cullen would have known if it were close. And away from it you're nothing but a witch.**

AUDREY: *(To SLOAN)* **They think I'm Mora.**

SLOAN: You've got your eyes, Doreen, I see that. Do you have your mind? Why would Mora come like this? This is Audrey and I am your cousin Sloan. *(CULLEN attacks again.)*

AUDREY: *(To ROBIN)* **Don't you know me? I know you! Why don't you know me?** *(SLOAN is slightly wounded.)*

SLOAN: *(To AUDREY)* **No, no, nothing wounded. Except my pride.**

DOREEN: Robin, help him. *(ROBIN steps up.)*

ROBIN: Why isn't she stopping us? Why didn't she come with

men if she can't use the crystal on Merinnis?

DOREEN: It's a trick! This is how she is!

CULLEN: I'll finish him, you take her.

SLOAN: *(To AUDREY)* **They're blind. Run back to the longboat. I'll hold them. Go on. Go!** *(CULLEN attacks, ROBIN hesitates. CULLEN wounds SLOAN in the side, he falls. CULLEN lifts sword to strike a fatal blow.)*

AUDREY: Sloan!

DOREEN: Not him, her. *(CULLEN turns to AUDREY.)*

SLOAN: Doreen! Don't do this to Errigal.

ROBIN: *(To CULLEN)* **Wait.** *(To AUDREY)* **I know you. How could I know you?**

AUDREY: Through the crystal. You know me through the crystal, you fool! How do you think I know you?!

DOREEN: Cullen — *(CULLEN starts to swing at AUDREY. ROBIN stops him.)*

ROBIN: No.

CULLEN: What? Let me go! *(AUDREY suddenly lunges at CULLEN with SLOAN's shield. He tries to duck and swing at AUDREY but ROBIN prevents him.)*

ROBIN: No! *(AUDREY bangs CULLEN in the head with the shield. He staggers backwards. She follows and slams him again in the head with the shield, knocking him out. ROBIN swings, hits shield, drives AUDREY back.)*

DOREEN: Cullen! *(ROBIN checks CULLEN. DOREEN moves to CULLEN, stays with him during the following.)*

SLOAN: Get to the longboat, Audrey, the crew will help you.

DOREEN: Don't let her go, Robin.

AUDREY: Robin, trust your own mind. *(He moves toward her. Dream music fades in.)*

ROBIN: Who are you?

DOREEN: Don't talk to her. Don't listen to her.

AUDREY: Audrey. I told you, Audrey. If I were Mora, I would have taken you by now. Don't you know anything?!

ROBIN: Why should I trust you?

AUDREY: You're supposed to know yourself — understand magic! Ask the old men. Ask your grandfather, old Egan's bones. Then you'll trust me.

DOREEN: She'll tell you what you want to hear. She's made herself look young, like Audrey would look but it's her.

ROBIN: Why have you come here?

AUDREY: Because I'm a fool!

ROBIN: How did you know where to find us?

AUDREY: We searched for you for years. Then a sailor brought news of two young men on Merinnis of your age and names.

DOREEN: Can you believe that, Robin?

ROBIN: What do you want?

AUDREY: You don't know anything!

ROBIN: What do you want? And don't lie. If you lie, somehow I'll know.

AUDREY: Lower your sword and I'll answer you. *(He doesn't.)* I never thought it would happen like this. I thought you'd say all those things I dreamt you'd say... *(Formally)* You are Robin of Errigal, the Inheritor of the Crystal, the Descendant Wizard?

ROBIN: One of them, but I don't have the crystal. I don't know anything about being a Wizard.

AUDREY: *(Again, formally)* You are Robin of Errigal, the Inheritor of the Crystal, the Descendant Wizard?

ROBIN: Yes.

AUDREY: I've come because I am of age now.

DOREEN: I should have thought she would have done it this way.

ROBIN: For what?

AUDREY: Stupid. Stupid. Stupid. We were given to each other at birth.

ROBIN: Given...You mean...

AUDREY: Yes.

ROBIN: You and I...

AUDREY: Yes. *(Silence)*

ROBIN: Are you saying you and I...

AUDREY: I'm trying but I don't seem to be saying anything! *(He stifles, only partially successfully, a screech. He finds her news difficult to assimilate. He tries to speak but only makes strange sounds.)* It isn't law. We can refuse each other. And right now I think that's a perfect idea.

ROBIN: No, no. I... *(To DOREEN)* Is this true?

DOREEN: You were given to someone named Audrey who may look like her, but —

ROBIN: Why didn't you tell me? *(He moves closer to AUDREY, opens his mouth to speak, nothing comes out.)*

AUDREY: You see? You know me. You've seen me; maybe in dreams or daydreaming. Maybe you've drawn pictures — I drew pictures of you. That's how I knew you.

ROBIN: Yes! That's where I've seen you — here, with me. It's like I've talked with you before, but I didn't understand. I...I knew you were coming.

AUDREY: Since our first ceremony as babies we've been connected through the crystal.

ROBIN: *(Moving to CULLEN)* Cullen, wake up. I have to talk to you.

DOREEN: Robin... *(He looks at his MOTHER for a moment, then* back to AUDREY.)

ROBIN: *(Quietly)* **No.** *(He puts his sword on the ground, moves closer. They both look at each other, trying to discover the other.)* **You're...young.**

AUDREY: The same age as you.

ROBIN: You're...beautiful.

AUDREY: Oh; and you're...different.

ROBIN: *(In disbelief)* **You...were given to me?**

AUDREY: I've always felt for you even though we've grown up apart.

ROBIN: So have I, for a long time.

AUDREY: You did?

ROBIN: Yes, I've been waiting for you. *(This hits him.)* **You're what I've been waiting for! I've been waiting for *you*.**

AUDREY: And I was waiting for you! *(They laugh.)*

ROBIN: Is there a time when we're supposed to marry?

AUDREY: Last spring.

ROBIN: Last spring.

AUDREY: I waited for you, thinking the crystal would call you home if I didn't, but you didn't come for either of us. I haven't married anyone else, although someone asked.

ROBIN: *(He suddenly explodes with excitement, hooting and strutting. AUDREY is a little embarrassed but amused as well.)* **Look at you!** *(He hoots more, twirls, sits on the ground, calms himself. He looks up at her and broadly grins. She doesn't know exactly what to say so she smiles back. With a big sigh he falls on his back, spread eagle.)* **Oh, yes, yes, yes! This is a dream I like!** *(He jumps up, moves to her slowly. She reaches out, touches his hair; he carefully leans over and kisses her. It is a fairly short kiss and as he pulls away from her, we see that she was not quite ready for it to end. He floats away a little, making quiet humming noises, floats to the ground and sits again, looking up at her, grinning.)*

AUDREY: This is more like I expected.

ROBIN: It's not what I expected.

AUDREY: You don't have someone here, on this island?

ROBIN: No.

AUDREY: Have you made a promise to anyone?

ROBIN: No.

SLOAN: Then I hope you will consider we've come... *(SLOAN tries to rise, collapses. ROBIN moves to SLOAN, begins to undo his clothing to look at the wound. SLOAN pulls ROBIN's hand away.)*

ROBIN: I have to see your wound.

SLOAN: I have a physician aboard ship.

ROBIN: *(He rips open SLOAN's clothing, pulls it back, revealing the* *cut. He's not anxious over the sight of blood.)* **Your wound needs to be cleaned and sewn. Don't move.**

SLOAN: I don't think you have to worry. *(ROBIN runs off.)*

AUDREY: You've lived well on this island. This far north; that was clever.

DOREEN: If you are Mora, they're strong, both of them; stronger than their father. One of them will bury you. If you are Audrey, I'm sorry and I welcome you.

AUDREY: I'm Audrey and this is Sloan.

DOREEN: I remember him.

SLOAN: Then why, dear cousin, did you confuse your sons? They would have killed her.

DOREEN: I wouldn't expect you to understand. *(To AUDREY)* You look like your mother.

AUDREY: And you look like your sister. My father sends his love and respect.

DOREEN: Thank him for me. He has always had mine. *(CULLEN begins to come around.)*

AUDREY: Cullen...

CULLEN: What's happened to you, Robin? You're much prettier this morning. *(He looks again.)* I mistook you for my brother. Come closer and I won't make that mistake again.

AUDREY: I'm Audrey.

CULLEN: I'm dreaming.

AUDREY: I'm sorry I hit you but you attacked me.

CULLEN: I attacked you? I'm usually better with the ladies.

AUDREY: You fight well.

CULLEN: And you hit me?

AUDREY: With Sloan's shield.

CULLEN: Shield — *(He gets up quickly, is now much more alert. He picks up his sword.)* **Where's Robin?**

DOREEN: He'll be back soon.

CULLEN: Is he hurt?

AUDREY: No.

SLOAN: I am.

DOREEN: Hold your sword, Cullen.

CULLEN: Why? What's happened?

ROBIN: *(Entering with a pitcher of water, bandages, etc.)* **Cullen!**

CULLEN: Robin, you're not hurt.

SLOAN: I am!

ROBIN: This is Audrey, from Errigal.

CULLEN: What's happened? Why aren't we fighting?

ROBIN: This *is Audrey.*

CULLEN: How do you know?

ROBIN: I know.

AUDREY: And this is Sloan, from the court of Old Errigal.

SLOAN: We've met before. I must say your custom of greeting friends with your sword may be a reason Merinnis is near- ly uninhabited.

ROBIN: Audrey's come because, at birth, we were promised to each other.

CULLEN: Promised...you mean...?

ROBIN: *Yeeees!* Yes! Yes! Ha-ha!

SLOAN: And to bring you to Errigal to take back your crystal.

ROBIN: *(He sits next to SLOAN, opens his clothes further, cleanses his wound during the following.)* **To bring me back...**

AUDREY: Isn't that what you want?

ROBIN: Yes, but...to Errigal.

SLOAN: Old Errigal has vanished. Mora disbanded the ruling council, but she doesn't govern. The people run wild while she stays locked in the fortress, as disturbed as the rest of us. We need you; we need the crystal in your hands.

ROBIN: *(To SLOAN)* **I have to sew it.**

SLOAN: *(Trying to sit up)* **Bandage it. We'll sew it aboard ship.**

ROBIN: *(Gently pushing him back down)* **Walking will hurt it.**

SLOAN: I have better instruments on the ship.

ROBIN: These instruments work well.

SLOAN: *(Trying to sit up)* **I have my own physician aboard ship.**

ROBIN: I will be your physician! And a better one than him! *(Pushing him back)* **Stay still!**

CULLEN: Let him. He's a poor swordsman but a good physician. Audrey, were Robin and I both promised to you?

ROBIN: *(The idea suddenly hitting him with a sense of impending loss)* **Oh.** *(Seeing AUDREY hesitating in response)* **Both of us.**

AUDREY: You were given to Kate.

CULLEN: Kate...

ROBIN: Yes! Kate! You were given to Kate.

CULLEN: Is she as pretty as her name?

AUDREY: Yes.

ROBIN: Yes, oh yes, Cullen, just as pretty. Prettier.

CULLEN: Is she tall? Can she — she sings, doesn't she? I dreamt about a girl who sings.

AUDREY: She's known for her singing.

CULLEN: In my dream I saw her with red hair, very long; she was as tall as I am, and a voice, when she sang — I want- ed to die.

SLOAN: Yes. All that. But she never sang to me.

ROBIN: *(Who is now ready to begin the stitching)* **This will stop the pain while I sew.** *(He touches wound with an ointment.)*

SLOAN: *(Grimacing in pain)* **Ah!**

ROBIN: Don't move. Stay calm.

SLOAN: What kind of a physician are you? Come here. *(He punches*

194

ROBIN.)

ROBIN: It should begin to numb.

SLOAN: *(The pain obviously subsides.)* **Yes...yes...**

ROBIN: Should I use more?

SLOAN: No! *(To AUDREY)* **Have a good life with this torturer.**

ROBIN: *(Laughs.)* **Stay still while I sew.** *(He stitches during the following.)*

CULLEN: *(To AUDREY, as KATE enters behind him.)* **Tell me more about Kate. I'd swim to Errigal if she's real.**

KATE: **Cullen?** *(She goes to him.)* **Just as I saw you. Just as beautiful and strong...** *(He starts to reach for her, stops.)* **I feel like I know you so well and...I don't know anything about you. You're exactly what I expected, yet...so different.**

AUDREY: Yes, different.

KATE: **I even feel I know this place. Do you spend much time here?...Can you speak?**

CULLEN: Ah...

KATE: **Cullen, I'm finally seeing you. This is you! You don't know how often I've imagined this. And look at you.** *(KATE impulsively embraces him.)*

CULLEN: You were given to me?

KATE: Yes.

CULLEN: You sailed here from Errigal to find me?

KATE: Yes.

CULLEN: And you're real.

KATE: **Yes...but...** *(She moves away from him.)*

CULLEN: What?

KATE: You're here!

CULLEN: Could you come back here a moment?

KATE: **Audrey knew we would find you but I didn't think we would. You are our hope. Everyone's hope. I wish I had known we would find you.**

CULLEN: **Why?** *(She doesn't answer. He looks to AUDREY.)* **What?**

KATE: **You...didn't come last spring — the time when we were to marry. I...decided to marry someone else.**

CULLEN: But you said we were given to each other.

KATE: But you didn't come.

SLOAN: But she still should have waited.

CULLEN: *(To AUDREY)* **Have you married someone else?**

AUDREY: I waited.

CULLEN: Why didn't you?

KATE: **We didn't know where you were. We even thought Mora found you and had you hidden somewhere. And there was someone I had grown up with, someone I've always cared for —**

CULLEN: *(Charging SLOAN)* **You?**

SLOAN: No, no. He's a humble tailor, who she hasn't married, yet.

KATE: But I've given my promise.

CULLEN: But now that you found me?

KATE: I'm sorry.

CULLEN: Then why are you here?

KATE: To give up my right to the bracelet. Audrey should wear it.

DOREEN: No.

CULLEN: What? What bracelet?

AUDREY: They don't know anything.

KATE: *(To DOREEN)* You didn't tell them about us? *(To CULLEN)* You didn't know I was waiting for you?

CULLEN: If I had known you were waiting for me...No!

ROBIN: Mother didn't want us to know.

AUDREY: The bracelet was created so the Wizard couldn't use the crystal against his wife.

SLOAN: All of Errigal needs that bracelet, if She's to heal.

AUDREY: Whoever wears it is protected from the power of the crystal. It's our only weapon against Mora. Your mother has it.

DOREEN: Ross took it before we sailed.

KATE: Doreen, please.

ROBIN: Mother, where is it?

DOREEN: He took it...If I had it I would give it to her. He took it.

SLOAN: Then Mora may have it after all.

AUDREY: Or Ross.

CULLEN: Damn! Why didn't you wait? Why didn't I know about you?! I should have known! Damn! Now I've lost you, too. I dreamt about you! You'd stand at the seashore —

KATE: Every day.

CULLEN: Singing — *(Just now fully admitting this)* Calling me back! That's what you were singing. You were calling me back.

KATE: I knew you heard me, but you didn't come.

CULLEN: I didn't know what I was dreaming. *(To DOREEN)* How was I to know? No one is here to teach us! Damn Father for leaving us! Damn the Elders of Errigal for not finding us and teaching us!

SLOAN: We searched since the day you sailed.

CULLEN: Damn you, Mother, for not telling us!

DOREEN: *(She slaps him.)* Cullen.

CULLEN: You lied to us!

DOREEN: Cullen, Cullen, what if I had told you? The pull of the crystal was enough but if you knew Kate and Audrey were waiting for you — I was protecting you.

CULLEN: You were stealing from me.

KATE: It was their right to know. It was our right that they knew. We waited for them.

DOREEN: How can you understand? You're a child yourself. You can't understand — not until you have children of your own. It hurt me to mislead them — to lie to them —even for their own safety. But I would still, if you hadn't come.

AUDREY: Do you think you could hide forever? They would have come to Errigal if I hadn't found them. The call to the crystal is in their bones. They'll go mad without it, just like their father.

ROBIN: My father?

DOREEN: What do you mean?

ROBIN: He's mad?

KATE: She's chained him in a cavern.

SLOAN: Since the day you sailed.

DOREEN: What?

ROBIN: I knew it was him.

AUDREY: He's dying. Mora needs one of you to take his place.

ROBIN: Needs us? *(To DOREEN)* But you said she wants to kill us.

KATE: The crystal's power must be channeled through you or she can't use it.

AUDREY: She wants to imprison one of you like your father. And kill the other.

KATE: That's what she'll do, if you let her.

DOREEN: *(To herself)* Imprisoned...he must have turned on her.

CULLEN: We sail today, Robin.

DOREEN: No, tonight; there's another island —

CULLEN: For Errigal. To take our crystal.

DOREEN: Didn't you hear what we said? She'll kill one of you and imprison the other.

CULLEN: It doesn't matter.

DOREEN: *(To ROBIN)* Talk to him. You understand more than he does.

CULLEN: I understand! I understand about you, about this father, and this girl.

DOREEN: If you do somehow take the crystal — and she won't let you near it — you have no experience. Your father, with all his knowledge, lost his mind to her. What do you think you can do?

AUDREY: What they have to, to take their inheritance.

DOREEN: What do you know? I gave up everything to come here and raise my sons in safety, and I've raised them well. Look at them. I won't let you and your ambitions — even your rights by birth — or their rights by birth — deliver them

197

to Mora.

CULLEN: Let's get what we need and sail.

DOREEN: No, no, no, no, no. *(As he starts off, DOREEN takes hold of CULLEN's arm. He pushes her violently away.)*

CULLEN: Let me go!

SLOAN: We have a cabin ready.

DOREEN: One of you go to Errigal. Let me take the other to another place. If she only has one, she won't kill you.

CULLEN: Which one sails to Errigal and which one goes with you, Mother? *(Silence)* You decide, Mother. Who goes to Errigal, who sails with you? *(Silence)*

DOREEN: Only one of you may hold the crystal. Just as there's only one bracelet, there's only one Wizard.

AUDREY: What I understand is one twin must give it to the other.

ROBIN: One...

CULLEN: Only one...

DOREEN: So one comes with me. *(Silence)*

CULLEN: Who stays with you, Mother? Who goes to Errigal? *(Silence. She looks at ROBIN.)*

AUDREY: *(To ROBIN)* If you stay, I won't stay with you. I didn't risk sailing here, my crew didn't risk their lives, so you could run away.

CULLEN: Which one, Mother? *(Silence. DOREEN stays focused on ROBIN.)*

ROBIN: I'm going to Errigal.

DOREEN: *Nooo!*

ROBIN: *(To CULLEN)* Someone has to protect you. I hear Mora's beautiful.

DOREEN: No, no, Robin —

CULLEN: Let's go.

DOREEN: *(Pulling ROBIN aside)* Let him go. Come with me. I know a perfect place — if you go I won't go with you.

ROBIN: You know you will.

DOREEN: I won't.

ROBIN: *(Directly to DOREEN)* Come on, we're going home. *(The directness seems to penetrate her panic.)* I have to go. *(She nods, lowers her head.)* To Errigal!

CULLEN: *(As they exit)* Do you know where she keeps our father?

AUDREY: We think inside a cavern, but no one has dared go into it...

DOREEN: *(All exit but DOREEN. She sings, as lights dim.)*
He is strong,
An oak in the wood.
And he is young,
A mother's son.

He is a heart,
A kiss for him. *(Speaks.)*
A kiss for him.
(End Act I, Scene 1)

ACT I
Scene 2

(Aboard ship, on deck. Midnight. Quiet sounds of the wind and the ship's wake. AUDREY runs on dressed in a white nightgown. She twirls in the sea breeze, charged with excitement.)

AUDREY: Robin. *(She fairly dances to the rail, looks out to sea.)*
Soon... *(A despondent KATE enters; AUDREY sees her, quietly backs into the shadows, watches her, unseen.)*

KATE: *(Looking out to sea, she sings.)*
When love takes its own sweet time
They say it lasts forever.
But can I wait even one more day?
I fear my answer's never.

Sometimes I feel I know you well.
Sometimes you are a stranger.
In my dreams I hold you safe
Though your days are filled with danger. *(AUDREY exits.)*

So if you sail the ocean
Or if you walk the land,
I'll give you my devotion.
Come and take my hand.

And when at last we're hand in hand —
(ROBIN staggers on, disturbed and confused, carrying his sword.)

ROBIN: Mora! *(This startles KATE. ROBIN runs around ship.)* **Mora!**
Here I am! Mora!
KATE: Robin?
ROBIN: You! *(Running to her, pointing sword at her)* **Who are you?**
KATE: Kate. Kate. You know who I am.
ROBIN: What are you singing?
KATE: It's a song I —
ROBIN: What is that song?
KATE: A song I used to sing waiting for Cullen.
ROBIN: Why are you on deck?
KATE: I couldn't sleep. And we're so close to Errigal, I came up
to see if I could see the fires. Has something —
ROBIN: *(Calling)* **Cullen!**

KATE: What's happened?

ROBIN: Did you see her?

KATE: Who?

ROBIN: In white; all in white — Mora!

CULLEN: *(Stumbling on deck, half-dressed, half-asleep, carrying sword, pulling up his trousers)* **What?**

ROBIN: Did you see her?

CULLEN: Who?

ROBIN: She was in our cabin.

CULLEN: Kate?

KATE: No.

CULLEN: *(To KATE)* **Were you looking for me?**

KATE: Not me.

CULLEN: And what did you want?

KATE: I wasn't in your cabin!

ROBIN: Could you smell her? Like dead, like she was dead — *(AUDREY enters; ROBIN raises his sword when he sees her.)* **There!**

AUDREY: Robin?

ROBIN: Who are you?

AUDREY: What?

ROBIN: Who are you?

CULLEN: It's Audrey. You see? Audrey.

ROBIN: She was in our cabin. Mora was in our cabin.

CULLEN: And she touched you.

ROBIN: On my shoulder and I couldn't breathe.

CULLEN: Then she floated out the window.

ROBIN: I yelled at her, her face went green, her eyes turned to fire and she floated out the window.

AUDREY: What?

ROBIN: *(To CULLEN)* **You saw her.**

CULLEN: You were dreaming.

ROBIN: No, I saw her, I felt her — and so did you — you saw her float out the window.

CULLEN: Every night, I'm resting, I'm asleep, I'm happy, and I'm dreaming, too, good dreams, and you jump up and ask me awful questions I can't answer like: "Whose bones are those in my bed and what's that song they're singing?" And: "Is our father a giant fish?"

ROBIN: I didn't ask you those questions. You were dreaming.

CULLEN: I was not. I know, because you were there and I'd never dream about you. And then you yell at me: "Cullen! Mora's here. She's floating above my bed. Stop her, she's floating out the window!" And you're sitting up, staring at me like *(He shows how)* **and you're not breathing, your eyes fall out of your head — you're dreaming, Robin, wake up!**

200

KATE: Walk with me. *(KATE pulls CULLEN; he goes with her.)*
CULLEN: He's killing me. No one cares. Who are you? *(They move to the other railing.)*
ROBIN: She was here.
AUDREY: Then where is she?
ROBIN: She was here.
AUDREY: What did she want?
ROBIN: The crystal...me...everything. She touched me and I couldn't breathe.

CULLEN: I was dreaming about you. We were — ha! — and we were very happy about it until Robin woke me up. *(Back to ROBIN)* **And *there* was the nightmare! "She's floating above our bed!"**

AUDREY: Robin... *(She strokes his forehead; he hits her hand away.)* **You're fevered.** *(She reaches out again.)*
ROBIN: *(Again slapping her hand away)* **What do you want?**
AUDREY: Robin? *(She reaches out again.)*
ROBIN: *(This time he grabs her wrist, pushes it away.)* **Leave me alone.**
AUDREY: Here... *(She persists, wipes his brow with her gown. He backs away from her.)*
ROBIN: What do you want?
AUDREY: Come here. Let me...
ROBIN: What? *(She moves to him, kisses him softly on the cheek.)*
AUDREY: Let me...take care of you. Robin, please...it's Audrey. I'm not going to hurt you.
ROBIN: I won't let you hurt me.
AUDREY: It's all right. *(She kisses his eyes.)* **Let me take care of you.** *(She carefully tries to take his sword.)* **You don't need this.** *(He jerks it away. Again she gently takes hold of hilt.)* **Let me have this.** *(She pulls the hand that holds the sword to her mouth, kisses it. He lets sword go. She puts it down. Again she touches his face.)* **You're burning up.** *(She lifts his shirt to take it off; he resists.)* **Help me. The breeze will cool you.** *(He allows her to take his shirt off.)* **You're covered with sweat.** *(She wipes his forehead with it, then his chest, then she kisses his chest.)* **Feel the breeze? The night-sea cools the air. And the moon — she's looking right at you. She's shining on you. She sees how young and beautiful you are.** *(She drops shirt, embraces him. He finally begins to respond.)* **Robin, I'm here.** *(He finally embraces her.)*
ROBIN: Audrey. *(He kisses her passionately.)* **I don't understand this.**
AUDREY: It's all right.
ROBIN: I thought she was here — in white — like you — all in

white.

AUDREY: Rest, now.

ROBIN: She'll kill me.

AUDREY: Nothing will hurt you. No one will come. They're dreams. Dreams can't hurt you.

ROBIN: I can't tell the difference, anymore.

AUDREY: I can.

ROBIN: I'm not going to be able to help Cullen.

AUDREY: What do you mean?

ROBIN: I can't think; I know I'll do something wrong and hurt him, too. I need to go back to Merinnis.

AUDREY: What?

ROBIN: It's his crystal more than mine. I've always felt that.

AUDREY: You're wrong. You have a light in you. I don't think you can see it. It's what Errigal needs; it's what I want. And it's strong. Stronger than her.

ROBIN: If only one of us can have the crystal, it will go to Cullen. Will you sail back to Merinnis with me?

AUDREY: No.

ROBIN: That's the only way everything will be all right.

AUDREY: I can't believe in that. I believe in you. I believe in you, Robin. And if you go back, I won't go with you. *(She moves from him, looks out to sea.)*

CULLEN: We were standing in the sea — this calm sea — under the moon — this beautiful moon — and you looked like you look now only...better. Ha!

KATE: In your dream.

CULLEN: And you said: "That humble tailor has never kissed me like that. Kiss me again or I'll die."

KATE: I said that?

CULLEN: Yes, to me. You said that to me. Don't you remember?

KATE: Or did I say: *(Dramatically)* "That humble tailor has never kissed me like that. Kiss me again or I'll die."

CULLEN: Oh. Oh, yes; yes, that's it. And yes, I will. *(He leans to kiss her. She pulls back playfully. He goes to embrace her, she grabs his sword, pulls it. He doesn't let go. She pulls it again; he holds on. She stomps his foot, pulls sword out of his hand.)*

KATE: *(Pointing sword at him)* Stay where you are.

CULLEN: Oh, help, Robin, oh, save me.

KATE: It's too late.

CULLEN: I see your strategy.

KATE: You do?

CULLEN: "I'll tell him I'm to marry someone else." Yes?

KATE: Yes?

CULLEN: Knowing I can't have you, making me want you

because I can't have you, singing those songs at night only
I can hear, planting dreams in my head, dreams about you
only better. You won't fool me.

KATE: I already have.

CULLEN: You won't fool me...kiss me you might. *(He knocks sword
from her hand, goes for her. She screams and runs to AUDREY.)*

KATE: Audrey! Audrey!

AUDREY: What?

KATE: Cullen had this terrible dream and now he — *(CULLEN,
who is crawling toward them, roars. KATE screams. KATE puts
ROBIN and AUDREY between herself and CULLEN.)*

CULLEN: Come here, Lovely One.

KATE: Never! Pig! *(CULLEN grunts and snorts over AUDREY and
ROBIN and, once there, crawls over them to get to KATE.)*

CULLEN: A kiss. Save me with a kiss.

AUDREY: Cullen, what are you doing?

ROBIN: Get off me.

KATE: Keep him away. He's a monster. *(She hides.)*

CULLEN: Ah, she loves me. Do you hear?

ROBIN: *(He wrestles CULLEN off him.)* Is no one safe from you?
(He pushes CULLEN.)

CULLEN: Nothing can keep her from me. *(He picks ROBIN up,
turns him upside-down, lets him slowly fall headfirst.)*

ROBIN: Cullen...Cullen!

CULLEN: Little snowflake falls slowly from the sky and when
he hits the ground — *(CULLEN lets him fall, makes an explo-
sive noise. ROBIN lands, sprawling over the deck.)* Kate? *(She
stays hidden. He stalks her.)* My love. My dream.

KATE: I'm sleeping in my cabin...and the door is bolted. *(He
moves closer; she screams and runs. He catches her, picks her
up, swings her around, carefully places her down. He picks up
sword, slams it on the railing.)*

CULLEN: *Errigal, I am your Wizard! I am the inheritor of the
crystal!* I will never go back to that island. To that black
dungeon. I wouldn't go back if you begged me to live there
with you.

KATE: Cullen, I want you to know, even though I —

CULLEN: What are you saying?

KATE: I want you to know —

CULLEN: She's begging! She's begging me! "Pleeease, Cullen,
pleeease forget the crystal, let Robin have it, sail back to
Merinnis and live with me forever."

KATE: I am not.

CULLEN: "Save me from the humble tailor, that snorting, root-
ing hog I promised I'd marry."

KATE: You are a pig! *(She swats him.)*

CULLEN: Can I refuse her? Could any man with heart and blood refuse her? Yes! Get off your knees, woman. I won't go back. I'll never go back! *(Short silence)* Kiss me I might.

ROBIN: I'll go on to Errigal...

CULLEN: I said kiss me I might. *(KATE stands looking at him in painful resignation.)*

ROBIN: I'll go on if you stay with me; close, no matter what happens.
AUDREY: You know I will. Always. Right here with you. I need you. *(They embrace.)*

KATE: *(Seriously)* That humble tailor's never kissed me like that. Kiss me again or I'll die. *(He moves to her, kisses her. Afterwards, he throws his hands in the air, walks away confused.)*
ROBIN: *(Seeing something dead ahead)* Errigal. *(He takes AUDREY's hand, runs to the foredeck.)* Errigal! *(CULLEN and KATE join ROBIN and AUDREY.)*
KATE: There it is. *(KATE takes CULLEN by the shoulder. He peels her off him, slowly pushes her away, then turns toward Errigal. Slow dim out begins. A light flashes, with the sound of a sudden rush of wind. It stuns ROBIN and CULLEN.)*
KATE: What was that?
ROBIN: Did you feel it, Cullen?
CULLEN: *(Pleasantly stunned)* What was that? Ho...
AUDREY: The crystal.
ROBIN: A greeting.
AUDREY: From who? *(Silence)*
ROBIN: She was here. *(Dim out. End of Act I, Scene 2.)*

ACT II
Scene 1

(The next morning on the shore of Errigal. Sounds of waves and sea birds. ROBIN, AUDREY, CULLEN, SLOAN, and KATE enter.)
AUDREY: Where is everyone? This time of the day — no one swimming, no children, no boats, no fishermen.
KATE: Where's Mora?
ROBIN: She knew we were coming. She knows we've landed. She could have met us at the anchorage.
SLOAN: She's got something in her darkened mind.
CULLEN: I'd feel better if your ship's crew were with us.
AUDREY: They took a great risk in sailing to Merinnis. They can't fight the crystal. This is yours to do.

KATE: I don't know why she's letting you near the crystal. The closer you are the more power you'll have.

CULLEN: But we don't know how to use it.

SLOAN: If we had the bracelet... *(To CULLEN)* If you were wearing it, you could walk right up to Mora and she couldn't do anything to stop you.

ROBIN: We should find Father; he could tell us what to do.

KATE: He may also know where the bracelet is.

AUDREY: The entrance to the cavern is in the fortress. I don't think Mora will let us —

KATE: There's also an entrance near the beach.

AUDREY: There is?

KATE: Yes.

AUDREY: I've never heard of it.

KATE: Everyone knows about it.

SLOAN: You can get through to Ross?

KATE: Yes.

ROBIN: Let's use that entrance.

AUDREY: Mora knows you'd go to your father first. It would be a perfect place to take you.

SLOAN: Once we were inside she could seal the doorways or flood the cavern with her men.

ROBIN: What else can we do? We have to talk to him.

KATE: This way. *(CULLEN doesn't move.)* This way. *(They exit. End of Act II, Scene 1.)*

ACT II
Scene 2

(A large cavern, dimly lit. ROSS, dirtier, more tattered, much less rational than in ROBIN's dream, is chained at the wrists to the cavern wall. The chains reach about ten or twelve feet. The tunnel into the cavern is blocked by a large, reinforced door with a two-foot square barred window in it. If no walls are used, ROSS could be chained to a large rock or group of rocks, the walls of the cavern being suggested by lighting.)

ROSS: *(Pacing erratically)* **Do I think they are here? They are here, I think.** *(Short silence)* **No one? No one, I thought before. They were here, before and no one; more time and no one.** *(He feels his robe.)* **Not dressed to see them.**

Welladay!
Every son outgrows his play.

I have a son. I remember, he's like no other boy...but one. And that's my secret. There may be two. *(He laughs to him-*

205

self.) **They are oaks; fish; great cats; clear jewels; they're light, they shine; they're old, very old young men now, with eyes and hands. Eyes of the dead. Their dead eyes see their time. I'll sit and wait.** *(He sits, waits in silence.)* **They're here.** *(Silence)* **What am I doing?...I'm waiting. Yes, I forgot. No, I didn't forget; if I could forget I'd die happy. I was seeing a girl. She came floating through a wall. I could see her hair and her bare feet. Her arm was a sword.** *(Suddenly, very sadly)* **They'll see me here. What will they do? They'll want to stake my head in the marketplace. Too much to forgive.** *(We hear them coming. Whispered)* **No, no, no, no, I waited too long. They found me.** *(Someone tries the door, then pushes on it, then kicks it. Silence. There is a thud against door. Then the sound of a sword hacking the door. Then two swords. The hacking stops. The door is heaved open.)*

CULLEN: *(CULLEN raises sword, comes forward, followed by ROBIN, KATE, SLOAN and AUDREY.)* **Someone should stay by the door.**

AUDREY: **I will.**

KATE: **Look at this place. Who could live here? There.** *(Points to ROSS.)*

CULLEN: **Ross?** *(No answer.)* **Is it him?**

SLOAN: **What she's left for you.**

CULLEN: **Robin, is it him — from your dream?**

ROBIN: **I think...yes, blind, you see?**

CULLEN: **Can this thing be our father?**

ROSS: **Who are you?**

CULLEN: **Cullen.**

ROBIN: *(ROBIN moves to him, reaches out, touches him.)* **And Robin.** *(ROSS shudders.)* **It's him.**

ROSS: **Both are here. Both. Here I am.** *(Firmly)* **Here I am.** *(Silence, as ROSS waits for a response.)* **What are you doing?**

CULLEN: **What?**

ROSS: **Why are you here?**

ROBIN: **We need your help.**

ROSS: *(Astonished)* **My help? You need my help?**

ROBIN: **Father.** *(He embraces ROSS.)*

ROSS: **My help? Oh, I — You both need my help? Robin.** *(To CULLEN)* **And you. My help. What do you know?**

ROBIN: **Nothing.**

CULLEN: **We don't know anything. What should we do?**

ROSS: *(To himself)* **What should we do?**

Welladay
Every son outgrows his play.

We will do such things. You will do, you will be able, I remember, to shine! But a girl. I saw a girl, with hair.

AUDREY: *(Taking his hand)* **Audrey. I'm honored to meet you. And I thank you for choosing me at my birth.**

ROSS: I remember. **And your father, he was — we were — in the time when we first knew each other —**

AUDREY: **He's never lost faith in you. He sends you his love and respect.**

ROSS: **Oh. He's more than my sons, I know. My sons are sons of — My sons are raised in the — somewhere, I don't know, but they say they need my help.**

SLOAN: **You see how Errigal lives.**

CULLEN: **Where is the bracelet?**

ROSS: **The bracelet is for her, but the — I don't know — the world is chained in a hole and mumbling, just words, mumbling, and when I can't know my sons...**

KATE: **I'm Kate.**

ROSS: **For Cullen.**

KATE: **You remember! The bracelet is for Audrey.**

ROSS: **But you — there were two, and —**

KATE: **When your sons didn't return for the wedding day, I chose someone else. Audrey will make a fine member of the New Council. Before your mother died, Audrey lived with her for three months and she taught Audrey. Could you give her the bracelet now, before the ceremony?**

SLOAN: **It's our only weapon against Mora.**

ROSS: **Your mother?**

CULLEN: **She wouldn't come.**

ROSS: **She was always in herself, not to believe me. And I see; I know what she means. There is too much to forgive.**

SLOAN: **Sir, the bracelet could keep the witch off your sons' backs while they restore the crystal to your house.**

ROSS: **I don't know. The bracelet? I don't know.**

CULLEN: **We're leaving here.**

ROBIN: **Lay the chain across the rock.**

CULLEN: **You'll never break through.**

ROSS: **No.** *(He holds out his hands, one to each of them.)* **Here.** *(They each take a hand.)* **Through you. The crystal, through you. Say this.**

ALL THREE: **Olnat ebrum cala soln.** *(A brilliant light flashes, the chain falls away. SLOAN cheers. Music.)*

ROSS: **Yes, yes, yes, gone, all gone, free and gone.**

ROBIN: *(Stunned)* **Cullen...**

CULLEN: *(Equally exhilarated)* **What was that?** *(He laughs.)*

KATE: **You cast!**

CULLEN: **Let's do it again.**

ROBIN: What was it we said?
CULLEN: How did we know what to say?
SLOAN: You're wizards.
ROBIN: And the chain broke!
CULLEN: Let's do it again!
SLOAN: We should proceed, gentlemen. Let's take him into the sun.
ROSS: Into the sun! Into the sky!
CULLEN: Ah, yes, we should go.
ROSS: *(As ROBIN and CULLEN begin to lead him out)* **"Welladay!"** My sons. My sons. *(They exit. End of Act II, Scene 2.)*

ACT II
Scene 3

(Late evening on the beach. CULLEN enters, followed by AUDREY, then ROBIN leading ROSS, then KATE and SLOAN.)
ROSS: No, no, no. No further.
ROBIN: He needs to rest.
CULLEN: Again?
ROSS: Yes, rest.
CULLEN: On the beach?
SLOAN: We can see anyone coming.
CULLEN: It'll be dark soon.
ROSS: She knows where we are.
ROBIN: We may as well stop here. *(ROBIN and AUDREY help ROSS sit on a rock.)*
CULLEN: What is she waiting for?
KATE: *(Shaking her head)* What do you think, Audrey?
AUDREY: Some reason known only to her.
CULLEN: She let us walk in and take him.
ROSS: What can we do to her?
AUDREY: The crystal is yours.
CULLEN: *(Increasingly frustrated)* We don't know how to use it!
ROBIN: You understood it and still she took it from you. What are we supposed to do? *(No answer)*
CULLEN: What are we supposed to do?
SLOAN: Can you help them, Ross?
ROSS: *(Sings.)*
A song of the bird of the highland, sings,
'Tis spring in lowland country,
Dead is my last year's lonely love,
Sing hi and a ho to your springtime maid.
(He smiles at AUDREY and KATE.) Hi and a ho.
KATE & AUDREY: Hi and a hey.
ROBIN: You made sense in my dreams; you called us here. You

208

must know something. Why is she waiting?

CULLEN: What were those words? Do they just come to us?

ROBIN: Are there books?

CULLEN: How much power do we have?

ROBIN: What do we do when we find the crystal?

CULLEN: How do we take it back?

ROBIN: How much more can you do?

CULLEN: What is she afraid of?

ROSS: Questions, good questions.

ROBIN: How can we take it?! *(Silence)*

CULLEN: Why is she waiting?

ROBIN: Answer!

AUDREY: Robin —

ROBIN: No.

ROBIN & CULLEN: You answer.

ROBIN: Now. I've waited seventeen years for answers from you.

KATE: And he's been chained for seventeen years waiting for you.

ROSS: Answer what?

CULLEN: You gave it away.

ROBIN: You would have given us to her.

CULLEN: You stole from us!

ROBIN: Why?

CULLEN: Talk to us!

ROBIN: You talk!

KATE: Maybe he would if you acted like his sons.

CULLEN: Why are you still alive; that's what I don't understand.

KATE: Cullen —

ROSS: *(To KATE)* No —

CULLEN: If she couldn't use the crystal without you, why are you still alive? Maybe if you had died she would have lost power and some good people like Sloan here would have taken this land back. Then, when we came for the crystal — and you knew we would — she wouldn't be here; it would be waiting for us. So you tell me, old man, why you're still alive. And don't you tell me it's for us. Don't you tell me you've done anything for us.

ROSS: For you.

CULLEN: God, keep me from him, Robin! I'll kill him!

KATE: It would have been easier to die.

ROBIN: For us? Where were you the last seventeen years? You can't help us, even now. You babbling old fool. You're too...*blind.* You killed us all. You did. You betrayed and killed us all. If you're no better than this why did you have children?

ROSS: For you.

ROBIN: *(He laughs.)* "For you." Oh, I am grateful, Father. That answers all my questions. "For you" gives me hope. "For you" will make all my dreams come true.

ROSS: *(Proudly)*
He is strong,
An oak in the wood
He is young
A father's son.

A kiss for him. *(Silence)*

Books...old books, wizard books. All burned.

KATE: Yes, remember? She burned them in the marketplace.

AUDREY: They burned for weeks. The fire was gold.

ROSS: But wizards, you're both wizards; you learn, from the air, the sun, you see the sun in the air; from the air you can see the old words, sometimes, and pictures, pictures that are answers to questions, and faces of the old men, eyes, hands, winking, pointing the way.

CULLEN: What's he babbling about?

ROBIN: I see pieces of things, in the air, maybe words or pictures, but I can't understand them.

KATE: You see? Listen to him.

CULLEN: *(To ROSS)* If we join together, like we did when we broke the chain, can we stand against her?

ROSS: You could, if you knew the old words, you could cast. Some. But the crystal is hers.

SLOAN: If they could take it, could you use it against her? *(ROSS indicates no.)*

ROBIN: It would still be yours, wouldn't it?

ROSS: I gave it away. And, my time with the crystal is almost over.

AUDREY: But she's still channeling it through you.

ROSS: You're of age, now. The crystal's turning to you. If you free it, it will look to you, not me.

ROBIN: There must be something about the crystal; some of those words —

CULLEN: — a weapon against her —

ROSS: She's made the crystal's energy hers. Without the crystal, she dies, now. And now it's turning. All these wizards around, drawing the crystal out of her; she's in pain; confused. She needs you to give it to her, then it'll stop fighting her.

CULLEN: But what can we do?

ROSS: Yes, what do we do?

Luck has gone, I walk with fate
Toward the dark house, where she waits.

Hey and a ho.
KATE: Hi and a hey.

CULLEN: **He can't help us. Let's go.** *(The sun is beginning to set; the scene begins to slowly darken.)*
ROBIN: **Where?**
CULLEN: **To the fortress?**
ROSS: *(Tiredly)* **Let me stay in the air.**
AUDREY: **He's too tired.**
CULLEN: **Then leave him.**
ROBIN: **I can't leave him.**
CULLEN: **Then stay with him.**
ROBIN: **We shouldn't separate.**
CULLEN: **Then what'll we do?!**
ROBIN: **Wait.**
CULLEN: **More waiting!** *(In ROSS' face)* **Where is that bracelet?!** *(He stomps away, followed by KATE. AUDREY moves to ROBIN. SLOAN stays near ROSS. The following conversations cannot be heard by the others.)*
KATE: **I think he's telling you more than you hear.**
CULLEN: **He's telling us nothing.**
KATE: **He can help you.**
CULLEN: **He can't. You can't. I should go on alone. Then if something happens to me, she can't hurt Robin. I should go on alone, like I always do.**

SLOAN: **They're young. And confused. That island was a wild place. I apologize for them. And for Errigal, who couldn't find them sooner.**
ROSS: **We do something then everything is wrong forever.**
SLOAN: **Not forever. No.**
ROSS: **Not forever.**

ROBIN: **The moon is up. Night's coming. All is well.** *(He turns to AUDREY. He suddenly embraces her.)* **I don't know what I'd do if you weren't here. I feel like you've always been with me.**
AUDREY: **I have.**
ROBIN: **If you know what I should do, tell me.**
AUDREY: **You're doing what you should do.**
ROBIN: **Am I?**
AUDREY: **Exactly what you should do.**

SLOAN: **Is there anything you can tell them about the bracelet?**
ROSS: **Nothing that would help them now.**

KATE: **Would you trust me...if I could help you...but you had to**

trust me and not tell the others?
CULLEN: What do you know?
KATE: You are so angry.
CULLEN: What do you know?
KATE: I know your father could help you.
CULLEN: What are you saying?
KATE: I'm sorry. You have every right to be angry. But you're not alone. Robin's here. Your father. I'm here. I could love you...very well. *(He turns, thinking he's heard something Off-stage, past ROSS.)*
ROBIN & CULLEN: *(Drawing)* **What was that?**
SLOAN: *(Drawing)* **What?**
ROBIN: *(He stares into the darkening seaside.)* **Audrey, did you hear that?**
CULLEN: I did.
AUDREY: Over there.
SLOAN: What did it sound like? *(There is an Off-stage rustle.)*
ROBIN: There. I'm going to see what it is. *(Pause. He doesn't move.)*
ROSS: "I'm going to see what it is." *(No one moves; silence.)* **I forgot; I'm blind.**
ROBIN: What was it?
ROSS: Oh, you've returned. What did you see?
ROBIN: What was it?
ROSS: You want me to go look? *(SLOAN laughs.)*
CULLEN: I'll look.
KATE: No. *(She holds on to him; CULLEN looks questioningly at her.)*
ROSS: Does anyone...have anything to eat?
ROBIN: What?
ROSS: A nightbird flew out of the grass. Do either of you have anything to eat?
CULLEN: A nightbird... *(ROBIN stands searching the dark. CULLEN crosses past KATE, takes her hand, walks her away from the others. Again, the conversations are inaudible to the others.)*
SLOAN: Still no bracelet, my lady.
AUDREY: I think Ross knows something.
SLOAN: How much farther do we dare go without it?

CULLEN: What do you know?
KATE: You cannot tell the others.
CULLEN: Tell them what?
KATE: I may know where the bracelet is. But you have to trust if I do, it will appear when you need it.
CULLEN: I need it now.
KATE: Your not having it may be what's protecting you. It may be why she's waiting. She's waiting for the bracelet to appear.
CULLEN: Give it to me now. No one will take it from me. *(She*

indicates no.) **You think I won't understand what to do?**
KATE: **That's not why I can't tell you.**
CULLEN: **Then why? And why can't they know? Why can't Robin know?**
KATE: **You have to trust I have reasons for what I'm doing. You see? You're not alone. I want you to know you're not alone.** *(She kisses him.)*
CULLEN: **Are you promised to someone?**
KATE: **Yes, but...**
CULLEN: **What? What is this?**
KATE: **You'll have to wait.**
CULLEN: **You tell me everything, now, or I tell them you have the bracelet.**
KATE: **If you tell them now, you may never get it.** *(Stymied, CULLEN moves away in frustration.)*

(From his pouch ROBIN takes out a small piece of bread, puts it in ROSS' hand; he eats.)
ROBIN: **It's old.**
ROSS: **It's good.**
ROBIN: **Your wife made it.** *(ROSS eats it hurriedly.)* **Eat that slow-ly. It's all the bread I have.**
ROSS: **Anything else?**
ROBIN: **Finish that first. Then if you're still hungry —**
ROSS: *(Stuffing all the bread into his mouth)* **Anything else?**
ROBIN: **My last...** *(ROBIN takes out a fig.)* **If you don't like this, I want it myself. It's my last —**
ROSS: *(Taking it)* **Fig! A fig!** *(He takes it, bites into it, smiles at ROBIN.)* **I love figs.**
ROBIN: **So do I.**
ROSS: *(Holding what's left out)* **Would you like a fig?** *(ROBIN starts to take it.)* **Yes, I would. Thank you.** *(ROSS puts the rest in his mouth.)* **The fig is good.**
ROBIN: *(ROBIN watches him eat.)* **In my dreams you were taller. You were blind, but not...You were strong.**
ROSS: **I'm here.**
ROBIN: **I know. We're grateful you're here.**
ROSS: **Yes?**
ROBIN: **Yes. We're grateful.** *(Silence)*
ROSS: *(Holding out his hand)* **Another fig.**
ROBIN: **I gave you the last one.**
ROSS: **One more.**
ROBIN: **How did you know I had one more?**
ROSS: **You're my son.** *(ROBIN gets it out, hands it to him.)* **Ah. Last one.** *(Holding out fig)* **Would you like the last fig?** *(ROBIN hesitates in taking it. ROSS laughs.)* **Yes. Thank you.** *(He bites it.)*

The last fig is good.

ROBIN: Since I gave you my last fig —

ROSS: Last two figs.

ROBIN: Will you answer one question?

ROSS: One question.

ROBIN: You will?

ROSS: Yes.

ROBIN: What...is a woman?

ROSS: But not that question.

ROBIN: Liar! You said you'd answer one question. What kind of father are you? I gave you my last fig.

ROSS: Last two figs.

ROBIN: Last two figs! Two figs for one answer.

ROSS: You won't believe me.

ROBIN: I'll believe whatever you say.

ROSS: What is a woman? All men should know this. It'll help them as they walk happily through life to understand their confusion and misery. Here's the answer: You already know. *(Short silence)* I'm still hungry.

ROBIN: You're lucky you're still alive. Just a moment ago I thought I might get both my figs back. *(ROSS laughs.)* What a poor answer!

ROSS: Dangerous question. Someone may be listening.

ROBIN: Cullen would have at least said something disgusting. *(ROSS laughs again. ROBIN studies him.)* I thought I'd be more...but, I'm not like you.

ROSS: *(Amused)* "I'm not like you."

ROBIN: You're...I don't know.

ROSS: What?

ROBIN: Hurt. *(ROBIN takes ROSS' hand.)* I feel the crystal more when I touch you. You seem to glow.

ROSS: What color?

ROBIN: Gold. *(ROSS indicates ROBIN is correct.)* Feels strong ...You're...my father...you're my...father...You've always been my father. Ever since...I was, you've been my father.

ROSS: I became your father; I remember the day. Here, on the beach. Sun and wind and Doreen and...sand, sand everywhere. *(He laughs.)* And hair; her long *(He indicates very long)* hair, everywhere. She was your age, now.

ROBIN: Is that true? My age?

ROSS: Close.

ROBIN: She's a good mother. Your parents chose well.

ROSS: I...was not. I thought you may kill me. Maybe it would help you, I thought. But, angry. You just cursed me. I liked that. And when you gave me your last two figs...Maybe there isn't too much to forgive.

ROBIN: I don't know...Why did you want to give us to Mora?

ROSS: I didn't. When I finally understood her, I kept her from you until you sailed.

ROBIN: But I thought —

ROSS: When Mora found you'd left, she couldn't kill me. She took my eyes, one for each of you.

ROBIN: But Mother said —

ROSS: You know what's true. You're a wizard. You always know.

ROBIN: Do I?

ROSS: It's time.

ROBIN: For what? I can't — that's what we need. Cullen and I need time with you. You're not as crazy as before.

ROSS: *(ROSS struggles awkwardly to stand.)* I'm sorry.

ROBIN: Why? You're not leaving again. *(ROBIN embraces ROSS.)* You're not going again!

ROSS: I'm not going.

ROBIN: *(Holding him tight)* You're not going.

ROSS: No, not again. I'm here.

ROBIN: Help me. He's going to be hurt, I know he is. Tell me what to do.

ROSS: You know.

ROBIN: Where is the bracelet? Why is she waiting?

ROSS: You know.

ROBIN: What does she want?

ROSS: You know.

ROBIN: I don't know.

ROSS: You're a wizard; you know through the crystal. You hear her feelings. You feel her mind. *(He pauses a moment.)* You look into the night and ask about her. You ask because you know she's in there; she's calling you. And the voice is sweet. So you go into the night and she's all around you; she surrounds you with her sweet voice and her touch. You can smell her. You want her. You want to fall deep into her river, and forget everything. You want to die for her. The crystal shines a light — it shines through you, *you* shine, you are a jewel — you can see, if you want, if you have the eyes, if you have eyes of the dead, of the Dead Old Men. *You have* the eyes. You have the blood in your hands to act. You can see her. *(He pauses for just a moment.)* She knows where you are. She knows what you want. She knows what you fear. And you know.

ROBIN: She's waiting for us.

ROSS: Yes.

ROBIN: She wants the bracelet.

ROSS: Yes.

ROBIN: Who has it? You?

ROSS: Do I?

ROBIN: It's...she's...if I knew where she was maybe I... she's...here. She's here.

ROSS: She is?

ROBIN: She's right here.

ROSS: Yes.

ROBIN: Cullen! *(CULLEN draws. ROBIN looks around the dark beach. SLOAN rises, slowly draws. The women rise.)*

CULLEN: What?

ROBIN: She's here!

CULLEN: Where?

SLOAN: Did you see her?

ROBIN: No, but she's here.

KATE: Where?

CULLEN: How do you know?

ROBIN: She... *(A realization begins to clear in his mind. He slowly turns to AUDREY, then looks at KATE. He looks back and forth at them. He crosses to AUDREY, stares at her.)*

AUDREY: What did he say?

SLOAN: What's that thought, Robin? *(He crosses to KATE, stares at her.)*

KATE: Where is she?

ROBIN: *(He crosses back to ROSS.)* I can't see. I can't see. Cullen, come here. Everyone else, over there. Over there!

CULLEN: Go on. *(The others move far from ROSS and ROBIN, except for CULLEN who joins ROBIN.)* What's bitten you, brother?

ROBIN: *(To ROSS)* Which one?

ROSS: Yes, which one.

ROBIN: Mora's one of them.

CULLEN: You can't believe anything he says.

ROBIN: He didn't tell me. Remember that feeling in the cave after we cast? Feel it and ask yourself where she is. *(CULLEN turns to the others.)*

CULLEN: It's so vague.

ROBIN: I could feel her. Almost hear her thinking. But I got confused.

CULLEN: If it's one of them, it's Kate.

ROBIN: Why?

CULLEN: Audrey loves you.

ROBIN: Yes, she does.

CULLEN: She does.

ROBIN: She does.

CULLEN: But why would Mora —

ROBIN: Because she doesn't know where the bracelet is. She's waiting for us to find it for her.

CULLEN: Yes. Mora may have learned Audrey and Kate were sailing for us then made herself look like Kate and came

216

along. That's why Kate stays with me! So we find the
bracelet for her.
ROBIN: Then let's not find it until we're standing next to the
crystal.
CULLEN: Let's go.
ROBIN: *(To ROSS)* Can you come?
ROSS: Yes.
CULLEN: *(To the others)* We're going.
KATE: What was it?
CULLEN: Dreams. He thought he saw Mora lurking in his mind
again. *(He takes her hand, kisses it.)* I see you may have rea-
sons for what you're doing.
KATE: Did Ross say anything about the bracelet?
CULLEN: Not to me.
AUDREY: Robin?
ROBIN: *(Embracing her)* It was nothing. I got confused, again.
AUDREY: Did Ross tell you anything about the bracelet?
ROBIN: No.
SLOAN: And what strategy has this joining of wizards produced?
ROBIN: None.
KATE: Then where are we going?
ROBIN: To the fortress!
KATE: With what plan?
ROBIN: No plan!
CULLEN: Hey ho! We're ready! Who goes first? *(Placing them in
the correct order)* Kate.
KATE: Why?
ROBIN: Then Audrey.
CULLEN: Good plan.
ROBIN: Then... *(ROSS waves frantically)* Father.
ROSS: Yes! The babbling old father!
CULLEN: Then Sloan, the Gallant Courtier. Then Sir Snowflake,
The Wizard Fool.
ROBIN: And last, the hero of this strange and tragical tale,
Cullen —
CULLEN: The Wifeless Conqueror.
ROSS: *(Sadly)* Oh...
CULLEN: I should never have left Kelly, the wheelwright's
daughter.
ROBIN: She was only twelve.
CULLEN: I could have gathered firewood while I waited. *(They
laugh. ROSS laughs. Everyone turns to ROSS. He laughs.)*
ROSS: *(Sings.)*

We go to join the marriage feast
Come you, come all, to the table.

ROBIN: **Let's go, old man. Light our way.** *(ROBIN helps ROSS. As they exit.)*
ROSS: *(Sings.)*
Eat and marvel at the tales
And dance as long as you're able.
(ROSS and SLOAN whistle.)
ROSS & SLOAN: **Hey.** *(ROSS and SLOAN whistle, pause for response.)*
AUDREY & KATE: **Hey la.** *(ROSS and SLOAN continue whistling song. Dim out. End of Act II, Scene 3.)*

ACT II
Scene 4

(The top hall of the fortress. Very dark. Steps lead up into the large, irregularly shaped room. In the shadows we see the crystal, really a cluster of crystals, growing up out of the rock. It is about six to eight feet tall and uncut — that is, the terminals are irregularly shaped. KATE enters upstairs, followed by AUDREY, SLOAN, then ROBIN and ROSS and CULLEN. It's too dark for them to see.)

KATE: **I've never seen the fortress like this.**
SLOAN: **Completely deserted; all doors opened for us.**
AUDREY: **Are you sure this is the way?**
CULLEN: **Can you feel it, Robin?**
ROBIN: **I feel it.**
AUDREY: **Can you see?**
CULLEN: **No.**
ROBIN:
"Toward the dark house
Where she waits."

CULLEN: *(They are inching their way into room.)* **Do you know where we are, Ross?**
ROSS: **A room.**
CULLEN: **More wisdom.**
SLOAN: **You've been here before — all of you — just after you were born — for your marriage promise. We're in the ceremonial hall. You can smell the centuries of incense. No one has been in here since I was a child.**
ROSS: **Tulla soln.** *(The crystal glows, lighting the hall.)* **The crystal.**
KATE: **I can feel it.**
SLOAN: **Beautiful.**
CULLEN: **It's much larger...**
ROBIN: **Just as I saw it.**
SLOAN: **Just as I remember.** *(They go up to it, touch it.)*
ROBIN: **This is what I've been feeling.**
CULLEN: **It shines through me. Like I'm floating. Like I could**

shoot fire out of my hands.

SLOAN: Look at what she's done. The hall was filled with statues, urns of the old wine, rows of coffers with the bones of the Old Men. The dead walked in this room. But now...

ROBIN: The words are scattered. She's clouding the air.

KATE: Where is she?

SLOAN: Where are her men?

ROBIN: *(To ROSS)* What do we do?

ROSS: The crystal knows you're here. It'll help you, both of you. Find its voice; the old one, the new one, your new voice.

KATE: Do you understand?

ROSS: Don't fear the dead ones; let them stand in your bones. Give them your hands. They'll help you. See with your dead eyes so you'll understand her.

CULLEN: What?

SLOAN: Sounds like words from the old ceremonies.

CULLEN: Sounds like one of Robin's stupid dreams. Dead eyes, singing bones. *(To ROBIN)* I'm surprised you don't see Mora floating around somewhere.

ROBIN: *(Looking up)* No.

CULLEN: Is there anything we can *do*?

ROSS: Don't become distracted.

ROBIN: From what?

ROSS: You'll know what to do. You both know what to do. *(In a silence they all look at one another.)*

CULLEN: *(To ROBIN)* Do you know what to do?

ROBIN: No. You?

CULLEN: No.

SLOAN: Good.

ROSS: You both know what to do. *(Silence)*

SLOAN: Ah, to have that bracelet. *(Silence)*

ROBIN: One of us knows something. *(Silence)*

CULLEN: *(To KATE)* I want to know what you know.

KATE: Cullen —

AUDREY: You know something, Kate?

CULLEN: She may know where the bracelet is.

SLOAN: Then, lady, tell us.

KATE: I trust you and this is what you do?

CULLEN: Do you have it with you? Or is this another lie.

KATE: What are you talking about — lies? I'm trying to help you.

AUDREY: Then tell us if you know something.

CULLEN: You think I don't understand anything.

KATE: You think I'm Mora? Is that what you meant on the beach?

CULLEN: My mother said you wouldn't be what we expected.

KATE: You should know who I am; a wizard would know the difference between Mora and me.

CULLEN: *(Drawing)* **All we need is that bracelet and we win.** *(He takes hold of her arm, pulls her away from the crystal, holds sword to her.)* **You trust me now.**

KATE: **Trust you? There's always a sword in your hand.**

ROBIN: **Cullen —**

AUDREY: **Kate, where is it?**

CULLEN: *(He raises the sword.)* **Who are you?**

ROBIN: **No. She's not —**

KATE: **I'm not Mora! I'm your —** *(He prepares to swing; she cringes.)*

ROBIN: **No!** *(He pushes AUDREY away, prepares to swing at her. AUDREY gestures, with a sound, the crystal flashes brightly. ROSS, KATE, CULLEN and SLOAN float to the floor, unconscious. ROBIN is repelled and stunned by the flash.)*

AUDREY: **They're asleep. I wouldn't hurt them.**

ROBIN: *(He holds sword to her.)* **You...I knew...I don't know how long I knew...**

AUDREY: *(Moving to the tip of his sword)* **Oh, Robin, no, no, understand what's important, what's very important, what's worth everything else. You and I are the only ones who are able to understand.**

ROBIN: **I understand.**

AUDREY: **Then why are you sad?**

ROBIN: **You stole our inheritance, you blinded our father, you forced us to hide on that island.**

AUDREY: **Long ago, before I knew you. I haven't hurt you since, and wouldn't.**

ROBIN: **Where's Audrey?**

AUDREY: **Here. She's here. I'm here. And look at me.** *(She twirls in front of him.)* **We were given to each other, you know.**

ROBIN: **Where's Audrey?**

AUDREY: **I'm here.**

ROBIN: **Where is she?**

AUDREY: **Far away. She has no memory of you or Errigal or of who she was, but she's happy. I knew you didn't want me to hurt her.**

ROBIN: **Not hurt her? You stole everything from her. Like you cheated me of my father.**

AUDREY: **What he did he chose to do.**

ROBIN: **I trusted you, and I** *believed* **in you. I believed you when you said you believed in me.**

AUDREY: **I do.**

ROBIN: **No! Lies! You lied to me! You're lying now. You are a lie. You're not Audrey, we weren't promised to one another. I don't know who you are. I don't know you!** *(He swings sword at her, with a sound the crystal flashes, seemingly repelling the blow. He swings again and again, each time the*

220

crystal flashes and the blow is repelled.)

AUDREY: Robin...these last years, through the crystal, I'd go to you, sit with you on the ocean side, walk with you on the cliffs. I'd listen to you, feel what was in your heart and mind. There's a part of you who listened to me, who knows all about me. That part of you — deep inside — told me this *(Indicating herself)* is what you wanted. And so I came to you as Audrey.

ROBIN: *(He laughs.)* I never wanted this.

AUDREY: We planned this together, you and I.

ROBIN: I didn't want this!

AUDREY: Part of you understands, part of you remembers. Ask yourself if it's true. Ask, Robin: did we plan this together?

ROBIN: I wouldn't...

AUDREY: Yes?

ROBIN: *(As the realization begins to come to him)* But I...

AUDREY: You see?

ROBIN: I did? *(Admitting the truth)* I did.

AUDREY: Yes.

ROBIN: *(He drops his sword.)* What?

AUDREY: You're confused, aren't you? You're beginning to understand your world is much larger than you ever thought. And the crystal is...an incredible mystery.

ROBIN: *(To himself)* How could I not know?

AUDREY: Who knows all the thoughts and feelings that pass through us every day? And every night, dreaming. And how much we have to hide from ourselves about what we want. But it wasn't someone else, Robin, it was just another part of you.

ROBIN: *(To himself)* Why?

AUDREY: What haunts you, Robin? What hangs over you like a sad fate? "No matter what I do I'm going to die. I'm dead." You brought that fear to me because you know as long as I have the crystal, you won't die.

ROBIN: That's impossible.

AUDREY: You feel it's true, don't you? You know, with me, you won't get sick or lonely or lost, and you won't die. *(She laughs.)* Not even a wizard can make you that promise.

ROBIN: *(Hopefully)* Can you?

AUDREY: We can do anything! How old would you say I am, Robin? Look... *(She models for him.)* I'm older than your father. And I can stop you from aging. Or we can age until we're as old as you want. But I like you as you are now. You don't have to age a day ever again. And you won't die.

ROBIN: Not die... *(She moves to him. ROSS awakens, sits up.)*

AUDREY: But I need the crystal to do this with you. And the bracelet. **Will you talk to the others and find the bracelet? One of them must have it...Yes, say yes, just say yes. It's our time, now. I'll bring everything to you. Live with me forever, Robin.** *(She kisses him.)*

ROSS: *(Dramatically)* **"Live with me forever, Robin."** *(He kisses the air.)*

ROBIN: *(To ROSS)* **Is it all true?**

AUDREY: Yes.

ROBIN: *(To ROSS)* **Is it true?**

ROSS: May's the merriest month of all.

AUDREY: Yes! It's the merry month of May, old man. And we couldn't be merrier!

ROSS: *(Dancing. AUDREY claps, dances.)*
  The woodland harp plays all day long
  The tools lie rusting while the dancers whirl
  The young man whispers in a twirl
  A song — an old song of love —

AUDREY: Yes —

ROSS: Into the mouth of a girl.

AUDREY: Hello, Ross. *(ROSS gestures towards AUDREY, the crystal flashes, AUDREY reacts as if she were slapped. The others begin to awaken.)*

ROSS: She has hopes for you. Does she know you?

ROBIN: Oh, she does. She does.

CULLEN: What happened?

ROBIN: She's Audrey.

SLOAN: What?

CULLEN: Audrey? I don't believe it. Mother was right.

KATE: Poor Audrey. Where is she?

ROBIN: Far away. I don't think she's hurt.

CULLEN: *(CULLEN sees AUDREY, starts for her.)* **Robin —**

ROBIN: *(Holding him back)* **No; you can't hurt her with your sword and she will hurt you.**

CULLEN: Then what are we doing? *(They group opposite AUDREY.)*

ROBIN: She says one of us has the bracelet.

CULLEN: I hope she's right. *(SLOAN, ROSS, CULLEN and AUDREY look to KATE.)*

KATE: If I had it I still couldn't give it to you.

ROBIN: Ross? Do you have it?

ROSS: Now that you see her. *(ROSS holds it out in his hand. ROBIN takes it.)*

AUDREY: There.

CULLEN: Put it on. Robin, put it on. *(ROBIN puts bracelet on.)*

ROSS: *(To KATE)* **You're a strong woman. A good choice.**

AUDREY: Well, Ross...how did you keep it from me?

ROSS: Under a rock, on the beach. Kate knew, if I couldn't get

it. *(To ROBIN)* **When Audrey said she knew where you were we thought Mora had decided to act; we didn't know how.**
KATE: *(To CULLEN)* **I promised your father I wouldn't tell anyone until he said it was time. I told everyone I'd marry someone else but only to fool Mora into believing I had lost faith in you, and that I didn't know where the bracelet was.**
CULLEN: **You're free?**
KATE: **Yes. And I hope you consider we were given to each other...You can refuse.**
CULLEN: **Refuse you?**
KATE: **I choose you.**
CULLEN: **Some of these dreams, Robin, are true.** *(He kisses her. ROBIN moves to AUDREY.)* **Robin, wait; wait for me —** *(ROBIN motions CULLEN to stay back, which he reluctantly does.)*
ROBIN: **If I gave you the crystal, would you let Cullen go, unhurt?**
CULLEN: **What?**
SLOAN: **Is this what we've come for?**
AUDREY: *(She's trembling.)* **Yes. And everything I promised would come true.**
ROBIN: *(To CULLEN)* **You wouldn't get hurt.**
CULLEN: **But you would.**
ROBIN: **That doesn't matter.**
CULLEN: **I'd have to go through both of you.**
AUDREY: **Robin, give me the bracelet.** *(He takes off bracelet, holds it out to her. The others watch in disbelief.)*
CULLEN: *(Completely disheartened)* **Robin...**
ROSS: **So you go into the night and she's all around you; she surrounds you.**
AUDREY: **Put it on the floor.**
ROSS: **You can smell her.**
ROBIN: *(He reaches for her wrist; she pulls her wrist back.)* **Let me put it on you.**
AUDREY: **Just put it on the floor.**
ROSS: **You want to fall into her and forget everything.**
ROBIN: **Mora...I want to believe you. I want to believe you.**
ROSS: **You can see, if you want, if you have the eyes. You know what's true.**
ROBIN: *(He turns and suddenly tosses bracelet to CULLEN. He catches it, quickly puts it on.)* **Keep it on; until you put it on her.**
AUDREY: **Robin!**
ROBIN: **That's what you have to do.**
AUDREY: **How could you tell him?**
ROSS: **She can't hold the crystal and bracelet. You put it on her, she'll die.**
ROBIN: *(To CULLEN)* **Then the crystal is yours. I give up my right. You are the wizard, not me.**

CULLEN: Snowflake, I may have to change your name.

AUDREY: *(To ROBIN)* Are you your father's son?

ROSS: *(Proudly)* My son!

AUDREY: Without me you're dead. They'll reach up out of the grave and pull you down. They want you. Those rotting old men. Look at him. Is that who you are?

ROBIN: My father.

AUDREY: I haven't hurt you, but I can. Why don't I clap you in chains or cut you to pieces? I want you with me. I-want-you-with-me.

CULLEN: Let's finish this. *(He starts for AUDREY, followed by SLOAN. From behind, SLOAN slices one of CULLEN's legs.)*

CULLEN: Ah!

KATE: Cullen! *(ROBIN and KATE run to CULLEN as SLOAN moves to AUDREY.)* Sloan!

SLOAN: There are certain charms in the world that are irresistible.

ROBIN: I should have known. *(CULLEN pulls himself up.)*

CULLEN: Coward! Stay back, they're mine. *(With a cry he lunges forward, engages SLOAN. CULLEN wounds SLOAN slightly, moves to AUDREY, grabs her by the arm, hauls her away from SLOAN.)*

AUDREY: Robin! Sloan! *(SLOAN kicks CULLEN in his wounded thigh, tosses him. CULLEN ends up near KATE and ROBIN.)*

KATE: Cullen, stop, you're hurt. It isn't a fair fight.

ROBIN: Give me the bracelet and she'll stop.

KATE: Yes, let Robin fight him.

ROBIN: Give me the bracelet. She'll kill you.

CULLEN: Stay back. You'll just get in my way. *(He engages SLOAN.)*

AUDREY: Stop him, Ross. You know he can't win. *(CULLEN is wounded in the shoulder, staggers back.)*

KATE: Can you help him?

ROSS: There's a long line of wizards inside of you. Find them. Listen to them. They'll help you.

CULLEN: As much as you've helped me? As much as they helped you? This...monster will not do to me what she did to you. I will not die like you; blind, babbling, thief.

ROSS: Too much to forgive. *(ROBIN attacks SLOAN.)*

CULLEN: Robin! *(CULLEN pulls ROBIN away. CULLEN attacks again. He is struck repeatedly by SLOAN, falls. ROBIN engages SLOAN.)*

AUDREY: Sloan, don't hurt him. No! *(SLOAN tries to retreat, to just defend himself. ROBIN trips him, mortally wounds him.)*

ROBIN: *(Moving to CULLEN)* I knew it. I knew it.

CULLEN: *(Giving him bracelet)* I give it to you. The crystal is yours. *(He faints. ROBIN holds the bracelet.)*

KATE: Cullen? He's still breathing. Can you help him? Ross?

ROBIN: *(To AUDREY)* **This is why you waited; why you led us here. You knew he'd never stop fighting. You made me watch, made it look like you were protecting yourself so some day I'd forgive you.**

AUDREY: **If I planned this, then it was for you.**

ROBIN: **I know.**

AUDREY: **It's what you wanted, too.**

ROBIN: **I know, but I was scared. I didn't know what I was doing. I didn't want to know. I just wanted...you. And for you to help me not know. So you made it look like everything was as it should be. Robin and Audrey. The two promised lovers. Everything is normal — all is well. But not Cullen. If you kill him, you kill me.**

AUDREY: **I could have you forget you ever had a brother. Would you like that?**

ROBIN: **Forget Cullen?**

AUDREY: *(Beginning to slowly move to him)* **Robin, will you give me the bracelet?**

ROSS: **There's a long line of wizards inside you. Listen to them. Join them. They believe in you.**

AUDREY: **I'll bring everything to you.**

ROSS: **You can wait.**

AUDREY: **Your wait is over.**

ROSS: **You can die waiting.**

AUDREY: **All is well.** *(ROBIN puts bracelet on her, holds it on. She stands for a moment, seemingly unaffected.)* **You're just a child. How will you live? You don't know how to live... because if you live, you'll die. You see?**

ROBIN: **I see.**

AUDREY: **I'll take care of you. I'll make everything all right.** *(The crystal dims and flickers. Both notice this.)* **The moment the crystal is yours, it will give you a vision; a vision of the day you will die.** *(He looks to ROSS.)*

ROSS: **Oh, yes.**

AUDREY: **You'll die, Robin.**

ROBIN: **You can't stop me from dying. Or growing older. Anymore than you could him.** *(ROSS)* **They're lies. I'd end just like him; a blind fool.** *(With a cry, she suddenly tries to pull away, struggles to get bracelet off; ROBIN holds it on. She gestures. With a sound, the crystal flashes. Again. She pulls ROBIN, then pushes him violently away. She moves from him, obviously in great pain, desperately struggling with the bracelet. The crystal flashes, flashes again and again.)*

AUDREY: **Off! Off! Off!** *(ROBIN again takes her wrist. She writhes in pain.)* **No! Robin!** *(Her energy is weakening. From behind, ROBIN wraps his arms around her, holding the bracelet on. The* *crystal flashes and flickers with a dimming light. She stops struggling, leans back into him, slowly slides to floor during the following.)*

You've been helping me, haven't you? You sailed to Errigal with me; you knew who I was yet you didn't tell the others; you gave the bracelet to Cullen; you wanted me to take it from him. Let me give you what I promised. It's what you want. Remember? *(She lies still. Music plays. The crystal's light concentrates into a single beam that shines on ROBIN. He stands entranced, feeling the energy of the crystal course through him. Another light hits ROSS; he turns to crystal, mumbles something inaudible, sings a short, nearly inaudible song. His light fades out. ROBIN stays entranced until the beam fades out and the crystal resumes its general glow. Music ends.)*

ROBIN: *(He bends over CULLEN, puts his hand on him. Almost inaudibly)* **Kultan Koren Gana Solt.** *(The crystal flashes. CULLEN takes a deep breath.)* **I think he'll live, if he wants to live.**

KATE: He will.

ROSS: *(Embracing ROBIN)* **Welladay...Wizard of Errigal.**

ROBIN: Thank you for waiting.

ROSS: For you. *(He turns away, lost in himself. Sadly)* **It's been a long, long time.**

KATE: You did it.

ROBIN: I did.

KATE: He did it, Ross. *(To ROBIN)* **And did you see the vision, like she said?**

ROBIN: Oh, yes.

KATE: How do you feel?

ROBIN: Like him. *(He points to ROSS.)* **Like that.** *(Points to crystal, as lights begin to fade, CULLEN struggles to sit up. ROBIN moves to ROSS. Fade out.)*

THE END

THE BOY WHO LEFT HOME TO FIND OUT ABOUT THE SHIVERS

BY MAX BUSH

CHARACTERS

BOY. . . . . A Teenager

SON. . . . . His Older Brother

FATHER. . . . . His Father

SISTER . . . . His Sister

SEXTON

SEXTON'S WIFE

ALICE

INNKEEPER. . . . . Alice's Husband

KING

PRINCESS

1 CAT

2 CAT

DOG

BRIDE

COUSIN

GHOST

LADY'S MAID

With doubling, all roles can be played by seven or eight actors.

TIME: Long ago.

PLACE: Various locations throughout Boy's journey: his house, a bell tower, the high road, an inn, and a haunted castle.

RUNNING TIME: Approximately sixty-five minutes.

NOTE: Because of the nature of the tale, the sets need to be suggested and fragmented, built to come on and off rapidly and simply. The costumes should be built to allow for movement.

There are a number of ways to bring scenic elements on and off during the castle scenes. The pieces could be brought on by a "shadow" or by many "shadows," or be moved by completely unseen hands. This would depend on concept and available resources.

Tune of the song, *Gather Your Rosebuds*, by W. Lawes (1802-1845). Lyrics from poem, "To the Virgins, to Make Much of Time," by Robert Herrick (1591-1674).

The Boy Who Left Home to Find Out About the Shivers was commissioned by the Nashville Academy Theatre and Hartford Children's Theatre. The play opened in Nashville, Tennessee, in October, 1994, with the following cast and crew:

CHARACTERS

BOY	Brandon Boyd
SON	Dobehi Lacaden
FATHER	Teddy Giles
SISTER	Jenny Littleton
SEXTON	Phil Perry
SEXTON'S WIFE	Persephone Felder-Fentress
ALICE	Rona Carter
INNKEEPER	Phil Perry
KING	Teddy Giles
PRINCESS	Jenny Littleton
1 CAT	Dobehi Lacaden
2 CAT	Persephone Felder-Fentress
DOG	Phil Perry
BRIDE	Jenny Littleton
COUSIN	Teddy Giles
GHOST	Rona Carter
LADY'S MAID	Persephone Felder-Fentress

PRODUCTION STAFF

DIRECTOR	Scot Copeland
STAGE MANAGER	Daniel C. Brewer
TECHNICAL DIRECTION	Scot Boyd
ASSISTANT TECHNICAL DIRECTOR	Raymond Speakman
TECHNICAL ASSISTANTS	Richard Neville, Laurie Powell
COSTUMERS	Ida Bostian, Tracey Howard
SOUND	Daniel C. Brewer

The play opened in Hartford, Connecticut, at the Hartford Children's Theatre, in October, 1994, with the following cast and crew:

CHARACTERS

BOY	Michael Pancheri
SON	Dan Affleck
FATHER	Jason Bush
SISTER	Kuhneena Sanko
SEXTON	Gregory J. Dixon
SEXTON'S WIFE	Nora Matthews
ALICE	Molly Pearson
INNKEEPER	Dan Affleck
KING	Jason Bush
PRINCESS	Quisi Kelly
1 CAT	Nora Matthews
2 CAT	Kuhneena Sanko
DOG	Gregory J. Dixon
BRIDE	Molly Pearson
COUSIN	Dan Affleck
GHOST	Jason Bush
LADY'S MAID	Molly Pearson

STAFF

DIRECTOR	Alan Levy
COSTUME DESIGN	Priscilla Putnam
STAGE MANAGER	Holly Stocker
TECHNICAL DIRECTION	Alan Levy
ASSISTANT STAGE MANAGER	Jamal James
MAKE-UP	Jeanette Wilson
LIGHT BOARD	Steven Hubbs

ACKNOWLEDGMENTS: The author gratefully acknowledges the following for their help in the development of this script: Phil Huber, Lynette Gallert, the drama students of Portland High School (Michigan), Lynn Rothrock, and the casts and crews of the first two productions.

Scene 1

*(At rise: SON, SISTER, SEXTON, SEXTON's WIFE and BOY are
sitting around the fire, listening to FATHER finish telling a ghost
story. The BOY sits apart.)*

(Simultaneously; a chorus of insistent voices)
SON: What happens next?
SEXTON: Don't stop there, sir!
WIFE: Heaven bless us, what happens?
SISTER: No, no, no, no, no.
BOY: Then what does he do?
FATHER: That's enough for now.

(In concert)
SON: What happens next, Father!
SEXTON: No, no, finish the story.
WIFE: You can't stop now.
SISTER: No, no, no, no, no.
BOY: I want to know what he does.

FATHER: You want me to go on?

(Again, simultaneously)
SON: Yes, what happens next?
SEXTON: Yes, finish the story.
WIFE: Yes, for heaven's sake.
SISTER: Yes, yes, yes, yes, yes.
BOY: Yes, what does he do?

FATHER: You're not too scared?
BOY: *(After a moment of silence)* **No.**
OTHERS: *(In chorus)* **Yes.**
SISTER: It gives me the shivers. But how does it end?
**FATHER: All he had to do was stay one more night in the cas-
tle, and the treasure would be his. He laid next to the fire
pretending to sleep. Scrape. Thump. Thump. Something
was being dragged across the floor towards him.**
SISTER: Get away. Get away!
FATHER: What was it?
SISTER: Don't just lie there, do something!
**FATHER: Falunk. Something dropped on the floor right next to
him.**
SON: I know what it is.
SISTER: Is it good?
FATHER: A filthy smell pierced his nose.

SISTER: *Nooo.*

FATHER: He jumped up and there lay the rotting body of his friend, the old Innkeeper, dragged up from the grave. Aaahh! *(He screams. The others, except the BOY, scream in response.)*

OTHERS: *Aaahhhh!*

FATHER: He screamed. And unable to bear it any longer, he ran up the stairs looking for a way out. He came to a window, jumped out into the darkness and fell down into the water-way — splash — where he drowned.

SISTER: No, that's terrible.

SEXTON: I knew he'd never get that treasure, not him.

SISTER: He drowned? That's what happened?

WIFE: It gives me the shivers.

SON: He wasn't brave enough.

SEXTON: He wasn't smart enough.

SISTER: I liked him. He should get the treasure. Father, tell it again and this time, he gets the treasure.

WIFE: Scared the poor boy out of his mind.

SON: Ah, that gives me the shivers.

BOY: You keep saying: "It gives me the shivers, it gives me the shivers!" It doesn't give *me* the shivers.

SEXTON: Well, it gives me the shivers, and I've heard the story before.

BOY: It must be another one of those tricks that I just can't learn.

FATHER: Well, that's all for the night.

SEXTON: And we must be going too.

WIFE: Thank you for the fine meal. But I'm afraid that story's going to keep me up all night.

FATHER: Sister, fetch the sexton's coat. Son, I'll need you to take a pair of new breeches to our poor cousin's house. *(SISTER goes to fetch light coats for SEXTON and WIFE. The FATHER picks up a pair of breeches.)*

SON: Our cousin, the one who has just died, Father?

FATHER: That's the one.

SON: Now?

FATHER: He's to be buried tomorrow, and they need these breeches for him to be buried in.

SON: Oh, no, Father, I won't go.

SEXTON: You will obey your father, Son.

SON: But I'll have to go through the graveyard to get to his house and it'll be dark by the time I get there. It'll give me the shivers.

WIFE: After that story, it would give any of us the shivers.

BOY: It wouldn't give me the shivers.

FATHER: *(To BOY)* But I can't send you to our cousin's house.

You'd get lost, or you'd go to the wrong house, or you'd come home wearing the breeches...and not know where they are. *(All the others laugh.)*

BOY: Yes, Father. *(Curiously, mostly to himself)* But I wouldn't get the shivers.

SEXTON: I can bring the breeches to your poor cousin in the morning before church.

SON: Thank you, sir.

FATHER: *(To BOY)* Listen, you over there in the corner, you're getting to be big and strong, and you eat a lot. You'll have to learn something to make a living by. Your brother is always working, helping me with the tailoring, but you're useless.

BOY: Oh, yes, Father, I'd be glad to learn something. If possible, I'd like to learn how to get the shivers. That's something I just don't understand.

SEXTON: As the twig is bent, so the tree will lean.

BOY: What does that mean?

SON: It means you're an idiot.

FATHER: *(A quiet scold)* Son.

BOY: But if I learned about the shivers I might make something of myself.

SISTER: A bigger idiot. *(SISTER laughs; SEXTON's WIFE laughs, unable to stop herself.)*

FATHER: *(A little stronger)* Sister.

SEXTON: *(To BOY)* If all you want is to learn about the shivers, I'll teach you, boy.

BOY: You will? I'd make a good student. I'll do just what you tell me.

WIFE: *(Genuinely concerned)* Are you sure you want to try to teach this boy something?

SEXTON: What can it hurt?

WIFE: Well, remember...

FATHER: *(To SEXTON)* He's bound to get something out of it if you teach him.

SEXTON: Sure, I'll teach you, boy. I'll teach you, tonight. And we'll have a good laugh, too.

BOY: Thank you. Then I'll learn something and then I'll know something, and then I'll make a living.

SEXTON: Good Lord, we'll all count our blessings.

FATHER: I have to see this.

WIFE: So do I.

SEXTON: Come on, Boy. Your prayers are answered!

(Music. The scene shifts around them to Scene 2, the bell tower. SON and SISTER exit. The FATHER, the SEXTON, his WIFE and BOY walk together. Under music)

BOY: **I'm going to get the shivers. I'm going to get the shivers!**
SEXTON: *(Once they near the tower, to FATHER and WIFE)* **Wait in our house until you hear the bell, then come out and join us.** *(FATHER and WIFE exit. BOY and SEXTON proceed to foot of tower. Music out.)*

Scene 2

SEXTON: **Now, you wait here and count to fifty. You can count to fifty, can't you?**
BOY: **Yes.**
SEXTON: **Well, it's a miracle.**
BOY: **What is?**
SEXTON: **Count to fifty then go up and ring the bell. Do you understand?**
BOY: **Count to fifty then go up and ring the bell.**
SEXTON: **It will be midnight and you must ring the bell so the people all over the countryside will know that all is well. Begin counting to fifty, now.**
BOY: **One...** *(He pauses.)*
SEXTON: **Two.**
BOY: **Oh, are you going to count with me?**
SEXTON: **No, I was helping you.**
BOY: **I can count to fifty by myself.**
SEXTON: **Then why did you stop?**
BOY: **I was wondering why I don't go up and ring the bell now. It's midnight. Do you know why I have to count? Is that part of getting the shivers?**
SEXTON: **If I say it is, it is.**
BOY: **Is it?**
SEXTON: **Yes it is. Count to fifty.**
BOY: **Should I start over?**
SEXTON: **No!**
BOY: **One — I mean two.** *(Slowly)* **Three, four, five...** *(Etc. The SEXTON quietly climbs the stairs. Once up, he wraps himself in a hooded, white shroud and stands in the corner.)* **Twelve...** *(He continues, amusing himself as he counts; then finishes last numbers in record time.)* **Fifty! Sexton?** *(He looks, doesn't see him.)* **Count to fifty then go up and ring the bell.** *(He runs up the stairs, comes to the bell rope and takes it in his hands. The SEXTON opens his arms, the BOY sees him.)* **Who's there?** *(Silence. SEXTON gestures in a ghostly fashion.)* **Answer me, or go away. You've no business here in the middle of the night. This is a church. I don't think you're supposed to be here. Who are you?**
SEXTON: *Oooo.*
BOY: *Oooo* **is no answer. What are you doing here? Are you here to learn about the shivers?**

SEXTON: *Oooo.*

BOY: **What language is that? That's not even church language. What are you doing here?**

SEXTON: *Oooo.*

BOY: **Answer me if you're an honest man, or I'll throw you down the stairs.** *(The SEXTON gestures wildly.)* **Who are you? What are you doing here?**

SEXTON: *Wooo!*

BOY: **All right, then.** *(The BOY charges SEXTON and they struggle. The BOY pushes the SEXTON down the stairs.)* **Out you go.**

SEXTON: **Ah! Ow! Stop it! No! Ow!**

BOY: *(BOY trips him and the SEXTON falls.)* **And stay out of this tower.** *(BOY pursues SEXTON, pushing him away from the bell tower. He punctuates the following words with pushes and swats.)* **Only honest men belong here. There's honest work, here. To ring the bell so the people know that all is well. And to learn about the shivers.** *(He breaks off his attack.)* **There you are. And I hope you've learned something.** *(The SEXTON lies groaning in a heap some distance from the tower. BOY goes back up bell tower and begins ringing bell. SEXTON tries to move, but collapses, holding his leg. FATHER and WIFE enter, move to foot of bell tower.)*

FATHER: **Boy!**

BOY: **Here, Father.**

FATHER: **What are you doing?**

BOY: **I'm ringing the bell but I don't feel any shivers yet.** *(WIFE goes up tower.)*

WIFE: **Where's my husband?**

BOY: **I don't know. When do I get the shivers?**

FATHER: **Stop ringing that bell!** *(He stops.)*

BOY: *(Checking himself out)* **I'm not shivering.**

WIFE: **Do you know what's become of my husband? He went up into the belfry ahead of you.**

BOY: **No, but somebody was standing on the stairs across from the sound hole, and when he wouldn't answer and wouldn't go away, I thought he was up to no good, so I pushed him down the stairs.**

WIFE: **You pushed him down the stairs?**

FATHER: **No, not again.**

WIFE: **Oh, heavens. Where is he?**

BOY: **He's down there somewhere. Go take a look. You'll see if it was him. I'd be very sorry.**

FATHER: *(They search the area.)* **Sexton?**

WIFE: **Where are you?**

FATHER: **Sexton?** *(The SEXTON groans.)* **There —** *(They run to SEXTON.)* **Sexton.**

WIFE: Are you hurt?

SEXTON: He hit me. He kicked me. He pushed me down the stairs. He broke my leg.

WIFE: Get that brute out of our church! *(The BOY has come down from tower.)*

FATHER: *(To BOY)* What godless thing have you done, now?

WIFE: You heathen! You're possessed!

FATHER: The Devil must have put you up to it.

BOY: Father, I'm perfectly innocent. He was standing there in the night like someone that's up to no good. I didn't know who he was and I warned him three times to say something or go away.

WIFE: He was pretending he was a ghost. He was teaching you about the shivers.

BOY: I didn't get the shivers.

SEXTON: It's not my fault. You can't teach a pig to fly.

WIFE: Ungrateful devil.

BOY: So I thought he wasn't an honest man and that I'd teach whoever it was a lesson. So I told him if he didn't answer me I'd throw him down the stairs. He didn't answer me, so I threw him down the stairs.

SEXTON: *(WIFE helps SEXTON up.)* I didn't think he'd do it, the brute.

FATHER: Heavens above, with you I'll never have anything but trouble. You understand nothing and you learn nothing. Get out of my sight. I don't want to see you any more.

BOY: Yes, Father, gladly, I'll go away and learn to get the shivers. Then at least I'll know something to earn a living by.

FATHER: Still the shivers!

WIFE: Heaven protect us.

SEXTON: You're a plague to everyone who knows you.

WIFE: You give me the shivers! *(She helps SEXTON off.)*

BOY: Lucky woman. Good-bye. *(WIFE and SEXTON exit.)*

FATHER: Learn whatever you like. It's all the same to me. Here ...here are fifty talers, take them, go out onto the high road and into the wide world. But never tell a soul where you come from or who your father is, because I'm ashamed of you.

BOY: Yes, Father, just as you say. If that's all you ask of me, it won't be hard to remember.

FATHER: Get some sense! I don't know how. Just get some sense!

(Scene change music. BOY starts out. FATHER exits. Bell tower is removed. Dawn breaks. As he walks)

BOY: The high road...on the high road...wide world...I'm in the wide world...but... *(Music out.)*

Scene 3

BOY: Oh, if I could only get the shivers. *(ALICE, a middle-aged woman, walks by.)* **If only I could get the shivers.**

ALICE: Were you talking to me?

BOY: I'm on the high road. I'm in the wide world. I'm getting some sense.

ALICE: What was that you were mumbling?

BOY: If only I could get the shivers, but no one can teach me how.

ALICE: Well, that's nonsense.

BOY: Then I could make my living.

ALICE: Good Lord, that's more nonsense. Are you all right?

BOY: Yes.

ALICE: Look at you, you're lost, aren't you?

BOY: I'm on the high road. I'm in the wide world. I'm getting some sense.

ALICE: That's nice. My name is Alice.

BOY: Hello, Alice.

ALICE: Who are you?

BOY: *(Truly)* I don't know.

ALICE: Where are you from?

BOY: *(Truly)* I don't know.

ALICE: Who's your father?

BOY: I mustn't say.

ALICE: Oh, I see. You're lost up here, too, *(Indicating her head)* aren't you. But such pretty eyes. You're just wandering, aren't you. And you have no idea who's on this road.

BOY: You are. *(Warmly)* Alice.

ALICE: Do you have a place to sleep the night?

BOY: Not yet.

ALICE: Then you come with me and I'll get you a place to stay. Doesn't that make sense?

BOY: It does to me. I'm getting some sense!

ALICE: Isn't that wonderful? *(They walk.)*

(Scene change music. The inn moves on which includes two tables, with food and mugs, and chairs. The INNKEEPER is setting a table. Music out.)

Scene 4

INNKEEPER: *(Sings.)*
"So raise your glass high,
We'll sing 'till we die.
Sing ho, sing derry,
I toast my dear Mary."

ALICE: **Here we are.** *(They enter the inn.)*
BOY: **It's an inn.**
ALICE: **Our inn. Welcome.**
BOY: **I have fifty talers, Alice, given to me by my father.**
ALICE: **You keep your money, my boy. Here, sit.** *(BOY sits as the INNKEEPER carries over a pitcher and pours a drink for the BOY and himself and ALICE.)*
INNKEEPER: **Welcome, traveler. How long have you been on the road?**
BOY: **I don't know.**
ALICE: **Where are you going?**
BOY: **I don't know.**
INNKEEPER: **You're...not like most people, are you, boy?**
BOY: **I'm not?**
ALICE: **Do you eat?**
BOY: **Oh, yes. I'm good at that.**
ALICE: **What a nice surprise.**
INNKEEPER: **And do you drink?**
BOY: **Yes.**
INNKEEPER: **What a man. So here — we drink to your health. A toast —** *(They all raise mugs. BOY rises.)* **To all good men — and good women — we say —**
BOY: **If only I could get the shivers!** *(He drinks a toast, slams mug on table, sits down, begins to eat. The others smile, drink.)*
INNKEEPER: **Exactly what I was about to say. A noble toast — the shivers.** *(Laughs.)* **If that's what you want, I believe it can be arranged.**
BOY: **How?**
INNKEEPER: **A haunted castle.**
ALICE: **Don't tell him such things, of all people. He's not been provided for.** *(Indicating his mind)*
INNKEEPER: **That's what the boy wants.**
BOY: **A haunted castle?**
ALICE: **No; think of all the foolhardy fellows who have lost their lives; what a shame if those pretty eyes were never to see the light of day again.**
BOY: **I don't care how hard it is, I want to learn, that's what I left home for.**
ALICE: *(To INNKEEPER)* **You see? He's adrift on some sea.**
INNKEEPER: **A distant sea.**
BOY: **Where is this haunted castle?**
INNKEEPER: **She's right. You'd die like the rest of them.**
BOY: **Did they get the shivers?**
INNKEEPER: **Ha — shivered their heads off, some of them.**
ALICE: **Shook their pretty eyes right out of their heads.**
INNKEEPER: **There's a haunted castle nearby — as a matter of**

239

fact, it's the king's castle — where a man — even a man as courageous as you — could easily learn all about the shivers —

ALICE: — if he was willing to spend three nights there.

INNKEEPER: The king has promised his daughter in marriage to the man who can do it. And she's the most beautiful maiden under the sun. Besides, there are great treasures in the castle —

ALICE: — guarded by spirits of the dead.

INNKEEPER: Those treasures would be set free and could make a poor man very rich.

ALICE: Many have already gone in — bigger and stronger ones than you, in full armor, and good fighters, too — but none have come out again. We've heard their screams as their souls passed beyond this world.

BOY: That's where I need to go. *(He starts off.)*

INNKEEPER: Then you must ask the king's permission. *(The BOY stops.)*

ALICE: But he travels from place to place, from inn to inn, because he has no castle. You'd have to find him.

BOY: All right. *(A royal flourish is heard.)*

ALICE: Oh, no.

INNKEEPER: Well, Boy, this is your lucky day. His Highness sleeps here, tonight.

ALICE: Bow. *(The INNKEEPER bows, ALICE bends the BOY over, then bows herself. The KING and PRINCESS enter inn, past BOY, and move to their table.)*

INNKEEPER: That's the king there, and that is his daughter. *(The BOY begins to move to KING and PRINCESS.)*

ALICE: *(Stopping him, affectionately)* Don't go, Boy. You have a place to stay here. And just because you're a loon doesn't mean you have to die.

BOY: Thank you, Alice. *(He kisses her.)*

INNKEEPER: Let him go, Alice. *(She lets him go. The INNKEEPER brings pitcher over to KING and PRINCESS, pours. The BOY moves to KING and PRINCESS, bows. ALICE watches from a distance.)*

BOY: Your Majesties.

KING: Who are you?

BOY: I don't know.

PRINCESS: Where are you from?

BOY: I don't know.

KING: Who was your father?

BOY: I mustn't say.

KING: Who let him in here?

ALICE: I did, sire. Isn't he a prince? *(The INNKEEPER exits.)*

KING: What do you want?

BOY: If you'd let me, I'd like to spend three nights in your haunted castle.

KING: I see why you mustn't say who your father is. He thinks you're an idiot.

BOY: Oh, do you know him?

KING: Ah, no, no. *(Laugh's at BOY's genuine innocence.)* No, I don't.

BOY: He told me to get some sense.

PRINCESS: I'm not sure, but I don't think you'll get any sense dying in our haunted castle. The powers of death haunt every corner, and they hate the living.

ALICE: And so I told him, Princess, but still he's determined.

KING: I see. You want to rescue our castle from death, and return it to your living king.

BOY: No.

PRINCESS: Then you want the treasures hidden there?

BOY: No.

KING: Then my daughter's hand in marriage.

BOY: Oh, no.

PRINCESS: Oh. No?

BOY: I want to learn about the shivers, sire, and I believe that is the place to do it.

KING: What?

PRINCESS: No?

BOY: If I learned about the shivers, then I'll understand something and then I'll be able to make my living.

ALICE: Like we've been saying, sire, he's a little lost.

PRINCESS: No...

ALICE: And may not know what he's saying.

KING: I like you, boy. You know your mind, what little there is of it. And you're honest. You can ask for three things to take with you into the castle, but they must be lifeless things.

BOY: Then, give me a fire, a ham and a woodcarver's bench with two vises — two vises made of iron — one on either end.

KING: A fire, a ham and a wood-carver's bench with two iron vises. You shall have them.

PRINCESS: Good-bye, young man. I'm sorry I won't see you again.

BOY: Your Majesties.

(He bows. Music. The KING and PRINCESS exit. ALICE gives him some bread and watches forlornly as BOY walks away. She exits as inn is removed and the KING's castle is brought on.

BOY mumbles, as there is food in his mouth, something we can't understand. Yet, by now, we have a pretty good idea of what it

241

might be. The BOY walks alone into the scene as it's being set around him. The bench and a sack containing the large ham are brought on. He moves to bench, tries a vise, then picks up the sack with the ham. He pulls ham out, checks it, puts it back in sack, then places ham away from the fire. He walks to fire and begins to add logs to it, from a pile of spare logs next to fire. The fire burns near the middle of a huge room. Two large, open windows rise behind him in the shadows. The castle walls are fragmented and dimly lit; a deep, empty darkness surrounds the fire. Music out.)

Scene 5

(The BOY leaves the fire to go exploring. The space is large, the quiet is oppressive. He sees a battle-axe sunk into a wall, portraits that have been slashed and stomped, a royal chair that's been overturned. Calling down a hall)

BOY: Hello. *(The sound echoes and dies out. He goes to the window, looks out and down, calls.)* **Is anyone down there?** *(He turns back to room.)* **Is anybody here?** *(Silence. He finds the head-piece to a suit of armor, picks it up, looks at its front.)* **Anybody in there?** *(He lifts the visor.)* **Nobody.** *(He drops it. It clangs; the clang echoes and fades away. He picks up royal chair, carries it to fire, sits in it. He hears whispers, first from one side, then the other. Then from above, then below. He hears the distant growl of an animal. Shadows move in the dark behind him. He turns to see what's there. The low growl, closer this time, turns him the other way. Movement elsewhere, he turns; what was there disappears. We hear sounds of animals: growling, yelping, panting, howling. Then a scream — a woman? A cat? Then complete silence.)* **Oh, if I could only get the shivers. But I won't learn in this place, either.** *(A large, fearsome, frenetic GHOST runs on, holding the leashes to two black CATS. The CATS, growling and hissing, pull against the leashes, struggling to free themselves, to get at the BOY. The GHOST is bigger than everyone and terrifying to look at. He's old and has a long white beard. The CATS have fiery eyes. The GHOST pulls them up short, some distance from the BOY.)*

GHOST: *(In an animated, lusty voice)* **It's a boy. It's another breathing boy, my angels! Oh, look at you; little, living human. Come to my castle, to win a queen and a kingdom. And a treasure for your deep peasant pockets. Welcome, Boy. We all welcome you.** *(The CATS moan.)* **Have you come to play? My cats want to play, we all want to play...with you.** *(As he unleashes the CATS. To CATS)* **My prince, my princess. You have him first.** *(To BOY)* **Have fun, little man.** *(He disappears into the darkness. The CATS prowl along the*

242

edge of the light.)

1 CAT: Miaow.

2 CAT: Miaow.

1 CAT: We're so cold!

2 CAT: Cold!

1 CAT: Miaow!

BOY: Fools. What's the good of screaming? If you're cold, come sit by the fire and warm yourselves. *(They take a leap into the firelight, move toward BOY.)*

2 CAT: Warm.

1 CAT: Warm. *(1 CAT rubs up against BOY.)* **Warm.** *(2 CAT rubs up against BOY, then pushes BOY out of chair, hisses.)*

BOY: Hey. *(They push him back and forth.)* **Hey! What are we doing?** *(2 CAT swipes at him, BOY ducks. 1 CAT swipes, misses; they swipe repeatedly, the BOY nimbly escapes.)* **What kind of game is this?** *(1 CAT jumps on BOY, knocking him down. He tries to crawl away, 2 CAT heads him off, swipes at him. The BOY tries another escape route, both CATS leap to block it. BOY tries to get up, they knock him down. He tries again, they knock him down. They cuff and paw him during the following.)*

1 CAT: Little bird.

2 CAT: Can't fly.

1 CAT: Can't fly away.

2 CAT: Fly away.

1 CAT: Little bird.

2 CAT: Fly away! *(BOY tries to escape, stand, they cut him off, knock him down, spit. They stand poised, ready to pounce.)*

BOY: I see. *(He jumps on both CATS. They squeal. 1 CAT escapes but BOY holds on to the other's back, laughing. 2 CAT fights furiously to free itself. Riding CAT)* **Hoooo, this is fun! I like this game. More. More!** *(2 CAT tosses BOY, he rolls away, stands. The CATS quickly regroup, turn back to BOY.)*

2 CAT: Would you...?

1 CAT: Would you like to play?

2 CAT: Would you like to play with us?

1 CAT: Would you like to play cards?

2 CAT: With us?

BOY: Cards? I like to play cards.

2 CAT: We'll play you for your life.

1 CAT: We'll play you for your death.

BOY: I'll play you for awhile. But first show me your paws. *(1 CAT swipes at him, the BOY catches the paw, looks at it.)* **What long nails you have.** *(The CAT swipes at him, he ducks.)* **I'll have to cut your nails before we play. Come on.** *(He hauls CAT over to the bench and vise.)* **In you go.** *(CAT doesn't want* *to go in.)* **I have to cut your nails or we can't play.** *(He holds 1 CAT's paw in vise, closes it, backs off. The CAT tries to pull paw out but can't.)* **And now you.** *(2 CAT paces in front of him.)*

2 CAT: "**And now you.**" **And now you. We'll play you for your death.** *(Spits and leaps at BOY. BOY dodges, he picks it up by the scruff of the neck, drags it to the other side of the bench and closes CAT's paw in vise.)*
(Overlapping each other)

2 CAT: Cards —
1 CAT: Cards, yes —
2 CAT: Yes; we'll play you—
1 CAT: You said cards —
2 CAT: Yes, cards —

BOY: Now that I've seen your paws, I don't feel like playing cards anymore. *(Both CATS howl and try desperately to pull themselves out of vise.)*
(Overlapping each other.)

1 CAT: Die.
2 CAT: You will die.
1 CAT: You will die, little bird.
2 CAT: Let us go.
1 CAT: Let us free.
2 CAT: Little bird.
1 CAT: You will die.

2 CAT: Free. *(BOY sits in the chair.)*
1 CAT: *(Calling into the darkness)* **Miaow!**
2 CAT: *(Calling.)* **Miaow!** *(Etc. A large, violent black DOG with a red-hot chain collar leaps out of the darkness at BOY. The DOG circles him, licking his chops.)*
BOY: What do you want? *(The DOG growls in his face.)* **What does that mean? I can't understand you. What do you want?** *(Another growl)* **Do you want to play cards, too?** *(Another growl)* **Yes, all right, but what does that mean?! Who could understand you? All you do is growl.** *(The DOG moves to fire, paws it, kicks a log off.)* **Hey, that's my fire! Leave it alone.** *(BOY gets up, puts log back on fire, the DOG moves into BOY's chair.)* **That's what you want. My chair. But that seat's mine. You have to get out.** *(DOG sits.)* **That seat's mine. There are other places for you to sit. Get out...All right.** *(The BOY grabs DOG, tries to pull it out of chair. The DOG holds his ground, tries to bite the BOY. BOY lets go, tries another body part, pulls it, but can't get DOG out of chair. BOY goes to sack*

and pulls out the large ham. He places it far from the DOG. DOG sits up, eyes riveted to the ham.) **Oh, I'm hungry. I'm so hungry.** *(He bites the ham.)* **And this ham is good. It is so good.** *(The BOY pulls off a piece and walks over to 1 CAT. He holds ham up.)* **Would you like a piece, Cat?**

2 CAT: **Of you.**

1 CAT: **A piece of you.**

2 CAT: **Piece of you.**

1 CAT: **We'll tear you to pieces.** *(The DOG is having great difficulty staying in the chair. He nervously paces, as much as is possible in a chair.)*

BOY: *(To CATS)* **Here, a delicious bite of ham. It makes me whine.** *(The DOG whines.)* **It makes me pant.** *(The DOG pants.)* **It makes me slobber.** *(The DOG slobbers.)* **It makes me howl.** *(The DOG howls and, unable to stand it any longer, leaps out of chair, gallops toward ham, grabs it in his jaws, and drags it toward the chair. BOY sees this, dashes to chair, sits in it before the DOG can get back with ham.)*

My chair. *(DOG drags ham over near chair, then he jumps up on BOY's lap and they struggle for chair. They both tumble out. DOG quickly snatches ham and gets into chair. DOG chews ham and watches BOY as he rises. When BOY approaches, DOG, still chewing ham, growls. BOY grabs ham, they struggle, BOY pulls it free. He clubs DOG with it and runs.)* **Here, dog. Ham! Ham!** *(DOG leaps out of chair, chases him around the CATS, around the fire, and toward the window.)*

Come on. Come on! Ham! Ham! Go get it! *(BOY throws ham out of window. The DOG starts after it, but stops. They look at each other for a moment then they both go for the chair, but the DOG is quicker and gets back in it.)* **That seat's mine. You have to get out.** *(BOY moves behind the chair, pushes on the back and tries to dump DOG onto floor. It hangs on for a time, but the BOY succeeds in dumping him out. The BOY then runs with chair. The DOG chases, waiting for BOY to put down chair. BOY runs, dodges, trying to get away from the DOG.)* **This is my seat! My seat, my seat, my seat!** *(He sets chair down, they scramble to get into it, the DOG wins again. The BOY stops to consider. He slowly walks around DOG; DOG eyes him fiercely. BOY moves to fire, picks up a burning log and moves toward DOG. The anxious DOG lowers its head, growls.)*

This is fire. That is my seat. Get out. *(The DOG doesn't budge.)* **All right. Hah!** *(He stabs the DOG with the burning side of the log. The DOG squeals but stays in chair.)* **Hah!** *(Again he stabs DOG, it squeals, but stays in chair.)* **Hah!** *(This time he holds it on DOG who squeals and jumps out of chair. BOY gets into it.)* **Ha! My seat. See? It's my seat!** *(DOG turns on BOY,*

245

but BOY holds log ready.) **My chair.**
2 CAT: Miaow.
1 CAT: Miaow. *(The CATS cry and moan. DOG leaps over to bench, swats a vise handle, it turns and a CAT is freed. He then frees the other. They all howl and run around BOY, hissing and pawing. He holds log ready. They trample the fire.)*
(Overlapping.)

1 CAT: Dark, dark, die.
2 CAT: You will die, in the dark.
1 CAT: In the cold, in the dark.
2 CAT: Die, in the cold, dark.

1 CAT: Die. *(They howl and kick at the fire, pull the logs off and stomp them. They work themselves into a frenzied dance, around, over and through the fire. The firelight fades, the lights dim.)*
BOY: Hey, that's enough. Hey, that's my fire. Don't put out my fire. *(They howl at him.)* **I'll get cold. I won't be able to see.** *(They stomp the fire.)* **All right.** *(He drops his burning log near fire, then jumps into the fray and grabs 1 CAT by the neck and back. He hauls it spitting and flailing to the window and throws it out.)* **Out you go and into the waterway.** *(The CAT's cry slowly dies out as it falls the long distance into the moat. He chases the other CAT. The CAT turns and hisses, then lunges, but the BOY grabs it, hauls it over to the window and flings it out.)* **Out you go and into the waterway.** *(We hear the CAT's cry fade as it falls. He turns to the DOG.)*

And now you. *(The DOG paces over and around fire. The BOY approaches, the DOG paws the burning log closer to the rest of the burning logs and moves into position to protect them. Suddenly they both go for the chair, the BOY gets there first, picks it up, runs, the DOG chases. BOY pulls away and sets chair down in front of window and sits in it. The DOG gets a running start and leaps at BOY and chair; but the BOY deftly picks up chair, moves to the side and the DOG flies howling out the window. DOG's howl fades away as he falls. BOY sets chair near fire, sits in it.)* **My seat.** *(He rebuilds fire, then blows on the coals; the flames and room brighten.)* **My fire.** *(He yawns and stretches.)*

Oh, I wish there was a bed. *(A bed rolls on.)* **Ah, just what I need.** *(He gets in bed.)* **I like bed. I like this bed. I like bedtime. Perfect.** *(He closes his eyes. The bed begins to move. It moves across the floor, around the entire room. He sits up, sees what's happening.)* **Even better. Faster. Faster.** *(The bed rolls and turns faster. The BOY laughs.)* **Better and better!** *(The bed makes a sudden turn, throwing him off, along with the blankets* *and pillows and mattress. They lay on him like a mountain. He crawls out from under them. A distant bell begins to toll the hour of twelve.)* **Now, if you want, you go on rolling. Let someone else do the traveling. I have to sleep.** *(He picks up a pillow and drags a blanket over to the fireside, makes his bed on the floor. The bed stops rolling.)* **Ah, the bell. Midnight. All is well.** *(He lays down, fluffs his pillow, covers himself with the blanket and falls asleep. The bell finishes tolling twelve. Firelight dies out.)*

Scene 6

(Lights brighten. The KING, PRINCESS and her LADY's MAID enter cautiously.)

KING: It seems quiet. *(Sees BOY.)* **There. What a pity. Such a handsome boy.**

PRINCESS: *(She goes to him.)* **He was different. He didn't deserve this. These spirits have no mercy.** *(She kneels, puts a hand on him. He opens his eyes.)* **Call the guards; we'll have to bury him.** *(He turns over and sees who is there.)*

BOY: Princess! *(The PRINCESS starts. He jumps up.)*

PRINCESS: Oh.

BOY: Don't bury me yet. I'm still here.

PRINCESS: You're still here.

BOY: *(Bowing)* **Your Majesties. Is it morning already?**

PRINCESS: Yes.

KING: Well, my boy, that's remarkable.

PRINCESS: I didn't think I'd see you alive again. How did it go?

BOY: Pretty well. I had some fun.

KING: Fun?

BOY: I played with the animals —

PRINCESS: *(Obviously she's met these animals.)* **The animals?** *(She scans room, anxiously.)*

BOY: Yes, and even if we didn't play cards, we did play a game about who sits in the chair. That was fun.

PRINCESS: You had fun with the animals?

KING: And did you learn about the shivers?

BOY: No, it's hopeless. If only someone could tell me.

KING: What a mind.

MAID: Excuse me, sir. Tell you what?

BOY: About the shivers. I don't seem to be able to get them.

MAID: That's what I thought.

KING: Will you stay, again, tonight?

BOY: I may as well.

KING: I'll inform the guards. Good luck, my boy. I hope you have as much fun tonight, and I'll look for you in the

morning. *(He exits.)*

PRINCESS: *(To MAID)* **Wait for me outside.**

MAID: Yes, my Lady. *(MAID curtsies, exits.)*

PRINCESS: You're not like the other men.

BOY: Yes I am.

PRINCESS: You're not after the gold, you don't want me, or to be the next king. Here... *(She takes off her jewelled necklace.)* **because you don't care about these things; and you had fun with the animals last night.** *(She puts the necklace around him.)* **It's very rich, from the king's treasury.**

BOY: Thanks.

PRINCESS: And a gift from me.

BOY: *(This gets his attention. He looks into her. Innocently)* **Would you like to stay for a while tonight? We could play something.**

PRINCESS: I like to play games.

BOY: We could play cards, or ninepins.

PRINCESS: I'm good at ninepins.

BOY: So am I. I'll bet you a couple of coppers I win.

PRINCESS: You haven't seen me throw. I can beat my father in ninepins and I can beat you.

BOY: You haven't seen *me* throw.

PRINCESS: I'd take all your money.

BOY: Ah, what fun we'll have! We'll play all night!

PRINCESS: I would love to stay and play —

BOY: Ninepins!

PRINCESS: — but there are spirits, here.

BOY: We could play with them, too.

PRINCESS: They'd hurt me, I know, because they have. This used to be my bedchamber. They came mostly at night — those horrible animals; and crawling, dead things; fierce ghosts.

BOY: Yes.

PRINCESS: They twisted my arms black and blue. And they'd lay across my face so I couldn't breathe. Sometimes they'd howl in my ears until I thought I'd lose my mind. And their games; I tried playing with them but their games...they're terrible, like nightmares.

BOY: Did you get the shivers?

PRINCESS: Oh, yes. I have them now.

BOY: You do? *(BOY touches her arm.)* **I feel them.**

PRINCESS: One night I called for my father and he came to protect me; he tried playing their games because he thought if he beat them, they'd go. The spirits broke his bones. They're strong, stronger than us. So we left our castle to them. *(The BOY continues to hold her arm.)* **That feels better.**

248

BOY: **Stay a while. We'll play ninepins.**
PRINCESS: **I can't. I hope to see you again, young man, whoever you are.** *(Music. She exits. The BOY tends his fire, the lights dim. Music out.)*

Scene 7

(He looks around castle, sees no one. He wanders Upstage.)
BOY: **Hello?** *(Silence. He picks up a long, iron rod.)* **A long, iron rod...to use against ghosts.** *(He whips the air.)* **Iron. A good choice.** *(He drops rod. He hears whispers and sees shadows moving in the dark.)* **Yes? I'm here.** *(He turns to see what's there.)* **Yes?** *(Movement elsewhere, he turns; what's there disappears.)* **Hello?** *(We hear whispers, then the long, distorted groan of a dying man.)* **If only I could get the shivers.** *(The clear sound of a female voice sings a lament. Out of the darkness a BRIDE, all in white and completely veiled, enters slowly, carrying a large bridal bouquet. The song is continuous; the dialogue is spoken while the BRIDE sings.)*
BRIDE: *("Marching" forward toward him, singing)*

**Gather your rosebuds while you may,
Old time is still a-flying;**

BOY: **Princess? Is that you, Princess?**

BRIDE: **And that same flow'r that smiles today,
Tomorrow will be dying.** *(She marches past him.)*

BOY: **Did you decide to stay awhile?**

BRIDE: **The glorious lamp of heaven, the sun,
The higher he is getting,**

BOY: **That's pretty...Is that a wedding dress? Are you getting married?**
BRIDE: *(She gestures for someone to proceed in front of her. A wooden coffin comes on, she follows it in procession.)*

**The sooner will his race be run,
And nearer he's to setting.**

BOY: **A coffin?**

BRIDE: **That age is best that is the first
While youth and blood are warmer;**

249

GHOST: *(Suddenly appearing. Wildly, but under the BRIDE's lament. The BRIDE and coffin are the main focus here.)* **I rule here. This is my castle. Because I'm stronger than any king. I'm stronger than any princess. I'm stronger than you, little, living man.**

BRIDE: Expect not the last and worst,
Time still succeeds the former.

GHOST: Stay, and you'll have some fun; stay, and you'll play games you only dream of. Shivers? You'll shiver yourself to pieces.

BRIDE: Then be not coy, but use your time,
While you may, go marry.

GHOST: *(Referring to BRIDE as she sings.)* **Isn't she beautiful? So beautiful and so sad. Do you like her? Do you want her? She's singing to you. Wouldn't you just die for her?** *(He slides into the darkness.)*

BRIDE: For having once but lost your prime,
You may for ever tarry.

(The BRIDE finishes her song, places her bouquet on the coffin, moves off.)

BOY: A coffin. Ha ha. That must be my cousin who died a few days ago. Cousin? Come out of there, cousin. *(No movement.)* **Come out, cousin, come out.** *(He knocks loudly on coffin cover.)* **It's your cousin, cousin.** *(No response. He unlatches the lid, lifts it just enough to stick his head in. Into coffin:)* **Are you coming out?...Don't you want to see me?...You'll hurt my feelings if you don't...Why won't you answer me...?** *(He opens lid all the way.)* **Cousin?** *(He pulls the dead body up and out of the coffin. COUSIN is very stiff, with a pale face and reddened, empty eye sockets; but he is well dressed. The BOY stands him up, holds him in place and touches COUSIN's face.)*

No wonder you didn't come out. You're cold as ice. I'll warm you a little. *(He carries COUSIN toward fire, sets him down, turns, lets COUSIN lean against his back, while he holds his hands out to the fire.)* **I'm glad you joined me tonight, cousin. I didn't know what was going to happen, but now, I'm much happier that you're here. I'll have a lot more fun with you.** *(He turns, touches COUSIN's face with his hands.)* **There. How do you like the new breeches my father made for you? They still look brand new; hardly used.** *(After a moment)*

Ah, you're still cold. I know. I'll warm you by the fire. Come
over and sit with me a while. *(BOY hauls COUSIN to fire, then
tries to make him sit on the floor, not the chair.)* Sit. Go ahead, sit.
(He has trouble making COUSIN's legs sit right as they are stiff.)
Bend your knees. *(COUSIN won't bend so BOY lays COUSIN flat
on his back, then lifts COUSIN up by the shoulders, trying to bend
him at the waist.)* Then bend your waist, bend your — bend.
Bend! *(COUSIN still won't bend. BOY lays COUSIN down flat on
the floor. He picks up a leg and tries to bend it.)* Bend...bend,
cousin...how can you sit if you don't bend? *(COUSIN won't
bend. He lets go of leg, it stays up, straight and stiff.)*

Have you been gone so long you forgot how to sit? You
always were stubborn. *(He pushes leg down, then sits on
COUSIN's legs, takes COUSIN's two arms, pulls and slowly,
with great effort and grunting, he bends COUSIN's upper half
up. COUSIN sits, legs straight out.)* That's it, bend. There.
Now, you'll catch the heat of the fire and warm up. *(The
BOY sits next to him, arm around him, holding him up.)*

So, how have you been, cousin?...Happy?...Busy?...
Dead? Yes, I know. But your joints get stiff if you don't use
them. Because, I'm sorry to tell you, cousin, you're stiff all
over. I can't blame you, laying in the ground with nothing
to do. You need exercise. We should play something to
loosen you up. Would you like to play ninepins? I'll see if
I can find a bowling ball. *(He stands, COUSIN falls over.)* No,
sit up. *(Sitting him up again)* I'll find us a bowling ball and
nine pins. *(He lets go, COUSIN stays there for the moment.
BOY moves away.)* Now, I'll find us a —*(COUSIN falls over.
BOY picks him up, considers what to do. He pulls COUSIN's arm,
straightens it. BOY lets go and arm stays where BOY put it. BOY
then moves arm down and out to COUSIN's side. BOY flattens the
hand out, bends the wrist flat. He then lets COUSIN go and backs
away; COUSIN starts to fall but his fall is broken by his stiff arm.
COUSIN stays propped up.)* That's it, cousin. Here, face the fire.
*(He twists COUSIN's head to face fire, then steps back to look at
him.)*

You still don't look happy. Why do they always make you
dead people look like that. What does that mean? *(He holds his
face next to COUSIN's in that expression.)* It just makes me think
I'm dead. *(He forces COUSIN's mouth up into a strange, frozen
smile. He steps back, looks at COUSIN.)* You look happy, now,
cousin. *(BOY smiles at COUSIN in the same fashion.)*

Now, ninepins. *(To the castle)* We need a ball to play
ninepins with! *(A skull comes rolling on.)* Look, cousin, a ball.
Now we can play. Yes, I'm happy, too. *(He smiles à la cousin
at COUSIN. COUSIN smiles back. To the castle.)* Thanks. *(He

251

checks out skull, looks in its face.) **Do I know you?...
Grampa?...No. Do you know me?** *(SKULL looks boy up and
down, then shakes itself "no."* **I didn't think so.** *(Holding skull
out to COUSIN.)* **Do you know who this is, cousin?...Me
either.** *(He puts his fingers through the eyes and nose, does a
couple of bowling-like gestures.)* **Not too bad.** *(A large thigh
bone falls near BOY.)* **A large thigh bone just fell near me.**
*(Another falls, then another and another. They come from all
directions, land all around him; then they stop.)* **Hey, that's
only eight.** *(The ninth one falls.)* **Nine. Ninepins!** *(He sets
them up.)* **Ninepins, cousin. Now we'll be able to bowl.
Whee! What a game we'll have! Did you want to make a bet
on the game? I bet I'll win. I'll bet you a couple of coppers.
Seven...eight...nine — Ninepins!** *(They are set up. He backs
up, takes ball in his hand.)* **Who's first? You want to go?...**
(He looks to COUSIN, who flashes him that happy smile.) **All
right. Don't get up. I'll go first. Watch.** *(He turns COUSIN's
head so COUSIN can see. He readies himself. To skull)* **You,
knock down all the pins over there. You see?** *(Skull turns to
look.)* **All down at once. All right.** *(He sticks fingers in ball,
takes a deep breath.)* **You can do it — you can do it — you
can do it — go get them!** *(He rolls skull at bones. He misses
everything. The ball doesn't roll straight and thunks as it rolls.)*
**This ball doesn't roll straight. And it thunks when it rolls.
And it doesn't listen. So don't even bother talking to it.**
(He gets ball.) **No wonder. It's not round.** *(He puts skull in
vise, tightens grip. Then he grabs the lower jaw, struggles and
pulls it off. Then he files down the edges with a file, blows on
it.)* **There, that's better.** *(He takes it out of vise, carries it to
COUSIN.)* **It should roll better, now. Here, you give it a roll,
cousin. See how you can do with it.** *(He holds it out to
COUSIN. COUSIN doesn't move to take it.)* **I'll help you.** *(He
puts ball down, then picks COUSIN up, faces him toward pins.)*
The ball. *(He sees ball a little distance from where they stand.
He steadies COUSIN, starts to go for skull, COUSIN starts to
fall, BOY catches him. BOY tries again, COUSIN starts to fall,
BOY quickly catches him. BOY then steadies COUSIN carefully,
measures distance, gets ready and picks COUSIN up, carries
him over to ball. BOY picks ball up, pulls out COUSIN's hand,
fixes his hand into a cup.)* **Hold this.** *(BOY puts ball in
COUSIN's hand. Then he carries COUSIN to the place from
which to roll. BOY takes other hand of COUSIN, fixes fingers,
then puts ball on the fingers. From behind, he holds COUSIN
around the waist, takes COUSIN's arm, swings it back and
forth.)* **Now, you're ready. Roll it like we know you can,
cousin. Put some spin on it, roll like thunder! Go!** *(COUSIN,*

with BOY's help, swings his arm to roll. At the peak of the arc, the ball falls out of COUSIN's hand directly down to floor.) **Not a very good roll.** *(Turns COUSIN's face to his.)* **Did you try?...No wonder. You're still too cold. I know. When two lie next to each other they warm each other.** *(The BOY carries COUSIN near fire.)*

    Sit. Bend. *(This time, he bends COUSIN, who sits.)* **That's better. See what exercise can do for you? Lay down.** *(BOY pushes COUSIN's back to the floor, COUSIN's legs go up in the air. BOY pushes the legs down, the upper body rolls up.)* **Lay down. Down.** *(BOY pushes on COUSIN's legs and chest until COUSIN lies flat on the floor. He wraps blanket around COUSIN and then lays next to him.)* **Now, cousin, you'll be warm in no time at all. Then we'll have a good game of ninepins. Because right now it wouldn't be fair. I'd win easily and take all your coppers.** *(COUSIN slowly begins to move his head.)* **Ah! You see? You're getting warm already.** *(COUSIN stretches out an arm, then a leg.)* **You see? You're warming up. I'm warming you, aren't I?**

COUSIN: *(Dryly)* **Aaaaiiiimmm...**

BOY: **You're talking now, see?**

COUSIN: **I'm...**

BOY: **"I'm."**

COUSIN: **Going...**

BOY: **"Going."**

COUSIN: **To...**

BOY: **Oh, this is wonderful. "To..."**

COUSIN: **Strangle you!**

BOY: **"Stra —"** *(The BOY jumps out from under the blanket. COUSIN slowly sits up.)* **What did you say?**

COUSIN: **I'm going to strangle you!** *(He is stiffly rising.)*

BOY: **What about our game of ninepins?**

COUSIN: **I'm going to kill you!** *(He begins — with arms reaching out — to slowly, stiffly advance on BOY. BOY backs up, keeping a safe distance.)*

BOY: **Is that my thanks? I took you out of your coffin, I warmed you up, I got us a ball to play ninepins, and you want to —**

COUSIN & BOY: **Strangle you!**

BOY: **You're ungrateful. I'm ashamed of you.** *(Backing away, toward the coffin. COUSIN is reaching for BOY's neck.)* **I'm glad my father isn't here. He'd be ashamed of you, too. So would your father. You ought to be ashamed of yourself. Are you?**

COUSIN: **I'm going to strangle you!**

BOY: **You never were much of a talker.** *(COUSIN grabs BOY around neck, choking him. They struggle. BOY pulls away leav-*

ing PRINCESS' necklace in COUSIN's hands.) **I would have given that to you if I'd known that's what you wanted. Why didn't you ask?**

COUSIN: *(With dark, shaking anger)* ***Aauugghh!***

BOY: I didn't understand what you just said, but I don't think that was thank you. Back you go into your coffin. *(BOY picks up the slow-moving COUSIN, trying to maneuver him back into the coffin.)*

COUSIN: You're going with me. You're going with me!

BOY: There's only room in there for one. *(BOY pushes him down flat, puts COUSIN's arms and hands in the customary position.)* **And here...** *(He gets skull and, when he approaches coffin, COUSIN sits up, reaching for BOY's throat. Instead, BOY puts ball in COUSIN's grasping hands.)* **You'd better practice. Then maybe next time we'll be able to play ninepins.** *(He shoves COUSIN down, closes lid of coffin, latches it. He begins to walk away, turns back, unlatches top, opens lid a short distance.)* **You couldn't tell me how to get the shivers, could you?**

COUSIN: I'm going to strangle you! *(COUSIN's hands shoot out, grab BOY by throat.)*

BOY: *(A little strangled, but we understand his words.)* **I didn't think so.** *(He pulls COUSIN's hands from his throat, closes lid, latches it. The distant bell begins to toll twelve.)* **I just can't get the shivers. I'll never learn how in this place, not if I live to be a hundred.** *(He listens. The coffin is moved off.)* **Ah, the bell. Midnight. All is well.** *(He puts the blanket over himself, fluffs his pillow, lays down and goes to sleep. The bell tolls twelve.)*

Scene 8

(The lights brighten. The KING, PRINCESS, and MAID cautiously enter.)

KING: There. I'm sorry.

PRINCESS: *(She runs to him, shakes him.)* **Young man?**

BOY: Princess.

PRINCESS: You're alive!

BOY: It must be morning. *(He stands and bows.)* **Your Majesties.**

KING: Still here!

PRINCESS: I knew you would be. How did it go?

BOY: Not as well I'm afraid. My cousin was here and we were going to play ninepins, but he was too cold and stiff.

PRINCESS: Was he dead?

BOY: Yes.

KING: Yes, I'm sure he was — and deadly.

BOY: No, ungrateful. I was ashamed of him.

KING: Ungrateful?

BOY: After all I did for him he wanted to strangle me.

KING: And yet, here you stand.

BOY: But it was good to see him again.

PRINCESS: You're right, Father. What a mind.

BOY: I would have had much more fun if you had stayed and played ninepins.

PRINCESS: Where's the necklace I gave you?

BOY: My cousin wanted it so I let him have it.

PRINCESS: *(Knowingly)* Your dead cousin. Oooo...

KING: Will you stay the third night?

BOY: I may as well. I hope I can learn something.

MAID: Excuse me, sir. What is it you hope to learn?

BOY: About the shivers.

MAID: That's what I thought.

KING: I'll inform the guards. Whoever you are, our hopes go with you. *(He exits.)*

MAID: I'll wait outside, My Lady. *(She curtsies and exits.)*

BOY: Would you like to stay a while tonight? You never know what's going to happen or who will come. Maybe you could teach me about the shivers.

PRINCESS: I want to stay and help you. I want to watch you with the spirits. You understand something, something that I don't, yet.

BOY: I don't understand about the shivers. You do. Will you stay and teach me?

PRINCESS: I want to stay, but I don't understand these spirits, or you. I will someday. But tonight, I'd be too scared. You'll do better without me.

BOY: If you change your mind, come back and we'll play something.

PRINCESS: There have been just two men who stayed the third night. Neither lived to see the morning. *(She embraces him.)* I hope I see you tomorrow. *(She kisses his cheek. She turns to go.)*

BOY: What? What was that?

PRINCESS: I hope to see you tomorrow. *(She doesn't kiss him. PRINCESS exits.)*

BOY: *(Shrugs it off.)* **Oh.** *(Music. BOY moves to fire, blows on it, builds it up. As he does, the lights dim.)*

Scene 9

(We hear the whispers, see the movements in the shadows. Abruptly all movements and whispers cease. The BRIDE is heard singing the lament. The BOY speaks while she is singing.)

BOY: Princess?

BRIDE: *(The BRIDE enters singing, carrying the bouquet, marching.)*
Gather your rosebuds while you may,
Old time is still a-flying,
And that same flow'r that smiles today,
Tomorrow will be dying.

BOY: What a beautiful dress. It's a wedding dress, isn't it. Is
that you, Princess? *(She stops singing.)* **Have you come back**
to teach me about the shivers? *(The BRIDE nods yes.)* **You**
have? That's great! The shivers. What do we do? *(The*
BRIDE gestures and a light, eerie, courtly music is heard. She
motions for BOY to come to her. As he does she raises her hands
to dance.) **You want to dance?** *(She motions yes, he takes her*
and they dance. He's not an accomplished dancer, but he
accepts the challenge.)
    I'm really happy you came back tonight, Princess. I was
thinking it was going to be a boring night, but now, the
shivers. I can't wait. Ha ha. *(He holds onto one hand, lets go*
of her waist. She twirls away, leaving her hand in his. That is,
her hand comes off in his.) **Oh, sorry, I...Who are you?** *(He*
goes to BRIDE, takes off her veil revealing a grotesque death's
head. The music dies out.)

BRIDE: *(Breathy, hissing)* **Kiss me.**

BOY: You're not the princess.

BRIDE: Kiss me.

BOY: Here I thought you were going to teach me how to get the
shivers. You told me you were going to teach me how to
get the shivers. You ought to be ashamed of yourself. Are
you?

BRIDE: Kiss me!

BOY: Is that all you can say: "Kiss me"?

BRIDE: *(Advancing on him)* **Come with me. Lie in the earth. Rest.**
Die. Die.

BOY: I'm not going with you. You're coming apart at the joints.
Here — *(He hands her her hand.)* **I'm through with you.** *(She*
takes it, tries repeatedly to stick it back on.)

GHOST: *(Running on)* **You insect!**

BOY: You, again.

GHOST: *(He rips double-headed axe out of wall.)* **Now you'll find**
out about the shivers because you're going to die!

BOY: Not so fast! If you want to kill me you'll have to catch me.

GHOST: I'll catch you, all right! *(With axe, he chases BOY. BOY*
starts off. 1 CAT leaps on, hisses, blocks his path. BOY tries
another direction, 2 CAT leaps on, blocks that path. GHOST
chops down at BOY with axe, hits the floor. The BOY steps on

axe, stomping it out of GHOST's hands, escapes. GHOST picks up thigh bones [ninepins] and throws them at BOY. The BOY dodges and tosses blanket and pillow in the air to block bones.)

BOY: **You can't hit me.** *(The BOY tries another way out, the CORPSE staggers on, arms reaching for BOY's neck, blocks BOY.)*

GHOST: **I can do anything I want with you. You stayed the third night. You're mine to play with. Ah, what's this, a chair?** *(GHOST picks up chair.)* **Whose seat is this? Aahh!** *(He throws chair at BOY.)*

BOY: **I told you, you can't hit me.** *(Now the BOY picks up bones, throws them at GHOST.)*

GHOST: **You can't hit me.** *(GHOST dodges bones.)* **Ah, this is fun! Isn't this fun? We needed fresh young blood to play with. Now I'm going to catch you.** *(He goes for BOY.)*

BOY: *(Running away)* **Take it easy. Stop bragging. I'm as strong as you are. Probably stronger.** *(The GHOST goes for him, he dodges away, starts to exit. The DOG jumps on, growls, blocks his path.)*

GHOST: **I'm stronger than you!**

BOY: **I'm stronger than you!**

GHOST: **Ha!** *(He chases BOY, gets close, the BOY suddenly kneels and the GHOST's momentum takes him flying over the BOY, headfirst. The GHOST finishes, however, with a graceful shoulder roll. They stand and challenge.)*

BOY: **You see, you can't catch me.**

GHOST: **Who's bragging now?**

BOY: **And I'm stronger than you, too.**

GHOST: **Don't say that. I hate when you say that. I hate everything that lives when you say that! I am stronger than you!** *(GHOST gestures and directly above BOY, a large block of granite falls from the darkness; the BOY moves and it just misses him.)*

BOY: **What did I tell you about bragging?** *(Another block falls, then another. The BOY moves away each time.)* **And you can't hit me.**

GHOST: *(Maddened)* **I can do such things to you. I have a great imagination. Arms, legs, heart, liver, spleen, skull, eyes —** *(He takes a deep breath and, from some distance away, blows out the fire. The darkness looms, moonlight streams in the windows.)* **There, little man.** *(The two CATS, the DOG, the CORPSE and BRIDE slowly begin to close in on him, surrounding him.)*

BOY: **What does that prove? I'm still stronger than you. Because, I'm stronger than you.** *(The CATS, DOG, CORPSE and BRIDE are all close, reaching, pawing, growling and hissing.)* **I'm stronger than you all.**

GHOST: **If you're stronger than I am, I'll let you go.** *(The SPIRITS* are close, they all reach for him.)

BOY: I accept the challenge.

GHOST: *(This stops the SPIRITS. They withdraw their paws and hands and sigh in anticipation. The GHOST gestures, the fire flares up, lighting the room.)* **Come with me. I will teach you a lesson. You need to learn a lesson. You need to get some sense.** *(He gestures, a platform appears with a saw horse holding a large log. An axe leans against log.)* **You stayed the third night. I'm grateful, little man. I'm enjoying playing with you. Here's a game you'll like. How many swings to cut the log. Agreed?**

BOY: This will be easy.

GHOST: I'm first. *(The SPIRITS surround them, watch. GHOST picks up the axe, prepares and swings. He cuts log off in one swing. The SPIRITS moan and growl in appreciation and anticipation. Intensely)* **There. You beat that, living man. Because if you don't, you're going to die, tonight. And you know what? You can't beat that. You're going to die tonight!**

BOY: Brag and more brag. *(Takes axe.)* **My turn.** *(To himself)* **An iron axe. Now, axe...Ahhh!** *(He strikes log with axe, but it doesn't break. He pulls axe out of log. The SPIRITS moan and growl.)*

GHOST: Yes, I won! I'm stronger!

BOY: No, I won.

GHOST: I won! I chopped it off in one blow and look at you.

BOY: Yes, look. Look here; I won.

GHOST: *(Moving to log, looking)* **There's nothing you could have done** — *(The BOY grabs the GHOST's beard, sticks it into the slit he just made, then chops the axe head into crack, where it stays.)*

BOY: Now I've got you. Now who's going to die?

GHOST: *(Pulling his beard, trying to get free)* **Let me out. You tricked me! I'm stronger than you.**

BOY: I don't think so.

GHOST: When I get out of here I'm going to kill you.

BOY: Hey, that's enough bragging. You're stuck in a log.

GHOST: I'm stronger than you!

BOY: *(He quickly looks for and finds the iron rod. The SPIRITS recognize its power, stay back.)* **Now who needs a lesson? Now who needs to get some sense?** *(He hits GHOST with the iron rod.)*

GHOST: Oh! Stop it!

BOY: *(Punctuating with an occasional strike of the iron rod)* **Stop that bragging. Stop saying you're stronger than me.**

GHOST: I'm stronger than you! I'm stronger than you!

BOY: Easy to say, easy to believe, when you know it's not true,

when you're stuck in a log. And stop saying you're going
to kill me. That's nonsense.

GHOST: I'm going to kill you!

BOY: Good Lord, that's more nonsense. *(Hitting him)* **Get some
sense. You should be ashamed of yourself. You terrible old
ghost.**

GHOST: I'll stop. I'll stop if you will. Stop, please, stop, I'll give
you riches, I promise you. I will, great riches. There are
great riches here, see — *(He gestures and three chests full of
brilliant gold appear.)* **One part is for the poor, one part is
for the king, and the third is for you. If you stop. And if
you set me free.**

BOY: Are you going to chase me?

GHOST: No.

BOY: Are you going to kill me?

GHOST: Yes — no. No.

BOY: Are you stronger than me?

GHOST: Yes! Yes, I am! *(BOY hits him.)* No! No I'm not!

BOY: **All right.** *(He drops the iron rod, pulls out the axe, then pulls
GHOST's beard from the log. The GHOST looks deep into BOY,
then bows to him. The DOG, CATS, CORPSE and BRIDE all bow
in their own fashion. BOY bows to them all. GHOST and SPIR-
ITS disappear into the darkness. BOY goes to chest of gold and
jewels. He picks up a handful of gold, looks at it, lets it fall back
into chest. From another he picks up a crown, looks at it, puts it
on.)* **"What a mind."** *(He takes off crown, sets it down. He picks
up a familiar necklace. The bell begins to toll twelve.)* **The
princess' necklace.** *(He puts it on.)* **Ah, the bell. Midnight. All
is well.** *(He lays near fire, goes to sleep.)*

Scene 10

(The lights brighten. The KING, PRINCESS and MAID enter.)

KING: Boy?

PRINCESS: Young man?

BOY: It's morning.

KING & PRINCESS: Alive!

BOY: *(Bowing)* **Your Majesties.**

KING: I don't believe it.

PRINCESS: Are the spirits gone?

KING: They must be, here he is. You've broken the spell. You've
returned the castle to the living. This time I'll wager you
learned what the shivers are.

BOY: What can they be? There was a bride here who pretended
to be the princess but whose hand came off. I don't think
she was even alive. And then an old man with a beard

259

came and we played some games; he showed me a lot of gold — there it is.

KING: The castle treasure.

BOY: One part is for the poor, one part is for you, and the other is for me.

PRINCESS: If you stayed the third night, and you're alive, then —

MAID: Congratulations, Princess.

PRINCESS: My husband? *(She laughs in innocent disbelief.)* My husband!

BOY: And here — *(He takes off her necklace.)* Your necklace. *(He gives it back to her.)* My cousin gave it back.

PRINCESS: Who *are* you?

BOY: I don't know.

PRINCESS: Where are you from?

BOY: I don't know.

KING: Who is your father?

BOY: I mustn't say.

KING: He would no longer be ashamed of you. You — *you* have set our castle free. You've earned a chest of riches. And you will marry my daughter and live in this magnificent castle. Your father would be proud of you. I am.

BOY: All right, but I still don't know what the shivers are.

KING: Ha, still on the shivers. What a mind. *(He laughs.)* Come, young man, let's prepare for your wedding. *(The KING exits with BOY.)*

MAID: Princess, if it's the shivers he wants, leave it to me, I'll give him the shivers.

PRINCESS: Oh, can you?

MAID: I'm sure I can.

PRINCESS: We would be eternally grateful.

MAID: Yes, my Lady. *(She curtsies; PRINCESS exits. MAID exits in another direction. Music. The room is reset to be the bedroom of the married couple. The bench, chair, saw horse are removed. The bed is decorated with lace and flowers. Two large bouquets are set on either side of the bed. MAID re-enters carrying a heavy pail, sets it down. She then arranges flowers on the bed.)*

Scene 11

(Lights come up as the BOY enters arm-in-arm with a BRIDE who is dressed exactly as before and carrying a bridal bouquet. The fire burns brightly. The BOY looks at BRIDE, pulls on her hand; it stays on. He pulls again, harder; it stays on. He stares at the veil, then suddenly pulls it back.)

BOY: Princess, it's you.

PRINCESS: You make a handsome groom. It was a wonderful wedding.

BOY: But it didn't give me the shivers.

PRINCESS: Still the shivers.

BOY: It's something that I just don't understand.

PRINCESS: You have all the gold you need, you're the next king, you're with me, *(He smiles at her)* you've won everything that anybody could ever want. And still —

BOY: *(Sits on bed.)* If I could only get the shivers.

PRINCESS: I'm sure there is wisdom in this somewhere. Maid! *(She crosses to the MAID. BOY doesn't hear them.)* You said you could give him the shivers?

MAID: I went to the stream that runs through the garden and scooped out a pail full of water and minnows.

PRINCESS: Minnows?

MAID: Yes, my Lady. Tell him to lie down and close his eyes. Speak softly to him. Then pour this on him and the little fishes will wiggle all over him.

PRINCESS: How could such a thing give him the shivers when all those horrible spirits couldn't? This is very strange, maid. *(MAID gestures toward BOY. PRINCESS looks at him.)* I'll do it.

MAID: *(Curtsies.)* Yes, my Lady. *(The MAID exits.)*

PRINCESS: Husband?

BOY: Yes?

PRINCESS: Lie down and I'll tell you an old story. *(He lies down.)*

BOY: My father used to tell us stories and everyone got the shivers but me. You're wasting your time.

PRINCESS: Close your eyes. *(He does. Stroking his head)* Rest ...my curious husband; my courageous one; my new, wise friend. *(She kisses his hand.)* Once upon a time, there was a strange young man, *(She picks up pail, carries it to the bed)* who came from nowhere, who didn't know who he was, *(Lifting pail)* who desperately sought something that would fulfill his life, and he finally found it. *(She slowly pours the entire bucket of water over him.)*

BOY: Ah! Oh! Ah! Princess! Why did — I'm all — What's this? I'm...I'm... *(He sits up.)* Ah! Dear wife, I'm shivering! I'm shivering!

PRINCESS: Yes, yes, at last!

BOY: I'm shivering! Oh, thank you! *(He jumps out of bed, shivering.)* Now I know what the shivers are!

PRINCESS: We're all so happy!

BOY: I'm shivering! I got some sense! I'm shivering! *(He embraces her, swings her around. He kisses her. Dim-out.)*

THE END

Rockway Cafe

by Max Bush

CHARACTERS

ROXANNE. 14
DELLA . . . . 38, Roxanne's Mother

TV CHARACTERS

ERIC . . . . 28, Rock & Roll Singer
RACHEL. . . . . 25, Eric's Girlfriend
JOHN. . . . . 45, Rachel's Father

TIME: The present.

PLACE: A suburb.

SETTING: The family recreation room; inside the television; and a recital hall stage.

MUSIC NOTE: The songs for *Rockway Cafe* can be performed by a live band or with music tapes which are available for purchase from the composer either in reel-to-reel (15 ips) or cassette. Complete music with original cast vocals may also be purchased from New Plays, Inc.; see "Credits" section at the end of the book for ordering information.

If a live band is used, five musicians are suggested: two guitars, drums, keyboard, and bass. Female back-up vocalists may also be used to strengthen the songs "Rockway Cafe," "Was It the Night?" and "I'm Ready for Love." If a live band is used, there can be interplay between band and players throughout. If the music tape is used with no live accompaniment, when the characters sing only part of a song, it is sung a capella.

For purchasing of cassette or reel-to-reel tapes, apply to the composer:

Dale Dieleman
362 S. Lakeshore Drive
Holland, MI 49424

DEDICATION: *Rockway Cafe* is dedicated to Dick and Barbara Parsaca, and Keith Oberfeld.

Rockway Cafe was commissioned by Grand Rapids Festival of the Arts, Grand Rapids, Michigan, and opened outside in the city's Calder Plaza on June 1, 1990 with the following cast and crew:

CHARACTERS

ROXANNE . . . . Amy Danles

DELLA . . . . Joanne Schreves

JOHN . . . . Wally Fleser

RACHEL . . . . Stacy Fuhs

ERIC . . . . Glen Danles

PRODUCTION STAFF

Director . . . . Max Bush

Assistant Director . . . . . Sondra Loucks

Stage Manager . . . . Sue Arterburn

Music Director . . . . Dale Dieleman

Music Producer . . . . . . Dave Zeoli

Design . . . . Keith Oberfeld

Producers . . . . Richard and Barbara Parsaca, Keith Oberfeld

Music & Lyrics . . . . Dale Dielman

ACKNOWLEDGMENT: Thanks to Debra Olsen for her help that day by the riverside, in the conception of *Rockway Cafe*.

(Rec room and TV area. Right is a couch, a coffee table, an end table with a phone. A practice mike stand with mike. Left is the TV area. The two worlds are clearly delineated; there is a strong contrast between the two. The TV ACTORS stand facing audience, unmoving, their heads down. The BAND and BACK-UP SINGERS wait far left, clearly visible to audience. When they are not playing and singing, they are unlit, but do not lower their heads and freeze as the TV actors do when the TV is off. ROXANNE enters, walks up to her practice mike stand and breaks into singing "Fantasy Man." The song potentially has a lot of energy, but ROXANNE sings it self-consciously and joylessly, going through the motions of choreography she's created for herself.)

ROXANNE: *(Sings a capella.)*
> **He's my fantasy man**
> **And girl he's always there**
> **He's my fantasy man**
> *(DELLA enters, unseen by ROXANNE.)*
> **When I need someone to care.**
> **He's my fantasy, fantasy, fantasy, fantasy man.**
> **He's my fantasy, fantasy, fantasy, fantasy man.**

DELLA: Well, that's a little better, Roxanne, isn't it?

ROXANNE: Hey, it's a lot better, Mom.

DELLA: But it's still not what you want, is it?

ROXANNE: I couldn't do better if I was Whitney Houston. It's a rank song.

DELLA: Who chose it for you?

ROXANNE: I did.

DELLA: Why did you choose a rank song?

ROXANNE: Because I love myself, Ma!

DELLA: I've heard you sing better, honey.

ROXANNE: I never sang it any better. I can't sing it any better. I will never sing it any better.

DELLA: Like when you're listening to headphones or watching *Rockway Cafe.* You sing loud, you jump around, you have fun. Try again.

ROXANNE: Don't you have court in the morning? *(DELLA indicates yes.)* Shouldn't you be figuring out your cross-exams?

DELLA: I've already done them.

ROXANNE: I hate Mr. Berry!

DELLA: Roxanne —

ROXANNE: You don't know what kind of teacher he is.

DELLA: He's letting you choose your own rank music.

ROXANNE: You know what Mr. Berry's first name is? It's Dingle. What does that tell you about his teaching methods?

DELLA: *(Covering a smile)* Roxanne, don't be rude. He doesn't

267

deserve that from you. Now, go ahead, sing. Only let yourself go. Have fun.

ROXANNE: *(Suddenly sitting on the floor. DELLA lets this run its*
course.) **Why does everyone have to sing? Why not just the**
best people in the class? I sing like a troll queen...giving
birth. *(Sings like a troll queen.)*
He's my fantasy man
More than a friend to me —
(DELLA throws a couch pillow, hits ROXANNE.) **I wish I had**
someone to sing with. Everybody was already stuck together
by the time Berry finished his sentence: "You can sing by
yourselves or with others." Zip, super glued in groups. "Ha-
ha, Roxanne." I'm the only one singing by her stupid self.

DELLA: *(Seeing she's finished)* **Come on. I'll help you.**

ROXANNE: **Don't you have a date?**

DELLA: **Not tonight.**

ROXANNE: **Well, shouldn't you go to the jail tonight and talk**
to that drug dealer?

DELLA: **Drunk driver.**

ROXANNE: **Or that cat burglar?**

DELLA: **Dog catcher.**

ROXANNE: **Don't you have to research something or update**
your folders or make some notes or look up some other
cases?

DELLA: **Always.**

ROXANNE: **Ma, you got to pick out your clothes!**

DELLA: **I will.**

ROXANNE: **You're perfect, aren't you?**

DELLA: **And I'd love to hear you sing.**

ROXANNE: **I want to watch *Rockway Cafe*.**

DELLA: **So that's it.**

ROXANNE: **I'll practice afterwards.**

DELLA: **Roxanne, you said you'd practice tonight because last**
night you had to watch *The Bradford Show* and *Our Times*
or you would die of television withdrawal.

ROXANNE: **But I've been looking forward to this episode for**
five months; ever since it was first on. You heard me talk
about it. Eric sings "I'm Ready for Love" to Rachel, tonight.
(ROXANNE sings romantically to DELLA part of the song with
more enthusiasm than her recital song.)

Please listen to this song,
'Cause it's the only way
To tell you how I'm feeling
And what I'm trying to say.
I'm ready for love.

(She kisses DELLA.)
The love that says there is only you.
Yes, I'm ready for love.
I give you everything, you know it's true.

DELLA: I'm worried about you and that TV.
ROXANNE: We're just going steady.
DELLA: I mean it, Roxanne.
ROXANNE: I'm worried, too. I'm worried about Eric. He's blowing it with Rachel. I keep telling him what he needs to do but he won't listen to me. Maybe he will tonight! Mom, I'll clean the porch or I'll do the laundry for a month or —
DELLA: Roxanne —
ROXANNE: I'll call Gramma and talk to her about her operations.
DELLA: You want to live to see your next birthday? *(ROXANNE sulks.)* Don't pull that face.
ROXANNE: What face?
DELLA: That thing you do with your eyes. It's just like your father.
ROXANNE: You mean this? *(She does it again.)*
DELLA: Stop it. You only do that to irritate me.
ROXANNE: I'm sorry. I am his daughter. I look like him.
DELLA: Roxanne, you chose to be in this class. You chose that rank song. You knew you'd have to sing in this recital.
ROXANNE: Dad lets me watch as much TV as I want at his house. He even watches *Rockway* with me sometimes.
DELLA: You sing that song through once — to me — we'll talk about it, then sing it again and you can watch TV. All right?
ROXANNE: All right.
DELLA: All right.
ROXANNE: After *Rockway Cafe.*
DELLA: Before *Rockway Cafe.* Before any more TV.
ROXANNE: It's almost time for it to start.
DELLA: Then tape it and watch it after you're done.
ROXANNE: I'll practice all night. I'll sing it to you three times! Mom! I'll have fun!
DELLA: Roxanne!
ROXANNE: I haven't won one argument since you became a lawyer.
DELLA: That's enough! You practice, now —
ROXANNE: I know.
DELLA: With or without me helping you.
ROXANNE: Without, please.
DELLA: Don't you think it would help you —
ROXANNE: Without, please.
DELLA: All right. Call me when you're ready to sing to me.

269

ROXANNE: All right.

DELLA: You can do this, Roxanne; the only thing stopping you is yourself. *(DELLA exits.)*

ROXANNE: "The only thing stopping you is yourself." God, Mom, what do you know? I'm on my deathbed! It's my last wish. *(She flops on couch.)* **Rockway Cafe...Rockway Cafe...** *(She dies. The phone rings. She sits up, checks her watch, picks up remote, turns on the TV.)* **Just starting.** *(The TV ACTORS animate. ROXANNE hears her mother coming, turns TV off, jumps up to mike and sings. The TV ACTORS put their heads down.)* **He's my fantasy man, More than a friend to me —**

DELLA: *(Entering)* **The phone's for you.**

ROXANNE: Who is it?

DELLA: Rob.

ROXANNE: Tell him I'm practicing.

DELLA: Why won't you talk to him? I think he's charming.

ROXANNE: Mom, I think I'd better accept the responsibility for things like practicing, don't you? *(Sings.)*

> He's my fantasy man
> He's what a friend should be...

(DELLA exits shaking her head. ROXANNE quickly turns on TV. The TV ACTORS animate. They are in the Rockway Cafe, preparing stage for ERIC to sing. RACHEL is setting up the floor mike.)

JOHN: Rachel, Eric is right. Listen to him.

RACHEL: What is it you think I haven't heard?

ERIC: I can help you, Rachel. Let me talk to Jackson, my promo man.

RACHEL: If you do I won't go to the audition.

ERIC: John, am I trying to do something wrong?

JOHN: No. Rachel, I don't know where this stubborn streak comes from. Certainly not me.

ERIC: What are you afraid of?

ROXANNE: She told you!

RACHEL: I told you. And I told you, Father.

ROXANNE & RACHEL: I want my talent to get me in the door.

RACHEL: I want my music to get this recording contract.

ROXANNE & RACHEL: Not you.

ERIC: I'm not singing for you, I'm just asking someone to listen to you.

ROXANNE: Eric, have amplifiers blown out your ears?

JOHN: You don't understand how the industry operates.

ROXANNE: You don't understand your daughter!

JOHN: I've worked in the studios and I know how they think.

ERIC: I came from the streets of nowhere and I needed lots of help.

ROXANNE: Eric, try not to talk.

ERIC: My music was always hot, but no one would hear it — until your father told them to listen. Suddenly, they had ears and contracts. But I still feel pride in my music; it's still mine.

RACHEL & ROXANNE: That's your story.

ERIC: *(Help)* John?

JOHN: Just let me tell them you're my daughter.

ROXANNE: I don't think so.

RACHEL: I waited — years — until my music was good enough — until I was good enough — to get this audition. My music got me in the door and now it's up to me to win a contract. It's time, Father. The mike is on.

ROXANNE: Just sing, Eric. That's all you need to do. *(JOHN steps up to the microphone, speaks directly to audience. RACHEL fixes ERIC's hair. Music intro to* Rockway Cafe *begins.)*

JOHN: Welcome. Welcome to Rockway Cafe! We know why you're here and we'll bring him right on. But first I'd like to personally thank this young man for not forgetting those who knew and loved him before he became a legend. Many have come through here, but none so hot, none with so much class. Hey! Returning to The Cafe where it started for him! Here's the man! The Rockman of Rockway! Eric Cortland! *(JOHN exits.)*

ERIC: It's great to be home! *(He points to some audience members.)* Hey, Steve, Richard — Lynn! *(He picks up his guitar.)*

ERIC & ROXANNE: Rockway Cafe!

ERIC: *(Sings "Rockway Cafe.")*
> Don't you worry 'bout tomorrow
> Don't you fret about today
> 'Cause there's a place you can rock tonight
> And roll your cares away.
>
> You can go there just the way you are.
> Join your friends who know you are a star.

(ROXANNE jumps up on couch, dances; RACHEL dances in the cafe.)
> Come on to the Rockway!
> Baby, it's your cafe!
> Come on to the Rockway!
> Baby, it's our cafe!

(He motions for RACHEL to join him; she does.)

ERIC & RACHEL:
> Come and meet me for the show tonight
> Leave your Monday world far below.
> Let your soul go sailin'

271

When the band starts wailin'
It's Friday night, let's go.

Join the beat that rocks the U.S.A.
Celebrate; get down; come out; come play.

(Come on, come on, come on)
Come on to the Rockway!
Get down at the cafe!
Join us at the Rockway!
Dancin' at the cafe!

Rock-way-Ca-fe *(Five times.)*

Take me to the Rockway!
Take me to our cafe!
Come on to the Rockway!
Baby, it's our cafe!

ERIC: **Thank you! Thank you! Rockway Cafe!** *(RACHEL steps away, applauds ERIC who bows. He takes off his guitar. Both ERIC and RACHEL slowly put their heads down, become inert.)*
ROXANNE: **Commercial. I hate —** *No commercials!* **Why don't they put them all at the beginning or the end.** *(She hits mute button, stands fidgeting for a time.)* **"You could sing while you're waiting."** **Oh, I didn't think of that. "Sure, let yourself go, jump around, have fun."** **Thank you. I'd rather eat my dad's socks.** *(She checks TV, then turns away in disgust. She sings absentmindedly.)*

Girls you know the story
You know all the rules
But there's nothing 'bout
(She suddenly jumps on end table charged with energy. She sings loud and rather than follow her choreography, she improvises movements athletically and fluidly.)

The game of love
That says we play the fools.

Yes, I may lose this game of love,
Out of sheer neglect —

(She glances up at rec room door, stops.) **Oh, no, I was singing!** *(She freezes. She begins to say something inaudibly, repeatedly, without moving her jaw. Finally we're able to understand what*

she is saying.) **Oil can. Oil can.** *(She loosens a couple of joints, then slumps. She checks TV, sees the commercials are still running. She resolutely sings, stiffly following her choreography.)*

He's my fantasy man
More than a friend to —
He's my fantasy —
He's my —

(She's made a couple of mistakes.) **I need help.** *(She takes a fistful of candy off the end table, stuffs it into her mouth with the wrappers still on. She sings with her mouth full.)*

He's my fantasy man
And girl, he's always there.
(Pieces fall out of her mouth to the floor.)
He's my fantasy man
When I need someone to care.

"Well, that's a little better, Roxanne, isn't it?" Yup. I never sang it better. I'm the star of the recital. *(She takes the last piece of candy from her mouth, offers it to her mother.)* **Would you like a piece of candy?** *(She sees the program is resuming, picks candy up, stuffs it back in candy dish.)* **That took forever.** *(Scene opens in the Rockway Cafe, late at night. RACHEL paces. ROXANNE hits mute button.)*

ERIC: Rachel —
RACHEL: Don't talk to me for a minute. *(Sings.)*
    Tell me, baby —
ERIC: How long will this take? The band is fried.
RACHEL: Until I have the song.
ERIC: Why don't you come out to the beach house, I'll turn on
    the jacuzzi —
RACHEL: Not now.
ROXANNE: I can make it. 555-4585! Say your name is Rob!
ERIC: After this?
RACHEL: I'm sure it will be too late.
ROXANNE: I bet it won't be too late for you, Eric.
ERIC: It won't be too late for me.
ROXANNE: I knew it. You're so predictable.
RACHEL: *(Sings to herself.)* **Tell me, baby, now** — *(JOHN walks on.)*
JOHN: Rachel!
RACHEL: I'm right here, Father, I wasn't hiding from you.
ROXANNE: What time is it, John?
JOHN: It's two o'clock in the morning.
ROXANNE: How's the band?

JOHN: The band is exhausted.

ROXANNE: I like fried better.

RACHEL: They're getting paid.

JOHN: How much longer —

RACHEL: Until we get it right.

ERIC: Great.

RACHEL: All night if I have to. The audition is next week. I want to be ready.

JOHN: *(Help)* Eric.

RACHEL: *(Sings.)* Tell me now, baby, is this all a dream?

ERIC: No. *(Sings.)* Tell me, baby, now —

RACHEL: Let me get it.

ERIC: But I hear it.

RACHEL & ROXANNE: I'll get it.

RACHEL: *(Sings.)* Tell me, baby, now, is this all —

ERIC: That's your mistake, right there.

RACHEL: Eric!

ERIC: I'm just showing you —

RACHEL: I'll find my mistake. I'm writing this song. It's my song.

ERIC: *(Sings.)* Tell me, baby, now, is this all a dream? Clean and simple, just how you like it. Now you have it, you can sing it and we can all get out of here.

JOHN: Thank you.

ROXANNE: Kill him! *(Infuriated, RACHEL pushes ERIC.)*

JOHN: Rachel! *(RACHEL tries to slap ERIC; he catches her arm. She swings the other, he grabs that wrist, too. They wrestle, she trying to get free of him and hit him, he protecting himself.)*

ERIC: What's wrong with you?

ROXANNE: She told you to let her do it!

RACHEL: Let me go! Let me go!

ROXANNE: Hit him!

JOHN: He was trying to help you!

ERIC: Rachel, Rachel!

ROXANNE: Kick him! Kick him!

RACHEL: Eric! Let me go! *(He pushes her away; she falls. He immediately tries to help her up. She scrambles away from him.)* Let me make mistakes! It's my song!

ERIC: I was helping you!

JOHN: He was only —

RACHEL: I make mistakes! They're my mistakes! I need to make them! Let me go! Let me go! *(She runs off.)*

JOHN: Rachel, he didn't mean...

ERIC: What was that?

JOHN: That was my sweet daughter.

ERIC: What am I doing wrong? Is it me, John?

ROXANNE: There's nothing wrong with her!

JOHN: Hey, she's seen a lot of rockers come through here; you're the only one she's written songs about.

ERIC: Maybe you can explain it to me.

ROXANNE: Let me explain it to you. Hah! *(She kicks at the TV. She then lets her hair down.)*

JOHN: This audition's made her crazy. I've seen it before, but in her mother.

ERIC: What do I do?

JOHN: I don't know.

ERIC: What did you do?

JOHN: I never knew what to do. I don't think it matters what you do. But it is a pleasure to see it's you in the middle of it and not me.

ROXANNE: Eric, it's my song. *(ROXANNE steps toward TV. The lights flicker and flash as ROXANNE moves into the TV and assumes RACHEL's character.)*

ERIC: Whatever I did, I'm sorry. I was just trying to help.

JOHN: I think that's true, don't you?

ERIC: Babe, you're just burning on nerves. Let's go to the beach house. You'll sleep forever.

ROXANNE: Father, you taught me it's my music, in my style, from myself. That's what people want; that's good music.

JOHN: Honey, you nailed it — three times in a row. Smooth and clean, just like you want it.

ROXANNE: But it didn't feel right. I'm not Eric. He rehearses a song once and he's ready. It comes hard for me. I have to work at it. *(To ERIC)* Will you wait? I'd like to sing it to you.

ERIC: Yeah. Yeah, I'll wait.

ROXANNE: Only if you want.

ERIC: I said I'd wait.

ROXANNE: Then maybe you should go —

ERIC: I said I'd wait.

ROXANNE: — both of you. I can do this myself.

JOHN: We'd love to hear it again.

ROXANNE: One and two and — *(She sings. At first she doesn't look at ERIC, but once she settles in, she sings to him clearly, with feeling: "Was It the Night.")*

Was it the night?
Was it the night?
Was it the night or the shine of your hair
In the candlelight?
Was it the night?

You're so free.
You're so free.

275

You're so free, good friends is all
I thought we'd be.
You're so free.

Tell me baby, now is this all a dream?
Or am I trapped inside some cruel scheme?
My mind says, baby, now don't you be a fool.
My heart says, baby, you'll lose him if you play too cool.
My heart says, baby, you'll lose him if you play too cool.
The moon was right.
The moon was right.
The moon was right and sent us on a magic flight.
The moon was right.

You came to me.
You came to me.
You came to me and you taught me all about harmony.
You came to me.

Tell me, baby, now, is this all a dream?
Or am I trapped inside some cruel scheme?
My heart says, baby, you'll lose him if you play too cool.
My heart says, baby, you'll lose him if you play too cool.
My heart says, baby, you'll lose him if you play too cool.
My heart says, baby, you'll lose him if you play too cool.

Was it the night?
Was it the night?

That was it, everybody! Thank you.

JOHN: *(Aside to ERIC)* **Was it any different?**

ROXANNE: That's how it goes!

JOHN: Let's pack it up. *(He exits.)*

ERIC: You sing it like that and they'll book your first world tour in a week.

ROXANNE: *(Embracing ERIC)* **Yes!**

DELLA: *(Entering rec room)* **Roxanne?**

ROXANNE: *(Aside)* **Mom...**

ERIC: That was strong. Clean as always but more from yourself.

ROXANNE: I felt more, like I was singing it for the first time.

DELLA: Roxanne?

ROXANNE: Having you listen made a difference. That's how you can help me. Just listen. *(DELLA picks up remote.)*

ERIC: You sing to me any time.

ROXANNE: Eric, you know that — *(To DELLA)* **No!** *(DELLA turns off TV. Slowly, as the scene fades out, ROXANNE and ERIC put* *their heads down, stay still.)* **Oh, no.** *(From that position, ROX-ANNE can see but not move.)* **I can't...** *(DELLA exits looking for ROXANNE.)* **Eric? Mother! Come back and turn on the TV! I'll miss the rest of the show. I'll miss the rest of my life! She never watches TV. I'll have to wait until Gramma comes over on Christmas to watch the Nutcracker. Maybe I...** *(She tries to move, can't. Laughing at herself)* **Oil can! Oil can! ...Mom?** *(DELLA enters the rec room.)* **Mom!** *(She picks up remote.)* **I don't believe it.**

DELLA: **Roxanne, come in here and turn this TV off yourself.**

ROXANNE: **I will, just turn it back on.**

DELLA: **You're smarter than this.**

ROXANNE: **I am! I am *sooo* smart!** *(DELLA turns TV on. ROXANNE and ERIC animate.)*

ERIC: **...take a walk on the beach. I have a new song I may want to sing to you.** *(ROXANNE begins to exit TV into rec room.)* **Rachel, talk to me, don't keep pushing me away.**

ROXANNE: **There are parts of my life you just don't understand.**

JOHN: *(Entering, carrying coat over his arm)* **All packed. Let's go home.**

DELLA: **Roxanne?**

ROXANNE: **I'm sorry, I have to go for a while.**

ERIC: **What?**

ROXANNE: **I'll meet you at the beach house tomorrow,** *(To herself)* **if I can.** *(To him)* **Then you can sing your new song.** *(The lights flicker and flash as ROXANNE steps out of TV into rec room.)*

ERIC: **Rachel, what are you doing? Where are you going?**

ROXANNE: **I'm right here.**

DELLA: **Well, Roxanne.**

ROXANNE: **I'm right here. I wasn't hiding from you.**	ERIC: **I wait all night for her, she finally sings the song and she runs away again.**

DELLA: **You were too hiding from me.**

ROXANNE: **All right, I was.**

DELLA: **Turn off the television.** *(Gives ROXANNE remote.)*

JOHN: **Let me talk to her.**

ROXANNE: **May we talk about this later?**	ERIC: **I don't care. I don't care.** *(He exits.)*
	JOHN: **Rachel —**

(JOHN takes a couple of steps toward ROXANNE; she turns off TV. JOHN lowers his head.)

DELLA: **Are you ready to sing to me?**

ROXANNE: **No.**

DELLA: **Have you been practicing?**

ROXANNE: No.

DELLA: Roxanne, what is the big deal? You agree you have to practice, you can't even answer the telephone because you're accepting the responsibility for things like practicing, then I catch you sneaking on the TV while I'm in the kitchen making your favorite brownies because you're practicing.

ROXANNE: I know.

DELLA: You be careful. You're going to grow up to sell real estate with a reputation like what's-his-name.

ROXANNE: "Dad."

DELLA: Sometimes I think he gives you an allowance to do things like this. Do you want to just sing to me now?

ROXANNE: No.

DELLA: *(Sitting next to her)* There must be something more I don't understand. What is it, Roxanne?

ROXANNE: Nothing.

DELLA: Then why won't you sing to me? *(A silence)* Do you like to sing?

ROXANNE: I love to sing.

DELLA: Why won't you sing to me then? *(Silence)* Come on, Rox, what is it? *(Silence)* Are you afraid you'll make a mistake? *(ROXANNE stares back at her mother.)* That's why you have to practice. I swear if you can't do something in two seconds you're sure you're going to fail. It takes work. Everyone has to practice. Even Rachel. Why can't you? And it isn't just this recital. It's your school work — remember that government project? And your art class? It's seeing something through to the end. *(ROXANNE looks away.)* Roxanne, you can sing. I can't imagine anybody being better than you at this recital. And you're interesting to watch, the way you move, your choreography. Do you know how many kids would give anything to have your talent? It's a shame to waste it all by not practicing. *(ROXANNE picks up cassette player and headphones and starts to leave room.)* Where are you going?

ROXANNE: I'm sorry, I have to go for a while.

DELLA: Stay here. *(ROXANNE drops cassette player and headphones on table.)* Where is the sheet music?

ROXANNE: Why?

DELLA: Do you have it in here?

ROXANNE: Why? *(She reaches in her pocket, takes out a wadded up piece of paper.)*

DELLA: *(She takes paper, opens it. She looks at music, hums tune.)* You know the song really isn't that difficult. *(DELLA taps some of it out, sings.)*

He's my fantasy man.

More than a friend to me.

ROXANNE: I can't sing that low.
DELLA: *(She belts out song in a higher register.)*

He's my fantasy man
He's what a man should be.

Come on, sing with me. Come on, Roxanne, sing with me.
(ROXANNE joins DELLA, begins singing half-heartedly and goes down from there until she's barely mouthing the words. DELLA notices this but pushes on with the song anyway, has a little fun with it.)
ROXANNE & DELLA:
He's my fantasy man,
And girls, he's always there
He's my fantasy man,
When I need someone to care.
(ROXANNE mocks DELLA, quits singing, sits on the couch.)
DELLA: **He's my fantasy, fantasy, fantasy, fantasy man;**
He's my fantasy, fantasy, fantasy, fantasy man.

(A big finish. DELLA laughs, looks at ROXANNE for applause.)
ROXANNE: **You sing it, then.**
DELLA: **I could, and I don't even know the rank song.**
ROXANNE: **Then you sing it and I'll stay home.**
DELLA: **I was just trying to help you.**
ROXANNE: **That's not helping me. You're not helping me.**
DELLA: **Because you won't be helped!**
ROXANNE: **You want to help me? Let me watch my program!**
DELLA: **That won't help you.**
ROXANNE: **Yes it will. Just let me watch my program!**
DELLA: **You need to practice!**
ROXANNE: **I don't want —**
DELLA: **No more argument! God, this isn't the end of the world, it's just a recital! It's just a recital! Now stop your poor Roxanne act and get on with it!** *(Silence)*
ROXANNE: *(Quietly)* **I have to do it myself, first. I have to sing it alone, first.**
DELLA: **What have you...? Fine. Fine. I don't have time for this.** *(DELLA exits.)*
ROXANNE: **Why do I do that? That's my mom. I'm the Original Daughter of Doom.** *(ROXANNE talks to JOHN who lifts his head, speaks back to her from inside the TV.)* **Maybe you can explain it to me.**
JOHN: **Oh, I think you're just a little confused, like the rest of us.**

ROXANNE: I am.

JOHN: *(He takes coat from his arm, puts it on.)* **I wish you could see what I see when I look at you. You'd know you're already a success in every important way.**

ROXANNE: **Yeah, I'm a success — at torturing my mother. It's this recital. Getting up in front of all those people, it scares me. Do you think I can sing?**

JOHN: **Do I know music?**

ROXANNE: **Yes.** *(JOHN steps out of TV into rec room. Lights flicker and flash.)*

JOHN: **Will you believe me if I tell you?**

ROXANNE: **Yes.**

JOHN: **You can sing.**

ROXANNE: **Then why don't I?**

JOHN: **Why don't you?**

ROXANNE: **I don't know. I just don't want to.**

JOHN: **What do you want?**

ROXANNE: **Why does everybody always ask me that? I'm doing what I want, all the time. Why else would I do it?**

JOHN: **Whatever you do, I'll feel exactly the same about you. Proud. Because I know whatever you're doing, it's what you need to do.**

ROXANNE: **You will?**

JOHN: **I get confused sometimes, myself, but I'm never confused about that.**

ROXANNE: **Is that true?**

JOHN: **It'll always be true. I promise.**

ROXANNE: **No, don't promise me.**

JOHN: **How do you want me to say it?**

ROXANNE: **Just don't promise me anything.**

JOHN: **Have you ever known me to break my promises?**

ROXANNE: **No, not you. Not you...What did you promise me?**

JOHN: **Whatever you do, I'll feel exactly the same about you. Proud. Because I know whatever you're doing, it's what you need to do.**

ROXANNE: **Thanks.** *(She embraces him.)*

JOHN: **Turn on the television.**

ROXANNE: **Oh, I don't think I should —**

JOHN: **They're on Eric's beach. Rachel's going to sing "Over Water." I think you'd really like to hear it.**

ROXANNE: **Yeah, but...**

JOHN: **It's all right. I'll sit here with you.** *(She considers, then picks up remote, turns on TV. "Over Water" music begins. RACHEL and ERIC enter beach. RACHEL is wearing a lovely summer dress.)*

ROXANNE: **She is *sooo* beautiful.**

RACHEL: *(Sings: "Over Water.")*
    Over water,
    Beyond the beach,
    Past the sunset
    Beyond its reach;
    There your troubles
    Are no more
    Than grains of sand
    On some distant shore
    (ERIC comes up behind her; she wraps him around her.)
    And no creature on the water, land, or sky;
    No woman, man, or child shall ever cry
    On this sphere,
    Without the water catching every tear.

ERIC: *(Speaking during music interlude)* **Look at this day...you can see forever...and that song is...You can sing** *(Indicating beach)* **this.** *(He looks directly at ROXANNE.)* **None of that other stuff matters.** *(To RACHEL)* **I could stay here with you forever.**

RACHEL: *(Sings.)*
    'N yes, the water
    Cool and clear
    Sings eternal
    For all to hear.

RACHEL & ROXANNE: *(ROXANNE mirrors RACHEL's movements.)*
    Sings a living mysery,
    Over every lake and every sea.
    'N yes, the water, cool and clear
    Sings eternal for all to hear.

RACHEL, ROXANNE, ERIC & JOHN:
    And no creature on the water, land or sky;
    No woman, man, or child shall ever cry
    On this sphere
    Without the water catching every tear.

RACHEL & ROXANNE: **Without the water catching every tear.**

RACHEL: **Without the water catching every tear.**

ROXANNE: **Sooo beautiful...** *(Commercial. The TV ACTORS put their heads down.)* **Thanks.** *(JOHN hugs ROXANNE, exits into the TV and out. Phone rings. ROXANNE turns off TV, sits, stares ahead dreamily.)*

DELLA: *(Enters.)* **It's Rob.**

ROXANNE: **Hmmm?**

DELLA: *(Picking up receiver, holding it out to ROXANNE)* **It's Rob. I told him you'd talk to him.**

ROXANNE: *(Refusing phone)* **I know what he wants and I don't —**
DELLA: **I told him you'd talk to him!**
ROXANNE: **Ma!** *(ROXANNE reluctantly takes phone. Her energy wilts. Tonelessly)* **Hello...hi, Rob...yeah...The dance? I can't...I can't because, um, my father promised he'd come to town to hear my recital and, ah, um, what?... Yeah, he's supposed to, um, close a big real estate deal on Friday but he's coming to my recital instead. So, I'm seeing him after the show...Yeah...Bye.** *(DELLA looks at ROXANNE.)* **What? Dad promised he'd come to my recital.**
DELLA: **But he isn't.**
ROXANNE: **He promised he would.**
DELLA: **But he isn't.**
ROXANNE: **He'd rather sell somebody a dog food factory.**
DELLA: **It's not you, Rox, it's him, that's just who he is.** *(ROXANNE isn't buying it.)* **Did Rob ask you to the dance?**
ROXANNE: **I hate dances.**
DELLA: **But you love to dance.**
ROXANNE: **I hate dances.**
DELLA: **But you dance here all the time.**
ROXANNE: **But I'll have to dance with Rob. He's too rich and famous for me. And besides, you have to *talk* at dances. I hate *talking*. And he's really interested in Francine, but she turned him down.**
DELLA: **Who's Francine?**
ROXANNE: **Nobody knows. No one's ever seen her. She wears so much makeup her face looks like a pizza. Besides, why do you want me to go on dates? I'm too young to go on dates.**
DELLA: **Maybe if you wanted to I wouldn't let you. I don't know. I just want you to do something. You're so unhappy. You spend so much time in here, alone.**
ROXANNE: **Yeah.**
DELLA: **I'm sorry about your father.**
ROXANNE: **I'm sorry I'm the Original Daughter of Doom.** *(DELLA starts to say something, stops, exits.)* **I wonder if he sang.** *(She gets remote.)* **Just to see what's happening, then I'll turn it off.** *(She hits remote, ERIC and RACHEL animate. Sounds of surf, wind and gulls; ERIC's beach again)*
ERIC: *(Calling)* **Rachel!**
RACHEL & ROXANNE: **I'm right here.**
ERIC: **Why did you walk off?**
RACHEL: **It's so peaceful; I wanted to be alone and think.**
ROXANNE: **Where have you been, Eric?**
ERIC: **I've been waiting for you.**
RACHEL: **I told you I'd see you later.**
ERIC: **No, I mean —**

ERIC & ROXANNE: I've been waiting for you.

ERIC: What do you want?

ROXANNE: Let me show you what I want. *(RACHEL embraces ERIC.)* Yeah, babe.

ERIC: How do I get you alone?

RACHEL: I'm here.

ERIC: Without your fears?

RACHEL: I'm not afraid of you.

ERIC: You're running away from me.

RACHEL: I'm not running away from you.

ERIC: Rachel —

RACHEL: We're fine. We're fine. What's your new song?

ROXANNE: *(Sings.)* I'm ready for lo-ve!

ERIC: I need to know the truth.

RACHEL: Sing it to me now.

ROXANNE: *(Sings.)* The love that says there is only you.

RACHEL: I can't wait until the Central Park Concert.

ROXANNE: Neither can I!

ERIC: Why? Aren't you going to New York? You're not, are you?

RACHEL & ROXANNE: Sing it to me now.

ERIC: Rachel, if we don't work this out we won't recover.

RACHEL: I'm no one, Eric. And look at you. You're glorious. Your fans want a rock princess or a movie star. You don't want me.

ERIC: I don't care what the world can see anymore.

RACHEL: Sing me your song, Eric.

ROXANNE: Sing!

ERIC: Run away with me.

ROXANNE: Yes! I'm already packed! Send over the limo!

ERIC: Rock and roll will be here when we get back. We'll go anywhere you want, stay there as long as you want. We'll write songs, play together, throw the guitars in the ocean, that's all right, I don't care...Marry me. *(He kisses her passionately.)*

ROXANNE: Yes, yes, yes, yes, oh yes, oh yes, oh yes!

RACHEL: I can't, now.

ROXANNE: "I can't, now?" Rachel! *(The TV ACTORS freeze. Intro to "I'm Ready for Love" is heard.)* Here it is! Oh, my God! Here it is! *(Quietly, as if DELLA were in the room)* Ma, watch. He's going to sing "I'm Ready for Love." Come on, Mom, you'll miss it. If you think Rob is cute, check out this Foxorama. *(JOHN enters, crosses to mike. Crowd noise comes up.)*

JOHN: And now — welcome him New York City — singing his newest gold — the Rockman of Rockway, Eric Cortland! *(Loud cheering. ERIC runs up to mike. RACHEL moves into crowd.)*

ROXANNE: Yes, yes, yes! This is it, Mom. This is it!

ERIC: New York City! *(A cheer)* For Rachel, wherever anybody

may find her. *(Sings, "I'm Ready for Love.")*

If I could take back all the words I said,
The ones that made you cry.
I would give you just this song, instead,
And hope that you will try
To listen to these words
'Cause it's the only way
To tell you what I'm feelin'
And what I'm tryin' to say.
I'm ready for love
The love that says there is only you.
Yes, I'm ready for love
I'd give up everything to show it's true.

(He sees RACHEL in crowd.) **Rachel?** *(He waves; she reluctantly waves back, frustrated she was seen. During the rest of the song ROXANNE walks into the TV, through the crowd, and up to RACHEL. RACHEL sees her, seems relieved that she's there, and starts to walk off. ROXANNE stops her, points to the rec room, pushes RACHEL in that direction. RACHEL agrees, walks through crowd, exits TV into rec room, sits on the couch. ROXANNE dances enthusiastically to the song. ERIC sings it directly to her. ROXANNE sees this and dances ecstatically.)*

So, here's my heart and here's my music
I lay the future in your hand.
Now, you say you need your distance,
I don't think I understand.
But listen to the song
It's the only way
To tell you what I'm feelin'
And what I'm tryin' to say.

I'm ready for love
The love that says there is only you.
Yes, I'm ready for love
I'd give up everything to show it's true.

Our time has finally come, love.
No more waiting, I need you now.
Turn this moment into a lifetime.
Take my hand, we'll make it somehow.

'Cause we're ready for love
A love that says, there is only one.

Yes, we're ready for love
A love that's dying or just begun?
...Or just begun?

(The crowd cheers. ERIC bows to crowd, then bows to ROX-
ANNE. She applauds enthusiastically.) **Thank you! Thank**
you, New York! *(Something begins to happen to ROXANNE,*
ERIC, and JOHN.)

ROXANNE: **Commercial.** *(ROXANNE, ERIC, and JOHN bow their*
heads.) **Ah...** *(ROXANNE, as before, is severely restricted in her*
movements. RACHEL stares blankly at TV.) **Oh, no. Turn off**
the TV. Rachel, turn off the television. *(RACHEL picks up*
the remote, turns off TV. DELLA enters carrying a plate with a
brownie and something to drink on it. DELLA stares at RACHEL
who smiles back at her.)

RACHEL: **Hi, Mom.**

DELLA: *(After a moment)* **What's going on in here?**

RACHEL: **Singing.**

DELLA: **Awfully quiet singing.**

ROXANNE: **Oh, oh. Say something to make her chill.**

RACHEL: **It's so peaceful; I wanted to be alone and think.**

ROXANNE: **Real good, Rachel.**

DELLA: **How's it going?**

RACHEL: **I sang it three times in a row.**

DELLA: **You did? How'd it go?**

RACHEL: **All right.**

DELLA: **It didn't sound like a troll queen?**

RACHEL: **Troll queen? No...but it didn't feel right. I just need**
to practice, even if it takes all night. *(ROXANNE groans.)*
I'm not Eric. He rehearses a song once and he's ready. I
have to work at it.

DELLA: **Yeah...**

RACHEL: **Is that for me?**

DELLA: **Yes, I thought you might —**

RACHEL: **A brownie! My favorite! You're my mom!**

ROXANNE: **My brownie...**

RACHEL: **I'm surprised you still made them after...**

DELLA: **Well...**

RACHEL: *(She bites it.)* **Oh, it's delicious! You're so good to me;**
so patient. I know I've been a pain lately.

DELLA: **Yeah.**

ROXANNE: **Thanks, Rachel.**

RACHEL: **It's this music — finally getting up there in front of**
those people — it scares me.

DELLA: **Of course it does. But I know you can do it.**

RACHEL: **So do I.**

DELLA: You do?

RACHEL: But I'm going to sing it the way I feel it.

DELLA: Well, of course.

RACHEL: And I want to sing it to you.

ROXANNE: What?

RACHEL: You don't have to say anything. You don't even have to like it. Just sit and listen. That's how you can help me.

ROXANNE: No!

DELLA: All right.

RACHEL: Thanks. *(Silence. She eats brownie.)*

DELLA: You want to sing to me now?

ROXANNE: *(Firmly)* No, Rachel.

RACHEL: Maybe not now.

DELLA: When?

ROXANNE: Rachel...

RACHEL: Sometime.

DELLA: *(Tiredly)* You said last night you'd sing it tonight.

RACHEL: Yes I did. *(To ROXANNE)* Yes I did.

ROXANNE: No.

RACHEL: But...

DELLA: When?

RACHEL: Oh —

ROXANNE: Never.

RACHEL: Soon. I promise.

ROXANNE: Don't — *No promises.*

DELLA: I thought you hated promises.

RACHEL: I don't hate promises. I hate broken promises.

DELLA: *(After consideration)* All right. I'll believe you.

RACHEL: Thanks. And thanks for putting up with me, and for being my friend. I need one right now.

DELLA: Roxanne, what a wonderful thing to say. *(DELLA hugs her.)*

ROXANNE: I have to practice now.

RACHEL: I have to practice now.

ROXANNE: So I need to be alone.

RACHEL: So I need to be alone.

ROXANNE: And I'd like another brownie for my friend in the television.

RACHEL: And I'd like another brownie for my friend in the television...please?

DELLA: Sure. I'll get it for you.

RACHEL: No. I'll get it.

ROXANNE: Rachel —

DELLA: That's all right. I'd be happy to —

RACHEL: It's my brownie. I'll get it.

ROXANNE: Rachel, not now.

DELLA: That's all right, honey, I'll get it for you while you practice.

RACHEL: I can practice and get my own brownie.

DELLA: They're in the kitchen.

RACHEL: Thanks. *(DELLA leaves. Pause)*

ROXANNE: *(Sweetly)* **Rachel?**

RACHEL: Yes?

ROXANNE: *Turn on the television!* *(RACHEL takes a big bite of the brownie, turns on television. ROXANNE and ERIC animate.)*

ERIC: I don't understand. Why did you follow me to New York?

ROXANNE: *(As she crosses toward rec room)* To hear you sing. Great song.

ERIC: Rachel... *(ROXANNE exits TV and immediately turns it off. ERIC puts his head down. RACHEL stuffs the rest of the brownie into her mouth.)*

ROXANNE: Wasn't that concert great! God, I loved it! And he sang that song to you. What did that feel like?

RACHEL: I loved it.

ROXANNE: So did I! You are so lucky he likes you.

RACHEL: Oh, he can be impossible, sometimes. He likes to take over — he's a man. And a successful man, so he thinks he's right all the time.

ROXANNE: I know, I heard that speech last week when you said it to your father. But when he sings "I'm Ready for Love" to you, none of that other stuff matters.

RACHEL: It matters to me.

ROXANNE: If Rob could sing like that to *me*, I'd marry him.

RACHEL: He's so good.

ROXANNE: So are you.

RACHEL: I hope so.

ROXANNE: Rachel, you can sing.

RACHEL: I want my audition to just send them flying.

ROXANNE: You sent them flying in the cafe tonight.

RACHEL: But that's not an audition, they're not you or Eric. They only know my music. And they only give you one chance.

ROXANNE: Oh, you're going to blow the audition. You're going to get so nervous you won't remember the words. I saw it four months ago. Yeah, then the only way you can get another audition is with Eric's help. You refuse. You wait and cry and take walks on the beach and cry — you cry a lot. And you write a couple of songs — one great one and one moldy one: "Can't Help But Cry Again." Gak. You meet another guy — Adrian — but he's really an alien who's smuggling drugs. Adrian — Alien — ha ha. And finally you ask Eric to help you but he won't because he thinks you'll hate him if he does but then you convince him that you really do want his help and he helps you and you get the audition. **This time you sing the song without mistakes. Then you get mad at Eric for helping you. You get so mad you break your arm.** *(Pause. Confused, she looks at RACHEL who is also confused.)* **You won't talk to him and you cry, some more, but you sort of get over it and on the last program you record your first song and ask Eric to marry you. He didn't answer but the wedding's probably in the first episode next fall, if your ratings were high enough.**

RACHEL: *(Who has listened to this without understanding a word)* **I just hope I do well in the audition.**

ROXANNE: But I just told you you're going to blow it.

RACHEL: It means so much; maybe you know how much.

ROXANNE: You're going to blow it.

RACHEL: It will be something that came from me. Something earned.

ROXANNE: You blow it!

RACHEL: *(A little desperate, looking for an exit)* **Well, I have to practice.**

ROXANNE: Wait. I guess it's reruns for me but not for you.

RACHEL: *(She spies TV; relieved, she crosses to it.)* **I have to practice.**

ROXANNE: I have to talk to you.

RACHEL: You know I'm always here for you to talk to.

ROXANNE: Why did you promise my mother I'd sing to her?

RACHEL: She'll help you; otherwise, you might blow it.

ROXANNE: *I* **might blow it?**

RACHEL: You might get so nervous you forget the words.

ROXANNE: Eek, Rachel. I'm not going to sing it to her. And... *(Getting an idea)* **And I want you to sing at my recital.**

RACHEL: I don't think they would understand.

ROXANNE: No, you don't understand. I want you to sing my recital song on Friday.

RACHEL: You want me to take your place?

ROXANNE: Isn't that what I just said?

RACHEL: Is that what you want?

ROXANNE: What did I just say?

RACHEL: "Isn't that what I just said?" But what do you want?

ROXANNE: Why would I ask you if that's not what I wanted!

RACHEL: If that's what you want.

ROXANNE: It is! *(Silence)* **Rachel?**

RACHEL: Yes?

ROXANNE: You ate my brownie.

RACHEL: Yeah. I love chocolate.

ROXANNE: So do I. *(Short silence.)*

RACHEL: There's more in the kitchen. *(They race to the kitchen. RACHEL screams.)*

ROXANNE: They're mine!

(Scene change music.)

(The scene changes to the recital stage. A mike and stand are brought Down Center. ROXANNE and RACHEL stand in the wings.)
RACHEL: Rob's out there.
ROXANNE: I know.
RACHEL: He waved at you.
ROXANNE: I know!
RACHEL: You can still change your mind.
ROXANNE: I — no. And I'm the first one on after intermission. Are you ready? You're not nervous — you won't forget the words — you won't cry, will you?
RACHEL: I don't think so. But it's one of the things I do best. *(ROXANNE panics.)* But Roxanne, you could do this. Frankly, most people in this program are not that talented.
ROXANNE: I can't. I just can't.
RACHEL: If you sang it like you did last night—
ROXANNE: I could sing better than that, I know I could.
RACHEL: Then sing. It's wonderful to sing to people.
ROXANNE: I want to. I want to but I just can't. I can't.
RACHEL: Why?
ROXANNE: "Why?"
RACHEL: Why can't you?
DELLA: *(Entering. RACHEL steps back into the shadows.)* You're on next. How do you feel?
ROXANNE: I'm fine.
DELLA: Well, I'm nervous.
ROXANNE: Mother, you won't believe how well it will go.
DELLA: I know, honey, I know.
VOICE: Ladies and gentlemen, Roxanne Walters, singing "Fantasy Man."
ROXANNE: I'm on. I'm on.
DELLA: Have fun.
ROXANNE: I will! I will!
DELLA: I'm here for you, Roxanne. If you get nervous just sing to me.
ROXANNE: *(She starts toward stage, stops, deliberates, turns back to DELLA.)* Sing to you?
DELLA: Have fun!
ROXANNE: *(This sinks her spirits. Aside to RACHEL)* Rachel. *(As DELLA glances at the crowd, ROXANNE steps back, puts her head down. RACHEL walks out on stage.)*
RACHEL: Hello. Hi, Rob. *(An inarticulate response from ROXANNE)* I know you're expecting me to sing "Fantasy Man" but I don't know that rank song. I'm going to sing a song called

"I'm Yours." And I'd like to dedicate it to a friend of mine, Eric. *(Music begins.)* For Eric, wherever we may find ourselves. *(Sings "I'm Yours" as DELLA watches.)*

And I am yours they say
Take his hand, you understand
Yes I am yours, today.
But what I know and the way I feel
Is all too real to hide away.

I feel I'm losing
When I take your hand
Losing my direction,
I don't understand.

And we're in love, they say
Take his hand, you'll understand.
Yes we're in love, today.
And what we hear and all we read
The picture's clear and you're what I need.

I'm not lost in the forest,
Calling out your name.
I'm not sleeping in a castle,
Beauty is not my name.
I'm not locked in a tower,
Longing to be free,
I'm not dreaming of princes
Dreaming of saving me.

Take heart, my love, I'm here,
There is nowhere else I'd rather be.
Take heart, my love, don't fear,
There is no one else I'd rather see.

If you got love, you say
You've got it all, you got it all.
Yes, we've got love, today.
But what I know and the way I feel
Is all too real to hide away.
I dream of beaches,
The wind and the sky.
But I can't see you with me.
And I don't know why.
I walk in the sunsets,
Dance in the sea,

I sail through the moonlight
Will you sail with me?
...Sail with me.

And I am yours, they say,
Take his hand, you understand...

(Applause) **Thank you. Thank you very much.** *(She moves toward DELLA who beams at her. Just before she gets there, ROXANNE steps up. RACHEL steps back.)*

DELLA: **When did you decide to sing that song? When did you practice it? Roxanne, that was very good.**

ROXANNE: **I knew you'd like it.**

DELLA: **I can't believe how well you did. I've never heard you sing like that before.**

ROXANNE: **I never did before.**

DELLA: **You little pain in the neck, I knew you could do it. That song's not exactly your style, you just stood there and sang but — so well.**

ROXANNE: **Can we go home?**

DELLA: **Don't you want to hear the other singers? Or talk to your friends? Next time you'll have to sing more — two or three songs, maybe in different styles, maybe you —**

ROXANNE: **Mom, I want to go home.**

DELLA: **Rob is here. I'm sure he'd like to talk to you. Come on, Roxanne. You did very well. Part of that is accepting the glory.**

ROXANNE: **I want to go home.**

DELLA: **All right. If that's what you want. Well, I'm going to congratulate you. Congratulations. You're the star of the show!**

ROXANNE: **Yeah.** *(They exit.)*

(Scene change music.)

(Scene changes back to rec room. JOHN and RACHEL are in their TV positions, head down in the TV area. ROXANNE sits on couch, depressed and confused. She picks up remote and turns on TV — actually the videotape of Rockway Cafe. *The first scene takes place in the dressing room in Rockway Cafe.)*

JOHN: *(To RACHEL)* **...could see what I see when I look at you. You'd know you're already a success. In every important way.**

RACHEL: **It's getting up in front of those people. I want my audition to just send them flying.**

JOHN: **You sent us flying in the cafe, tonight.**

RACHEL: **But that's not an audition, they're not you or Eric.**

They only know my music. And they only give you one chance. *(ROXANNE freezes frame.)*

ROXANNE: **One chance...** *(She hits play and they go on.)*

RACHEL: **It means so much; maybe you know how much. It will be something that came from me. Something earned.**

ROXANNE: *(Sadly)* **You blow it.**

RACHEL: **Do you think I can sing?**

ROXANNE: **You can sing! God, how could you be so stupid!**

JOHN: **Do I know music?**

RACHEL: **Yes.**

JOHN: **Will you believe me if I tell you?**

ROXANNE: **No.**

RACHEL: **It shouldn't matter whether I believe you or not — or even the studio; just that I believe myself.**

JOHN: **Do you?**

RACHEL: **Why is this so difficult?**

ROXANNE: **Duh.**

JOHN: **Because you're smart and talented and you have the courage to do what you believe is right for yourself.**

RACHEL: **Do I?**

JOHN: **Just like your mother. She wanted more than a rock and roll club and when I turned down the big studio, she left. She now has what she wanted. It isn't us, but—** *(ROXANNE freezes the frame, stares at it. She hits stop, the TV ACTORS put their heads down, then she hits fast forward. She hits play. The scene is backstage in Central Park.)*

RACHEL: *(To JOHN)* **...but he saw me in the crowd.**

JOHN: **It sounds like you're avoiding something.**

RACHEL: **Avoiding what?**

JOHN: **Oh, I think you can figure it out.** *(ERIC enters.)* **There he is.** *(RACHEL moves to ERIC, embraces him.)*

RACHEL: **They loved you!**

ERIC: **I don't understand. Why did you follow me to New York City?**

RACHEL: **To hear you sing. Great song.**

ERIC: **Rachel —** *(ROXANNE hits reverse. The TV ACTORS reverse motions. ROXANNE hits play.)*

RACHEL: **They loved you!**

ERIC: **I don't understand. Why did you follow me to New York City?**

RACHEL: **To hear you sing. Great song.**

ERIC: **Rachel —**

ROXANNE: **Tell him the truth.**

RACHEL: **I didn't come for you. I came for myself.**

ERIC: **That's got to be true.**

RACHEL: **You're right; I have been running away from you,**

even lying to you, and myself.

ERIC: **Yeah.**

RACHEL: **But I want to stop. It hurts me, too.** *(ROXANNE hits reverse, the TV ACTORS reverse their motions. ROXANNE hits play.)*

RACHEL: **...hear you sing. Great song.**

ERIC: **Rachel —**

RACHEL: **I didn't come for you. I came for myself.**

ERIC: **That's got to be true.**

RACHEL: **You're right; I have been running away from you, even lying to you, and myself.**

ERIC: **Yeah.**

RACHEL: **But I want to stop. It hurts me, too.**

ERIC: **That's good to hear.**

RACHEL: **I want to love you; I'm just not sure how.** *(She holds out her hand to him. ROXANNE hits slow motion. RACHEL slowly moves closer to ERIC, who is slowly turning toward her. ROXANNE pauses tape; then turns off the TV, the TV ACTORS put their heads down. JOHN lifts his head, walks out of TV into rec room.)*

ROXANNE: **What are you doing here?**

JOHN: **I'm not sure.**

ROXANNE: **What do you want?**

JOHN: **What do you want?**

ROXANNE: **I don't know.**

JOHN: **Everything worked out well.**

ROXANNE: **Everybody thought I was great. Mom thought I was great.**

JOHN: **I'm proud of you.**

ROXANNE: **But I didn't...I don't...**

JOHN: **It sounds like you're avoiding something.**

ROXANNE: **Avoiding what?**

JOHN: **Oh, I think you can figure it out.**

ROXANNE: **Why is this so difficult?**

JOHN: **Because you're smart and talented and you have the courage to do what you believe is right for yourself.**

ROXANNE: **I...I don't think I do.**

JOHN: **What?**

ROXANNE: **I didn't sing "Fantasy Man" because she wanted me to. "You chose this song, you practice, you practice, you sing it perfectly, with no mistakes — here, let me show you how — then sing more songs, in different styles —" Well, I didn't sing it. Ha ha.** *(Short silence)* **I wanted to but I didn't.** *(To JOHN)* **I miss you. Do you miss me?** *(No response)* **No answer? That's typical. Do you miss me? You missed my recital, liar.**

JOHN: **I'm sorry your mother and I wanted such different lives.**

ROXANNE: Then why did you marry her? Why did you move so far away? Why do you keep breaking your promises! You say I'm avoiding something — you're avoiding me. If you would have come to my recital I would have sung that rank song.

JOHN: Is that true?

ROXANNE: No, but what do you care?

JOHN: You know I care.

ROXANNE: No I don't. And I'm not going to listen to what you say, anymore — I'm going to avoid listening to you. I'll only believe what you do.

JOHN: I know it's —

ROXANNE: Go away.

JOHN: *(He checks his watch.)* Well, I have to introduce the next act.

ROXANNE: Go away! *(He exits rec room into the TV, puts head down. DELLA enters carrying a wrapped present.)*

DELLA: Hey, Rocker.

ROXANNE: Hey, Mom.

DELLA: Congratulations. *(Hands her present.)*

ROXANNE: What's this?

DELLA: Something for all your work and courage.

ROXANNE: Oh, Mom, no, I don't deserve anything.

DELLA: Sure you do. Open it.

ROXANNE: Now?

DELLA: Yeah. I think you'll be surprised at your moldy mom. *(ROXANNE opens package. Even before ROXANNE has opened it:)* "The Greatest Hits of Rockway Cafe, Volume One!" It has all those songs you love on it. Even "I'm Ready for Love" by that foxorama Eric.

ROXANNE: Thanks, Mom. I... *(She hugs DELLA.)*

DELLA: Shall we play it? Then I can hear what's been so important in your life.

ROXANNE: This is really great. I can't believe how patient you've been with me.

DELLA: Well, I have a secret. You're not the Original Daughter of Doom. *(She points to herself.)*

ROXANNE: You? What did you do?

DELLA: I don't want to give you any ideas. If you do what I did... *(She gestures to show ROXANNE what she'd do.)*

ROXANNE: Well, I make mistakes. I...make mistakes.

DELLA: Well, you can always do better.

ROXANNE: May I sing to you?

DELLA: Now?

ROXANNE: Yeah, right now. I want to sing you "Fantasy Man."

DELLA: But I thought you didn't know that rank song.

ROXANNE: I know.

DELLA: You want to sing that song to me now, the song I couldn't get you to sing, the song you'd rather die than sing to me?

ROXANNE: I'm not singing it for you, I'm singing it for myself. Will you listen?

DELLA: Of course.

ROXANNE: You don't have to say anything. You don't have to like it. Just sit and listen. That's how you can help me.

DELLA: Ready.

ROXANNE: *(Steps up to her mike. Sings.)*

> **Girls, you know the story**
> **You know all the rules**
> **But —**

(She stops.) **No, that was Rachel.** *(She tries again, in a different, strident style.)*

> **Girls, you know the story**
> **You know all the rules**
> **But there's nothing 'bout**

(Again she stops.) **Sorry. That was Tiffany from** *The Bradford Show.*

DELLA: Tiffany.

ROXANNE: *(She starts again.)*

> **Girls, you know the story**
> **You know —**

(Stops.) **Allyson, from** *Our Times.* *(She tries again, searching for the song inside herself. She makes mistakes but pushes through them. The music comes in quietly underneath and gradually gets louder as she finds the song.)*

> **Girls, you know the story,**
> **You know all the rules**
> **But there's nothing 'bout the game of love**
> **That says we play the fools.** *(She's hitting a rhythm.)*

> **Yes, I may lose this game of love,**
> **Out of sheer neglect.**
> **But I've someone who treats me right**
> **And shows me some respect.**
> *(Music is up full. She's having much more fun, enthusiastically doing her choreography and spontaneously expanding on it.)*

He's my fantasy man, he's more than a friend to me
He's my fantasy man, he's what a man should be.
He's my fantasy man and girls, he's always there.
He's my fantasy man when I need someone to care.
He's my fantasy, fantasy, fantasy, fantasy man.
He's my fantasy, fantasy, fantasy, fantasy man.

Someday some man may come by here
An' turn my head around.
But girls, 'til then I'm satisfied
With the one I've found.
His promises he keeps, it's true,
I never have to plead,
And I can say, he's ready today
To give me what I need.

He's my fantasy man, he's more than a friend to me
He's my fantasy man, he's what a man should be.
He's my fantasy man and girls, he's always there.
He's my fantasy man when I need someone to care.
He's my fantasy, fantasy, fantasy, fantasy man.
He's my fantasy, fantasy, fantasy, fantasy man.
He's my fantasy, fantasy, fantasy, fantasy man.

DELLA: Rox, that was great! I like that rank song even more
than the other one.
ROXANNE: Yeah.
DELLA: Yeah. You sang loud, you jumped around, you had fun.
ROXANNE: Thanks for listening.
DELLA: I had fun, too, just listening to you.
ROXANNE: *(After a moment)* Let's go out!
DELLA: Oh, I don't know, honey —
ROXANNE: Oh, come on, Ma, yeah!
DELLA: I think I have a date. Why don't you go to the dance?
There's still plenty of time.
ROXANNE: The dance?
DELLA: Sure. We'll drop you off.
ROXANNE: *(She looks at the TV ACTORS; they raise their heads,
look at her in confusion and hope.)* The dance...?
DELLA: Only if you want. *(ROXANNE considers. Pause)* What do
you say?
ROXANNE: *(Apprehensively)* All right.
DELLA: Let's go.
ROXANNE: *(To herself)* I'm going to the dance. *(They start off
together. DELLA exits. ROXANNE turns, looks at room and TV
ACTORS. Anxiously)* I'm going to the dance. *(She walks off.*

They lower their heads.)

THE END

(Reprise during curtain call: first half of "Rockway Cafe.")

ENSEMBLE: Don't you worry 'bout tomorrow
    Don't you fret about today
    'Cause there's a place, you can rock tonight
    And roll your cares away.

    You can go there just the way you are.
    Join your friends who know you are a star.

    Come on to the Rockway!
    Baby it's your cafe!
    Come on to the Rockway!
    Baby it's our cafe!

    Come and meet me for the show tonight
    Leave your Monday world far below.
    Let your soul go sailin' when the band starts wailin'
    It's Friday night, let's go.

    Join the beat that rocks the U.S.A.
    Celebrate; get down; come out; come play.

    (Come on, come on, come on)
    Come on to the Rockway!
    Get down at the cafe!
    Join us at the Rockway!
    Dancin' at the cafe!
    (CAST exits as music continues.)

RAPUNZEL

by

Max Bush

CHARACTERS

HELGA . . . . Rapunzel's Mother

THEO . . . . Rapunzel's Father

MOTHER GOTHAL . . . . . The Witch

RAPUNZEL

PRINCE DERRICK

BALLARD. . . . . Old Man, Servant to Prince

NARRATOR

SETTING: The Witch's garden and Theo and Helga's house. Later a tower in a woods and a wilderness. Long ago.

PRODUCTION NOTES: Settings can be quite simple. For the house, Theo's chair, a wood bin, perhaps something indicating a wall. For the garden, the large rock, and something representing an actual garden holding the radishes. A cut-away wall of stone stands between them. All the business concerning the window can be mimed.

The tower contains a bed, a chair, and a small table. A practicable stump sits in the woods. The tower itself is large and round — large enough to allow for the physical action — again suggested by a cut-away wall. A platform sits just inside the window to aid in the illusion of height.

The wilderness can be played anywhere on an open floor.

Stage lighting is useful but not necessary.

CASTING NOTES: All roles can be played by four actors — two males, two females.

The Narrator can be played by one or more of the actors.

Rapunzel was comissioned by the Grand Rapids Circle Theatre of Grand Rapids, Michigan, and opened there in August, 1986, with the following cast and crew.

CHARACTERS

HELGA . . . . Jane Hobart

THEO/BALLARD . . . . Mark Jones

WITCH GOTHAL . . . . Wendy Pestka

RAPUNZEL . . . . Lisa Blanchard

PRINCE DERRICK . . . Kevin Abbott

NARRATOR

PRODUCTION STAFF

Director . . . . Penelope Victor

Assistant Director/
Stage Manager . . . . Sondra Loucks

Assistant Stage Manager. . . . . . . Sallie Loucks

Costumer. . . . . Sue Leatherman

Properties . . . . Sondra Loucks

Sound Design . . . . Timothy Parsaca

Light Design. . . . . Timothy Parsaca

Scenic Design . . . . D. Robert Green

Carpenter . . . . Tacey Boucher

Managing Director . . . . Joseph Dulin

Art Work . . . . Penelope Victor

DEDICATION: *Rapunzel* is dedicated to Debra Olsen with gratitude, love and congratulations.

(Spot up on NARRATOR who holds a large book.)

NARRATOR: *(Opening book)* **"The Frog Prince"... "Sleeping Beauty"... "Cinderella"... "The Golden Bird"... "Rapunzel."** *(Reading)* **There once was a man,** *(Looking up to audience)* **Theo, in our story today,** *(THEO enters, paces intensely. Reading)* **and his wife,** *(Looking up)* **Helga, we'll call her,** *(Reading)* **who wished for a child to be born to them.** *(HELGA enters.)*

THEO: *(Stopping pacing, anxiously)* **Yes?**

HELGA: *(Wistfully)* **No.** *(She exits.)*

NARRATOR: **They had long wished for a child. Month after month passed and there were no hopeful signs. Month after month they waited, still wishing, still longing for a child.** *(THEO's pacing is gradually slowing.)* **Month after month after month...** *(THEO, exhausted from pacing, paces very slowly. HELGA enters.)*

THEO: **Yes?**

HELGA: **No.** *(Exits. THEO falls into his chair.)*

NARRATOR: **One day —** *(THEO sleeps in the chair. HELGA enters. THEO opens one eye.)*

THEO: **Yes?**

HELGA: **Yes!**

THEO: **Yes?**

HELGA: **Yes! Our wish has been granted!**

THEO: **A child!**

HELGA: **Our child!**

THEO: **Helga! I'm proud of you.** *(Out window)* **We're going to have a child! I'm going to have a daughter!**

HELGA: **Or a son.**

THEO: **Both!**

HELGA: **We'll have twins!**

THEO: **I'm going to tell everyone in town! Everyone I meet!** *(Heading out door)*

HELGA: **Theo!**

THEO: *(Seeing someone on the road)* **Roland, Dagmar, wait! The world has changed! A child!** *(He is gone.)*

HELGA: *(A little embarrassed, but still delighted at his exuberance)* **Theo...** *(She starts after him. The NARRATOR stops her.)*

NARRATOR: **There was a little window in their house overlooking a beautiful garden,** *(HELGA crosses to window, smiles, full of satisfaction)* **full of lovely flowers and shrubs. It was, however, surrounded by a wall and nobody dared enter it because it belonged to a powerful witch who was feared by everybody.** *(HELGA's smile fades away.)* **One day, Helga, standing at the window and looking into the garden, saw —**

HELGA: **Rampion...fresh...red...radishes...** *(She dismisses them, turns from window, crosses away.)*

NARRATOR: **This longing increased...** *(HELGA stops)* **day after day...** *(HELGA returns to the window.)*

HELGA: **Rampion...**

NARRATOR: **...after day...**

HELGA: **...rampion...**

THEO: *(Entering, carrying a baby toy)* **Helga, see what I've made!**

HELGA: **Theo, it's perfect!**

NARRATOR: **...after day...** *(HELGA turns back to window, as THEO plays with toy.)*

HELGA: **Theo!**

THEO: **What is it, dear wife?**

HELGA: **Out the window.**

THEO: *(Crossing to window)* **In the witch's garden?**

HELGA: **Red radishes, fresh rapunzels.**

THEO: **Helga, what's making you pale?**

HELGA: **I want some rampion.**

THEO: **Then I'll go to market and buy you —**

HELGA: **I must have *that* rampion.**

THEO: **How are you going to get them?** *(She turns to him.)* **You know what happens if Witch Gothal catches someone in her garden. She scratches out their eyes, or turns them into a rock, or locks them inside a tree.**

HELGA: **If I can't have any of that rampion...I'll die.**

THEO: **You mean you'll stop breathing and we'll bury you?**

HELGA: **I shall die, Theo.**

THEO: *(Surprised and concerned)* **Then you'll have that rampion tonight.**

HELGA: **Now.**

THEO: **The sun is just setting. Wait until after dark and —**

HELGA: **Now.**

THEO: **I'll go now, if that's what you need.**

NARRATOR: **In the twilight, he set out.** *(THEO crosses to wall.)*

THEO: **Theo...before you let your good wife die, you'd better bring her some witch's rampion...now...** *(He looks over the wall)* **no matter the cost.** *(He climbs the wall, slips, falls over into garden.)* **Oh! I fell over the wall. I'll just climb back over...** *(He crosses to wall, stops, listens.)* **Witch Gothal?** *(The cry of a night bird startles him. He dives behind rock.)* **Theo...before you let your good wife die...** *(He crosses to rampion.)* **Here...** *(He pulls one out. From the direction of the WITCH's house comes the sound of a single recorder or possibly a harp, playing a slow, sad melody. THEO starts, freezes.)* **Music?...Witch's music! Magic! She's casting a spell!** *(He runs to wall, listens, looks at himself.)* **I'm still here. I'm still**

304

Theo. It's not a spell for me. *(He quickly gathers six radishes, shakes them out, covers the holes, begins sneaking towards the wall. The music stops abruptly. He stops. Silence. He bolts to the wall, climbs over frantically, enters the house.)* **Witch's rampion! For my dear wife!**

HELGA: *(Taking the rampion)* **Oh, Theo, you've saved my life.** *(She begins to eat one.)* **Mmmm...oh...Theo, they're strangely delicious; like no other rampion I've tasted.**

THEO: **Please, Helga, eat them slowly.**

HELGA: **I can't.**

THEO: **And I can't go back for more. Did you hear the music?**

HELGA: **Rampion, rapunzels. Oh, Theo, they taste better than anything I've ever eaten.**

THEO: *(Sitting in the chair)* **Witch's music...shouldn't be heard by any man...steal his mind...make him eat grass...**

NARRATOR: **She ate them all and was very happy.**

HELGA: **I'm happy.**

NARRATOR: **The rapunzels were so good the next day her longing for the witch's rampion increased three times what it was.** *(HELGA crosses to window. THEO sleeps. HELGA turns to THEO, looks at him, back out window, back to THEO.)*

HELGA: **Theo!**

THEO: *(Falling out of his chair)* **What? Who — what is it? Helga? What's wrong? Did you call me? Someone — I was asleep — did you call me?**

HELGA: **You must get more rampion.**

THEO: **If I go back she'll turn me into a rock, like the one in her garden now.**

HELGA: **If you don't get me more —**

THEO: **Don't say it, Helga.**

HELGA: **If you don't get me more of that rampion —**

THEO: **She'll lock me inside a tree!**

HELGA: **If you don't get more of her rampion...I shall die.**

THEO: **There it is, Theo. Before you let your wife die, you must fetch her more rampion,** *tonight, after sunset —* *(Starting to sit)*

HELGA: **Now.**

THEO: *(Stops mid-sit, pulls himself up.)* **— now, no matter the cost.**

HELGA: **Now...now...**

THEO: *(Picking up bag)* **Watch, and if she catches me, come and speak to her.**

HELGA: **I will.**

NARRATOR: **In the twilight he set out again.**

THEO: *(He crosses to wall, looks over. Calling)* **Witch Gothal?** *(Louder)* **Witch Gothal?** *(He carefully climbs over wall, hides* behind a rock. Music resumes.) **I didn't want to hear that.** *(He realizes he's touching rock, pulls his hands back.)* **Oh, I'm sorry.** *(He looks up.)* **Before you let your wife die...** *(He crosses to rampion. HELGA peeks out window. He pulls up a rapunzel, music stops abruptly.)* **Good. Good?**

HELGA: *(A loud whisper)* **Good!**

THEO: *(Reassuring himself)* **Good.** *(He pulls up some rampion. The WITCH suddenly appears.)*

WITCH: **How dare you come into my garden like a thief and steal my rampion!** *(HELGA screams and runs off.)*

THEO: **I...I was...I...** *(He runs to window of his house.)*

WITCH: **Stop!**

THEO: **Helga!** *(He runs to wall.)*

WITCH: **Stop!** *(She claws the air like a large cat. He grabs his chest in pain as if she scratched him. He turns to run again. Again she claws him in his back.)* **Stop, I say!**

THEO: **I've stopped.**

WITCH: **You'll pay for this.** *(WITCH GOTHAL is a lonely social outcast; a plain and unattractive spinster who walks with a slight limp. Which doesn't mean she isn't powerful and threatening and capable of acting violently from her anger. She is and does. But she's also more vulnerable and human than one would assume; certainly much more than she tries to show the world.)*

THEO: **I had to steal them.**

WITCH: **No one steals from me.**

THEO: **Then Witch Gothal, may I buy some of your rampion? My wife —** *(Calling)* **Helga!** *(To WITCH)* **— craves your rampion, saying she would die if I didn't get it for her. And "Now! Now!" And since she's going to have a baby, I thought it was my duty as a father and a husband —**

WITCH: **Your wife —**

THEO: **Yes.** *(Calling)* **Helga!**

WITCH: **— is going to have a child?**

THEO: **We have long wished for one.**

WITCH: **Long wished for a child...**

THEO: **So you see I had to take this rampion.**

WITCH: **If what you say is true, take as much as you like.**

THEO: **As much...you are kind, Witch Gothal.**

WITCH: **Yes...**

THEO: **I'll only take six.**

WITCH: **Take them all, if she'll die without them.**

THEO: **I will! All! I'll take them all!**

WITCH: **On one condition.**

THEO: **What condition?**

WITCH: **You must give me the child your wife is about to bring into the world.**

THEO: I can't give you our child.

WITCH: You will, neighbor.

THEO: Not to a witch!

WITCH: A witch who will curse you with a foul spell if you don't.

THEO: I'm not afraid of you. Or your spells. I won't betray my wife and child to a hag!

WITCH: **Hah!** *(She claws him again. He starts to run.)* **Down!** *(He quickly falls on his back, spread eagle.)* **Stay!** *(He is stuck on the ground, struggles to get away, can't.)*

THEO: Witch Gothal, please, I only took a few radishes.

WITCH: I want your child.

THEO: There are other children. Children of the poor —

WITCH: I want your child.

THEO: I'll find you an orphan. Two orphans. As many orphans as you need.

WITCH: Agree, now, or you'll die.

THEO: You mean I'll stop breathing, and they'll bury me?

WITCH: You shall die.

THEO: Then...I agree. The child will be yours.

WITCH: Rise. *(He does.)* **Give me your hand.**

THEO: I'm a man of my word.

WITCH: Give me your hand, Theo.

THEO: *(Bravely)* **Here.**

WITCH: *(Taking his wrist)* **You needn't worry. All will be well with the child. I will raise it in kindness, love it dearly.** *(She cuts his palm with her fingernail.)*

THEO: Ah! *(She cuts hers, then places them together.)*

WITCH: There. The bargain is sealed in our blood. The rampion is yours. *(He quickly takes rampion.)* **Take it all...it will protect the growing baby...until I come for it...** *(He climbs over the wall)* **good neighbor Theo.** *(She exits. He crosses into house.)*

THEO: Helga! *(HELGA enters.)*

HELGA: *(Taking bag)* **Did you get them?**

THEO: Why didn't you come when I called?

HELGA: The bag is full! Oh, Theo! You got them all!

THEO: Why didn't you come when I called?

HELGA: *(Eating)* Oh, they're even more delicious than the others.

THEO: Enjoy your rampion, Helga. We've paid dearly for them.

HELGA: What have we paid?

THEO: Our child.

NARRATOR: And he told her the story. *(HELGA puts rapunzels down.)*

HELGA: Our child? After we waited so long? Theo...

THEO: I've heard of ways to stop a witch.

307

HELGA: Witch!

THEO: Salt.

HELGA: Yes.

THEO: Witches turn stiff when sprinkled with salt...and holly branches.

HELGA: Holly branches burn witches!

THEO: Set out salt in every room in the house. I'll cut some holly branches. One of them has to work against her. *(They exit.)*

NARRATOR: And so they prepared for the day when the witch would come for their child. *(HELGA and THEO re-enter, place salt and holly branches around their house.)*

THEO: Here...here...and here...and here, by the door...

HELGA: See where I put this? Here...And here...that should be enough.

THEO: Now let her come. *(They exit.)*

NARRATOR: Yet they lived in fear of the witch. Month after month they waited but she didn't appear...until one morning... *(THEO enters with baby, sits, rocks the baby, speaks baby talk to it. Then he tries to teach it to speak.)*

THEO: Pa...pa. Pa...pa. Say papa...not gaga, *papa*...Theo... Thee...o...not oo-goo. *(He puts his hands over his face, pulls hands away.)* **Papa.** *(He laughs at the child's apparent delight. This happens again. On the third time he growls at baby instead of saying "Papa." This apparently startles it.)* **Oh! No, no. Quiet. No. No.** *(He rocks it.)* **Yes...gaga, yes...** *(The WITCH enters; witch's music comes up, quietly plays under the following scene.)*

WITCH: Theo.

THEO: *(Moving quickly out of chair)* **Gothal!**

WITCH: I've heard the wonderful sounds of a new child.

THEO: Yes, a new...yes.

WITCH: Let me see it.

THEO: What a pleasant surprise to have you visit, neighbor. How are you?

WITCH: Show your child to me. *(He does.)* **A girl?**

THEO: A girl.

WITCH: A lovely girl...

THEO: Fate has been kind. We — after waiting so long, we're very happy.

WITCH: What have you named her?

THEO: We haven't, yet, as we're waiting for her right name to come to us.

WITCH: How pretty...how very, very pretty.

THEO: She looks like her mother, don't you think?

WITCH: No matter.

THEO: Oh, you think she looks like me. So do I.

WITCH: Let me hold her.

THEO: She's very young and I...

WITCH: I will be gentle.

THEO: She'll cry, away from me.

WITCH: *(Gravely)* Give her to me.

THEO: You can't expect me to give you our baby.

WITCH: You forget our bargain.

THEO: I'm her father.

WITCH: What do you know of the matters of children? Or witchcraft? This child is mine. Be grateful you still live, you trembling little thief of a man! *(He picks up salt and throws it on her.)* Salt?

THEO: Yes, salt, witch!

WITCH: To make me stiff?

THEO: Yes! *(He throws more on her. It has no effect.)*

WITCH: Do you believe every old tale you hear? Where are your red ribbons to prevent me from entering your house? Where are your ashes to turn me to dust? Nothing will keep your child from me. *(He picks up holly.)* Good neighbor Theo, you are a simple, sad man. Give me the girl before you anger me. You don't want me angry at you again. *(She starts for him. He holds holly up.)* Enough of this, Theo. Put that down and give me the child. *(Silence)* Theo! *(He puts down holly. She crosses to him, begins to take the baby. He quickly picks up the holly, strikes the WITCH with it. It burns her and she recoils. He keeps child.)* Ah!

THEO: Holly! Holly burns you!

WITCH: You think that will help you?

THEO: *(He lunges for her; she backs up.)* Out of my house, witch!

WITCH: The spell is cast!

THEO: Out! Out! *(He is striking out at her. She's avoiding the holly.)*

WITCH: We sealed our bargain in blood!

THEO: Out!

WITCH: Our blood!

THEO: Out!

WITCH: *(She turns on him.)* Ah! *(She gestures directly into his face. He becomes instantly entranced.)* Drop the holly. *(He does.)* Give me the child. *(He does. She carefully takes it. She slaps THEO hard and he falls on to his chair. To him.)* Sleep... *(He sleeps)* and dream a terrible dream of loneliness...and loss. *(Looking at baby)* Oh, my lovely child. I will care for you like a loving mother; all will be well. You see, Theo? She doesn't cry with me. *(As she's exiting)* Such a lovely baby...wants a lovely name. I'll name you after the rampion. Rapunzel will be your name, my child. Rapunzel...Rapunzel... *(Witch* *music fades out.)*

NARRATOR: The witch raised Rapunzel as her own child, watching over her carefully. When Rapunzel was twelve years old the witch shut her up in a tower which stood in a wood. *(Music. Scene changes to tower and forest. NARRATOR continues once tower is in place.)* **The tower had neither a staircase nor doors and only a little window quite high in the wall.** *(RAPUNZEL enters with a doll, sets it on bed, looks out.)* **In here Rapunzel lived alone, passing her days singing, weaving wreaths of wildflowers the witch brought her, telling herself stories, or playing with her old toys.** *(Music out.)*

RAPUNZEL: *(Standing at window, talking to the doll on the bed)* **You're awake. I thought you were going to sleep all day. It's time to get up. Oh, no. Up!** *(Crossing to doll, picking it up.)* **Look at you...hair all tangled. You have such long, lovely hair.** *(She fixes the doll's hair.)* **There. Look outside. It's a beautiful morning.** *(They both look out window. Both yawn. Doll rests her head on RAPUNZEL's shoulder.)* **Wake up.** *(She pushes doll away, shakes it.)*

Wake up! Don't you remember what day it is? Your birthday! Yes, your birthday. And I have a surprise for you. *(They turn away from window.)* **Look...yes...a horse! The most beautiful horse in the kingdom...in the world. We have to name it something beautiful...Star, just Star. Yes. Ride her.** *(She puts doll on imaginary horse.)* **You don't have to be afraid.** *(Doll rocks unsteadily back and forth.)* **There. That's it. Now, ride...ride...yes...** *(Now she narrates.)* **And as she rode Star through the city everyone turned and watched her. Someone rode up on his horse and became her friend. Many people rode up and became her friends. They rode together far...and fast...very fast...all the way to the sea.** *(She indicates riding, splashing in the water.)* **They galloped up a mountain. When they got to the top she spurred her horse to jump.** *(It jumps.)* **Higher.** *(Again, higher)* **Higher!** *(Again, higher)* **And then it flew! Her horse could fly. She flew away! High into the sky! Flew away to wherever she wanted —** *(She stops abruptly; they are both staring out the window. Pause. WITCH enters woods, crosses to tower.)*

WITCH: Rapunzel, Rapunzel, let down your hair.

RAPUNZEL: Mother Gothal! *(To doll)* **Mother's here!** *(To WITCH)* **Coming!**

WITCH: Let down your hair.

RAPUNZEL: Here... *(She lets down her hair and the WITCH climbs up.)*

WITCH: *(Kissing RAPUNZEL's cheek)* **I've brought your breakfast,**

my Rapunzel. Your favorite fruit pie.

RAPUNZEL: Will you stay and eat it with me?

WITCH: Of course. Did you miss me?

RAPUNZEL: You know I did, Mother Gothal.

WITCH: Did you see anyone in the wood this morning?

RAPUNZEL: *(Looking out window, as WITCH sets out food)* Just the deer and squirrels and the mother owl, again, making her nest on top of the tower. Could I go out today, just for a short time? I want to walk; run. Surely running in the woods wouldn't harm me.

WITCH: There are thieves, sometimes a knight, in this woods. You are safe here.

RAPUNZEL: Then, Mother, may I have a friend?

WITCH: Aren't I your friend?

RAPUNZEL: I want to play with someone when you're not here.

WITCH: I'll come more often.

RAPUNZEL: Bring me a friend, Mother. A boy from the village.

WITCH: A boy...This desire will disappear in a short while and you will be happy here, with me. What games would you play with a friend?

RAPUNZEL: Leapfrog...or tag...

WITCH: Then we'll play, before we eat.

RAPUNZEL: You will?

WITCH: Of course.

RAPUNZEL: What game?

WITCH: You choose.

RAPUNZEL: Tag. I'll chase you. Run, Mother. *(The WITCH shuffles more than runs. RAPUNZEL easily runs up to her.)* Run... faster!

WITCH: I'm running.

RAPUNZEL: Try to get away.

WITCH: You can't catch me. You can't catch me! *(RAPUNZEL tags her.)*

RAPUNZEL: Caught. Now you catch me.

WITCH: I know the game. *(RAPUNZEL easily eludes her.)* Come here...come here...

RAPUNZEL: Catch me. Catch me! *(RAPUNZEL laughs.)* Come, Mother. Run. Run!

WITCH: I'm coming.

RAPUNZEL: Mother, run!

WITCH: I am!

RAPUNZEL: But it isn't any fun if you're this slow. Hurry!

WITCH: I'll catch you. *(RAPUNZEL runs near her.)* There!

RAPUNZEL: Missed!

WITCH: I almost got you.

RAPUNZEL: But you didn't. Come again. *(They begin running in*

a circle.) **Run, Mother...run...**
WITCH: You see? I can play with you.
RAPUNZEL: Faster! Run faster!
WITCH: This is a wonderful game.
RAPUNZEL: You can't catch me!
WITCH: Rapunzel...Rapunzel...
RAPUNZEL: *(Playfully)* **You'll never catch me! You'll never catch me!**
WITCH: Rapunzel...I have to...stop... *(She stops, sits on bed, trying to catch her breath.)*
RAPUNZEL: Mother? What is it? Don't you feel well? *(She goes to WITCH. WITCH hits RAPUNZEL.)*
WITCH: Got you!
RAPUNZEL: But you —
WITCH: *(Crossing to breakfast)* **I told you I would catch you.**
RAPUNZEL: But Mother Gothal, you —
WITCH: That's all for now.
RAPUNZEL: But I thought you —
WITCH: Let's eat while it's still warm.
RAPUNZEL: Yes, Mother.
WITCH: That was fun, wasn't it?
RAPUNZEL: Yes. After breakfast we'll play leapfrog.
WITCH: Perhaps tomorrow, Rapunzel...perhaps tomorrow. *(WITCH exits tower.)*
NARRATOR: Rapunzel had no friends visit her that day nor any other day. It happened a couple of years later, *(PRINCE runs on in forest)* **the king's son, Prince Derrick, walked through the forest with his manservant, Ballard.**
BALLARD: *(Off)* **My Lord! My Lord!**
PRINCE: Here, Old Ballard. *(BALLARD enters, out of breath, using a walking stick.)* **Why do you follow me?**
BALLARD: If you continue running, I'll never follow anyone anywhere again. Have mercy on an old man. *(He sits on the ground.)*
PRINCE: It's not that I want you to die, old friend, but I want to run, or crawl, or jump if I wish — *(He leaps over BALLARD.)*
BALLARD: Princes do not jump.
PRINCE: — without someone watching over me. *(BALLARD rises.)*
BALLARD: The king has commanded me to follow you.
PRINCE: *(He sits.)* **I am never alone. There are always servants.**
BALLARD: The king fears your young mind, my Lord. I am here to serve as your good judgment. And I say again we shouldn't have entered this wood. They say a witch inhabits these trees and the Black Knight himself hides out here.
PRINCE: Witch...Shall we walk?

BALLARD: If you wish, my Lord.
PRINCE: I wish to walk alone.
BALLARD: Not today, my Lord.
PRINCE: Then come, my faithful dog. **Follow at my heels.** *(The PRINCE barks and walks. BALLARD follows. From the tower, RAPUNZEL sings.)*
RAPUNZEL: Why do you search?
My knight, my friend.
Where do you travel?
What is your end?

Across the desert
The wood, the city
Over the mountains
Far from me.

Why do you search?
What must you see?
Here is my hand.
Are you searching for me?
PRINCE: Listen.
BALLARD: I hear it.
PRINCE: It's beautiful. This way.
BALLARD: My Lord, you don't know who it is...or why it is. *(RAPUNZEL stops.)*
PRINCE: Quiet! Listen! *(Silence)* It's stopped.
BALLARD: Come, my Lord, back to the horses.
PRINCE: I'll wait until I hear it again.
BALLARD: This is what your father fears. Your young mind lured into dangerous, foolish —
PRINCE: Quiet. *(RAPUNZEL begins again.)* There...this way. *(He moves, BALLARD follows. They see the tower.)* From the tower. Stay here. I'm going to enter it.
BALLARD: My Lord, let's ride back to the castle. There I'll find two knights to enter this tower. If the witch is inside they will face her. If not and it's safe, then you may enter.
PRINCE: You give good advice, sir.
BALLARD: Thank you, my Lord.
PRINCE: And I will be wise to follow it.
BALLARD: Then let's return to our horses.
PRINCE: But, poor fellow, I'm a fool with a young mind. Wait here. *(He moves to tower, goes around it, followed by BALLARD.)* There's no doorway...no stairs.
BALLARD: You see? It's no ordinary tower. Enchantment is here. Return to the castle. We'll send two knights — *(The WITCH enters. BALLARD spies her.)* The witch! *(They hide.)*

313

PRINCE: She's going to the tower.

BALLARD: I knew this was an evil place...and that an evil song.

PRINCE: But how will she enter?

BALLARD: With her spell!

PRINCE: I'll move closer to learn it.

BALLARD: My Lord! She's a witch! *(The PRINCE moves closer. BALLARD reluctantly follows.)*

WITCH: Rapunzel, Rapunzel, let down your hair.

RAPUNZEL: *(Despondently)* Mother. *(RAPUNZEL stops singing, lets down her hair. The WITCH climbs up.)*

WITCH: Rapunzel...I brought you something... *(They sit. Brightly)* This! *(The WITCH gives RAPUNZEL a toy.)*

RAPUNZEL: *(Hollowly)* It's...thank you, Mother.

WITCH: Don't you want...? *(RAPUNZEL turns sadly away from the WITCH.)* We'll play with it another time. *(WITCH takes her hand, holds it. No response from RAPUNZEL. The PRINCE and BALLARD move away.)*

PRINCE: Did you hear?

BALLARD: *(Lying.)* No.

PRINCE: And did you see?

BALLARD: Nothing.

PRINCE: Then you must be dead, old man.

BALLARD: Not dead; wise.

PRINCE: What beautiful hair.

BALLARD: It will entangle you in its spell.

PRINCE: What a wonderful thought.

BALLARD: My Lord, you wouldn't —

PRINCE: No, Ballard, my old dungeon master, I won't try her "spell"...with the witch up there. I'll wait until tomorrow. *(He laughs, runs off, followed by BALLARD. WITCH exits.)*

NARRATOR: Early the next morning, they returned. *(PRINCE crosses to tower, followed by BALLARD.)*

PRINCE: Watch for the witch.

BALLARD: I won't help you in this, my Lord.

PRINCE: Call to me if she comes.

BALLARD: What monster must it be if a witch must keep it shut up in a tower?

PRINCE: *(As much like the WITCH as possible)* Rapunzel, Rapunzel, let down your hair.

RAPUNZEL: Mother, you're early. *(She lets down her hair.)*

PRINCE: She does!

RAPUNZEL: *(As he climbs up)* Why have you come so early?

PRINCE: *(In the WITCH's voice)* I...I have a wonderful surprise for you. *(He enters tower.)*

RAPUNZEL: *(Terrified)* Who are you?

PRINCE: *(Stunned)* Who are you?

RAPUNZEL: Did Mother Gothal send you?
PRINCE: Who is she? The witch? The witch is your mother?
RAPUNZEL: You tricked me.
PRINCE: Only to meet you.
RAPUNZEL: Are you a thief?
PRINCE: I'm not a thief and you're not a witch.
RAPUNZEL: What do you want?
PRINCE: I heard you singing. You sang so beautifully I had to meet you.
RAPUNZEL: You have to go. Mother Gothal mustn't see you.
PRINCE: I have a servant watching for her. If she comes he'll warn me and I'll go.
RAPUNZEL: Go now. I don't know you.
PRINCE: *(With a courtly bow)* I'm Prince Derrick, son of the king. Is your name Rapunzel?
RAPUNZEL: Yes.
PRINCE: *(Starting toward her)* Now that we know each other —
RAPUNZEL: Stand there!
PRINCE: I will. Here.
RAPUNZEL: Turn away. *(He does. He now looks away from her.)* Don't move.
PRINCE: You would make a good queen. "Stand there! Turn away! Don't move!" Whatever you command, my Lady.
RAPUNZEL: Don't speak. *(RAPUNZEL approaches him, looks him over. She reaches out her hand, touches his shoulder. He reaches up, takes her hand. She pulls it back, he holds on.)* Let go! *(She hits his hand sharply. He lets go. She backs off.)* Are you a man?
PRINCE: Yes.
RAPUNZEL: I've never seen a man before.
PRINCE: I won't hurt you.
RAPUNZEL: Do all men look like you?
PRINCE: Well, most men aren't quite as, how should I say —
RAPUNZEL: What's it like where you live?
PRINCE: I live in the castle with —
RAPUNZEL: Have you ever traveled to a mountain?
PRINCE: Last year, during the —
RAPUNZEL: Do you ride a horse?
PRINCE: Yes, a horse named —
RAPUNZEL: Do people sing in your castle?
PRINCE: *(Catching on)* Yes.
RAPUNZEL: Are there dances?
PRINCE: Often.
RAPUNZEL: Do you dance?
PRINCE: Very well.
RAPUNZEL: Show me.

315

PRINCE: **I would be honored.** *(He crosses to her. She doesn't move. Bowing)* **May I have this dance, my Lady?**

RAPUNZEL: **Yes.** *(He holds out his hand. No response from RAPUNZEL. Pause)* **Dance.**

PRINCE: **You have to dance with me.**

RAPUNZEL: **I don't know how.**

PRINCE: **I'll show you.**

RAPUNZEL: **Yes, show me. Dance.** *(She sits on bed, picks up her doll, holds it.)*

PRINCE: **With you...I need...here...** *(He takes doll, puts it back on bed. He pulls her up, tentatively moves in to her, into the dance position. She becomes confused and frightened and slowly pushes him to the floor. He allows this as he is also confused. Once he's on the floor, RAPUNZEL backs up.)* **No, Rapunzel, you don't understand...** *(Rising)* **When we dance...** *(He moves in to her again)* **we stand close —** *(She pushes him down, sharply, backs away quickly.)*

RAPUNZEL: **I want you to dance!**

PRINCE: *(As he rises)* **A man doesn't dance alone. Where I live two people dance together, a man and a woman.**

RAPUNZEL: **A woman...show me.** *(She crosses to him, stands close and ready. He positions their hands carefully.)*

PRINCE: **You won't push me down again, will you?**

RAPUNZEL: **I don't think so.**

PRINCE: **Now...move this way...and this...and this way...** *(She doesn't move.)* **You must move with me, together...this way... and this...** *(They slowly dance. Faint courtly music fades in.)*

RAPUNZEL: *(Disappointedly)* **Do you enjoy this?**

PRINCE: **Yes...if I am fond of the person I'm dancing with.**

RAPUNZEL: **Are you enjoying this now?**

PRINCE: **Very much.**

RAPUNZEL: **Oh.**

PRINCE: **Are you?**

RAPUNZEL: **Oh, yes...yes...it's a wonderful dance...** *(They dance. Suddenly)* **Faster.** *(She leads him faster.)*

PRINCE: **But with this dance...yes!...and then we dance faster!** *(RAPUNZEL laughs.)*

RAPUNZEL: **Faster! Dance faster! Jump! Jump! Fly! Fly!** *(They spin around. RAPUNZEL fairly throws the PRINCE down. He quickly stands, regaining his dignity as she laughs.)*

PRINCE: *(Bowing)* **Thank you for a wonderful dance. You dance like no one I've ever danced with before.**

RAPUNZEL: **What is the place like where you live?**

PRINCE: *(Sitting with her)* **The castle stands high on a hill overlooking a river and valley. The river leads to the ocean...** *(They continue their conversation inaudibly. The WITCH enters* *humming to herself. Music dies out.)*

BALLARD: The witch! *(Running to tower)* **My Lord...My Lord...** *(The PRINCE is too engrossed in RAPUNZEL to hear him.)* **My —** **Ah!** *(BALLARD runs away from the tower as the WITCH approaches it.)*

WITCH: *(Sniffing the air)* **Who has been here? An old...dog?** *(She looks around, sniffs her way toward BALLARD.)* **No, an old man!** *(BALLARD, in terror, moves away, exits, followed by the WITCH, stalking him.)*

PRINCE: Will you have me for your husband?

RAPUNZEL: *(To herself)* **He will love me better than old Mother Gothal.** *(To the PRINCE)* **Yes. And I would gladly go with you but I don't know how I'm to get down from this tower.** *(Looks out window.)* **Each time you come bring silk. I will twist it into a ladder and when it's long enough I will descend by it. Then we can ride away on your horse.** *(BALLARD runs on.)*

PRINCE: When does the witch see you?

RAPUNZEL: During the day. You come in the evening...my prince.

PRINCE: My Lady.

BALLARD: My Lord!

PRINCE: My servant!

RAPUNZEL: *(Out window)* **My mother!**

ALL: Ah!

BALLARD: The witch!

PRINCE: Where?

BALLARD: Coming there!

PRINCE: Distract her!

BALLARD: I have!

PRINCE: Then continue! *(BALLARD runs away, hides.)*

RAPUNZEL: *(To PRINCE)* **Don't let her see you. You don't know what she'll do!**

PRINCE: I think I do. *(WITCH enters.)*

RAPUNZEL: She's here. *(WITCH crosses below window.)*

WITCH: Back again! An old man? *(Calling)* **Rapunzel? Rapunzel?**

RAPUNZEL: *(Moving to window)* **Mother Gothal! Good morning! Oh, it's a beautiful day. Isn't it a beautiful day, Mother?**

WITCH: I'm pleased to see you this happy, Rapunzel.

RAPUNZEL: I'm very happy.

WITCH: Have you seen an old man near the tower?

RAPUNZEL: An old man? No, Mother.

WITCH: One has been here.

PRINCE: *(To himself)* **Ballard** — *(To RAPUNZEL)* **My servant.**

RAPUNZEL: I haven't been watching.

WITCH: I see...Let down your hair.

RAPUNZEL: Oh, Mother, I...

PRINCE: You can't, Rapunzel.

WITCH: What is it?

RAPUNZEL: I would much rather come down. May I walk in the woods this morning?

WITCH: You know there isn't a way for you to come down. And there's a man in the woods. Let down your hair.

PRINCE: Rapunzel.

RAPUNZEL: I...Mother...ah... *(Stepping back, speaking to the PRINCE)* Hide!

PRINCE: Where?

RAPUNZEL: Anywhere! *(He searches around the room, then jumps under the covers of the bed.)* No.

PRINCE: *(Getting back up)* There isn't anywhere!

WITCH: Rapunzel? Let down your hair.

RAPUNZEL: I can't, Mother.

WITCH: Why?

RAPUNZEL: I can't because...there's a man...

WITCH: What? A man?

PRINCE: Rapunzel!

RAPUNZEL: Yes, Mother, a man.

PRINCE: A young fool.

RAPUNZEL: An old man in the woods. *(BALLARD stifles a scream.)*

WITCH: Where?

RAPUNZEL: *(Pointing away from BALLARD)* By the fallen tree.

PRINCE: I love you.

WITCH: I don't see him.

RAPUNZEL: Neither do I, now. He's hiding. Mother, what are we going to do? There's a man in the woods! What if he's come for me? Mother! Help me!

WITCH: I'll find him. Hide in the tower! *(She exits.)*

RAPUNZEL: A man! A man! *(BALLARD moves to window.)*

BALLARD: *(Stage whisper)* Now, my Lord.

RAPUNZEL: Now. *(RAPUNZEL lets down her hair, the PRINCE starts down.)* No! *(He re-enters tower, BALLARD hides. WITCH re-enters, searching. RAPUNZEL stands in the window, suddenly points off.)* There he is! There he is! Mother! *(WITCH crosses quickly out.)* Now. *(The PRINCE kisses RAPUNZEL, climbs down, helped by BALLARD. BALLARD and PRINCE move around tower, as RAPUNZEL lifts up her hair. The WITCH re-enters, just misses seeing her hair. The WITCH stops, the men stop. The WITCH starts moving one way, the men hear and move to avoid being seen, then the WITCH reverses her direction quickly as do the men. As the WITCH moves again, the men are divided as to which way to go.)*

BALLARD: This way —

PRINCE: But the witch went that way.

BALLARD: We'll follow behind her.

PRINCE: **This way.**

BALLARD: **My Lord, I am your counselor and I counsel you to go this way.**

PRINCE: **Go, then. Go.** *(The PRINCE starts off, behind and with BALLARD, but then turns, runs other way, exits. The WITCH meets BALLARD who screams and begins to run off in the PRINCE's direction. The WITCH quickly takes BALLARD's walking stick, trips him, pushes him down and begins to kick him and hit him repeatedly with stick as he tries to crawl away.)*

WITCH: **Caught you!**

BALLARD: **Help! Help!**

WITCH: *(Kicking, hitting)* **Stalking around my woods!**

BALLARD: **Stop! Stop!**

WITCH: **Disgusting old dog!**

BALLARD: **I haven't done anything!** *(She stops hitting him.)*

WITCH: **Stay where you are!** *(He stops moving.)* **What do you want, old man?**

BALLARD: **I'm lost!**

WITCH: **You've been walking in circles.**

BALLARD: **I'm lost!**

WITCH: **Where are you going?**

BALLARD: **To the king's castle.**

WITCH: **You're lost!**

BALLARD: **I know!**

WITCH: **It lies that way, old fool.**

BALLARD: **That way?**

WITCH: **Follow the morning sun.**

BALLARD: **I'm grateful to you.**

WITCH: **Be gone now, and never return for if I see you again, it's a dog you'll be; a slobbering, howling hound.**

BALLARD: **Never again. You won't see me. Not me.** *(He starts off.)*

WITCH: **Old fool... "I'm lost! I'm lost!"** *(She laughs.)*

BALLARD: **A good morning to you, Madam.** *(She spits like a large cat at him, he squeals, she chases him off as they both exit.)*

NARRATOR: **And so, unknown to the witch, the prince visited Rapunzel every evening.** *(The PRINCE enters, crosses to tower.)*

PRINCE: **Rapunzel, Rapunzel, fairest of the fair.**
Rapunzel, Rapunzel, let down your enchanting hair.

RAPUNZEL: **Derrick! The sun has almost set. Where have you been?**

PRINCE: *(As he climbs)* **I had to make a purchase along the way.** *(He enters tower, they kiss quickly.)* **Here, more silk.**

RAPUNZEL: **Look.** *(She pulls the silk ladder out from under the bed.)* **Another month and it will be long enough for me to**

climb down.

PRINCE: Another month?...I brought you something. *(He holds his hands behind his back.)*

RAPUNZEL: *(Putting away silk)* **You know you shouldn't bring me things. Mother Gothal may find them.**

PRINCE: I'll give it to you if you promise to sing to me tonight.

RAPUNZEL: What is it?

PRINCE: Promise me.

RAPUNZEL: You know I will. What is it? *(He opens his hands. Nothing is there.)* **I don't see anything.**

PRINCE: Look outside near the fallen tree.

RAPUNZEL: Outside? What did you... *(Runs to window, looks out.)* **A horse! You brought me a horse!**

PRINCE: Your own horse.

RAPUNZEL: She's beautiful.

PRINCE: The most beautiful horse in the kingdom.

RAPUNZEL: In the world.

PRINCE: Her name is —

RAPUNZEL: Star.

PRINCE: We call her —

RAPUNZEL: Star!

PRINCE: Yes. Star. That's her name. She'll be waiting for you the night you leave with me.

RAPUNZEL: And we'll ride to a mountain.

PRINCE: To wherever you want. *(They embrace.)*

NARRATOR: The prince brought her silk every evening and the ladder grew longer. *(PRINCE exits tower. WITCH enters, crosses to tower. RAPUNZEL sleeps on bed.)* **The witch discovered nothing until one morning...**

WITCH: Rapunzel, Rapunzel, let down your hair. *(Pause)* **Rapunzel? Rapunzel!**

RAPUNZEL: *(Waking some)* **What? Oh...yes, Mother.**

WITCH: Let down your hair.

RAPUNZEL: Yes, Mother. *(Sleepily doing so. The WITCH pulls it hard, hurts RAPUNZEL.)* **Oh!** *(Once the WITCH is up, still half asleep, crossing to bed, falling on it)* **Tell me, Mother Gothal, how can it be that you are so much heavier than the prince?**

WITCH: Oh, you wicked child. What did you say?

RAPUNZEL: I...I said...What did I say?

WITCH: Who comes here?

RAPUNZEL: *(Startled, completely awake)* **Oh! I wanted to tell you. I'm happy I've told you. There's a prince, Prince Derrick, who visits me here.**

WITCH: When?

RAPUNZEL: Every evening.

WITCH: What?

RAPUNZEL: But you musn't think —

WITCH: I thought I had separated you from all the world.

RAPUNZEL: He's a kind man, Mother.

WITCH: You deceived me!

RAPUNZEL: I was lonely!

WITCH: I came every day!

RAPUNZEL: He's different from you.

WITCH: Ungrateful child!

RAPUNZEL: He asked me to marry him.

WITCH: What?

RAPUNZEL: And I said yes.

WITCH: Without speaking to me!

RAPUNZEL: He's my husband.

WITCH: What have you done!

RAPUNZEL: I was afraid you wouldn't allow it. Mother Gothal, I like this man. There's nothing wicked in my seeing him.

WITCH: Lying to your mother? What have you done to me? Wicked child...And what will I do to you. *(Getting large scissors)*

RAPUNZEL: What are you doing? *(WITCH slowly advances toward RAPUNZEL.)* What do you have in your hands?

WITCH: Come here, my child.

RAPUNZEL: I didn't want to hurt you.

WITCH: And I never wanted to hurt you...until now.

RAPUNZEL: I've done nothing wrong! *(The WITCH goes for RAPUNZEL who runs. The WITCH chases her.)* **Scissors? Why? What are you going to do?** *(Again WITCH goes for RAPUNZEL; again RAPUNZEL gets away.)* **You can't catch me. Remember? You'll never catch me!**

WITCH: Rapunzel! *(Another miss)*

RAPUNZEL: See? You can't catch me. *(RAPUNZEL throws dolls and toys at WITCH.)* **Not until I want you to. Not until you're not angry any more and you'll listen to me!** *(WITCH sits on bed, closes her eyes.)*

WITCH: *(Quietly)* **Rapunzel...**

RAPUNZEL: Mother? You're not going to fool me again. Mother? Mother Gothal, that trick won't fool me! *(RAPUNZEL keeps her distance.)*

WITCH: *(Sadly)* **Rapunzel, why...?**

RAPUNZEL: Don't feel sad. I'm still here with you. I'm still your — *(Suddenly the WITCH leaps up, starts to go one way, goes another and, quick as a cat, grabs RAPUNZEL by the hair.)* **No!**

WITCH: Caught you! You see? I caught you! *(She drags RAPUNZEL by her hair to the bed.)*

RAPUNZEL: Mother, that hurts! Let go! Please! You're hurting me! You're hurting me.

WITCH: On the bed.

RAPUNZEL: What are you going to do? Mother Gothal, why — *(The WITCH throws RAPUNZEL on the bed, turns her on her stomach, puts her knee on RAPUNZEL's back, holds her down. She then takes RAPUNZEL by the hair and cuts it off.)* No! Not my hair! Mother, please! I won't be able to see him! I won't be able to see you! My beautiful hair! *Nooo!*

WITCH: You're correct, my child. You'll never see him again. And it's the last you'll see of me. Come! *(WITCH twirls with RAPUNZEL out of the tower. Sounds of a windswept desert. Lights out in tower then up in wilderness, isolating an area.)*

NARRATOR: She took Rapunzel far from the tower into a wilderness. *(WITCH pushes RAPUNZEL down.)*

RAPUNZEL: Where are we? What is this place?

WITCH: *(Looking around)* Yes...few trees...dry sand...burning sun...

RAPUNZEL: Why have you brought me here?

WITCH: Here you'll stay, my lady love, and live out what's left of your miserable life.

RAPUNZEL: You're going to leave me here? How will I live? What will I eat?

WITCH: Swift justice for an ungrateful child! You'll find out how much you need me.

RAPUNZEL: I'll die here!

WITCH: What do I care whether you live or die? When you care so little for me.

RAPUNZEL: *(Taking hold of WITCH's dress.)* I love you, Mother.

WITCH: Let go! *(WITCH pushes RAPUNZEL down, backs away.)*

RAPUNZEL: Mother! *(The WITCH stands for a moment looking down at RAPUNZEL, then exits.)* Mother Gothal?...I'm hungry...I'm hungry...Did you go?...You left me?...Come back! Come back! I don't want to stay here! I don't like it! *(A silence)* You're right! I was wicked and ungrateful! I won't see him again! I'll live in the tower alone! With just you! *(Angrily)* Mother Gothal! You old witch! *(Beat)* I won't live here! I won't eat anything and I'll die! You'll see! I'll die! You bitter old witch! You ungrateful old hag! Mother Gothal! *(She falls on her back, pounds the ground with her hands and feet furiously, rolls over, continues pounding. She screams and flops on her stomach, stops pounding. She lies there a moment, then laughs. She laughs heartily at herself as she sits up. She sees something, carefully and quietly picks up a long stick. Sweetly)*

Come here...little...rabbit. I won't hurt you. You see? I'm just very hungry and I'd like to — *(She runs at it, tries*

322

repeatedly to hit it with stick.) **Eat you!** *(She chases it around, swinging more and more desperately, but it gets away.)* **Come back! Come back!** *(She stops in frustration, then sees she must continue to hunt. In spite of her frustration, she goes on.)* **Here...little...toad...** *(She hits it, then forces herself to look at it, pick it up, pull off one of its legs, and eat it. She stands, looks around wilderness. The wind blows stronger. Anxiously.)*

How will I live here? *(Calming herself)* **I need to build a hut. I can use sticks and branches...and I'll need water...** *(Beginning to panic again)* **Where would there be water here?** *(Again calming herself, trying to think)* **I'll dig under a tree — or follow animals to where they drink water...and to eat?** *(She looks at toad, throws remainder away in disgust.)* **No!...roots...rabbits. First...eat.** *(Confidently)* **No. First I'll build a hut.** *(She picks up a stick, selects a spot.)* **Here.** *(As she begins to put stick in place a wolf howls. She drops stick in fear.)*

Wolf! Mother Gothal! *(She screams and runs, stops just before exiting, turns, comes back. She picks up stick, slowly walks toward wolf, shakes stick at it.)* **This is my house.** *(She growls at wolf.)* **Away. Away! Hah! Hah!** *(She holds stick high, the wolf howls, she screams and runs off the other way.)*

NARRATOR: **On the evening of the day on which she banished Rapunzel, the witch returned to the tower.** *(The WITCH twirls into tower.)*

WITCH: **Ah, here he comes, my little mouse, into the claws of the cat.** *(PRINCE enters.)*

PRINCE: **Rapunzel, Rapunzel, let down your hair.**

WITCH: *(In RAPUNZEL's voice)* **Yes...yes, my prince...** *(In her own voice)* **Come up to the cat.** *(She lets down hair from hook. He climbs up. In RAPUNZELs voice.)* **I have a surprise for you.** *(PRINCE enters tower.)*

PRINCE: **Mother Gothal!**

WITCH: **Yes...**

PRINCE: **Yes...you frightened me...I'm pleased to meet you. I'm Derrick, son of King Ludvic II, and Crowned Prince.**

WITCH: **Yes...**

PRINCE: **A...friend of Rapunzel's.**

WITCH: **I'm...pleased to meet you. You know who I am.**

PRINCE: **Yes...** *(Looking around)* **Rapunzel? Rapunzel?**

WITCH: **Ah! You have come to fetch your ladylove, but the pretty bird is no longer in her nest.**

PRINCE: *(Still innocently)* **Where is she?**

WITCH: **Thief!** *(She scratches him in the chest. He recoils in pain.)* **She's lost to you! She'll sing no more for you!**

PRINCE: **What have you done to her?**

WITCH: **What I may do to you.**
PRINCE: **Is she still living?**
WITCH: **Yes, my prince, still living. But where For how long?**
PRINCE: **Where have you put her? Mother Gothal, please, I must know.**
WITCH: *(Mocking him)* **Please, I must know.**
PRINCE: **I'll do anything you ask. Just let me see her.**
WITCH: **Never again, for the cat has seized her and it will scratch your eyes out.**
PRINCE: *(Drawing his dagger.)* **Where is she?**
WITCH: **Look at you, my little mouse, angry at the cat.**
PRINCE: **Tell me! Or, as much as it's against my nature, I will use this. Where is she?** *(She scratches at his eyes. He recoils, screams in pain, falls to his knees, drops his dagger.)* **My eyes! I can't see!** *(He gropes for his dagger, finds it, stands, listens for WITCH.)* **Witch!**
WITCH: **Here, my mouse.** *(PRINCE lunges for her, she moves, he stabs bed. She moves near window, calls to him in RAPUNZEL's voice.)* **Help me! Save me, my prince. Save your Rapunzel!** *(He lunges for her, she pushes him out window. He falls on to the ground.)*
PRINCE: *(Slowly rising)* **Rapunzel...Rapunzel...**
WITCH: *(Sadly, picking up RAPUNZEL's doll.)* **Rapunzel...** *(WITCH exits tower, the PRINCE staggers off.)*
NARRATOR: **The prince wandered blind through the lands, eating nothing but roots and berries, sad over the loss of his wife. After living for a time in the wilderness, Rapunzel gave birth to twins, a boy and a girl.** *(RAPUNZEL enters carrying two babies.)*
RAPUNZEL: **You're finally quiet. Sleep, yes, sleep. In the morning we'll walk all the way to the nut tree and have our breakfast there. Sleep...Dream gentle, good dreams...** *(She sets them down, sings her song to them. The PRINCE enters, blind and disheveled.)*
PRINCE: *(As RAPUNZEL sings. He stops.)* **I know that voice...No, it's different. It's been so long since I heard her sing.** *(He begins walking away.)* **I felt she would be this way, but —** *(He stops again.)* **That song...** *(He hums with her, sings some with her.)* **Rapunzel? Rapunzel!**
RAPUNZEL: **Derrick? Derrick!** *(They embrace.)*
PRINCE: **Rapunzel...**
RAPUNZEL: **You're here! You found me.** *(Seeing his face)* **What's happened to you?**
PRINCE: **When I came for you in the tower the witch blinded me.**
RAPUNZEL: **That's why you haven't come.**

PRINCE: I've wandered everywhere, searching for you, listening for you. *(He slides down to his knees, holding her.)*

RAPUNZEL: And I've waited for you. I knew you'd find me, Derrick. I knew you'd find me.

PRINCE: *(Looking up)* You're crying. *(Enchanted by this)* I feel your tears...I...my eyes... *(He rises, looks at her.)* I can see. I can see!

RAPUNZEL: Derrick! *(He swings her around.)*

NARRATOR: She told him the story of her life in the wilderness and of their children. *(They cross to children, each pick one up, exit.)* Then he took her to his kingdom where they were received with joy and they lived long and happily together. *(NARRATOR closes book.)*

THE END

RAPUNZEL'S LAMENT

Words: **Max Bush**
Music: **Dale Dieleman**

Almauria:
Voyage of the Dragonfly
— by Max Bush —

CHARACTERS

Queen Meaghan

Cynric . . . . The Magician

Mariana . . . . The Magician's Daughter

Captain Taran

Brian . . . . First Mate

The Beast

The Hag-Witch

NOTE: The Beast can be doubled with the Magician; the Hag-Witch can be doubled with the Queen. Musicians are optional. The music can be live, recorded, or both. If live, the musicians remain in view of the audience.

TIME: Long ago.

PLACE: Scene 1 — Queen Meaghan's castle and a promontory overlooking the sea.

Scene 2 — Aboard the "Dragonfly," about three weeks later.

Scene 3 — The island of Aalmauria, later that day.

Scene 4 — Aboard the "Dragonfly," the next morning.

PLAYING TIME: Approximately seventy-five minutes.

DEDICATION: *Aalmauria: Voyage of the Dragonfly* is dedicated to David Avcollie.

The premiere production of *Aalmauria: Voyage of the Dragonfly* was presented on April 23, 1984, at the DePaul/Goodman School of Drama, Chicago, with the following cast and crew:

CHARACTERS

MAGICIAN	Stephen Smith
MARIANA	Laural Paxton
ARIA.	Lynn C. Schwarzbach
QUEEN.	Cynthia J. Orthal
CAPTAIN	Jim Krag
MATE	Craig Hassebrock
BEAST	Dave Saperstein
	Kevin C. White

PRODUCTION STAFF

Director	David Avcollie
Fight Choreography . .	James Finney
Scenic Design.	Jeff Bauer
Costume Design	Kathryn Wagner
Lighting Design	Joel A. Monaghan
Assistant Director. . . .	Todd Schmidt
Stage Manager	Michelle C. Armamentos
Sound Design.	Kevin Snow

Scene 1

(The throne room of the QUEEN's castle. Dark, damp, cold atmosphere. A throne sits Right Center, a large old book is on the floor next to it. The QUEEN's cape is spread out on the throne. The QUEEN, young, attractive and strong, runs on, sword in hand. A loud wind courses through the castle. She shivers, turns toward the entrance and calls.)

QUEEN: Mariana? *(No response)* **Mariana! Come!** *(MARIANA, younger than the QUEEN, appears.)* **I'm freezing.** *(MARIANA fairly drags her sword as she enters.)* **Raise your sword.**

MARIANA: I'm a lady of your court, Queen, not a lord or knight.

QUEEN: Higher.

MARIANA: We do not sword fight.

QUEEN: In my court we do, and will. Prepare...now! *(MARIANA lowers her sword. Although MARIANA clearly expresses an ambivalence toward the QUEEN, it is not weighted in either direction. As well as the more obvious conflicted stance against the QUEEN, MARIANA will express warmth, care and respect. The QUEEN obviously cares deeply for MARIANA, despite the frustrations, and exhibits an infinite patience with her.)* **Mariana, when your mother died, I gave her my oath I would watch over you. You are bright-minded and beautiful, but you must prepare yourself for the world as it is. Now, defend yourself.**

MARIANA: As you command, Meaghan. *(They raise swords.)*

QUEEN: Now! *(MARIANA turns away with a cry and lunges with her sword, stops, freezes. The QUEEN stops her swing, looks at MARIANA, then hits MARIANA's sword down. MARIANA, still turned away, lifts it again with energy and a small vocal challenge.)*

MARIANA: Hah.

QUEEN: To help you, imagine I'm a dragon.

MARIANA: That's not difficult, Meaghan. *(They both laugh.)*

QUEEN: *(She growls. Then in a dragon voice)* **Maiden...**

MARIANA: Yes, Queen Dragon?

QUEEN: *(Dragon voice)* **I will devour you.**

MARIANA: Please, do not.

QUEEN: *(Dragon voice)* **Then raise your sword.** *(She growls and advances on MARIANA, who lowers her sword and suddenly bolts.)*

MARIANA: Help!

QUEEN: *(Her own voice)* **Who do you call?**

MARIANA: My father.

QUEEN: I've sent him from the castle. His magic will not always rescue you. Therefore, imagine me a dragon. *(She*

331

lunges at MARIANA who screams and runs. The QUEEN chases her. In a dragon voice) **You can't escape!**

MARIANA: **Help! Help!**

QUEEN: **Come back!**

MARIANA: **Someone help!**

QUEEN: *(QUEEN chases her. In her own voice.)* **No one will save you. Defend yourself!** *(They stop running.)*

MARIANA: **No!**

QUEEN: **Why?**

MARIANA: **I don't want to hurt you.**

QUEEN: *(Laughing)* **Mariana! I command you to fight. Now.** *(They fight.)* **Yes!...Well aimed!...Head up. Hold your head up.**

MARIANA: **I can't.**

QUEEN: **Open one eye! Protect yourself!**

MARIANA: **No!**

QUEEN: **Then die!** *(She whacks MARIANA in the arm with her sword.)*

MARIANA: **Oh!**

QUEEN: **Dishonorable faint-hearted hag!** *(MARIANA sits on floor.)*

MARIANA: **Meaghan, my arm...**

QUEEN: **Oh, Mariana...come off the cold floor.** *(MARIANA stands without allowing QUEEN to help her.)* **Rub it gently and the pain will...Let me —** *(Touching MARIANA's arm. MARIANA pulls away.)*

MARIANA: **Must you strike me?**

QUEEN: **If you are to learn swordplay.**

MARIANA: **I don't want to learn.**

QUEEN: **You'll be grateful I taught you...someday.**

MARIANA: **Are we to play again?**

QUEEN: **No, that's the end; although it did warm me —** *(A loud wind courses through the castle.)* **for a time.** *(They put swords down. QUEEN sits in throne.)* **Cold.**

MARIANA: **And colder.**

QUEEN: *(Curling up in throne, wrapping up in her cape)* **I'd give all our castle's gold for one summer's day.**

MARIANA: **Some say it will never be summer here again.**

QUEEN: **Not true.**

MARIANA: **The snow still falls —**

QUEEN: **Oh, I am sick to death of these cold, dark walls. And lonely.**

MARIANA: *(A little remorse)* **With me here?**

QUEEN: **For someone a little more handsome than you, dragon-face. A man.**

MARIANA: **Oh.**

QUEEN: *(Holding out her hand to MARIANA. MARIANA takes it.)* **But who would come to this icen land. Did I hurt you?**

MARIANA: **Not much.** *(CYNRIC, the magician enters.)*
CYNRIC: **Queen Meaghan.** *(He bows.)*
QUEEN: **Magician.**
MARIANA: **Father —** *(She embraces him.)*
QUEEN: **What have you found?**
CYNRIC: **As far as we traveled — east and west — snow covered all ground. To the north the ice still flows downward toward the castle. I'm sorry, but I'm certain a long age of ice is descending on these lands. There'll be no summer again this year, nor any as long as we live.**
MARIANA: **We must all move south.**
CYNRIC: **Yes. Mariana will be leaving tomorrow.**
QUEEN: **Mariana...no...**
MARIANA: **You must leave, Meaghan, or you'll freeze.**
QUEEN: **I will not move south!** *These* **are my lands.**
CYNRIC: **Then I'll remain in the castle to serve you as I can.**
QUEEN: **Cynric, what would give enough power to your magic to stop this ice age?**
CYNRIC: **We've attempted everything.**
QUEEN: **What in all the world would have the power?**
CYNRIC: **Something magic itself...a source of extreme energy or heat, but —**
QUEEN: **A fire with power —**
CYNRIC: **Yes —**
QUEEN: **As I thought. Here...this morning...** *(She retrieves the large book.)* **In one of your ancient manuscripts...I read of such a flame, burning in a cave.** *(She opens book.)* **It's on an island...within the Isles of Mist... called —**
CYNRIC: **Aalmauria.** *(Aalmauria music, lyrical and alluring, fades in.)*
QUEEN: **You know this island?**
CYNRIC: **Yes.**
QUEEN: **Is there such a flame?**
CYNRIC: **Aalmauria is an island of enchantment. The flame, the forest, certain rocks and streams, but —**
MARIANA: **Would this flame help you, Father?**
CYNRIC: **For me it would be a great source of power.**
QUEEN: **Why haven't you spoken of this before?**
CYNRIC: **No one can enter the cave to retrieve the flame. A Beast guards it, and a powerful hag-witch.**
QUEEN: **I'll face them.**
CYNRIC: **Meaghan, many have tried — I have tried — and failed. Few escape; most fall before the beast or hag and are slaughtered without mercy.**
QUEEN: **I'll face them.**
CYNRIC: **And they're not the worst you'll face. The greatest**

danger is the flame itself. It must be used correctly or it will turn against those who possess it and destroy them. Yet no one can be sure what is correct.

QUEEN: I'll discover what is correct.

MARIANA: Doesn't Aalmauria lie far across the sea?

QUEEN: Yes. *(They share some excitement over this.)* **The captain who sailed you and me south last year** — *(The CAPTAIN, RANDOLF TARAN, enters a promontory on an island.)*

MARIANA: Captain Taran —

QUEEN: Would he sail us to Aalmauria?

MARIANA: Yes. I've spoken to you of him, Father. *(The MATE, BRIAN, joins the CAPTAIN on the promontory.)* **He'd sail anywhere!**

CAPTAIN: Dolphins, mate, there! Look at those creatures!

MATE: The sea's creatures.

CAPTAIN: As free as the sea.

CYNRIC: Would he agree to such an impossible voyage? *(Aalmauria music out.)*

MARIANA: He's sailed the world and knows its secrets. He'll save our lands.

QUEEN: If he refuses we will find another ship. But I'll ask this man first.

CYNRIC: How well do you know him?

QUEEN: Only from our voyage south last year, but —

CYNRIC: Didn't you tell me he's like the sea itself; wild, willful? *(TARAN swats BRIAN, moves away.)*

QUEEN: Yes, but...

CYNRIC: Can we trust him?

MARIANA: I do.

CYNRIC: For your people, I urge you to be cautious. He won't understand the laws that rule Aalmauria's magic as you will. If he is wild he'll endanger everyone.

QUEEN: If he accepts the voyage, prepare me a charm, Cynric, a magical charm to use against him if I must.

MARIANA: What type of charm?

QUEEN: *(To MARIANA)* **Only if I must.**

MARIANA: You won't.

QUEEN: Now, I want to call him here, to the castle. He's somewhere at sea.

CYNRIC: We'll use a song as we've done in the past.

QUEEN: Come, let's prepare. *(To MARIANA)* **Aalmauria! This is our hope!**

MARIANA: *(As they exit)* **And to see Taran again!**

QUEEN: I dreamed of it. *(MARIANA stops. CYNRIC and QUEEN*

have gone.)

MARIANA: *You* **have?** *(MARIANA exits. Focus shifts to TARAN and BRIAN on promontory. Sounds of waves and gulls)*

MATE: Feel that, Captain?

CAPTAIN: Aye, mate, it's a cool breeze.

MATE: Winter won't be late.

CAPTAIN: No; we're in for a frost.

MATE: And an early snow.

CAPTAIN: It's a good wind, sir, and a good day.

MATE: Aye, Captain.

CAPTAIN: But in my bones, mate, I feel...

MATE: What?

CAPTAIN: Like this chilled wind. Have we lost our way?

MATE: Captain, the seas are ours; we're free to follow the winds as we will.

CAPTAIN: Aye...

MATE: It's this strange seacoast we're on, this deserted island; it makes us...

CAPTAIN: Lonely.

MATE: With your mate right with you?

CAPTAIN: For someone prettier than you are, you ugly fish head. A lady.

MATE: You're not thinking of leaving the sea?

CAPTAIN: Never. Never. But...Do you remember Queen Meaghan, mate? From last year? As beautiful as the sunset to look on.

MATE: I remember she troubled you.

CAPTAIN: She's not been out of my mind these last days. And at night I dream — I see her, floating above the waves in the winds. She calls me, but I —

MATE: *(Suddenly alarmed)* **Captain!**

CAPTAIN: *(Rising abruptly)* **Aye?**

MATE: Look there.

CAPTAIN: Where?

MATE: A mermaid!

CAPTAIN: What?

MATE: Floating on the waves! I think she calls you. *(He becomes a comical portrait of a mermaid. In a falsetto)* **Captain!**

CAPTAIN: *(Finally understanding him)* **Ah!**

MATE: *(As mermaid)* **Captain, are you lonely? Aaawww! Come down here, you old dog-fish! Come here, and I'll give you a salty kiss!** *(He puckers and smacks his lips, laughs, and then calls.)* **Raaaannndoooolff!**

CAPTAIN: Don't call me that, mate.

MATE: *(As mermaid)* **Randolf, come here!** *(As BRIAN)* **She calls you, Captain. Do you hear? "Randolf!" she says.**

CAPTAIN: Don't call me Randolf! You know I hate it.

MATE: **You don't want her? No? Then I'll take her, Captain.** *(He now becomes the CAPTAIN.)* **No, you won't, mate; she's mine.** *(As himself)* **She's mine, Captain! You'll not have her!** *(As CAPTAIN)* **Mine, mate!** *(As MATE, drawing his sword)* **Then draw, you love-sick sailor, draw and fight for her.** *(He whacks TARAN with his sword.)*

CAPTAIN: **Not now, mate.**

MATE: **Aye, you cowardly sand bug.** *(Another whack)*

CAPTAIN: **Mate, not now.**

MATE: **Draw, you barnacled buccaneer! Or I'll throw your cowardous shanks to the sharks — Randolf!**

CAPTAIN: *(Drawing sword)* **Clam yourself shut, you jigglin' jellyfish!**

MATE: **A jellyfish am I?** *(As they are facing off)* **Come for me, Randolf, you lovesick sea cow!**

CAPTAIN: **Lovesick am I? Randolf am I? She's *my* mermaid!** *(They sword fight playfully, energetically. BRIAN wins.)* **Yours.**

MATE: **Shall we sail, Randol —** *(TARAN stops him with gesture of his sword.)* **Captain?**

CAPTAIN: **Aye.** *(They speak simultaneously during the following, moving and pointing in their appropriate directions.)*

CAPTAIN: **We'll head south, mate.**	**MATE:** **We'll head north, Captain.**
Aye, north, aye. Well, south, then. What's our course to be, mate?	**Aye, south, aye. Well, north, then. What's our course to be, Captain?**

CAPTAIN: *(Lying on the hillside)* **Ah, let's sit on this isle a little longer and watch the dolphins play.**

MATE: **Aye. Perhaps this day something will come.**

CAPTAIN: **Aye, this day.**

MATE: **A strong wind.**

CAPTAIN: **To take us where?**

MATE: **Aye, where?**

CAPTAIN: **A strong wind.**

MATE: **To take us where?** *(A loud wind courses through the castle as MAGICIAN and MARIANA enter. MARIANA carries a lantern and hourglass, CYNRIC his staff and a chest of jewels.)*

MARIANA: **But, Father!**

CYNRIC: **Put them there and lower your voice.**

MARIANA: **But I want to sail with Captain Taran. I'm old enough to make that choice.**

CYNRIC: *(Drawing a pentacle on the floor with his staff)* **The voyage will be unpredictable and dangerous.**

MARIANA: **But I want to be near him.**

CYNRIC: **Be patient...wait. If it is meant to be, he'll come for you to be your prince. Remain here, in the safety of the cas-**

tle. For me? *(He kisses her forehead, leaning out of the pentacle.)*
MARIANA: *(For now)* **Yes.**
CYNRIC: **That's my princess.**
QUEEN: *(Entering)* **Magician, you'll present our offer to the captain when he appears. Mariana and I will withdraw. I want to see him before he sees me.**
CYNRIC: **As you say.**
QUEEN: **Be kind to him. I value this man.** *(BRIAN whistles a melancholy tune.)*
CYNRIC: **In raising this staff, I summon all forces that serve me; I assume the powers of the ages and command them to flow through me, their master.** *(He makes a pass with his staff, the lights alter.)*
Hail, I summon you, I call you to obey
Give power to our music
To find its way
Across the lands, across the sea.
To Captain Taran —

— Listen to me, to what I say —

Between there and here
Open the way.

Begin!
(CYNRIC twirls out of the pentacle and the QUEEN twirls into it. The musicians begin a rhythmic beat on the tympani. Instantly the CAPTAIN hears it. MARIANA and CYNRIC stand on opposite sides of the QUEEN.)
CAPTAIN: **Mate!**
MATE: *(He stops whistling. He doesn't hear drums.)* **What?**
CAPTAIN: **What is that sound?**
MATE: **It was me, whistling.**
CAPTAIN: **Thunder? Is it a storm, mate?**
MATE: **I can't hear.**
CAPTAIN: **Listen...do you still not hear it?**
MATE: **Nothing but the gulls.** *(Drum beats. CYNRIC, MARIANA and QUEEN begin to sound out a melancholy chorus without words. The CAPTAIN searches the horizon, points off.)*
CAPTAIN: **There!**
MATE: **Where?**
CAPTAIN: **Voices! Song!**
MATE: **It's the gulls.**
CAPTAIN: **Gulls? No!**
MATE: **Then it's this strange isle, or an evil spirit. Come, let's return to the ship.**

337

CAPTAIN: **I'll hear more.** *(Musicians improvise a rhythm with the percussion instruments. The QUEEN makes passes causing the lights to alter, and sings.)*

QUEEN: **"Spirits, hear our cry**   CAPTAIN: **Spirits...**
Come to us, to our castle
fly Spirits, hear our plea   MATE: **Spirits? Why do you**
Come to us and you will   **say spirits?**
see."

CHORUS: *(CHORUS consists of QUEEN, CYNRIC, and MARIANA.)*
"We're calling in our time of need"

QUEEN: **"The cold is in the**   CAPTAIN: **Castle...they sing**
castle walls   **of a castle.**
Do you hear the people's
call
Winter is blowing through
Oh, Spirits, we ask of you."

CHORUS: **"We need a light**   CAPTAIN: **...and a light.**
that's warm and new."

QUEEN: **"The captain!"**

    CAPTAIN: **They're calling my**
CHORUS: **"Taran!**   **name.**

(TARAN moves to escape the sound. He covers his ears.)
"We need a light that's   MATE: **Who? What do they**
warm and new."   **say?**

QUEEN: **"Captain!"**
CHORUS: **"Taran!**   CAPTAIN: **Again — my name.**
Sailing the skies and
oceans blue."

QUEEN: *(Whispers.)* **"Captain"** —
CHORUS: *(Whispers.)* **"Captain"** —
QUEEN: *(Whispers.)* **"Captain"** —
CHORUS: *(Whispers.)* **"Captain"** —

(TARAN draws his sword. During the following exchange between TARAN and BRIAN, QUEEN and CHORUS begin to whisper and crescendo the word "Captain" until TARAN exits. During the following, TARAN runs wildly about, BRIAN following him, trying to calm him.)

CAPTAIN: **Do you see them?**
MATE: **Who?**
CAPTAIN: **I can't!**
MATE: **There is no one but the sea!**
CAPTAIN: **They're calling me!**
MATE: **Who?**
CAPTAIN: **I can't see them!** *(To voices)* **Show yourselves!**
MATE: **Return to the ship, Captain!**
CAPTAIN: **Who are you?!**

MATE: It may be an evil spirit of the isle. To the ship!

CAPTAIN: What do you want of me?

MATE: To the ship, Captain! *(He grabs TARAN's arm, pulling him Upstage. TARAN breaks the MATE's grip.)*

CAPTAIN: Leave me! *(He runs off with sword drawn. The MATE scans the horizon and then follows. The chorus of "Captain" peaks.)*

CHORUS: "We-need-you."

QUEEN: "Captain, Taran, we need you.
Spirits, Spirits, call him to."

CHORUS: "We-need-you."

QUEEN: "Captain, Taran, join us here.
Within the castle walls appear."

CHORUS: "Within the castle walls appear."

QUEEN: "We need a light that's warm and new."

CHORUS: "Winter is coming, we're cold, leave your crew. Captain" —

QUEEN: "Taran —"

CHORUS: "Hear! Captain —"

QUEEN: "Taran —"

CHORUS: "Here! Captain —"

QUEEN: "Taran —"

CHORUS: "Appear! Appear! Appear!" *(There is a flash of light, a gong sounds, and in the castle the CAPTAIN appears, sword in hand and confused, with the MATE holding tightly on to him. QUEEN and MARIANA silently withdraw into shadows.)*

CYNRIC: Captain.

CAPTAIN: Yes...the captain...but he knows not where he is... nor how he got here...

MATE: Cold, Captain...

CAPTAIN: Nor does he know you.

CYNRIC: I have brought you here, far from the "Dragonfly."

CAPTAIN: Yes, you have. What are you, that you can call me from my ship?

CYNRIC: A magician. And I need you and your ship. Here is your gold. *(He throws the CAPTAIN a purse.)*

CAPTAIN: Gold.

MATE: But for what crime?

CYNRIC: To sail us to Aalmauria.

MATE: Aye.

CYNRIC: To the cave of fire.

CAPTAIN: To Aalmauria.

CYNRIC: To catch the flame in this lantern and return us here.

CAPTAIN: Aye, but not for a purse as little as this. *(He throws purse back to CYNRIC.)* **Aalmauria lies through the Isles of Mist.**

339

MATE: Where countless ships have sunk against the rocks.

CYNRIC: I'll show you the way through the mist.

CAPTAIN: Still we'll not get the flame. The cave is guarded by a beast that eats men.

MATE: And an evil hag of a witch.

CYNRIC: This... *(He retrieves an hourglass, about a foot and a half tall)* hourglass, when smashed, will stop time. You'll smash it, enter the cave past the Beast and Hag, catch the flame in the lantern, and walk back to the ship, safely.

MATE: Aye, but will it do as you say?

MARIANA: *(Stepping forward, unable to hold herself back any longer)* Trust us, Captain Taran.

CAPTAIN: Mate, it's...

MATE: Mariana?!

CAPTAIN: That's who she is.

MATE: You live here?

MARIANA: With my father, the magician.

MATE: I'm happy to see you again.

MARIANA: And I you, and you, Captain Taran. *(She moves up to him, does a deep, formal curtsy.)* Welcome. Do you remember me?

CAPTAIN: If this is your castle, Mariana, then Queen Meaghan —

QUEEN: *(Stepping out)* — Is here, Captain.

CAPTAIN: Meaghan!

QUEEN: I called you from the "Dragonfly."

CAPTAIN: You...called...me...It was your voice I heard.

QUEEN: I told the magician of your bravery, Taran, and that you would... *(She is getting lost in staring at him.)* ...you would...help us. I've missed you, Randolf.

MATE: Randolf!

QUEEN: And thought of you.

CAPTAIN: Meaghan, you called me.

QUEEN: If you will sail us to the island, I will face the Beast and the Hag.

CAPTAIN: And they'll be the last you face.

QUEEN: We've no other choice. The ice flows to our doors.

CAPTAIN: I feel the cold of this place.

CYNRIC: Return us with the flame —

MARIANA: And this also will be yours. *(CYNRIC pushes MARIANA forward and she presents a large coffer of jewels.)*

CAPTAIN: Brian...

MATE: A pirate's riches...

CYNRIC: But only if we return with the flame.

MARIANA: I'll sail with you.

CAPTAIN: If we will go.

QUEEN: There are others I know who would make this voyage.

But I want to take it with you. *(She kisses him.)*

CAPTAIN: Aye...but...to...Aalmauria...I, ah...mate!

MATE: Here, Captain.

CAPTAIN: Will we venture this? What do we say?

MATE: I'll sail to this shore, if that's your mind.

CAPTAIN: Then, good lady, we'll find your flame.

QUEEN: Come, stand with me as I announce our voyage to the people. Everyone must know of this.

CAPTAIN: *(Aside to MATE)* Is this what we dreamed of, Brian?

MATE: She's your mermaid. *(They laugh and exeunt with the QUEEN. As they do, the MATE turns for a moment to MARIANA, then exits.)*

MARIANA: He didn't remember me and when Meaghan appeared, for him I disappeared.

CYNRIC: Mariana...

MARIANA: Did you see her just kiss him?

CYNRIC: I saw.

MARIANA: That wasn't the act of a queen. More like a beggar than a lady.

CYNRIC: She is as willful as he is.

MARIANA: More! I trust him more than her.

CYNRIC: I'm afraid of her strong feelings for this man.

MARIANA: Why?

CYNRIC: She will need all her powers of mind and heart for this voyage to succeed. Her love for him may only confuse her. Perhaps I should prepare a charm to use against Meaghan as well —

MARIANA: A charm —

CYNRIC: — to use only if it's needed.

MARIANA: I'm going on this voyage, Father.

CYNRIC: Don't you see? There's almost no chance we'll return.

MARIANA: He won't allow us to be harmed.

CYNRIC: You know nothing of these matters. Take the chest and hourglass.

MARIANA: I could learn.

CYNRIC: I know what's best.

MARIANA: I could help you.

CYNRIC: Mariana... *(They are off. End of Scene 1)*

Scene 2

(Aboard the "Dragonfly," three weeks later. MATE is at the helm. CAPTAIN is looking seaward through the spyglass and referring to a chart. MARIANA stands next to him.)

MATE: *(Singing, passing the time)*
"A mermaid called to me one day

Oh, Brian, won't you come and play
So I followed her into the sea
We swam together merrily."

CAPTAIN: Starboard, mate, ten degrees... *(He moves, MARIANA follows him, staying very close to him.)*

MATE: *(Continuing to sing as he follows order)*
"She led me to a distant shore.
She kissed me once and then no more.
She swam away and left me there
Alone and lost and in despair."

CAPTAIN: ...and hold her steady.

MATE: "There's not a mermaid 'round for me
I'll love no other than the sea
But if this mermaid calls again —"

QUEEN: *(Off)* Brian!

MATE: *(MATE starts.)* **What? Who?** *(QUEEN runs on.)* **Ah... Meaghan.**

QUEEN: *(She laughs.)* Another glorious morning!

MATE: The winds still favor us.

QUEEN: I had forgotten how bright and warm the sun is. *(To CAPTAIN)* Do you see the Isles of Mist?

CAPTAIN: Nay, but we'll see them today and Aalmauria lies just behind them. We're almost at their shores.

QUEEN: Although I understand little of sailing, Mariana, I understand the sea. Will you teach me, Taran? About charts and winds and ships?

CAPTAIN: If you wish.

MARIANA: *(To QUEEN)* He's been teaching me. Do you know what a mizzen mast is?

QUEEN: We'll sail everywhere, Mariana! Is it true, Taran, that there are lagoons with whales that sing to you while you swim?

CAPTAIN: I've heard them.

QUEEN: What do they sound like?

CAPTAIN: Like whales singing.

QUEEN: What does it sound like when a fish sings?

MARIANA: Meaghan...

MATE: Aye, we want to hear.

CAPTAIN: Mate. *(MATE grins broadly at him.)*

MATE: Aye, Captain?

MARIANA: You needn't listen to them, Captain Taran. And you were explaining your chart. *(The CAPTAIN sings quietly and shortly.)*

QUEEN: Sing. Loudly. *(He starts, MATE laughs, he stops, glares at MATE. MATE stifles himself.)*

CAPTAIN: Whales are under water as you know and I...am...not, as you can see.

QUEEN: So we see.

CAPTAIN: We think they are calling one another from a great distance.

QUEEN: As when I called you to the castle?

CAPTAIN: *(Crossing to her)* Aye, but now you're so close.

QUEEN: *(She moves far from him.)* Sing. Call me.

MARIANA: Meaghan! Why do you insist he play your fool? *(Silence. He finally sings like a whale loudly and clearly. All burst into laughter.)*

QUEEN: I want to swim those lagoons with you, Randolf.

CAPTAIN: Whales sing better than me.

MATE: So do the ducks.

CAPTAIN: Brian!

MATE: Aye, *Randolf?*

CAPTAIN: Mate! Calm your winds!

QUEEN: Will you sail with me to such places, Taran?

CAPTAIN: To wherever you say. You're more beautiful than ever this morning.

QUEEN: If I am more beautiful, it's the sea....or you. *(She kisses him.)*

CAPTAIN: I think it's me. *(The MATE hoots.)* So does Brian.

MARIANA: Am I more beautiful this morning, Brian? *(She pulls a face, indirectly at the CAPTAIN; MATE laughs.)*

QUEEN: It is all this, you, the sea, the voyage for the flame. There is now hope for my people.

CYNRIC: *(Entering during her last speech)* Meaghan, may I speak to you alone for a moment?

QUEEN: You may speak freely here.

MARIANA: What is it, Father?

CYNRIC: It concerns the castle and is meant only for our queen.

QUEEN: Very well. *(They move from the others.)*

CAPTAIN: Mate, the chart. I've finished setting our full course. *(The MATE and the CAPTAIN look over chart. MARIANA will wander near CYNRIC and QUEEN and attempt to hear their conversation.)*

QUEEN: What is it, Cynric?

CYNRIC: I've prepared the charm you ordered for the captain.

QUEEN: I see...I won't need it.

CYNRIC: *(Taking it out)* It's a potion to rub on your lips. If you kiss him with this, he'll do as you say.

QUEEN: And I say now I won't need it.

CYNRIC: Meaghan, until now our voyage has been well-favored, but we're nearing the Isles of Mist and Aalmauria. You understand something of magic and may know more than he what must be done. Take it, as a precaution and —

QUEEN: He's a good man who'll listen to what I say. He would not endanger this voyage, or me.

CYNRIC: Follow me below where I'll place this in your cabin. Then, if you need, you'll know where to find it.

QUEEN: Cynric —

CYNRIC: This is all I ask.

QUEEN: Very well... *(She smiles at his concern.)* but I'll hear no more of this. *(Turning to CAPTAIN)* Taran, call me when we sight the Isles of Mist.

CAPTAIN: I will.

QUEEN: Come, Cynric, quickly. *(QUEEN and MAGICIAN exit below. MARIANA exits after them.)*

CAPTAIN: What do you think of Meaghan, mate?

MATE: She's a fine lady.

CAPTAIN: Wise, strong, curious about all things. She's learning magic, she says, and she wants to learn about sailing. Did you hear?

MATE: She is fine. But you...I worry.

CAPTAIN: Why?

MATE: *(Coming down from helm)* "Why?" Look at your splendid self. *(The CAPTAIN looks at himself.)* "Aye, Queen," you say. "Nay, Queen. Whatever you say, Queen. You are more beautiful than ever, Queen. Are you sad? May I fall down for you to cheer your heart?" *(He falls down.)* "May I act like a fish trying to walk on the shore?" *(He flops about.)* "May I sing you the love song of the whale?" *(He sings loudly the love song of the whale.)* Sounds more like a whale dying to me. *(He sings like a dying whale.)*

CAPTAIN: *(Truly a little worried)* Is it true? Do I appear like this?

MATE: Nay, Captain. Not with this queen.

CAPTAIN: At times I feel I do.

MATE: It's worse with this Hag-Witch! *(He pinches the CAPTAIN's side, runs. The CAPTAIN goes for him.)*

CAPTAIN: Avast! You'll not call her a Hag-Witch! *(The MATE laughs. CAPTAIN picks him up as if to throw him over the rail.)* Over the rail with you!

MARIANA: *(Entering)* Captain Taran?

MATE: Mariana! *(CAPTAIN puts down MATE. They straighten themselves.)*

CAPTAIN: Brian was just teaching me...

MATE: ...a certain dance...

CAPTAIN: ...from a southern island...

MATE: ...a strange southern island...

CAPTAIN: ...to present...

MATE: ...at your court.

MARIANA: May I speak to you?

CAPTAIN: Aye...we had finished.

MARIANA: For helping our people, I want to give you this, *(She removes her medallion.)* **my medallion. It will help bring you a safe voyage.** *(The MATE gives a small bow of concession to the CAPTAIN, moves to helm.)*

CAPTAIN: That's kind of you.

MARIANA: May I put it on you? *(She motions for him to kneel; he does. She puts it around his neck.)* **Wear it and know that I am with you, always.**

CAPTAIN: A worthy gift, Mariana.

MARIANA: I would have nothing hurt you. Watch over yourself.

CAPTAIN: I will.

MARIANA: And... *(Short silence as she considers this, then:)* **Beware of the queen.**

CAPTAIN: What? Why?

MARIANA: I can't say more, but...don't be deceived.

CAPTAIN: Why, Mariana, beware of Meaghan?

MARIANA: My father has taught her much of magic.

CAPTAIN: As she says.

MARIANA: We are nearing the Isles of Mist and Aalmauria. She will use magic if she feels she must. Beware. That's all I can say. *(She kisses him.)*

CAPTAIN: That is kind of you, but — *(She turns, begins to exit. He takes her by the arm, stops her.)* **Mariana, what is this?** *(Silence)* **Do you trust me?**

MARIANA: Oh, yes.

CAPTAIN: Then tell me.

MARIANA: *(After a moment)* **Meaghan ordered my father to prepare a charm to use against you.**

CAPTAIN: What?

MARIANA: It will rob you of your mind and you will do as she says. What it is, I don't know. They wouldn't tell me.

CAPTAIN: Meaghan would not do this.

MARIANA: I wouldn't, but she has.

CAPTAIN: I can't believe it of her. *(CYNRIC enters.)*

MARIANA: There — ask my father. Father! Taran wants to ask you a question.

CYNRIC: Yes, Captain?

CAPTAIN: Mariana has told me Meaghan asked you to prepare a charm to use against me.

CYNRIC: Mariana!

CAPTAIN: Just as I thought.

MARIANA: Is this true? *(Beat)* **Father, is this true?**

CYNRIC: Yes.

CAPTAIN: What?

MARIANA: You see?

345

CYNRIC: It was simply a precaution.

CAPTAIN: What kind of charm?

CYNRIC: She won't use it, Captain. She refused to take it.

CAPTAIN: What is the nature of this charm?

CYNRIC: A potion to rub on her lips.

CAPTAIN: For what purpose?

CYNRIC: What does it matter?

CAPTAIN: For what purpose?

CYNRIC: If she would kiss you with it, you would follow only what she says.

MARIANA: *(To CAPTAIN)* I'm sorry to dishearten you. But I feel you deserve the truth.

CYNRIC: The potion was prepared only to protect this voyage.

CAPTAIN: But against me.

CYNRIC: Captain, make no more of this.

CAPTAIN: Against me.

MARIANA: Now you feel my concern.

CYNRIC: We would have prepared it for anyone. Captain, I prepared one for Meaghan as well, to ensure... *(He stops.)*

CAPTAIN: What was that?

CYNRIC: You see, Captain, we can't allow anyone's feelings to further endanger this voyage.

CAPTAIN: You distrust your own queen this much? To prepare a charm against her?

MARIANA: He does.

CAPTAIN: What is this charm? *(Short silence)* Show it to me. *(Short silence. To MARIANA)* What is it?

MARIANA: I shouldn't say.

CAPTAIN: I will have it.

MARIANA: Why, Taran?

CAPTAIN: *(Back to MAGICIAN)* You will give it to me —

CYNRIC: You won't understand its use.

CAPTAIN: You'll teach me. And I will have it, now, by the seas, or this voyage ends.

CYNRIC: *(He takes out a large black cloth.)* It's a shroud. Cover her with this and she'll grow weaker and weaker until she'll do as you say.

CAPTAIN: Brian — *(He gives it to BRIAN.)* keep it hidden. *(BRIAN takes shroud, hides it near the helm.)*

CYNRIC: But, Captain, be wise. Understand what's true in this.

CAPTAIN: Leave me.

MARIANA: I hope you're not angry with me.

CAPTAIN: Both of you, clear the deck.

MARIANA: As you wish.

CYNRIC: *(As MARIANA and MAGICIAN exit)* Mariana, I told you you shouldn't have come!

MARIANA: I didn't order the charm! I trust him!

CYNRIC: And I trusted you! *(They are gone.)*

CAPTAIN: I would not have believed this, Brian. I thought I knew them. I thought I knew her.

MATE: Captain —

CAPTAIN: I saw something of this on our voyage south last year.

MATE: Captain —

CAPTAIN: What if...what if she's already used this potion against me? You said I do as she says: "Aye, Queen! Nay, Queen!" you said.

MATE: I was only jesting.

CAPTAIN: Mate! Back in the castle — she kissed me and it was *then* I agreed to this voyage!

MATE: As I did, but I don't remember Meaghan kissing me.

CAPTAIN: And I sang like a whale! As she asked! Me! Blubbering like a whale! That may have been a test to know if the potion will work on me.

MATE: You are not magically charmed. What you do you choose to do.

CAPTAIN: Where's the shroud?

MATE: Here.

CAPTAIN: If we must use it, I will signal you by...by offering Meaghan this medallion. When she kneels to receive it, you'll throw the shroud over her.

MATE: Aye, but, Captain—

CAPTAIN: And we'll sail in peace. I'll have no one else commanding this ship.

MATE: I'll do as you say, but how will you know it's needed?

CAPTAIN: If she uses her charm.

MATE: But the magician says she refused this potion.

CAPTAIN: If she tries to kiss me. I'll know she's using the potion if she tries to kiss me.

MATE: That's not enough. She has kissed you before.

CAPTAIN: Aye, but Mariana said now may be the time Meaghan will use it as we are nearing the Isles of Mist. *(He hears something.)* She's coming. Remember, if ever I offer her this medallion. *(He turns seaward. The QUEEN runs on.)*

QUEEN: She's a handsome ship, Taran — "The Dragonfly..." I feel at times as if we are flying — like we are on the back of a dragon with her wings spread wide flying across the sea. Have you ever felt that?

CAPTAIN: Aye, but that is not what the name "Dragonfly" means.

QUEEN: I know, but it's what I feel, sailing with you; strong and free — *(She sees medallion, recognizes it. Lightly)* What is that?

CAPTAIN: What?

QUEEN: Around your neck.

CAPTAIN: This medallion?
QUEEN: Who gave it to you?
CAPTAIN: A friend.
QUEEN: *(Teasing)* Would that be Mariana's medallion?
CAPTAIN: Ah...nay.
QUEEN: Taran, why would you...?
CAPTAIN: What?
QUEEN: Is there something...you seem...
CAPTAIN: What do I seem?
QUEEN: *(She dismisses it.)* It's a fine medallion. And another fine day for sailing. Will you kiss me this grand morning?
CAPTAIN: *(Looks at MATE, backs away.)* Ah...not here on deck.
QUEEN: Brian, gaze seaward, if you will...and now?
CAPTAIN: It's not...not now.
QUEEN: Why? I won't turn you to stone. I may not ask again.
CAPTAIN: Meaghan, why do you insist?
QUEEN: I...enjoy it. Why do you resist? Come, Randolf, I'll only ask once more. Will you kiss me?
CAPTAIN: Not now.
QUEEN: As you wish.
CAPTAIN: But...I would like to give you this medallion that you think is so fine. *(As he speaks, the MATE crosses with the shroud around behind her.)*
QUEEN: You want to give that to me?
CAPTAIN: If you kneel, I'll put it on you.
QUEEN: Put it in my hand. *(MATE takes out shroud, gets ready.)*
CAPTAIN: It's a magical ornament that will protect you on our voyage if it's worn. Kneel and I'll put it around your neck.
QUEEN: You're quick to offer gifts of the heart, Captain.
CAPTAIN: Not as quick as you to steal a good sailor's heart. May I put it on you?
QUEEN: As you wish. *(She kneels, the MATE readies the shroud, the CAPTAIN prepares to put the medallion on her.)*
CAPTAIN: Now, mate! The shroud! *(She stands as the MATE goes to cover her. She backs up, he misses.)*
QUEEN: Taran, what is this?
CAPTAIN: Again, mate! Throw it over her! *(The MATE goes for the QUEEN, she ducks, he misses.)*
MATE: Watch her there!
QUEEN: Why, Taran? What has happened?
CAPTAIN: You'll not enslave me!
QUEEN: What? Why are you angry?
MATE: Magician! *(The QUEEN makes a move to go below.)*
CAPTAIN: Stay where you are.
QUEEN: I'll go where I will.
CAPTAIN: Not aboard my ship.

QUEEN: I am a queen! I'll do as I wish!

CAPTAIN: You're not queen aboard my ship! You'll have no power here! And not over me!

MATE: *(Calling)* **Magician!**

CYNRIC: *(Entering with MARIANA)* **What is it? Have we sighted the Isles of —** *(Next two lines are simultaneously delivered.)*

CAPTAIN: Take care of her, Magician.

QUEEN: Magician, did you give him that shroud?

CAPTAIN: She's yours. I'll have nothing more to do with her.

MARIANA: What?

CYNRIC: What has happened here?

QUEEN: He tried to cover me with that shroud.

CYNRIC: Captain!

CAPTAIN: *(To QUEEN)* And why?

QUEEN: I don't know.

CAPTAIN: Hah.

CYNRIC: Meaghan?

QUEEN: I did nothing, I tell you. He attacked me, unprovoked.

CAPTAIN: That's not true.

QUEEN: What have I done?

CAPTAIN: You won't fool me.

QUEEN: How, Taran?

CAPTAIN: With your charm.

QUEEN: How do you know of a charm? *(Short silence)* I would not have used it.

CAPTAIN: You ordered it.

QUEEN: And I refused it.

CAPTAIN: You have it now.

QUEEN: But who told you of it? Cynric?

CYNRIC: Meaghan —

QUEEN: And did you give him the shroud?

CYNRIC: Yes, Meaghan, but —

QUEEN: Traitor!

CYNRIC: I'm no traitor.

QUEEN: Then why this shroud?

CYNRIC: I was afraid your feelings for him would endanger this voyage. It was a precaution as the potion was.

QUEEN: Against your queen?

CAPTAIN: Aye, and against your captain!

CYNRIC: On my oath I'm loyal.

QUEEN: To him or to me?

CYNRIC: To this voyage.

QUEEN: To yourself.

CYNRIC: And to you.

QUEEN: Then give me the shroud.

CAPTAIN: You'll not have it.

349

QUEEN: I will, one way or another.

CYNRIC: Give me the shroud.

CAPTAIN: *(Drawing)* No one'll have it but me!

QUEEN: *(Drawing sword from rack)* We'll see! *(All shout at once.)*

CYNRIC: Wait. Listen to me. Silence! *(All are quiet.)*

MARIANA: Captain, this is not what I wanted. This is all wrong.

CYNRIC: Lower your swords. *(No one moves.)*

MARIANA: You must do as he says for the success of this voyage.

CYNRIC: Lower your swords.

MARIANA: Listen to him.

QUEEN: He's a traitor to his queen. And you, Mariana, are you against me?

MARIANA: No.

CYNRIC: No one is against you.

QUEEN: *(To MAGICIAN)* He wears her medallion and lies that it isn't hers. *(To MARIANA)* Is it yours?

MARIANA: Yes, but Meaghan, I don't know why he —

QUEEN: *(To all)* You've all formed some plan, sworn some pact against me.

MARIANA: I wouldn't.

CYNRIC: I'll explain everything but we can't speak until you lower your swords.

QUEEN: Lower your sword.

CAPTAIN: You'll not tell me what to do.

CYNRIC: Both of you.

QUEEN: I'll have that shroud first!

CAPTAIN: Then come for it! *(All shout at once again, as CAPTAIN and QUEEN go for each other and are held back by everyone else.)*

CYNRIC: Stop!

MATE: *(Who happens to glance up)* Land ahoy! The Isles of Mist. There they lie, Captain, within the clouds. We're almost upon them. *(Silence. The QUEEN and the CAPTAIN are still faced off.)*

MARIANA: *(To CAPTAIN)* Will you continue this voyage?

CYNRIC: For the jewels?

QUEEN: You gave your oath, Taran.

MATE: Captain?

CAPTAIN: For the jewels and because I said I would. *(To MATE)* Turn her windward.

CYNRIC: And the flame? Remember, all you need do is smash the hourglass to stop time and enter the cave.

QUEEN: *I* will enter the cave.

CAPTAIN: If that is all, why don't you do it?

CYNRIC: The spell of the hourglass may not be strong enough.

CAPTAIN: Just as I thought.

MARIANA: It may be.

CAPTAIN: I'll bring you the flame whether it is or not, if you keep her from me until this voyage ends.

QUEEN: *(They remain in a face-off.)* **Am I to be ignored? I called for this voyage, not you, Cynric. You knew of the flame yet dared nothing. I am queen and for my people I will enter the cave! And you will keep *him* from *me!* Now, Captain, I'll only ask once, will you give me the shroud?**

CAPTAIN: It stays with me.

QUEEN: Very well. *(She moves away. To herself)* **What can I believe? Are they all against me? Taran, how could this happen?** *(She looks at him as MARIANA goes over to him. Mist begins to appear on the ship.)*

MARIANA: Captain, I'm sorry.

CAPTAIN: *(The QUEEN is unable to hear them.)* **Do you see what comes of trust? What cold wind was it that blew her to me?**

QUEEN: *(To herself)* **I don't know what has happened. But I won't sail in fear of that shroud.** *(She draws out a pentacle with her sword, makes passes and mumbles during the following.)* **Now spirits...come to my call...**

MATE: Mist, Captain, beginning to rise. *(Lights are gradually dimming.)*

CAPTAIN: Turn her portside, mate, we'll ease her into the fog.

MATE: How will we avoid the rocks in this mist?

CYNRIC: I'll show the way.

CAPTAIN: Steady as she goes.

CYNRIC: If you'll trust what I say.

CAPTAIN: I will now, by the mast.

QUEEN: *(Turned away from the others, quietly)*
Until the spell is past
Let them not know
That magic is cast.

Let them not hear
The words or the song
Let them sail on
As if nothing were wrong.
(She sings, strongly, lyrically.)
"Spirit, I'm calling you
Rise and touch their eyes
Let the men not see,
The ship or the sea."
(The mist is becoming thick. Lights dim farther.)

QUEEN: *(Sings. They begin to respond by blinking, rubbing eyes,*

looking skyward.)
"Spirit in the mist
Rise unto the men
Cover their light   CAPTAIN: My eyes...
Blind their sight
Turn their day into   MATE: And mine. Is there
The darkest night.   something in the
       mist?
Cover their light   CAPTAIN: What could there
       be?
Blind their sight
Turn their day   MATE: Dark...
Into darkest night.
     CAPTAIN: And darker. Is the
       mist covering the
(She sings the first   sun?
section again under   MARIANA: No, it's not that
the dialogue. Mist   thick. What is it?
continues to thicken.)   CAPTAIN: Is there something
       from the Isles?
     MATE: Magician, do you
       know what this could be?
     CYNRIC: The queen has done
       this!

(QUEEN stops singing.)

MATE: Captain, my eyes! I can't see!

MARIANA: What?

CAPTAIN: Magician?

CYNRIC: Neither can I.

QUEEN: Nor can you, Captain. And that's how you'll stay, until
you give me that shroud.

CYNRIC: *(Speaking simultaneously)* This is not the way —

MARIANA: Meaghan, no —

CYNRIC: This is what I feared.

CAPTAIN: Mate, to the foredeck. Find me here!

MATE: Aye!

QUEEN: Brian! *(QUEEN crosses to MATE, pushes him down.)*

MARIANA: Father, do something.

CYNRIC: Can *you* see?

MARIANA: Yes.

CYNRIC: Lead me to the helm, then you'll guide the ship.

MARIANA: Here —

QUEEN: Give me the shroud, Captain, and we'll sail to
Aalmauria in peace.

CAPTAIN: You'll not order me!

QUEEN: All I ask is you give me the shroud. It is not in my

mind to harm you.
CAPTAIN: Mate!
MATE: *(Who is not near him)* **Here, Captain.**
CAPTAIN: Come this way.
QUEEN: *(Returning to MATE)* **Brian. Hah!...** *(Concerned, as she has thrown him toward the rail.)* **Brian! The rail!** *(Crosses back to CAPTAIN.)* **Captain —**
CAPTAIN: Back, Meaghan. You have your weapon. The shroud is mine. *(She takes hold of shroud and pulls it.)*
QUEEN: Taran!
CAPTAIN: Now this is mutiny! *(He swings his sword in a broad arc, misses everybody.)*
MARIANA: Captain, no! Father, they're too angry —
QUEEN: *(Crossing behind MATE, pulling him away from CAPTAIN)* **Back, Mate.**
MATE: Let me go, Meaghan. I mean what I say!
MARIANA: The mist — I won't be able to see the rocks.
CYNRIC: Is our course clear now? *(He takes the wheel.)*
MARIANA: For as far as I can see, but —
CYNRIC: Run below, bring me the hourglass. *(She runs below.)*
QUEEN: The shroud, Captain.
CAPTAIN: Find me, mate.
MATE: Here. *(QUEEN trips the MATE; he falls toward the CAPTAIN.)*
CAPTAIN: This way!
MATE: It's me, Captain.
CAPTAIN: There. The shroud is here.
MATE: I feel it. *(They stand together, the CAPTAIN sheathes his sword and they hold shroud between them.)*
CAPTAIN: Now —
QUEEN: Taran, I will have that shroud.
CAPTAIN: Follow me — *(They lunge. She moves. They stalk her.)*
MATE: Here! *(They move rapidly toward her; she backs away. MARIANA runs on with the hourglass.)*
MARIANA: *(As QUEEN prepares to attack)* **Here, Father, the hourglass.**
CYNRIC: Are you able to see the rocks?
MARIANA: Not through the mist. *(QUEEN goes for the shroud. She, the CAPTAIN and the MATE all wrestle.)*
CAPTAIN: Hold it, Mate!
MATE: I have it!
QUEEN: Give it to me! *(They wrestle wildly, shouting.)*
MARIANA: Stop! Meaghan! Captain Taran! Do something, Father! I can't stop them!
CYNRIC: Listen to me! All of you! You'll destroy everything! Don't make me use the hourglass! *(He smashes the hourglass. Lights dim. Everyone freezes except the MAGICIAN.*

Lightning fills the air. The CAPTAIN, QUEEN and MATE are a frozen picture of angry grappling.) **You're mad! All of you! You'll destroy everything! The ship, the voyage, Mariana, yourselves. Everything!** *(He rubs his eyes.)* **There.** *(He can now see.)*

Look at you. You say you love each other. Look at you! Tearing at each other's throats, as angry as the beast. I knew it would come to this. And you forced me to smash the hourglass! What will you do when you face the beast? Ah! *(He pulls shroud away, puts it down, then pulls the CAPTAIN from the others. He goes for MATE and does same thing. They come to a position and freeze again.)* **Until we anchor off Aalmauria, you won't see each other, you won't speak to each other, you won't know each other!** *(Looking upward, he picks up his staff, makes a pass.)*
Hail, magic in the mist, give me power
To sail in peace for this one hour.
See these warriors, let rest their hearts
Fill them with music and hold them apart.
(Music plays; a dreamy, soothing melody that will also suggest sailing through the mist.)
Turn their heads from each other to the sea
Let them not speak except to me.
Give strength to their eyes
Their vision assist
To see rocks as we sail
Through the waters and mist.
Let us pass from sea to the shore,
To Aalmauria we sail, then their minds I'll restore.
(A final pass, then:)
Time pass. *(MARIANA, the CAPTAIN, MATE, and QUEEN awaken to time in a trance. They are filled with the music, and move with it.)* **To the fore rail.** *(They all move Downstage, evenly spaced out at the prow of the ship.)* **I'll sail the direction you say. Call out what you see, what rocks lie in our way.** *(MAGICIAN takes helm. Mist is quite thick.)*
QUEEN: *(Pointing, after a moment. All are still entranced.)* **There.**
CAPTAIN: Off the port bow.
MATE: Turn her starboard.
CAPTAIN: Harder.
MATE: Steady as she goes, now. *(They sail. Pause)*
MARIANA: Another.
QUEEN: There.
CAPTAIN: Steady.
MATE: She'll pass close by. *(Pause)*
MARIANA: And another.

354

CAPTAIN: Turn her starboard once more.
MATE: Aye...Steady... *(Silence)* **Steady...** *(End of Scene 2.)*

Scene 3

(On Aalmauria. Shoreline, with a cave Upstage. The interior of the cave ends out of sight. We can, however, see the shadows of flames flickering within the cave. Distant music — the Aalmauria music — is heard. The CAPTAIN enters, sword drawn, reconnoitering. He dashes behind a rock, peers out, waves to the MATE, who appears, joins him. The MAGICIAN follows. They speak in hushed tones.)

MATE: Aalmauria...
CAPTAIN: A beautiful isle.
MATE: Enchanting.
CAPTAIN: Is that faint music I hear?
MATE: I hear it. It makes me smile.
CAPTAIN: What dangers can there be in this magical place?
MATE: The isle seems to welcome us.
CYNRIC: There is danger here, that you will face. *(Points.)* **The cave.** *(They crouch down.)*
CAPTAIN: But where is the Beast?
MATE: And the Hag-Witch?
CYNRIC: Somewhere near. You may meet one or the other, or they'll both appear.
MATE: How shall we pass into the cave if it's the Hag we meet?
CYNRIC: If she sees you, don't run from her or attack her. The Hag-Witch is powerful and can easily destroy you both. Talk to her. She'll offer you three things.
MATE: Three.
CYNRIC: To defeat her, do not take the first or the second offering. Take the third.
CAPTAIN: The third offering.
CYNRIC: But even then stay close on your guard. There may be a trick or a twist to the third thing. *(A noise is heard from within the cave, they react.)*
MATE: And if it's the Beast we meet?
CYNRIC: Then you are unlucky, because I destroyed the hourglass.
CAPTAIN: There must be another way. *(Aalmauria music fades out.)*
CYNRIC: In an ancient manuscript I read he will let you pass if you speak the correct words.
CAPTAIN: What are they?
CYNRIC: What I tell you may not be exact. The writing was faint, in parts worn away.

CAPTAIN: **What could you read?**

CYNRIC: **"The cave is open**
Rest your fear
Lay down your weapon
The path is clear."

MATE: **The Beast carries a weapon?**

CYNRIC: **A sword or club.**

CAPTAIN: **"The cave is open, rest your fear."**

MATE: **"Lay down your weapon, the path is clear."**

CAPTAIN & MATE: **"The cave is open**
Rest your fear
Lay down your weapon
The path is clear."

CAPTAIN: **We have it.**

CYNRIC: **Say it to him and attempt to pass into the cave.** *(A noise from within the cave)* **Here's the lantern to hold the flame.** *(The MATE takes it.)*

CAPTAIN: **And the shroud? I'll go no further without it.**

CYNRIC: *(Producing it)* **If I give you this, you will give me the flame.**

CAPTAIN: **I will.**

CYNRIC: **If Meaghan uses the flame against you, it may destroy us all.**

CAPTAIN: **What do you fear? She is in your trance aboard ship.**

CYNRIC: **She may awaken and, if so, she'll come here.** *(CAPTAIN takes shroud, hides it behind rock.)*

MATE: **We'll give the flame only to you.**

CYNRIC: **Then I'll return to the ship.**

CAPTAIN: **Nay. You'll stay and instruct us.**

MATE: **Protect us!**

CYNRIC: **In years past, I instructed other good men only to see them fall to the Beast or the Hag. These powers are beyond my knowledge. Follow your own mind. Good luck to you both. The hopes of our people are all on you.** *(He exits.)*

CAPTAIN: **Avast, mate. Here we are. "You may meet one...or the other..."**

MATE: **Let's hope it's the Hag we meet.**

CAPTAIN: **The Hag it will be. For today is our lucky day.** *(The MATE jumps up, runs to the mouth of the cave. The CAPTAIN does the same to the opposite side.)* **Do you see anything?**

MATE: **The glow of the fire. I feel the warmth of the flame.** *(The CAPTAIN steps out, takes a closer look. The MATE jumps ahead of the CAPTAIN. The CAPTAIN hears something, turns, stops.)*

CAPTAIN: **Mate! Hold!** *(He points off as MATE jumps back.)* **I thought...nothing. There's nothing there.** *(They return to the mouth of the cave. The MATE steps into mouth.)* **And?**

MATE: Nothing.
CAPTAIN: Go further.
MATE: Me?
CAPTAIN: Better you than me. I'll watch for the Hag.
MATE: You go. I'll watch for the Hag.
CAPTAIN: I'll bargain with you.
MATE: What bargain?
CAPTAIN: Whoever goes first shall have Mariana, if she'll take him.
MATE: Then I'll go first, for Mariana.
CAPTAIN: I thought that was the way the winds blew. Good luck with *your* mermaid.
MATE: *(Taking another step in)* **Still nothing.**
CAPTAIN: Then our fortune is made. This *is* our lucky day.
MATE: *(Another step, and another)* **Nothing still.** *(He starts to whistle, relax; they both move closer.)*
CAPTAIN: You'll have Mariana and —
MATE: Captain, stay! *(We hear a loud growl and the CAPTAIN and the MATE bolt out of the cave.)* **Back!** *(The BEAST runs on carrying a club. He is fierce, large, angry; when he rears up he's imposing and threatening.)*
CAPTAIN: The Beast! *(The BEAST guards the mouth of the cave, growling, pacing, threatening. He charges.)*
MATE: Captain! *(They back further off.)* **Look at that! Bring us the Hag. We'll face her instead!**
CAPTAIN: Together, mate; we'll close in and try saying the words the magician gave us.
MATE: Aye. *(They approach the BEAST. The BEAST prepares to attack.)*
CAPTAIN: Now!
CAPTAIN & MATE: "The cave is open, rest your fear." *(They both stop dead, turn to each other, mouths wide but silent. Then:)*
MATE: What'll be next?
CAPTAIN: I forgot!
MATE: You didn't!
CAPTAIN: "The cave is open, rest your fear," — mate! What is it?!
MATE: I can't remember.
CAPTAIN: Think!
MATE: "Let rest your fear —"
CAPTAIN: Mate! "Lay...Lay..."
MATE: "Lay down your weapon!"
CAPTAIN: There it is!
MATE: "Lay down your weapon, the path is clear." *(The BEAST stops, stands in what appears to be puzzlement.)*
CAPTAIN: It heard us. Again.

CAPTAIN & MATE: "The cave is open
    Rest your fear
    Lay down your weapon
    The path is clear."
    (The BEAST crouches down, but does not take his eyes off them.)

MATE: **He lays his club on the ground.**

CAPTAIN: **Come, while he stays down.** *(They slowly advance towards the cave entrance. As they pass the BEAST, he jumps up with a terrible growl and lunges at them.)*

MATE: **Captain!** *(They fight the BEAST. Their swordplay, they learn, is ineffective. Suddenly the BEAST lunges at the MATE. As the MATE backs off in fear, the CAPTAIN steps in front of him and the BEAST knocks him down. The MATE then whacks the BEAST who has the CAPTAIN pinned, trying to draw him away from the CAPTAIN. This doesn't work.)* **Captain!** *(The MATE charges the BEAST, fights, is succeeding at drawing BEAST away. The CAPTAIN begins to free himself, then the BEAST turns back on him, knocks sword from CAPTAIN's hand.)*

CAPTAIN: **Brian!**

MATE: **Hah! Hah!** *(MATE closes in and this time is struck, stunned.)* **Captain...** *(He falls.)*

CAPTAIN: **Brian!** *(The BEAST prepares to destroy the CAPTAIN. The QUEEN runs in, faces BEAST, fights. She moves up toward the cave, drawing him to her. He goes for her; she avoids his club, skillfully fighting him.)*

QUEEN: **Now, Captain! Move away!** *(The CAPTAIN, stunned, crawls away. She runs over, helps him away. He rises unsteadily.)*

CAPTAIN: **Mate...** *(He moves to MATE. The QUEEN keeps her guard on the BEAST.)* **Brian...**

MATE: *(Regaining consciousness.)* **Captain, you freed yourself.**

CAPTAIN: **With Meaghan's help.**

MATE: **Meaghan...?**

CAPTAIN: **Aye.**

MATE: **But —**

CAPTAIN: **I don't know how...or why.**

QUEEN: **Perhaps the Beast would chase me. Then you could run in behind him.**

CAPTAIN: *(To MATE)* **Are you able to fight?**

MATE: **I'll go with Meaghan.** *(The CAPTAIN gets lantern. They set themselves.)*

QUEEN: **Now —** *(They crisscross. The BEAST at first goes for the QUEEN and MATE, but then he goes for the CAPTAIN.)*

CAPTAIN: *(Retreating)* **He'll stay near the cave.**

MATE: **Then what'll we do?**

QUEEN: **The way is open to us. I feel it.** *(They come together, far* *from cave. MATE guards the BEAST, who rocks rhythmically back and forth, growling in the mouth of the cave.)*

MATE: I thought the words were our entry, but —

CAPTAIN: Perhaps we said them wrong.

MATE: We said them exactly as the magician told us.

CAPTAIN: Then perhaps he read them wrong. The writing was worn, he said.

MATE: Then they are no help to us.

QUEEN: What were they?

CAPTAIN: "The cave is open..."

MATE: "Rest your fear..."

QUEEN: I read these words in the magician's book.

MATE: We said them to the Beast with no luck.

QUEEN: There must be some truth in them..."The cave is open..."

CAPTAIN: "Rest your fear..."

QUEEN: But the Beast wouldn't rest his fear.

MATE: He'll kill us.

QUEEN: "Rest your fear..." Does it mean... *(Suddenly occurring to her)* Does it mean to rest the fear in the Beast? Or us?

CAPTAIN: I see. We thought the Beast.

QUEEN: What comes next?

MATE: "Lay down your weapon..."

CAPTAIN: "The path is clear." The Beast's weapon? Or ours?

MATE: The Beast's. His club.

QUEEN: What if the meaning is ours?

CAPTAIN: Aye, what if wé are to lay down our weapons and our fear?

MATE: And just walk past the Beast? Unarmed?

CAPTAIN & QUEEN: *(Together)* Aye. Yes.

CAPTAIN: I think that is what is meant. We don't say the words —

QUEEN: — we *do* them.

MATE: Don't put down your sword. The Beast will kill you.

CAPTAIN: Not if I can walk past him without fear.

QUEEN: *I'll* do it. I need the flame. Stand clear and —

CAPTAIN: We'll both go.

QUEEN: It's my castle. I must go. Give me the lantern. Stand away. *(He gives her the lantern. She moves toward the BEAST, then stops. She begins to go in, the BEAST rears and roars; she stops. She begins again. The BEAST growls, she stops. She backs away calmly.)* Taran, you must enter with me.

MATE: She's afraid.

CAPTAIN: Nay.

QUEEN: No, two must enter. Together.

CAPTAIN: That'll be right. Two.

MATE: How do you know?

CAPTAIN: I just feel it to be so. *(Giving MATE his sword)* Take my

sword.

MATE: **What if you're wrong?**

CAPTAIN: **You'll save me from him.**

MATE: **I won't. I won't save anyone ignorant enough to lay down his sword. This must not be the way.**

QUEEN: **It is. I feel it.**

CAPTAIN: **Aye...** *(With a smile)* **But be ready, Brian.** *(He moves to QUEEN, taking hold of lantern with her. They begin to walk toward BEAST and cave opening. The BEAST prepares to attack.)*

MATE: **Captain, no!**

CAPTAIN & QUEEN: *(Together)* **Don't. No.**

QUEEN: **Don't call out.**

CAPTAIN: **Let us go.** *(The CAPTAIN and QUEEN move closer together. They continue. The BEAST leaps at them, then growls at them, jumps in their path, always just missing them. The BEAST tries various ploys to rattle them. They continue on their way until they're within the cave.)*

MATE: *(In a small voice)* **Captain?...You've entered!** *(The BEAST pauses, then turns toward the MATE. The MATE lays down his weapons, fixes his tunic, stands as tall as he dares, begins to walk toward the cave opening. The BEAST charges him, he screams and bolts back toward the two swords and picks them up. He wheels, facing the BEAST.)*

    Come on, then! I'll fight you like a sailor! Come on! Pirate! Do your worst! Aah! Hah! *(The BEAST turns and moves into the cave.)* **Coward! Hah! Run away!** *(Silence. Victory is short-lived. He worries about the CAPTAIN. He crosses to opening, listens. Quietly calling)* **Captain? Meaghan?** *(He moves into opening, holding out both swords. He advances, stops, quickly retreats, stands ready at opening to swing sword at whatever comes out. It is the QUEEN and CAPTAIN slowly walking out. The MATE begins a terrible swing but stops before hitting the CAPTAIN. Aalmauria music fades in.)* **Captain!**

CAPTAIN: *(They are both holding lantern and both are dazed.)* **Brian...did you see?**

MATE: **The Beast stopped me. The flame?**

QUEEN: **Burning here.**

MATE: **Avast! You let rest your fear.**

QUEEN: **I'm grateful you remained, Brian.**

CAPTAIN: **She feared you may not wait.**

MATE: **Wait?**

CAPTAIN: **We would have returned long before, but the wonder within...**

MATE: **But you only just entered.**

CAPTAIN: **Nay; half the day —**

QUEEN: And all the night —
CAPTAIN: We passed in the cave.
MATE: You entered not a moment ago.
QUEEN: I see...
CAPTAIN: It was wonderful, mate.
QUEEN: Like I've not felt before.
CAPTAIN: Warm —
QUEEN: Bright —
CAPTAIN: Glow —
QUEEN: It filled me with its light.
CAPTAIN: We put our hands into the fire — we held it in our hands — but it didn't burn us.
QUEEN: We walked through the flames and we didn't burn.
MATE: Captain, the ship, we must return. And the flame...
CAPTAIN: Here...burning bright red.
MATE: Nay, Captain, *the flame.* Remember what the magician said. *(Aalmauria music fades out.)*
CAPTAIN: Magician, aye, but...
QUEEN: What did Cynric say?
MATE: Awaken to where you are. Remember.
CAPTAIN: I do; but I don't feel, now, that's the way.
MATE: Trust me, Captain; make your stand.
CAPTAIN: I must...take it, Meaghan.
QUEEN: What?
MATE: Aye, do as we planned.
CAPTAIN: ...this...flame.
QUEEN: From me? But it's for my castle. It's why we came.
CAPTAIN: Aye, that'll be right.
MATE: Remember, Captain, aboard ship?
CAPTAIN: The fight. This comes with me. *(He pulls flame from her.)*
QUEEN: But we're different now. Do you feel this change?
CAPTAIN: I do.
QUEEN: Then, here...trust these feelings. *(She holds out her hand. He keeps flame, backs a little further away.)*
CAPTAIN: But would you use it against me on the ship?
QUEEN: No, I wouldn't. Nor could I. It must burn in a large fire for its power to be released.
CAPTAIN: Then, mate, we can give —
MATE: She could build a large fire on the island. Keep your mind, and your word.
CAPTAIN: *(To QUEEN.)* I can't.
MATE: *(Stepping in front of CAPTAIN, facing QUEEN)* **And do not try to take it, Meaghan. You'll not get past both of us.** *(Gives sword to CAPTAIN.)*
QUEEN: **Then I'm betrayed again.** *(She gets her sword.)* **I am**

sorry, Captain. I am sorry. Beware of the Hag, Captain. The flame will attract her. She may not allow you to leave with it. *(She exits.)*

MATE: You've done well, Captain.

CAPTAIN: I feel we've run aground.

MATE: She would have used it against you.

CAPTAIN: She saved me from the Beast.

MATE: She needed your help.

CAPTAIN: What should I do? I'll need to think.

MATE: There is no time. The Hag-Witch —

CAPTAIN: I'm not afraid of her.

MATE: Then become so. The magician said the Hag is too dangerous. Captain! The Hag will come. Let us go.

CAPTAIN: I see the way. Let's return to the "Dragonfly"... where I'll just give Meaghan the flame.

MATE: But —

CAPTAIN: I can't say why! *(He starts off, in the wrong direction.)* But I know it goes to her.

MATE: Captain... *(Taking him by the arm)* The ship lies this way. *(As they start off, the HAG appears. She wears a hood that covers her face and a full-length cloak. She shuffles toward them, bent over, leaning on a twisted cane.)*

HAG: Men...

CAPTAIN: Mate!

MATE: The Hag!

HAG: Stay!

MATE: Run! *(They begin to run.)*

HAG: Stop...stop!

MATE: She's seen us. *(They stop.)*

HAG: One...two...

CAPTAIN: Then we face her.

HAG: I knew...men... *(Approaching)*

CAPTAIN: Aye, Hag. Good men.

HAG: With the flame of the cave. Ah, you are brave, men.

MATE: What is it you want?

HAG: I am old, as you see, and the touch of the enchanted flame will make me young again.

CAPTAIN: What do you offer for it?

MATE: Aye, that's the game.

HAG: I offer you a safe passage back to your ship if I may touch your flame.

MATE: Not for that.

HAG: Then perhaps this cup, made of gold and covered with rare, red jewels. *(She holds up a jeweled chalice.)*

CAPTAIN: Not that either.

MATE: What is your next offer?

362

HAG: I have nothing more.

CAPTAIN: But you must.

HAG: Nothing.

MATE: Captain? The magician said three things.

CAPTAIN: Come, what is your third offer?

HAG: Offer you...my warm-hearted friends. You'll not help an old woman without receiving something in return?

CAPTAIN: We know what you are, Hag. What else do you offer?

HAG: All I have left is a kiss. One kiss for each of you.

CAPTAIN: That's it.

MATE: *(With some trepidation)* **Aye, the third offer.**

CAPTAIN: I thought this was to be our *lucky* day. We accept.

HAG: Then let me kiss you. *(The MATE steps forward. The HAG stops, shies away.)* **But you must drop your swords. I fear you might attack and rob me.** *(They drop their swords.)* **Then come.** *(They both move toward her.)* **First you.** *(She lifts her head and hood just enough to kiss the MATE, who then freezes.)* **And now you.** *(The CAPTAIN closes his eyes, is about to kiss her. He opens them as she lifts her hood to kiss him. He suddenly pulls back her hood to reveal the QUEEN.)*

CAPTAIN: Meaghan! Avast, mate! It's the queen!

QUEEN: *(Removing Hag-Witch robe)* **He can't hear you.**

CAPTAIN: Mate! It's Meaghan! Do you see? Dressed as the Hag!

QUEEN: Call as loud as you will. He won't hear.

CAPTAIN: What have you done to him?

QUEEN: What I had to do.

CAPTAIN: The potion! The magician's potion is on her lips. Mate! Hear me! Can you hear me?

QUEEN: Taran, you forced me to play the Hag, don't you see? What is your plan with Mariana and the magician? Why would you give them the flame and not me? *(Earnestly, without anger)* **Taran, tell me.**

CAPTAIN: I'll tell you nothing.

QUEEN: Then I must believe you plan to take the flame. Captain, I need it, for my people. Give me the lantern and I will free your mate.

CAPTAIN: I should have known what you were when I first saw you.

QUEEN: *(Still without anger)* **I am not your enemy, Taran. Give me the flame and I swear we'll sail in peace.**

CAPTAIN: Peace!

QUEEN: Trust me, Taran.

CAPTAIN: *(Retrieving shroud)* **You deceiving thief! You've stolen my mate!**

QUEEN: The shroud!

CAPTAIN: Aye, witch, the shroud.

QUEEN: Mariana said the magician had hidden it from you. So I see you all *are* against me. *(He advances on her. She goes for swords, but CAPTAIN gets there first, picks them up and puts them near the flame, on the ground.)*

CAPTAIN: There's your flame. Come for it. *(The QUEEN circles, makes a move.)* **Hah!** *(He leaps at her.)* **I'll not be as easy as Brian! Come; come on, you heartless, icen Hag! Hah!** *(He goes for her with the shroud, throwing it out in front of him. She avoids it. He goes again, she grabs the shroud, he holds on, she pulls.)*

QUEEN: Give it to me! Why must you hate me?

CAPTAIN: Hah! *(The CAPTAIN lunges at her with the shroud, she ducks, lets go, he moves away.)*

QUEEN: Very well, Captain. *(He goes for her, she moves.)* **Kiss me.**

CAPTAIN: Nay.

QUEEN: Kiss me! Kiss me! *(He goes for her, she trips him, runs to flame, picks it up, turns, sees he is close, backs up, but he is too fast and he covers her.)*

QUEEN: *Ooooohhh...*

CAPTAIN: Avast, witch! I have you! I've won!

QUEEN: *Nooo...*

CAPTAIN: Be calmed here, then, and put down the flame. *(She does.)* **Mate...I have her! Mate!** *(Remembering)* **Avast, mate, do you hear me?**

MATE: *(The MATE begins to move. Disorientedly)* **Meaghan?**

CAPTAIN: It's your captain. What colors are you flying?

MATE: Meaghan?

CAPTAIN: She's fogged your brains. Brian!

MATE: Captain...?

CAPTAIN: *(The Aalmauria music plays until end of scene.)* **Aye, here, with you, mate. Are you well?**

MATE: I don't know.

CAPTAIN: Do you know where you are?

MATE: Near the cave.

CAPTAIN: Ah! Then with the shroud over her, you'll not be her slave. Take the lantern. Return to the "Dragonfly" and set our course east. We've beaten them both, the Hag and the Beast. *(End of Scene 3.)*

Scene 4

(Back aboard the "Dragonfly," the next morning. QUEEN is under shroud. Chains are wrapped around the shroud with a large lock holding them on. The MATE stands looking at the QUEEN throughout the scene with MARIANA. Sounds of waves and sea birds. MARIANA runs on.)

MARIANA: Another beautiful morning! With a fair wind! Has Taran arisen?

MATE: *(Distantly, but clear-minded. He is no longer foggy but obsessed.)* **Not that I've seen.**

MARIANA: I knew he'd succeed — to face the Beast and enter the cave. Our people will welcome you with a feast, praise you as brave heroes. They'll present you more gifts than your treasure-hold will carry. Once the ice melts, I'll show Taran the majesty of our lands and the gracious pleasures of our court — music, dancing. I'll treat him as a true lady does a lord. *(She turns to QUEEN.)* **How is Meaghan?**

MATE: In pain.

MARIANA: It hurts me she is chained. *(A very distant, low rumble is heard. For the first time the MATE looks away from the QUEEN, skyward. MARIANA follows his gaze upward. He returns to watching the QUEEN. She moves closer to the QUEEN, kneels in front of her.)* **Meaghan, I never wanted this. To see our proud queen locked in chains. This saddens me more than you believe. But what can I do? You blinded the men. You played the Hag —**

QUEEN: *(A call for help)* **Mariana —**

MARIANA: I can't help you. *(The CAPTAIN is heard off, singing with great heart.)*

CAPTAIN: *(Off)* **"A mermaid called to me one day"**

MARIANA: *(Jubilant again)* **Captain Taran!**

CAPTAIN: *(Off)* **Said, "Taran, won't you come and play!"** *(He appears.)*

MARIANA: *(Curtseying)* **Randolf!**

CAPTAIN: "So I followed her into the sea
We swam together merrily."
(He boots the MATE playfully.) **Avast, you wave-gulping snail! Look like you're breathing!**

MATE: *(Distantly)* **Aye, sir.**

CAPTAIN: What? Has your blood turned to salt? From just one kiss?

MATE: Aye.

CAPTAIN: Then shake your sails, you sea slug! Our fortune is made! Our cargo is secure! The day carries us full sail seaward! *(He grabs MARIANA, swings her around, kisses her.)*

MARIANA: Randolf! You must ask me first!

CAPTAIN: What, sir, have you scuttled your Captain? Then draw, you... *(The CAPTAIN draws his sword)* **...scheming mutineer and I'll throw your traitorous shanks to the sharks!**

MATE: Not now, Captain.

CAPTAIN: Come, you quivering cabin boy; draw! Draw or die

where you stand!

MARIANA: **Oh, mate, a cabin boy! Fight for your honor!**

MATE: **Not now.** *(A distant rumble is heard. The MATE lifts his head to listen. The CAPTAIN pauses a moment, then continues.)*

CAPTAIN: **Mate, look there.**

MATE: **What?**

CAPTAIN: *(Indicating MARIANA)* **There. It's your mermaid. She's calling you.** *(He moves behind MARIANA.)*

MARIANA: **What do you mean? Why am I his mermaid?**

CAPTAIN: *(The CAPTAIN comes out from behind MARIANA as Hag-Witch, using his sword as her walking stick.)* **Brian, my warm-hearted friend, come to me. I have something to offer you.**

MARIANA: **Oh, I see, the Hag.**

CAPTAIN: *(As MATE)* **Help! Captain, help! It's the Hag-Witch! It's the Hag-Witch!**

MARIANA: **I am not the Hag-Witch!**

CAPTAIN: **Brian, come and I'll give you one wicked kiss!** *(He kisses air, laughs like Hag. As himself)* **You unmanly jellyfish! Will you take this?** *(He raises sword at MATE.)*

MATE: **Not now, Captain.**

CAPTAIN: *(In a quieter tone)* **Where would your heart be, mate?**

MATE: **Lost at sea.**

CAPTAIN: **Aye...** *(A distant, low rumble is heard. They all hear it, responding for just a moment to look down and away. They then return their attention to the ship. The CAPTAIN holds up the key from around his neck.)* **Would you like the key to unlock her?**

MATE: **Nay.**

CAPTAIN: **I'm glad to hear it. For I could almost release her myself. It's strange to have so wonderful an enemy.**

MATE: **Wonderful...**

CAPTAIN: **But let her go. She's nothing but a storm in your heart.**

MATE: **I wish I could.**

CAPTAIN: **The magician will unlock her in the castle after we depart, rich as pirates. And we'll never set eyes on this Hag-Witch again.**

MARIANA: **Then you won't be returning?**

CAPTAIN: **Never again.**

MARIANA: **Will you remain for a time at court?**

CAPTAIN: **For what reason?**

MARIANA: **We'll hold a feast. You'll receive gifts...** *(He indicates no.)* **I ask you to stay a time, for me. I want to show you our lands, the pleasures of our court.**

CAPTAIN: **Mariana, I won't.**

MARIANA: **For me.**

CAPTAIN: I won't.

MARIANA: And when you depart — may I sail with you? I want to sail with you.

CAPTAIN: I'll sail with no one but Brian. *(He removes medallion, gives it to her.)*

MARIANA: I see. *(Another low rumble is heard, this time more pronounced.)*

CAPTAIN: Is that thunder?

MATE: The skies are clear.

CAPTAIN: Then what could it be?

MATE: I heard it twice earlier. *(The CAPTAIN looks through spyglass, scanning the horizon.)*

QUEEN: *(Quietly)* Brian...

MATE: *(Turning to QUEEN, as others look seaward)* Meaghan?

QUEEN: The shroud...it hurts me. I'm growing weaker and weaker.

MATE: What can I...he...

QUEEN: Open the lock.

MATE: I haven't the key.

QUEEN: Where is the key?

MATE: It's...

QUEEN: Where?

MATE: Around his neck.

QUEEN: Unlock these chains.

MATE: But —

QUEEN: Remove these chains.

MATE: I can't listen to you.

QUEEN: Take off this shroud.

MATE: Captain, can't you hear her? What should I do?

CAPTAIN: Fight her, mate. Her spell will wear away in one more day, perhaps two. Then she'll be so weak she'll do as I say.

QUEEN: *(Quietly)* Brian...

MATE: She calls me. I can't keep fighting her.

CAPTAIN: You can and for me you'll do it.

QUEEN: Brian...

MARIANA: Is there no other way, Taran? Must she be shrouded and chained?

CAPTAIN: If she were free, she'd shipwreck us, as you have seen.

MARIANA: But the shroud — it hurts her. If you locked her in her cabin —

CAPTAIN: She'll use her charms and spells against me, as she did Brian. *(The low rumbling is louder. The CAPTAIN and MATE scan the horizon and ship.)*

MATE: Captain...

CAPTAIN: I feel it. *(They seem to be quaking.)*

MATE: The ship — it shakes.

MARIANA: What is this?

CAPTAIN: Is the magician casting magic? Would that bring this?

MARIANA: I don't know. Father! Father! *(She starts off. He runs on from below, carrying lantern.)*

CYNRIC: What is causing this, Captain?

CAPTAIN: You don't know?

CYNRIC: How would I know?

CAPTAIN: It's not your magic?

CYNRIC: No, what is it?

MATE: Captain?

CAPTAIN: I don't know. Take the helm. Turn her portside, full sail! It may — *(A very loud explosion is heard, and a red glow covers the stage.)*

MATE: *(Pointing directly ahead)* **There!**

CAPTAIN: The sea explodes!

CYNRIC: Fire!

CAPTAIN: A volcano!

MATE: That's what she is!

CAPTAIN: She's cracked open the sea. *(Another explosion)*

MARIANA: There again! Look how high!

MATE: She's an angry one! She'll blacken the sky!

CAPTAIN: Hard to port! Or she'll sink us for sure.

MARIANA: Are we in danger?

CAPTAIN: Not if we sail quickly away. Portside, mate! Put her behind us!

MATE: **Aye, aye!** *(Another eruption. As he turns the ship the red glow shifts to the side of the sails and the constant roar and explosions gradually become quieter.)*

CAPTAIN: Look at her! The water is on fire!

MARIANA: The sea is boiling.

CYNRIC: *(Mostly to himself. MARIANA just happens to be close enough to overhear what he says.)* **Just as I feared.**

MARIANA: *(They whisper.)* **What?**

CYNRIC: The flame has brought this volcano.

MARIANA: Its power is that strong?

CYNRIC: I told you it would turn against us. We don't understand it.

MARIANA: But we're sailing away.

CYNRIC: The flame will somehow draw us into the volcano. We must do something...but what?

MARIANA: You don't know?

CYNRIC: I told you — no one knows what is correct.

CAPTAIN: Hold her there.

MARIANA: The old manuscript. Would it say?

CYNRIC: The writing is worn; I could understand nothing. If I had entered the cave, I may know.

MARIANA: Taran entered the cave.

CYNRIC: He knows nothing of magic.

MARIANA: Meaghan.

CYNRIC: If she knew, would she say the truth?

MARIANA: *(Crosses to MEAGHAN.)* **My father believes the flame has brought this volcano. You entered the cave —**

QUEEN: **Uncover me. That's what is needed. What other answer could there be?** *(Beat)* **Help me.**

MARIANA: **Father —**

CYNRIC: **I knew that's what she'd say. If she were free, they'd fight. No.**

MARIANA: **Then what must be done?**

CYNRIC: **I don't know.**

MATE: **Captain, the winds.**

CAPTAIN: **I feel them.**

MATE: **They begin to slow.**

CAPTAIN: **Hold our course. Steady as she goes.**

MARIANA: **The winds are changing.**

CYNRIC: **And so it begins.**

MARIANA: **Father, do something.**

CYNRIC: **And what should I do?**

MARIANA: **Strengthen the winds, blow us a safe course.**

CYNRIC: **I've tried! I'm not strong enough to go against the power of the flame. No, we must do what is correct.**

MARIANA: **But what is that?**

CYNRIC: **I don't know!**

CAPTAIN: **Hold our course.**

MATE: **I can't, Captain, without wind. The current pulls us.**

MARIANA: **I feel as if all this is my fault. If I hadn't told the captain of the potion, none of this may have followed.** *(Firmly)* **I will stop this.**

CYNRIC: **How?**

MARIANA: **I've heard only one answer.** *(To CAPTAIN)* **Taran, you must uncover her.**

CAPTAIN: **Mariana —**

MARIANA: **My father warned you of the power of the flame. It has brought this volcano and it will destroy us unless we uncover her.**

CAPTAIN: **I feel your concern for your queen, but she stays as she is.**

QUEEN: **Brian...** *(Everyone hears her. The MATE immediately crosses to QUEEN.)*

CAPTAIN: *(Relying on his friendship more than command)* **Back to the helm, mate. Hold our course.** *(MARIANA picks up sword and crosses to helm and turns wheel while others focus on*

369

MATE *and* QUEEN.)

MATE: Meaghan, you called me.

QUEEN: Listen to Mariana. Uncover me. The "Dragonfly" will burn.

MATE: Captain...the "Dragonfly." She says we'll burn unless we uncover her. Give me the key, and I'll unlock her.

CAPTAIN: *(Quietly)* I tell you I'll have no more mutiny aboard my ship. Take the helm.

QUEEN: Brian —

MATE: Captain, you must unchain her. Do you see? For me, take off this shroud.

CAPTAIN: I won't. And I'll not say again — take the helm. *(MAR-IANA lashes the wheel and raises her sword.)*

MARIANA: Look what course we're on, Captain.

MATE: She's turned us toward the volcano.

MARIANA: And that's our course until you unchain her.

CAPTAIN: Mate, turn the helm.

QUEEN: Brian, no.

CYNRIC: Mariana, this is not what is needed.

MARIANA: You don't know.

CYNRIC: *(Moving to her. She holds sword to him, stopping him.)* **Turn the wheel.** *(The sails begin to redden, the volcano rumble increases in volume. The rumble will continue through the end of the play, modulating in volume.)*

MARIANA: Stay away! I'll fight you if I must. Unchain her. That may be what is correct.

CAPTAIN: Brian? *(MATE stands still.)*

MARIANA: *(To CAPTAIN)* Unchain her. There may be no other way. Do you want to burn?

CYNRIC: **(**The MAGICIAN makes a pass with his staff, mumbling.) Hail spirits, I call you to obey. Give power to my will to —

MARIANA: Father! You won't turn the ship! *(MARIANA moves quickly to him, knocks the staff out of his hands with her sword. She picks it up, keeps sword on MAGICIAN, puts staff behind helm.)*

CYNRIC: Mariana — against me?

CAPTAIN: *(To MATE)* Will you allow this to go on?

MARIANA: Your queen has commanded you. Uncover her.

CAPTAIN: Turn the helm, mate. *(MATE crosses to helm.)*

MARIANA: *(Raising her sword)* Stand back.

QUEEN: Brian, no.

MATE: What?

CAPTAIN: Don't listen to her.

QUEEN: Head for the volcano. *(Volcano explosion)*

MATE: Meaghan.

CAPTAIN: Don't listen to her.

CYNRIC: *(To QUEEN)* **Is this what you want? All of us destroyed? Your people frozen?** *(To MATE)* **Turn it, mate.**

MARIANA: **No.**

CAPTAIN: **Brian.**

MATE: **I can't, Captain.**

CAPTAIN: **The winds blow stronger. We're coming upon the volcano. Turn her windward.** *(Explosion)* **Don't abandon ship! Turn her!**

MATE: **I can't.** *(The sails are reddening into a deep, flickering crimson. The roar of the volcano is louder.)*

CAPTAIN: **By the seas, I'll turn her myself.**

MATE: *(The MATE suddenly raises a sword, stopping the CAPTAIN.)* **Hold!**

CAPTAIN: **What?**

MATE: **No further, Captain.**

CAPTAIN: **Will you draw on me?**

MATE: **I told you I can't stop myself.**

CAPTAIN: **What has she done?**

CYNRIC: **Meaghan, release him.**

CAPTAIN: **Will you go against me? Where's your heart, man? Don't let her do this to you. Brian...** *(Explosion. He moves to the end of BRIAN's drawn sword. The MATE quickly reaches out and takes key.)* **Mate! Listen to me. Do you know what you're doing?**

MATE: **Unlocking her, as she says.**

CAPTAIN: **Look at yourself. Look at me — Randolf.**

MATE: *(In great indecision)* **Captain...**

CAPTAIN: **Give it back to me. Drop your sword. This is mutiny.** *(The MATE stands strong, gives MARIANA the key.)*

MATE: **Unchain her.**

CAPTAIN: **I see what course you're on. Then die for her!** *(The CAPTAIN and MATE sword fight as MARIANA guards the helm and unlocks the chains. The MAGICIAN tries to get to the wheel but the MATE also helps run him off. Explosion.)* **Avast, you foul mutineer! Turn on your captain! Hah!** *(The MATE wounds the CAPTAIN lightly. The MAGICIAN helps MARIANA uncover the QUEEN.)* **Ah!**

MATE: **Captain...** *(They fight furiously. Incensed, the CAPTAIN knocks the sword out of the MATE's hand, then wounds him. The MATE stands easy victim to the CAPTAIN.)* **Go on, Captain.**

CAPTAIN: *(Anguished)* **Brian...** *(He pushes him out of the way just as the QUEEN is uncovered by MARIANA.)*

MARIANA: **She's free.**

QUEEN: *(Picking up sword)* **The flame!** *(The CAPTAIN takes it from the MAGICIAN. A loud eruption from the volcano rocks the ship;*

371

all catch their balance.)

CAPTAIN: **The helm...**

QUEEN: **No!** *(She jumps in front of him, raises sword.)* **Mariana...** *(MARIANA retrieves a sword, protects the helm.)* **Keep Cynric from the helm.**

CYNRIC: Mariana —

MARIANA: **Stay back.**

CYNRIC: **With Meaghan uncovered, the volcano remains. Turn the helm.**

MARIANA: **We won't alter this course until she commands it.**

QUEEN: **Give me the lantern.**

CAPTAIN: **I'd rather burn.**

QUEEN: **The flame, Captain. Then you may turn your ship.**

MARIANA: **Listen to her, Taran.**

CYNRIC: **Give it to her, Captain.**

MATE: Captain —

CAPTAIN: **All of you stay back! I'm going to turn my ship. If she will try to stop me, let her do her worst.** *(Turning to QUEEN)* **But by the mast, if you strike first, woman or not, I'll strike last.**

CYNRIC: **Meaghan, you entered the cave. Is this the nature of the flame?** *(The CAPTAIN starts toward helm, with sword and flame in hand. The QUEEN attacks him, he defends. They separate.)* **Is this correct? Will this save us from the volcano? Think of your people. What does the flame require?** *(Explosion. Angered, the CAPTAIN puts down flame and strikes back. Quickly it appears as if the CAPTAIN is about to win. The QUEEN escapes the CAPTAIN but she has heard what the MAGICIAN has said. As they face off again.)* **Meaghan.** *(The QUEEN makes a decision and drops her sword upon the deck, steps toward the CAPTAIN completely vulnerable. He raises his sword high, hesitates.)*

QUEEN: *(Calmly)* **Is this what you want?**

CAPTAIN: **You've brought this upon yourself.** *(He starts to strike, hesitates.)*

QUEEN: **Is this what you want?**

CAPTAIN: **Why did you drop your sword?**

QUEEN: **What is stopping you?**

CAPTAIN: **Why did you drop your sword?**

QUEEN: **Taran...to enter the cave...lay down your weapon. Mariana, turn the wheel.** *(The QUEEN finds shroud, tosses it to CAPTAIN. Gradually, as they sail away, the volcano rumble dies out.)*

CAPTAIN: **Why give me this?**

QUEEN: **So you'll destroy it. And the potion. I'll throw what remains in the sea.**

CYNRIC: *(Looking toward volcano)* **This may be correct.**

QUEEN: **Taran, on my honor as queen, I will not fight you again.**

CYNRIC: **Captain, you entered the cave. Remember? Is she correct? If she is...** *(An explosion from the volcano. The CAPTAIN deliberates, then drops his sword. He stands stunned and confused.)*

QUEEN: **Brian, I won't trouble you again. The potion will wear away soon.**

MARIANA: **Father...**

CYNRIC: **Mariana, the volcano is dying away. You were correct; you understood what I didn't.**

MARIANA: **Captain, I only wanted you to know how I felt.** *(No response)* **Forgive me.** *(Moves to QUEEN.)* **Meaghan, you are safe.** *(MARIANA and QUEEN embrace.)*

QUEEN: **And you are brave.**

MARIANA: **It was you who taught me; and I am grateful.**

MATE: **Captain...?** *(The CAPTAIN still stands stunned, not responding, looking seaward.)*

QUEEN: **Accept this.** *(She gives MARIANA a bracelet.)* **Now you are our princess...and perhaps our next queen.**

MATE: *(To CAPTAIN)* **Your wound?**

CAPTAIN: *(Without looking at MATE)* **Nothing. And yours?**

MATE: **Not deep.**

MARIANA: *(Crossing to MATE)* **Let me see.**

MATE: **Nay, it's noth — aye, you'd better look; it's very painful.**

QUEEN: *(To CAPTAIN)* **But you...What course shall you and I set?**

CAPTAIN: **Take the helm, mate.**

MATE: **On what course, Captain?**

CAPTAIN: **Full sail ahead.**

MATE: **Aye, aye, sir.**

CAPTAIN: **To the castle.** *(The MATE crosses to helm, turns it. MARIANA stands alone looking seaward. The MAGICIAN watches the dying volcano. The CAPTAIN crosses to the rail, looks seaward, still stunned and confused. As lights dim, the QUEEN crosses to the rail near him.)*

THE END

The Call

A Mermaid Called

Words and Music by Max Bush

A mer-maid called to me one day. "Oh Bri-an, won't you come and play." So I fol-lowed her in-to the sea; we swam to-geth-er mer-ri-ly.

CAPT: Starboard, Mate, ten degrees. . .

She led me to a dis-tant shore. She kissed me once and then no more. She swam a-way and left me there, a-lone and lost and in des-pair.

CAPT: . . .and hold her steady.

There's not a mer-maid 'round for me. I'll love no o-ther than the sea. But, if this mer-maid calls a-gain.......

QUEEN: BRIAN!

Spirit

Words and Music by Max Bush

PERFORMANCE RIGHTS AND ROYALTY INFORMATION

13 BELLS OF BOGLEWOOD © 1987. The possession of this book, without written authorization first having been obtained from the publisher, confers no right or license to professionals or amateurs, to produce the play publicly or in private, for gain or charity. In its present form the play is dedicated to the reading public only, and not to producers. However, productions of this play are encouraged, and those who wish to present it may secure the necessary permission by writing to Anchorage Press, Incorporated, P.O. Box 8067, New Orleans, LA 70182. This play is fully protected by copyright, and anyone presenting it without the consent of the Anchorage Press will be liable to the penalties provided by the copyright law. Professional producers are requested to apply to the Anchorage Press for royalty quotation. Whenever the play is produced, the names of the authors must be carried in all publicity, advertising, fliers, and programs. Also the following notice must appear on all printed programs: "Produced by special arrangement with The Anchorage Press, of New Orleans, Louisiana."

RAPUNZEL © 1987. Reprinted here through special arrangement with New Plays Inc. This play is fully protected under the copyright laws of the United States of America and all other countries of the copyright union. All performances, whether professional or amateur, including performances given by non-profit groups, are subject to a royalty. All rights, including photocopying, reprint, television, radio broadcasting, motion pictures, and translation into foreign languages, are strictly reserved. Arrangements for production and for obtaining scripts must be made in writing with New Plays Inc., P.O. Box 5074, Charlottesville, VA 22905.

PUSS IN BOOTS © 1986. Reprinted here through special arrangement with New Plays Inc. This play is fully protected under the copyright laws of the United States of America and all other countries of the copyright union. All performances, whether professional or amateur, including performances given by non-profit groups, are subject to a royalty. All rights, including photocopying, reprint, television, radio broadcasting, motion pictures, and translation into foreign languages, are strictly reserved. Arrangements for production and for obtaining scripts must be made in writing with New Plays Inc., P.O. Box 5074, Charlottesville, VA 22905.

VOYAGE OF THE DRAGONFLY © 1989. The possession of this book, without written authorization first having been obtained from the publisher, confers no right or license to professionals or amateurs, to produce the play publicly or in private, for gain or charity. In its present form the play is dedicated to the reading public only, and not to producers. However, productions of this play are encouraged, and those who wish to present it may secure the necessary permission by writing to Anchorage Press, Incorporated, P.O. Box 8067, New Orleans, LA 70182. This play is fully protected by copyright, and anyone presenting it without the consent of the Anchorage Press will be liable to the penalties provided by the copyright law. Professional producers are requested to apply to the Anchorage Press for royalty quotation. Whenever the play is produced, the names of the authors must be carried in all publicity, advertising, fliers, and programs. Also the following notice must appear on all printed programs: "Produced by special arrangement with The Anchorage Press, of New Orleans, Louisiana."

ROCKWAY CAFE © 1992. Reprinted here through special arrangement with New Plays Inc. This play is fully protected under the copyright laws of the United States of America and all other countries of the copyright union. All performances, whether professional or amateur, including performances given by non-profit groups, are subject to a royalty. All rights, including photocopying, reprint, television, radio broadcasting, motion pictures, and translation into foreign languages, are strictly reserved. Arrangements for production and for obtaining scripts must be made in writing with New Plays Inc., P.O. Box 5074, Charlottesville, VA 22905.

HANSEL AND GRETEL © 1993. The possession of this book, without written authorization first having been obtained from the publisher, confers no right or license to professionals or amateurs, to produce the play publicly or in private, for gain or charity. In its present form the play is dedicated to the reading public only, and not to producers. However, productions of this play are encouraged, and those who wish to present it may secure the necessary permission by writing to Anchorage Press, Incorporated, P.O. Box 8067, New Orleans, LA 70182. This play is fully protected by copyright, and anyone presenting it without the consent of the Anchorage Press will be liable to the penalties provided by the copyright law. Professional producers are requested to apply to the Anchorage Press for royalty quotation. Whenever the play is produced, the names of the authors must be carried in all publicity, advertising, fliers, and programs. Also the following notice must appear on all printed programs: "Produced by special arrangement with The Anchorage Press, of New Orleans, Louisiana."

GHOST OF THE RIVER HOUSE © 1995. The possession of this book, without written authorization first having been obtained from the publisher, confers no right or license to professionals or amateurs, to produce the play publicly or in private, for gain or charity. In its present form the play is dedicated to the reading public only, and not to producers. However, productions of this play are encouraged, and those who wish to present it may secure the necessary permission by writing to Anchorage Press, Incorporated, P.O. Box 8067, New Orleans, LA 70182. This play is fully protected by copyright, and anyone presenting it without the consent of the Anchorage Press will be liable to the penalties provided by the copyright law. Professional producers are requested to apply to the Anchorage Press for royalty quotation. Whenever the play is produced, the names of the authors must be carried in all publicity, advertising, fliers, and programs. Also the following notice must appear on all printed programs: "Produced by special arrangement with The Anchorage Press, of New Orleans, Louisiana."

THE EMERALD CIRCLE © 1997 by Max Bush. Published by Dramatic Publishing Company. This play is fully protected by copyright, and

ABOUT THE PLAYWRIGHT

Max Bush is a Michigan writer whose plays have been widely produced on professional, educational, and amateur stages across the United States. He graduated in English from Grand Valley State University and earned his M.F.A. in directing from the University of Michigan in 1985. He has won numerous awards for his work including the Distinguished Play Award from the American Alliance of Theatre and Education, and Individual Artist Grants from the Michigan Council for the Arts and the Iupui National Playwriting Competition. His scripts have been performed on such prestigious stages as the Honolulu Youth Theatre, the Kennedy Center, the Goodman Theatre, the Emmy Gifford Theatre, the Nashville Academy Theatre and elsewhere. In addition to writing, Max is also active as a guest director for many theatres, having staged plays for the Boarshead Theatre in Lansing, Michigan, Purdue University, and the Magic Circle Theatre in Grand Rapids, Michigan. When he is not busy writing new scripts for his many commissions, or directing for other theatres, or taking long walks in the southwest Michigan countryside where he lives, Max plays a mean game of Gus Macker basketball wherever the competition presents itself.

ORDER FORM

MERIWETHER PUBLISHING LTD.
P.O. BOX 7710
COLORADO SPRINGS, CO 80933
TELEPHONE: (719) 594-4422

Please send me the following books:

_____	**Plays for Young Audiences by**	**$16.95**
	Max Bush #TT-B131	
	edited by Roger Ellis	
	An anthology of widely produced plays for youth	
_____	**Multicultural Theatre #TT-B205**	**$14.95**
	edited by Roger Ellis	
	Scenes and monologs by multicultural writers	
_____	**Scenes and Monologs From the Best**	**$14.95**
	New Plays #TT-B140	
	edited by Roger Ellis	
	An anthology of new American plays	
_____	**Everything About Theatre! #TT-B200**	**$15.95**
	by Robert L. Lee	
	The guidebook of theatre fundamentals	
_____	**The Scenebook for Actors #TT-B177**	**$14.95**
	by Dr. Norman A. Bert	
	Collection of great monologs and dialogs for auditions	
_____	**One-Act Plays for Acting Students #TT-B159**	**$15.95**
	by Dr. Norman A. Bert	
	An anthology of complete one-act plays	
_____	**Theatre Alive! #TT-B178**	**$24.95**
	by Dr. Norman A. Bert	
	An introductory anthology of world drama	

These and other fine Meriwether Publishing books are available at
your local bookstore or direct from the publisher. Use the handy
order form on this page.

NAME: _____

ORGANIZATION NAME: _____

ADDRESS: _____

CITY: _____ STATE: _____

ZIP: _____ PHONE: _____

❑ **Check Enclosed**
❑ **Visa or MasterCard #** _____

Signature: _____ *Expiration Date:* _____
(required for Visa/MasterCard orders)

COLORADO RESIDENTS: Please add 3% sales tax.
SHIPPING: Include $2.75 for the first book and 50¢ for each additional book ordered.

❑ *Please send me a copy of your complete catalog of books and plays.*